THE LEARNING MYSTIQUE

THE LEARNING MYSTIQUE

A Critical Look
at "Learning Disabilities"

Gerald Coles

PANTHEON BOOKS
NEW YORK

 Published in the United States by Pantheon Books, a division of Random House, Inc., New York, and simultaneously in Canada by Random House of Canada Limited, Toronto.

Library of Congress Cataloging-in-Publication Data

Coles, Gerald S.
The learning mystique.

Bibliography: p.
Includes index.
1. Learning disabilities. I. Title.
LC4704.C62 1988 371.9 87-43061
ISBN 0-394-54898-1

Designed by Claudia DePolo

Manufactured in the United States of America

9876543

DEDICATION

To the memory of my father-in-law,
Alfonso Iannacome, a tailor from Celano,
whose art embodied his favorite saying,
"Work makes one noble."

Contents

Acknowledgments

When I think of the path between my shaky early school years and this book, I appreciate the opportunity to give public thanks to teachers to whom I have always been privately grateful. Sidney Bloomgarden, my sixth-grade teacher, probably made all his students feel special (in the best sense of that word), but I only remember how special he made me feel. Harry Kroiter, my freshman English professor, was a teacher, counselor, and friend, whose wisdom and love were there when I most needed it. William Yates, although never formally my teacher, was a profound and encouraging educator at a pivotal time in my life and has remained a valued friend. I owe an immeasurable debt to Michael Simmons, a philosopher of education, for what he taught me about the deeper meaning of schooling (and for providing a memorable forum in which we graduate students could argue without restraint about issues raised in his classes).

I am frankly at a loss to express fully my appreciation for the contribution of Wendy Wolf, my editor. Acknowledging her judgment, skill, criticism, guidance, and good humor in the preparation of this book falls short of describing her qualities and my gratitude. I am most fortunate to have worked with her.

The manuscript benefited greatly from a careful and critical reading of an earlier draft by Jonathan Cobb. His comments combined intelligence and caring, and were consistently correct—sometimes to my chagrin, always to my benefit.

I also want to acknowledge the contribution of Tony Borden, a fine copyeditor, who helped produce a more readable manuscript.

My thanks as well to John Marciano, an historian of education and a dear friend, who helped me formulate many of the ideas in the book.

My clinical work at the University of Medicine and Dentistry of New Jersey has been integral to my writings on learning disabilities for the past decade. I am especially indebted to Gary Lamson, Vice President for Mental Health Services, for his constant support of my clinical work and writing—especially the writing of this book.

The completion of this book also owes much to colleagues at the UMDNJ-Community Mental Health Center at Piscataway. My thanks to Boaz Cohen, Lorna MacDougal, and Barbara Dillon.

To my family—Coleses, Iannacomes, and Reinhardts—I extend my love for their love. In addition, my sons Romand, Terence, and Jeremy, my brother-in-law Walter and sister-in-law Katia, and my brother Michael all made substantive contributions to the book. My mother-in-law, Josephine, and mother, Lee—with lasagna from the former, and rugaluch from the latter—also made substantive contributions to the author.

My wife, Maria, a poet, quotes Gabriela Mistral in one of her poems. I quote the lines here to convey some of what Maria has given to this book and me:

I open the bread to its softest part
and give it its warmth;
I turn it over
and give it its breath.

Introduction

Learning disabilities were virtually unknown as a field until the mid-1960s. During the past two decades, however, millions of children have been identified in school and clinical programs as "learning disabled" and have been treated for their "condition" by educators, psychologists, and medical doctors. Some say that one in ten children of school age may be undiagnosed victims. Many of these professionals have also contributed to an ever-growing body of learning-disabilities research, and both specialized publications and the popular media acclaim this research for contributing to the diagnosis and instruction of children and adults who have severe academic learning problems.

The learning-disabilities field seems to present a more "scientific" explanation of learning and literacy problems than has generally been provided in remedial instruction. Underlying causes of learning failure are attributed to a variety of complicated perceptual, neurological, and thinking processes, processes to which remedial educators have often given little, if any, attention. For those who have endured the anguish and embarrassment of persistent learning failure, and for many professionals who have struggled to help them, the explanation offers hope.

The essence of this explanation lies in the alleged identification of *minimal neurological dysfunctions* that biologically disable youngsters whose serious academic difficulties apparently cannot be explained by those factors that commonly create learning difficulties in other children—including intelligence, sensory ability, and family. In other words, for learning-disabled children—who perform within the normal range on IQ tests, have normal sensory functioning (e.g., no hearing loss), come from "good" (e.g., middle-class) environments, and have been taught with methods that are generally successful with the average student—this field of research provides a "clinical" response.

Of course it is critical whether the neurological explanation is indeed correct, for this is no mere academic argument. Both research and discussion in the field are tied to a widespread practice of diagnosing children for a debilitating neurological condition and treating them for it with remedial classes and medication. The crux of my argument is that the very existence of this "condition" has been virtually unproven, with only the shakiest of evidence reported, and that it has certainly been claimed in far greater proportion than it actually occurs. After decades of research, it has still not been demonstrated that disabling neurological dysfunctions exist in more than a minuscule number of these children. A review I published in 1978 illustrates the point: most studies of the ten major diagnostic tests have not proved that the tests can differentiate between learning-disabled and non-learning-disabled children; the few studies that do claim to validate the tests have serious methodological flaws.[1]

There is no question that the children identified as learning disabled do indeed have serious learning difficulties that commonly begin in the early grades. These difficulties generally span the entire gamut of school subjects. Reading, however, is the most common disability, so much so that calling a child learning disabled is understood to mean reading disabled. The seriousness of these difficulties is hard to exaggerate. The youngsters will probably be confounded by many letter-sound associations in phonics instruction. As a rule, the children will not be simply marginal achievers, somewhat below the average ability of their classmates. Rather, again using reading as an example, learning-disabled children will either not learn to read or will learn so poorly and slowly that each year they will fall farther behind classmates who are normal learners.

For a child classified as learning disabled, the identification process usually begins when a youngster's serious academic difficulties induce a teacher to refer him or her to a multidisciplinary team for an evaluation. The team is frequently made up of a school psychologist, an LD specialist, a school social worker, and other professionals whose expertise might have a bearing on the child's problems. If the respective members reach a mutual agreement that the child is learning disabled, the team will meet with the child's parents, tell them of their conclusions, and present a remedial plan. The schemes vary, but most include a special-education program through which a child may spend all or part of the day in a learning-disabilities program. As a part of the treatment, the child is also likely to be given medication, generally the psychostimulant Ritalin.

These children generally come from middle-class families; indeed, "learning disabled" is the category into which middle-class children are most likely to be placed if they are judged to require a special-education program. As I will demonstrate, neither of these outcomes is surprising when one considers the historical context of the evolution of the LD diagnosis. The category was introduced in U.S. schools in the 1960s as one of the means of explaining a handicapping condition which many professionals and middle-class parents considered unaddressed by existing educational classifications.

Many professionals and middle-class parents thought that special-education classifications such as "mentally retarded" or "emotionally disturbed" and prevailing social-science categories for explaining academic failure such as "culturally deprived" seemed more appropriate for children from minority and poor communities, not children from the middle class. The variety of problems afflicting minority groups and the poor were said to affect the emotions and intellect of children in ways that explained their difficulties in school. An applicable but *different* explanation was needed for children who had grown up in the suburbs, with the advantages of middle-class life, and who, despite their academic problems, often appeared to be good learners outside of school. The learning-disabilities explanation—that the problem was caused not by retardation or other exclusionary factors, but by a minor neurological "glitch"—made sense to many. The explanation also offered different advantages to different interests: it was less pejorative than other special-education categories and it did not consider or criticize any role schools, families, or other social influences might have had in creating the learning disabilities.

Despite the middle-class bias, in recent years the LD label has been used much more broadly. Once the category was institutionally incorporated into the existing field of special education, it began to be applied increasingly to minority and poor children as well. While this might appear to have been an effort at a more accurate diagnosis of children who had been misclassified, studies suggest otherwise. The learning-disabilities classification of minority and poor children appears to have been used defensively against criticism of and challenges to special-education diagnoses, particularly in the category of mentally retarded.

Fortunately, although learning-disabled children are diagnosed and treated in schools and clinics for a condition that appears to be more conjecture than fact, a number of the children have been helped, thanks by and large to excellent teaching that has *not* been based on a neurological diagnosis. Most of them, however, have been helped very little. They enjoy minimal academic success throughout their school years, and as learning failure deepens, so does frustration, disappointment, and insecurity. Their reading and other learning problems are likely to continue into adulthood, with destructive effects on their feelings of self-worth, personal relationships, and job opportunities and performance. The personal and psychological turmoil often continues to increase exponentially and, for a learning-disabled adult, can reach critical levels.

Persistent academic failure is no surprise. The invalid assumptions behind the learning-disabilities explanation center almost exclusively on what is happening inside children's heads and misdirect the diagnoses and remedial programs. At the same time, they hinder the pursuit of other explanations, of preventative strategies, and of truly effective methods for addressing the problems when they do occur.

In writing this critique of the learning-disabilities explanation, I by no means blankly condemn those professionals associated with the field or parents who, through organized groups, have encouraged the creation of learning-disabilities programs and the propagation of the learning-disabilities explanation. Many investigators, as my examination of the research will show, have done exemplary work evaluating learning-disabilities theories and programs in schools and clinics. Many parents, concerned about a child's failure, have been motivated by the earnest belief that more and different programs in the schools are the only way to brighten that child's future. And as I have already suggested, many teachers—often not by overtly confronting the validity of a school's learning-disabilities program but by quietly disregarding neurological interpretations and invalid labels—have provided exceptional remediation.

Furthermore, my critique is not meant to impugn the scientific legitimacy or *potential* value of research into neurological dysfunctions that might cause learning disabilities. Little is known about the neurological and mental processes involved in successful learning—indeed, how any child actually learns to read remains, on the whole, something of a mystery—leaving altogether too much room for speculation. Properly conducted scientific inquiry into the possible biological substrates underlying mental processes could conceivably explain why some children have trouble learning in school. Moreover, even if causal connections were not found, we could understand more fully other kinds of associations between biological functioning, mental processes, and an individual's academic activity—and help break down that mystique of how children learn as well as fail. Regrettably, the legitimacy and value of the present research into the learning-disabilities explanation has been undermined by a fundamental flaw: the overwhelming majority of research is *not* a disinterested examination of a scientific question but a collection of tracts intent on making the child or the child's neurology responsible for his or her learning problems. As I will show, the LD theorists have, by excluding from the start other avenues of exploration, actually rendered the learning mystique even more opaque.

The very notion of a learning disability should be situated within several contexts embracing broad theoretical and practical issues. The claim that normally intelligent children can have a specific intellectual disability is associated with an ongoing controversy over the nature of intelligence. Here, the learning-disabilities explanation is congruent with the general theory that the brain is composed of "multiple intelligences," each differing in quality and relatively unconnected, rather than being composed of a level (or quality) of intellectual functioning that is uniform throughout the brain. Similarly, the question of why more boys than girls have reading problems (again, the primary form of learning disabilities) may be subsumed within broader interpretations of the differences between males and females. On a practical level, the influence of family and schools on child development is also part of a far-reaching context within which research on the learning-disabilities explanation may be located. In actuality, however, these issues are secondary to two interrelated contexts, one converging around a theoretical issue, the other a practical one.

The primary theoretical argument is whether numerous social problems have fundamental biological or social causes. Among the problems that have been attributed to biological makeup are aggression, poverty, racial inequality, and patriarchy (which is not seen as a "problem" by those who account for it biologically). Learning disabilities, with their own explanation via neurological dysfunction, fit within this larger set of biologically based descriptions of social organization.

In a practical context the contradiction must be explained between the great opportunity ostensibly available to everyone and the short change actually received by various individuals and groups. Men and women, whites and blacks, rich and poor, educated and uneducated, are among the obvious social distinctions proving that the same achievements and rewards are not equally open to all. As I have said, learning disabilities became prominent in the 1960s as a biological explanation of academic inequalities within the middle class. This explanation led to the establishment of methods and programs for ameliorating "the problem" without demanding any structural changes in society—while at the same time suggesting that these children were bound to attain less. The practical solutions that were proposed all remained within the existing framework of the institutions involved. New classrooms might be opened to help "disabled" students get around their biological flaws, but the school—and the school system—remained unchanged.

I will begin with an overview of the history, definition, and extent of learning disabilities in the first chapter. The subsequent chapters are divided into two parts. In chapters two through six, I review the research on the fundamental question to be answered before any conclusions about learning disabilities can be drawn: Can children be identified as "learning disabled" according to a formal definition that posits minimal neurological dysfunctions as the cause of the problem?

Because research in support of the learning-disabilities explanation has concentrated on mental functioning, usually by isolating it from the social context in which learning difficulties develop, my critique will also focus on mental functioning, and will explore the various explanations that have grown out of this approach. I begin with the more familiar perceptual-deficit explanation of learning disabilities (the most common symptom thought to be the "reversal" of letters and words) and proceed to the more rarefied work on brain-cell abnormalities and genetics. Generally, I have organized the interpretations to move from less to more technical, and from older to newer, and grouped them where feasible by similarities of explanations (e.g., perceptual explanations). This categorization is somewhat arbitrary, however, because of the overlap among specific aspects of the learning-disabilities explanations (e.g., dysfunctional brain hemisphere theories, use of diagnostic technology, evaluation of empirical data). On the whole, what chapter a specific theory appears in is less important than its place in the comprehensive picture of a body of work that shares a basic assumption about brain dysfunction.

The research critiqued here was not chosen at random nor because it was weak, "straw man" evidence which poorly represents the learning-disabilities explanation. In fact, I discuss the work that advocates of respective explanations themselves use as validating evidence, and which professional books and textbooks most commonly cite.

Assessing this work meant covering a considerable body of research. Nevertheless, I have, for three reasons, chosen to discuss thoroughly many relevant studies, rather than allow myself brief summaries. The first two reasons pertain to a critique of the literature; the third, to the alternative theory I will propose. First, only by the most careful examination can one conclusively evaluate the extent to which the research supports learning-disabilities explanations. My purpose is to present a thorough and all-encompassing statement on the field, for which cursory summations would not have been sufficient. Second, critical appraisals are always open to criticisms. To be frank, I have opted to give particular attention to the details of the research to head off the charge that certain findings have been skimmed over in an effort to prove a point. I do not want subsequent studies to take me to task by complaining, "What about this research here?" However, to prevent the text from becoming too detailed, I have included in the footnotes even greater discussion and documentation. Third, I intend to show that within the body of research on the neurological deficits underlying learning disabilities, evidence actually can be found to support an alternative theory. This evidence is not readily available; it can be uncovered only by sifting through the experiments.

The second section of this book, beginning with chapter seven, presents this alternative theory of learning disabilities, one that attempts to understand "LD" within the context of the child's social life. This explanation does not dismiss biological functioning as unimportant to a theory of learning disabilities, nor does it seek to replace biological determinism with social determinism. Put succinctly, the alternative perspective suggests that learning difficulties, and any neurological dysfunctions associated with them, develop not from within the individual but from the individual's interaction within social relationships. Brain functioning is both a product of and a contributor to the individual's interactions, it is not a predetermined condition.

This kind of critique requires that I clarify from the start whether I believe anyone has a disability as formally defined by professionals in the field. The numbers have not been estimated, but there is a modicum of evidence suggesting that a very small portion of the children identified as learning disabled do have some degree of neurological dysfunction that may interfere with learning and academic achievement. Research shows, however, that the actual extent of the problem is quite small compared to the millions of children who have been diagnosed as learning disabled. It is quite difficult to understand, therefore, why this diagnosis should have produced the pedagogical and psychological extravaganza we have seen in recent years. The point can be made by drawing an analogy to a learning problem that may be as pervasive. Strabismus, or lazy eye, can cause some people difficulty in learning to read. Though their number is quite small even compared to the total number of persons with strabismus problems, it is well known that eye-muscle imbalance must nonetheless be appraised when assessing a person who has a hard time learning. Still, no one has thought to conceptualize "strabismus disability" as a prominent cause of learning failure, and certainly no one has attempted to use it as the basis for a professional field.

Most of the differences in brain activity found between normal and disabled learners are just that—differences. They are not neurological abnormalities; they are simply biological distinctions that might be found between any two groups of people with different abilities. Because a person is a biological creature, his or her individual behavior is at the same time social and biological. Consequently, differences in normal social behavior are concomitant with biological differences. For example, the brain activity of two people reading a Spanish text would be different if one understood the language and the other did not. They would be "reading" in different ways and thus the mental activity in the left hemisphere of their brains would also be different.

With the introduction of the alternative theory, so-called learning disabilities will be discussed with respect to specific and broad social contexts. I do not intend to present another kind of reductionism, in which the largest social contexts, through the mediation of decreasingly smaller ones, determine the learning ability of individuals. The alternative theory attempts to be the opposite of reductionism by interweaving the interactions of the individual within a variety of social relationships, and explaining the development of the individual's learning problems and neurological makeup as part of the totality of these interactions.

A final word about qualifying key terms such as "learning disabilities" and "learning disabled." Because this book is critical of these and associated terms, they ought to be accompanied by quotation marks to denote doubt about their validity. For the sake of keeping the text uncluttered, however, the terms will be written without quotation marks, in the expectation that my position will be evident and omission of the quotation marks will not be construed as approval of either the use or the meaning of the terms.

THE LEARNING MYSTIQUE

1

■ ● ▲

Hinshelwood's Legacy

In 1907, a schoolmaster in Glasgow, Scotland, mentioned to a county Medical Officer of Health that he was "greatly puzzled" about four of his students.[1] They were the four youngest brothers in a family of eleven children and, unlike their seven siblings, had "experienced the greatest difficulties in learning to read." The schoolmaster was perplexed because, while "the boys seemed so intelligent," in his long experience in schools he had never before encountered such a problem in teaching reading.

Upon learning about this "remarkable case"—but without actually seeing the boys himself—the medical officer "at once recognized" the "true nature of the difficulty": congenital word-blindness, a reading disorder caused by a genetic defect. His quick determination that "the four boys were typical cases of this condition" was made possible because the medical officer was a former pupil of James Hinshelwood, the Glasgow ophthalmologist who today is cited as the first major figure in what would become the field of learning disabilities. Hinshelwood had since 1895 been studying and writing about congenital word-blindness, attempting to analyze and explain its symptoms in detail in order to place its diagnosis on a "scientific basis," and to show how to teach children with this condition. The medical officer referred the boys to his former mentor to confirm the diagnosis and provide the schoolmaster with expert help.

The oldest two boys, sixteen and eighteen years old, respectively, had worked in the local coal mines since leaving school, at fourteen. The eighteen-year-old was particularly interesting to Hinshelwood, because even though the schoolmaster said the boy had had "insuperable difficulty in his learning to read," the young man had improved his reading on his own during the four years he had worked in the mines. This seemingly extraordinary change was stimulated by his enthusiasm for football (soccer) and his desire to read about the game. Since leaving school he had religiously bought a sports newspaper that gave detailed accounts of all football matches, and every night after coming home from the mines he "would spend a large part of the evening in poring over this newspaper," sometimes with the help of family members.

Hinshelwood found that the young man had great difficulty reading a child's first primer or an "ordinary book," but when asked to read football news, "he could do this much better, as he could recognize by sight a much greater number of words," such as *goal, goalkeeper, forward backs, runs, dribbling,* and the names of various clubs. On his own, then, he had "mastered to a great extent the vocabulary of football teams" and could "read these football reports fairly well." According to Hinshelwood, this young man's "persevering effort" demonstrated "what can be done by steady application even in apparently very hopeless cases."

This information could have led Hinshelwood to postulate several possibilities about why the young man had, as a child, become an "apparently very hopeless" educational case. He might indeed have had congenital word-blindness and have compensated for it by only memorizing certain words, without gaining facility in reading. Or, given how much he improved when reading about football, his earlier problems might have been because the schoolmaster had used reading materials that had failed to motivate the boy.

There were still other plausible explanations for the boys' reading difficulties. Perhaps by the time the eighth child came along, the parents of this large mining family had been too busy and too tired to provide the nurturing they had given the others. Perhaps a large family dependent upon a small salary had become increasingly poor as the family grew, and the diminishing financial means relative to family needs had adversely affected the youngest children.

Hinshelwood's analysis was similar in all of his discussions of clinical cases. In his diagnosis of the four brothers, Hinshelwood rejected or ignored any hypotheses about school, family, and other environmental conditions. He reasoned that—because the reading problems were clustered in one family, and because the four boys had normal general intelligence, lacked visual problems, had good visual memory except for letters and words, had a family life which had not impeded their siblings' learning, but had failed to read with school instruction that had been successful with their siblings—the medical officer's preliminary conclusions could be confirmed: the boys indeed had congenital word-blindness, a condition that "frequently assumes a family type," that probably was hereditary, and that was caused by a defective language-related area of the brain. Because the boys, like other children with congenital word-blindness, had good mental abilities in areas other than reading, it was "evident that their cerebral defect was a purely local one, . . . that it was strictly confined to the cerebral area for the visual memory of words and letters, the left angular gyrus, and did not extend at all beyond that."

Hinshelwood found similar "confirmation" of congenital word-blindness in the case of a twelve-year-old boy who, after seven years of school, had progressed only to a second-grade reader, even though he was normally intelligent and had good auditory memory, etc.[2] Hinshelwood examined the boy and obtained an educational and social history from the boy's mother; she was concerned about the constant classroom humiliation and impediment to learning the boy suffered because "the other boys laughed at him when he read in class, and when he became excited his reading was worse than ever." To rectify the congenital word-blindness he diagnosed, Hinshelwood advised the schoolmaster "to make no further attempt to make the boy read in class with the other boys" and to employ individual, short, frequent lessons rather than one long one. This advice was Hinshelwood's *only* treatment intervention, but it was sufficient; "under this line of treatment, he . . . made splendid progress." When, after two years, the boy could read at a fourth-grade level—a two-year reading improvement in as many years, compared to the five years he had needed to reach a second-grade reading level—Hinshelwood interpreted the boy's progress as evidence of the validity of his diagnosis.

Hinshelwood concluded that the root of congenital word-blindness lay in children's brains because he had observed that dysfunctional reading symptoms found in adults with brain lesions were analogous to those of certain children with reading problems.[3] If an inability to recognize and remember letters and words, or to unite recognizable letters into syllables or into words, was acquired word-blindness, a symptom of localized brain damage in adults, the same reading problems in generally normal children could be symptoms of similar brain damage.

The medical profession at the time had limited means of directly studying the brains of normal persons, and certainly did not have the technology to detect a language-related localized cerebral defect related to reading problems in otherwise normal children, so Hinshelwood was unable to verify his analogy. Consequently, he devised a diagnostic procedure that served to exclude other influences that could have caused reading disabilities until, in his mind at least, only congenital word-blindness remained as the possible cause. His logic, based on what he considered to be "scientific criteria," went as follows: If it was clear that sensory functioning, intellectual functioning, and environmental conditions could be excluded as causes of the reading disability, and if the reading symptoms were similar to those of acquired word-blindness, it was "evident" (Hinshelwood's exact word), not just possible, that the problem was caused by localized brain damage that was probably hereditary.

From an examination of Hinshelwood's overall work and an understanding of the time in which it was done, one could say that although Hinshelwood's conclusion was presumptuous, his thinking did have a sensible logic and his work ultimately made a contribution. After all, analysis by exclusion is not necessarily unsound as an indirect, preliminary way of identifying the cause of a problem, particularly when more direct means are unavailable. Apart from his extravagant claims, perhaps Hinshelwood should at least be commended for advancing our understanding of reading disabilities as far as was possible at the turn of the century. One way to evaluate the appropriateness of this judgment would be to appraise how thoroughly he examined information that was directly available to him, such as the potential causes he excluded or ignored in formulating his diagnosis.

By this measure, Hinshelwood does not fare well. For example, from his discussion of the four brothers it appears that he hardly thought about their family. Since two of the boys were miners, one might assume that their father was also a miner, but this is not certain since Hinshelwood said nothing about their father's occupation or about whether their mother worked outside the home at any time. Similarly, nothing is mentioned about their economic condition, such as whether the family had been able to make ends meet with seven children but not with eight, nine, ten, or eleven. Nor did the reading development of the oldest boy after leaving school lead to any question about the boy's education, such as whether he was simply too bored by the material to learn. If a youngster could improve his reading solely by working hard to read material of interest to him, without using any unusual instructional method, why should this achievement be interpreted as evidence that he had overcome a localized brain dysfunction? If the presumed dysfunction had been severe enough to prevent successful learning under a skilled schoolmaster's instruction, why did it not equally impede self-instruction?

Similarly, in the case of the twelve-year-old boy, Hinshelwood did not rebuke the school for its part in creating the reading problem. Even if the schoolmaster did not know that the boy might have had congenital word-blindness, shouldn't he have known better than to enforce the almost perverse daily demand that the boy read aloud? Yet Hinshelwood does not recognize this shoddy instruction. His criticism of schools was confined to what he saw as a failure to know how to treat congenital word-blindness. He criticized crowded schools, for example, but only because an excessive number of children in the classroom prevented a schoolmaster from recognizing and helping the congenitally word-blind. As was true of his interpretation of the reading development of the eighteen-year-old football fan, Hinshelwood regarded the twelve-year-old's progress, following a few basic changes in the mode of instruction, as evidence that pathology existed and that the pathology itself had been overcome with proper treatment. The circular reasoning here is obvious, as is the probability, never raised by Hinshelwood, that removing the child from the classroom had salutary effects unconnected to pathology.

In short, in all his writings, Hinshelwood, an eye surgeon keen enough to identify the angular gyrus as the brain area related to congenital word-blindness, appeared blind to other explanations he could barely avoid tripping over.[4]

■●▲ Recent Assessments of Hinshelwood

Throughout the twentieth century and especially during the past two decades, all accounts and references to the history of the learning-disabilities field regard Hinshelwood as its major progenitor.[5] Recent assessments of Hinshelwood have noted that his 1895 paper on congenital word-blindness, published in *Lancet,* a major British medical journal, was the first of two decades of articles and books on the subject, and while he did not originate the term, first suggest it could be a hereditary condition, or report the first case of the condition, he was the only one at the turn of the century to have continued to publish work on it and to have helped stimulate research and publications on congenital word-blindness throughout Europe and elsewhere.[6] Today, Hinshelwood is said to have "contributed not only to the growing body of knowledge regarding clinical manifestation of congenital word blindness" and to have set "the stage for the development of remedial programs," but also to have helped make it "an accepted fact that cases of congenital word blindness existed, perhaps in far greater frequency than had even been imagined."[7] One recent author quotes a long section from Hinshelwood's case description of the twelve-year-old boy "because it remains one of the best descriptions around of dyslexic behavior."[8]

Researchers after Hinshelwood replaced "congenital word-blindness" with other terms thought to define reading disabilities more accurately, and research in the past two decades has developed more and more elaborate theories using an array of psychometric tests, complex experimental methods, and modern technology to study the brain directly.[9] Various questions have been raised about Hinshelwood's work: whether the angular gyrus is the portion of the brain responsible for reading disabilities, whether the term "word-blindness" is precise enough to describe reading disabilities or too narrow to include other language disabilities, whether there is one kind of learning disability or many, and whether learning disabilities are inherited. However, Hinshelwood's predominant thesis about the causal relationship between brain deficits and learning and reading problems remains alive and well: "Hinshelwood may have been wrong in various neuroanatomical particulars, but he was probably correct in principle—more so than he recognized at the time."[10] Another recent assessment emphasized the later work he helped stimulate: "The early medical literature concerned primarily with congenital word blindness led to basic understanding as to how brain deficits could be associated with processes important in reading."[11] These quotations illustrate the view commonly held in the learning-disabilities field today that Hinshelwood's work was a sturdy effort that helped launch a progressive understanding of neurologically derived learning disorders in otherwise normal children.

However, it should be clear by now that something is amiss in the continued laudatory portrayal of Hinshelwood's work. Even if subsequent research had proved Hinshelwood right about brain dysfunction, he would have been right for the wrong reasons. The way he considered the parallel between the reading problems of brain damaged adults and those of generally normal school children was reasonable, but his conclusions were illogical, failing the simplest syllogistic test, "If A causes B, then is B *necessarily* caused by A?" His exclusionary diagnosis is further discredited by his failure to follow the clear trail of more obvious explanations of reading disabilities. With such a forefather, the learning-disabilities field certainly got off to a shaky start. And it is unknown whether the progeny of Hinshelwood regard his analytic method as a skeleton in the closet, because his work, though frequently mentioned, is never discussed more than superficially.

■●▲ Classifying Children "LD" Today

So what? What difference does Hinshelwood's actual theory make at the present time? What is the point of resurrecting and criticizing work nearly a century old, work that now seems quaint compared with modern methods of studying brain and behavior, work that presumably has long been corrected by Hinshelwood's heirs? An answer to these questions requires a preliminary overview of Hinshelwood's legacy.

The small number of cases of congenital word-blindness identified by Hinshelwood and others at the turn of the century pales in comparison to the number of children now identified as having learning and reading disabilities due to neurological deficits. Currently in U.S. schools, an estimated total of 1.8 million children are categorized as learning disabled, approximately 42 percent of the 4.3 million children formally identified as educationally handicapped. The learning-disabled category contains a considerably larger number of children than the 750,000 classified as mentally retarded or the approximately 362,000 classified as emotionally disturbed. Moreover, the number of children categorized as learning disabled continues to grow rapidly. The figure for 1985 is more than twice the approximately 800,000 children who were in this category in the 1976–77 school year. This leap of approximately 127 percent was much greater than the relatively modest 27.9 percent increase for the emotionally disturbed or the 22.6 percent *decrease* in children classified as mentally retarded during the same ten-year period.[12]

These numbers represent the children formally classified in special-education categories, not the total number of children who professionals estimate could and should join the ranks of the learning disabled. For example, 5.1 percent of Colorado's school children were classified as learning disabled, about the same as the percentage of children in this classification nationally.[13] However, in a prevalence study of learning disabilities in Colorado and seven other Rocky Mountain states, approximately 15 percent of second-grade children were judged to have symptoms of learning disabilities. This was a slightly higher estimate than that of an earlier study by the same researchers, who found that in the Greeley, Colorado, schools, the prevalence rate was 11 percent, still higher than the classified rate for the state as a whole.[14] Other studies have supported the 15 percent estimate.[15] Two organizations that publicize information on the subject have also estimated that the problem is much greater than the formal numbers reflect. The Orton Dyslexia Society states that "at least one in ten otherwise able people has serious [dyslexia] problems."[16] For the Foundation for Children with Learning Disabilities, "LD children represent more than 10 million of the total population in the U.S."[17]

Learning and reading disabilities are not regarded as a problem only in the United States. Australian reports estimate 10 percent of "otherwise fully capable children" have a reading disability. In England the percentages vary from 4 to 10 percent, the latter percentage found among children in London. In South Africa a committee appointed by the Minister of National Education set the percentage at 15 percent. In Canada the estimate is between 10 and 16 percent.[18] While these figures vary because of differing definitions and research methods, taken together they suggest that millions of children worldwide are suffering from a disability that has been diagnosed in an increasing number of children and which should properly be recognized in even more.

What exactly is the disability? Since Hinshelwood established the term "congenital word-blindness," the condition has had a multiplicity of names, including strephosymbolia, word amblyopia, bradylexia, script-blindness, primary reading retardation, specific reading disability, developmental reading backwardness, analfabetia partialis, amnesia visualis, genetic dyslexia, reading disability, dyslexia, and learning disability.[19] (Some of these could have been written in plain English as simply slow reading, partial illiteracy, and visual amnesia; instead, Latin and Greek mumbo jumbo lends an air of medical authority.) Most of these have now been discarded in favor of the last three, with "learning disabilities" (LD) as an overall term for language, math, spelling, and reading disabilities; and "dyslexia" or "reading disability" as synonymous terms for learning-disabled children who specifically have trouble reading. However, while learning disabilities encompass several areas of difficulty, both in practice and in research children placed in this category have primarily had a reading problem.[20]

■•▲ Definitions and Exclusionary Factors

Ever since Hinshelwood, a learning disability—by any name—has always been formally defined as a specific subset of low academic achievers whose serious academic failures could not be accounted for by their sensory functioning, intellectual ability (as measured by IQ tests), or emotions, which are generally normal. Nor can unfavorable circumstances or experiences explain the disabilities. These children by and large come from the middle class. Their homes usually seem to be materially comfortable and free of family or emotional problems; their schools seem to provide normal instruction which benefits most children. In learning-disabilities jargon, these sensory, intellectual, emotional, and environmental conditions are known as exclusionary factors, and excluding them as causes of the problem establishes or at least paves the way for a diagnosis of a genuine learning disability. Experts recognize that in some learning-disabled children the exclusionary factors might be evident, but in these instances they are judged to be a consequence, not a cause, of the disability. The disability might create emotional problems in the child, initiate conflict in an otherwise intact family, or lead to low scores on intelligence tests because the child's learning has been hindered. Again, however, these conditions are not said to explain the disability itself, even though they may compound it. A cardinal requirement of the field is to eliminate "exclusionary criteria." In formal definitions and in actual diagnosis, determining what has *not* caused the severe academic problems is as important—and often more important—than identifying what has.

Defining a learning disability does not stop with exclusionary factors. There is also an affirmative part of the definition: learning-disabled children are said to have a *neurological dysfunction.* This has been the prevailing definition since Hinshelwood, even though among the public and among professional groups in the field, "learning disabilities" is sometimes thought to refer to serious academic problems. "Restricted brain dysfunction" and the absence of exclusionary criteria—not just low academic achievement, regardless of severity—have been and remain the core of any definition of "learning disability" or "dyslexia."

A sampling of the observations of some leaders in the field illustrates the prescience of Hinshelwood's thinking.[21] Perhaps the most succinct expression recently of the causal relationship between neurological dysfunctions and learning disabilities can be found in the foreword to a 1980 book by one noted researcher, which explains, "Neurological dysfunction leads to perceptual processing deficits which, in turn, result in a variety and complexity of learning disabilities . . . *Learning and perception are neurological.*"[22] While many would contest making perceptual processing deficits the middle and only link in the LD equation, there is considerable agreement about the causal association between the first and last parts of the equation. For example, in a major 1981 book propounding the view that there are multiple causes of learning disabilities—rather than a single cause such as perceptual processing—the authors state: "Reading disabilities could result from the impairment of specific abilities that are associated with specific neurological dysfunctions . . . [D]ifferent types of neurological dysfunction can lead to different types of reading disabilities."[23] While many theorists argue about the precise nature of learning disabilities, they remain in general agreement that underlying neurological deficits are to blame. The summary statement of an international conference held in Denmark noted that the many views expressed about the causal role of neurology were not necessarily incompatible but rather "coalesced as building blocks in a theory of a neuropsychology of learning disorders."[24]

While laying greater stress on new research techniques and accomplishments, a recent book on dyslexia finds a similar convergence of conclusions: "Computerized tomographic procedures, refined electrophysiological mapping techniques, postmortem studies, and extensive neuropsychological research have provided convincing evidence that for the dyslexic child, associated neurodevelopmental deficits exist within the functional system of reading."[25]

An important formal expression of the meaning of "learning disabilities" was developed in 1968 as part of congressional work to prepare learning-disabilities legislation. The National Advisory Committee on Handicapped Children, a multidisciplinary group, was asked to define LD, and with only a few insignificant changes, their definition was used as the standard in the field and in federal legislation on the problem for the next decade:

> Children with special learning disabilities exhibit a disorder in one or more of the basic psychological processes involved in understanding or using spoken or written language. These may be manifested in disorders of listening, thinking, talking, reading, writing, spelling, or arithmetic. They include conditions which have been referred to as perceptual handicaps, brain injury, minimal brain dysfunction, dyslexia, developmental aphasia, etc. They do not include learning problems which are due primarily to visual, hearing, or motor handicaps, to mental retardation, emotional disturbance, or to environmental disadvantage.[26]

The wording is altogether vague, relying on exclusion and on synonyms that were no more precisely defined elsewhere.[27] Despite ambiguities, the central idea is apparent: a learning disability is a language-related disorder caused by a neurological problem within normal children living within normal environmental conditions.

This definition remained preeminent from 1968 until 1981, when cumulative dissatisfaction with its imprecision prompted the six professional organizations concerned with LD to form the National Joint Committee for Learning Disabilities and to hammer out a new definition. After "prolonged discussion and compromise" the committee issued the following:

> Learning disabilities is a generic term that refers to a heterogeneous group of disorders manifested by significant difficulties in the acquisition and use of listening, speaking, reading, writing, reasoning or mathematical abilities. *These disorders are intrinsic to the individual and presumed to be due to central nervous system dysfunction.* Even though a learning disability may occur concomitantly with other handicapping conditions (e.g., sensory impairment, mental retardation, social and emotional disturbance) or environmental influences (e.g., cultural differences, insufficient/inappropriate instruction, psychogenic factors), it is not the direct result of those conditions or influences.[28]

Comparison of the 1968 and this new definition reveals some differences. For example, the 1968 guideline assumed normal intelligence whereas now below-normal intelligence became a concomitant condition. Their differences, however, are minor compared with their similarities. Because the National Joint Committee was concerned with precision and sought to avoid "inadvertent misinterpretation," the definition was published with phrase-by-phrase explanations, one of which, although it repeats somewhat the phrases it is supposed to elaborate on, is worth quoting so that there can be no doubt about the committee's thinking. The sentence emphasized above

> means that the source of the disorder is to be found within the person who is affected. . . . The cause of the learning disability is a known or presumed dysfunction in the central nervous system. . . . The phrase is intended to spell out clearly the intent behind the statement that learning disabilities are intrinsic to the individual.

This intrinsic causality was stated explicitly because, the committee felt, this view was "the original intention" of the 1968 definition but had not been spelled out clearly.[29]

The committee's explanation of "intrinsic neurological dysfunction" acknowledged that "attempts to determine the [central nervous system] cause of the LD problem become difficult and are often speculative." Still, concluded the committee, "speculative" diagnosis should not prevent the LD field from citing the central nervous system (CNS) as the origin for a child's learning problem:

> the Committee agreed that hard evidence of organicity did not have to be present in order to diagnose a person as learning disabled, but that no person should be labelled LD unless CNS dysfunction was the *suspected cause.*[30]

This definition was reviewed and endorsed by five of the six organizations on the committee. The sixth, the Association for Children and Adults with Learning Disabilities (ACLD), refused to endorse it, and in September 1984 its board adopted a definition of its own, one which illustrated the proverbial much ado about nothing. Specific learning disabilities, ACLD said,

> is a chronic condition of presumed neurological origin which selectively interferes with the development, integration, and/or demonstration of verbal and/or non-verbal abilities.
>
> Specific learning disabilities exists as a distinct handicapping condition in the presence of average to superior intelligence, adequate sensory and motor systems, and adequate learning opportunities. The condition varies in its manifestation and in degree of severity.[31]

As the National Joint Committee had, ACLD also provided an accompanying explanation or "rationale," one portion of which referred to the past and present professional consensus: " 'neurological origin' was inserted because early and recent authors of definitions have agreed to a central nervous system basis."

Presumably, the authors of the definitions felt there was a body of evidence that, although not conclusively documenting that neurological deficits caused learning problems, was substantial enough to promote agreement that this relationship existed and therefore that diagnosing children as LD on the basis of professional suspicion was justified.

■●▲ Current Reasoning and Research

As the next five chapters will show, despite assertions to the contrary, even if the learning disabilities explanation is judged on its own terms—that is, on its own body of work—current evidence of a causal intrinsic neurological dysfunction is no more convincing than that produced in Hinshelwood's day. His work, in its essentials, has not been the seed for a flowering body of knowledge but the template whose pattern has been ceaselessly copied in reading and learning disabilities research and practice. This pattern includes an unswerving postulation that the source of the individual's problem lies within the individual's neurology; a proclivity for "finding" biological causes; a disregard for experiential explanations; illogical reasoning about the relationship between behavior and the brain; a misinterpretation of symptoms; and a readiness to apply a medical label to superficially diagnosed and insufficiently understood academic problems. This misdirected thinking has contributed to a fundamental misunderstanding of children's learning difficulties, which in turn has necessarily produced professional procedures that have misdiagnosed learning-disabled children and have failed to solve their problems or possibly prevent them from occurring.

More elaborate research methods and statistical analyses, more tests and instruments for studying learning, and more technical and sophisticated methods of understanding the brain have only further mystified our understanding of children's learning problems. The form of current research claiming to corroborate the LD explanation contributes to the mystification by working from the assumption that neurological deficits are the primary cause of the condition. It relies on an empirical, "scientific method" that implicitly legitimatizes a blindness to any other possible explanations.

New and abstruse neuropsychological techniques also make the research harder for many professional and most general readers to comprehend and evaluate. Some of the current methods for studying the brain in LD research include electroencephalography (EEG) or computerized axial tomography (CAT scans), brain autopsies, complicated neuropsychological test batteries, genetic analyses, and various approaches for studying right/left brain lateralization. It is true that many of these technological advances have contributed to other valid medical diagnoses and could contribute to more insights into LD if the focus of the research were not as limited and circumscribed as it has been. However, as is often true for technology generally, the fancy hardware has another edge, that of making professionals and the public acquiesce to experts. In LD research, the abstruse technology has failed to provide scientific confirmation but, because it seems so formidable, has nevertheless silenced dissent and in this way worked to validate the learning disabilities explanation.

Perhaps without realizing it, Hinshelwood obscured the meaning and cause of children's learning difficulties. His seemingly concrete explanation actually abstracted neurological processes from the truly concrete individual activity and social context in which they are embedded. To this day, out of the fog is pulled a reified explanation that makes LD a corporeal entity—a *thing,* either a defective brain tissue, a malfunctioning oversized or undersized brain area, or a bad gene—an entity having an existence or force of its own. Social relationships are considered, but only as consequences of the biologically caused learning disabilities, only as reactions to the response by parents, teachers, and others to the child's behavior.

Certainly, neurological dysfunctions and learning disabilities are connected for some children diagnosed as learning disabled. As stated in the introduction, there are many children identified as LD who do have inordinate difficulties with reading and other school subjects. The question is, Why? I do not intend to argue that LD is a myth, and that children are classified as learning disabled solely for cynical reasons, such as a school system's need to qualify for federal special-education funds or to placate or fend off criticism of classroom instruction from irate parents. Influences external to children's abilities are involved in the classification of LD children, but the children would not be so classified if they did not have serious academic difficulties in the first place.

In criticizing past and current biological explanations, I do not reject the need to study the biological mechanisms in learning and learning problems. The learner is not a "black box" in which biology is unimportant for understanding learning or only important for neuropsychologists, if not for educators. Some research on the neuropsychology of learning is critical for understanding learning disabilities, and, again, for some children there is an association between neurological dysfunction and LD. However, that association is not the cause of the child's problems. Some professionals would not agree that neuropsychological research in the LD field is needed. These critics, who espouse a pragmatic view of learning disabilities, are concerned with children's pressing academic problems. They want the field's fascination with causes to be replaced by greater concentration on the amelioration of learning problems. These, they emphasize, remain to be solved no matter what diagnosis or label is applied. For me, the question of causes is a critical one, and it requires neuropsychological research as *part* of its answer. However, to find the answer, neuropsychological research must be placed within a theory that considers learning difficulties to be created not through one or another side of a defunct biological-social dualism but through the complex interactions that always include both the social and the biological in numerous relationships. The failure to validate the neurological thesis is not merely an empirical one, in which proof is lacking because researchers do not yet have the necessary methodological and technical means. Given the present conception of the relationship between biology and learning within the discipline, an empirical confirmation will, probably in another ninety years, only further mystify what learning-disabilities empiricism has obscured during the field's first ninety years.

■●▲ LD Popularized

Most professionals who work with the learning disabled, and professionals and nonprofessionals who work with popular organizations publicizing the cause, base their practice on the results LD researchers have claimed. These claims are often accepted because the research is perceived not as a fog created by researchers, unwittingly or otherwise, but as the necessary smoke behind which the scientific wizards can discover the effects of malefic neurology.

The impact of these claims is evident in the coverage given the subject by newspapers, popular magazines, radio, and television. A special supplement to the *New York Times* devoted almost entirely to learning disabilities carried articles with headings such as "New Awareness of a Growing Problem" and "Brain Studies Shed Light on Disorders," all of which portrayed LD as a pervasive problem requiring greater public attention.[32] The introductory article noted that "there is now an emerging consensus among researchers that they [learning disabilities] constitute neurological problems, some of which seem to have genetic bases."

Family Circle, a magazine sold at supermarkets, carried an article titled "Solving the Mysteries of the Mind," written by a physician and a faculty member of a major medical school.[33] Its "brief guide to brain disorders and their most up-to-date treatments" explained that a dyslexic is a child "who, because of one or more minor brain malfunctions, is unable to process in a normal way the information he receives through his eyes or his ears."

On a national nightly news program, coinciding with school openings across the country, a report titled "Blind to Words" stated that one out of ten people suffer from reading disabilities not related to intelligence or retardation. It concluded that just as some will never learn to draw or sing, some will never learn to read.[34] Just before a morning news program on national TV, a public affairs ad was run, showing a boy about ten years old, with a distressed look on his face, reluctantly walking to school. A background voice says, "All across America there are bright kids who have trouble learning, making school a problem." The boy looks up at a "SCHOOL" sign alongside the street, scrunches his eyes, and tries to read it. The screen shows the sign as the boy perceives it: "OƧHOOⱢ." The narrator explains, "These kids have learning disabilities. Often the problem's as simple as seeing letters and numbers reversed or in the wrong order." The youngster reappears on the screen, standing with a frustrated, pathetic look on his face, and the voice continues: "If nobody recognizes this problem, it can make every word a stumbling block, every school day a disappointment. These kids can overcome this problem and grow up the bright kids they really are. Write to the Foundation for Children with Learning Disabilities for information about special programs." Once more the school sign is shown with letter sequence and forms reversed, as the narration concludes: "If this is how you saw school, you'd hate it too."

The foundation was established in 1977 by Carrie Rozelle (wife of football commissioner Pete Rozelle), whose concern for the learning disabled, a foundation pamphlet says, "grew out of her own sons' experiences with learning disabilities."[35] For responding to the TV ad, parents received *Their World,* a foundation magazine containing information about learning disabilities, success stories of the learning disabled, and encouraging ads from a number of major U.S. corporations that also provide funds for the foundation.

Perusing the magazine, parents would come across an ad from the Hertz car rental company, demonstrating that the parents' child was not alone and, in fact, was in the company of one of the best minds of the human race. The ad pictures a chalkboard, in front of which is printed, "This is how Einstein really saw the theory of relativity." On it is the famous formula, only it is written as Einstein is thought to have seen it: $^2CM = E$. And why did Einstein see it this way? Because, says the ad, "Einstein was dyslexic." Thus, this ad also depicts the perceptual reversal of linguistic material, often regarded as a major symptom of LD. Since Einstein never said he saw the formula that way, the ad could of course be taken as Madison Avenue hyperbole. But granting the hyperbole, this diagnosis of the physicist is part of a speculation that each year seems to move more and more into the realm of lore. In addition to Einstein, other legendary dyslexics are said to include Thomas Edison, Rodin, Woodrow Wilson, William James, William Butler Yeats, and Gen. George Patton. Among the more old-time dyslexics, Karl XI (1655–97), "one of Sweden's wisest Kings," has been identified as a "well-adjusted ex-dyslexic."[36] A case has also been building for adding Leonardo da Vinci to the list, on the theory that his dyslexia was symptomatic of hyperspatial abilities that underpinned his creative powers.[37]

It is not surprising that with the fellowship of these men—whose eminence suggested to the mother of one dyslexic that the problem "could almost be called the affliction of geniuses"—some people diagnosed as learning disabled and dyslexic feel less stigmatized and are encouraged to disclose their problems.[38] A few years ago the first dyslexia confessional was published. In the triumphantly titled *Reversals: A Personal Account of Victory Over Dyslexia,* Eileen Simpson describes the effect dyslexia had had on her life and how she was able to overcome it and go on to get a Ph.D. in psychology, become a psychotherapist, and write critically praised short stories, a novel, and a literary history of American poets she had known. With real accomplishments like these, some readers might wish dyslexia had befallen them.

There are also instances of "coming out" by dyslexics who do not boast of that kind of intellectual "eminence." Reinforcing General Patton's example that real men can be dyslexic, a set of twin brothers are trying to achieve an eminence of a different sort. Each weighs over 250 pounds, all muscle, has a sixty-inch chest and twenty-inch biceps, and they call themselves the Barbarians. In the popular weekly magazine *People* and in a nationally distributed bodybuilding magazine with a monthly readership of over 1.7 million, the brothers divulged that their roughshod ride to barbarian size and strength—and, it seems, their appearance in movies, TV shows, and the marketing of Barbarian posters and dolls—began when, at the age of six, both were "diagnosed as having dyslexia, an impairment of the brain that affects reading ability." Made to feel "stupid and inadequate," as one of them put it, "we took out our frustrations physically." Added the other, "In the long run it proved to be an advantage. Since we were nearly unable to memorize, we were forced to use our creativity."[39]

Unfortunately, not all LD life stories turn out as well as those of the men of eminence, Eileen Simpson, and the Barbarians. One school of thought, for example, sees a strong link between learning disabilities and juvenile delinquency. First, a neurological dysfunction produces academic failure; that in turn creates low self-esteem and anger, which are transformed into antisocial feelings and behavior and, in the end, criminal acts. A study by the National Institute for Juvenile Justice and Delinquency Prevention reported that approximately 32 percent of adjudicated youngsters have learning disabilities, that learning-disabled adolescents have a significantly higher rate of violent acts, and that male adolescents with learning disabilities are more likely to become juvenile delinquents than non-LD male adolescents. In 1983 the House of Delegates of the American Bar Association passed a resolution "recognizing that there is a correlation between children who suffer from the handicap of learning disability and children who are involved in the juvenile justice and child welfare system." Recently the Foundation for Children with Learning Disabilities awarded over $100,000 to the American Bar Association and related groups for educational and research programs on the link between LD and delinquency.[40]

Probably the worst-case example of a purported association between learning disabilities and crime was made by Lloyd J. Thompson, a psychiatrist widely published in the LD field and leading proponent of the men-of-eminence theory, who suggested that Lee Harvey Oswald might have been dyslexic and that this disability could have been a strong influence leading to the assassination of John Kennedy. After studying Oswald's published Russian journal and other writings about him, Thompson made a tentative diagnosis of dyslexia and concluded that dyslexia and consequent years of frustration in school—and the fact that Oswald did not understand his condition—might have been a fundamental reason for his hostility against society and figures of authority.[41] Perhaps it is the link between LD and potentially disastrous ends that has led to an increasing propensity to find LD in ever younger children. Louise Bates Ames, head of the Gesell Institute of Human Development in New Haven, Connecticut, explains that the youngest learning disabled child brought to the institute was a boy slightly over one year old, whose candidacy for adoption had been approved by a local clinic. Unexpectedly, one week after approval, the clinic contacted the biological parents and said that during its examination of the child, the youngster had "cast objects and did not seem to concentrate." From this behavior the clinic concluded that he might later be a "learning-disability child with emotional problems" and, therefore, seemed a poor risk. It is not unique for the Gesell Institute to see learning-disabilities diagnoses in youngsters almost this young. Ames describes similar cases of children three years old and under who were diagnosed with evidence equally superficial and by professionals not even trained in LD.[42]

These examples are not merely instances of extreme LD interpretations. Rather, they—along with the nearly 2 million children diagnosed as learning disabled each year, the large number of families and relatives of the learning disabled, and the array of professionals associated with these children—show the extent to which LD has become an increasingly familiar and "widespread" malady.

■●▲ The History of a Diagnosis

If my analysis is correct, and LD research has in fact failed to support its neurological-deficit thesis, how has the field grown and gained in credibility and influence in recent years? Why are millions of children diagnosed as learning disabled? If, in the words of Edna St. Vincent Millay, "impetus is all we have," why hasn't everyone seen the emptiness of the movement? To provide an initial answer and to place the forthcoming chapters on research and practice within the proper context, I will sketch the outline of LD's historical and social development and its connection with other explanations of human behavior. The story begins, of course, with Hinshelwood.

Hinshelwood's work never had a big impact on either educational theory or practice during his lifetime or for several decades afterward. At its inception, the learning-disabilities field nearly expired from infant-death syndrome. In 1925, William S. Gray, the doyen of the reading profession, chaired the Research Committee of the Commonwealth Fund and produced the first of a series of state-of-the-art bibliographic reports on reading.[43] In this *Summary of Investigations Related to Reading,* the committee discussed numerous causes of reading retardation, but only one of its 436 references, that for Hinshelwood, drew any attention to organic or inherited deficits that might prevent normal children from learning to read. In later editions and in other writings, Gray continued to give little credence to the idea that brain dysfunction caused reading problems.[44]

Ironically, the year Gray published his first *Summary* was also the year the neurologist Samuel T. Orton began to develop a theory that would become the next milestone in LD history. The event ushering it in was simple enough: a routine examination of a young patient who was having inordinate difficulty learning to read. In a recent retrospective view of the event, the late neurologist Norman Geschwind explains that Orton saw before him a "remarkable phenomenon." He "recognized that his historic patient was in fact suffering from the same condition that had been described by the English neurologist, James Hinshelwood." Others had read Hinshelwood, but had assumed that the condition he described "was some unusually rare and curious disorder that might be encountered only once or twice in a lifetime." But not Orton. In a short time he discovered many other cases, wrote his first paper on a neurological explanation of reading disability, and within a year of publishing it, received a grant from the Rockefeller Foundation to carry on research about "this previously neglected disorder."[45]

Orton, who went on to become a neuropathologist on the staff of many hospitals and schools, including Harvard Medical School and the College of Physicians and Surgeons of Columbia University, supplanted Hinshelwood's congenital word-blindness with an explanation of his own: "strephosymbolia," or mixed symbols. Relying solely on his own observations of children's reading behavior, Orton proposed that reading disabilities were caused by a child's failure to establish dominance for language in the left hemisphere of the brain. When reading, the disabled (or dyslexic) child's nerve impulses produce equal language records in both brain hemispheres, rather than predominantly in the language-dominant one. The dual records were complicated further because both hemispheres

> are reversed in pattern, that is, the left hemisphere bears the same relation to the right hemisphere that the left hand does to the right hand. It seems logical, therefore, to conclude that the records (or engrams, as they are called) of one hemisphere would be mirrored copies . . . of those in the mate.

This neurological mixed dominance could cause perceptual confusion in spatial orientation and direction "in reading and in a lack of prompt recognition of the differences between pairs of words which can be spelled backward or forward, such as was and saw, not and ton, on and no and the like"—that is, reversals.[46] Subsequent researchers failed to confirm Orton's theory of strephosymbolia and it is now generally rejected, even though "reversals," as a symptom of dyslexia, remains—seemingly with a life of its own. Regardless, Orton, in the words of one of his former students, had been "a downright and forthright organicist."[47] And even though the specifics of strephosymbolia were rejected, he is said to have contributed a theory whose basic tenets were sound. For example, Geschwind's remarks, made in 1982, included the following: "It is particularly fascinating to me and to my co-workers to realize that the fundamental concepts of the work that we have been carrying out are essentially identical to those formulated by Orton." In other words, it is the organicists of today who look back and find Orton—regardless of the forsaken part of his explanation—to be the standard-bearer for the fundamental concept that many poor readers have defects in the language-related areas of their brains.

Unfortunately for Orton, full appreciation and application of even this basic organic tenet came only retrospectively. Orton's fate, at least in the short run, was similar to Hinshelwood's: he did stimulate some new research, some instructional materials and methods, and some "schools for dyslexics." Those undertakings, however, were minor compared to all the remedial-reading research and instruction in the field. It remained Orton's destiny that neither during the period he wrote, from the 1920s to the 1940s, nor for about two decades afterward, did his work have much effect on schooling or on most professionals concerned with reading problems. Other figures in LD history at about Orton's time left a similar stamp.

The attitude of LD professionals in the 1950s can be seen clearly in the major reading-diagnosis and remediation texts used in colleges at the time. A good example is a text published in 1957 by Cambridge

University Press and written by M. D. Vernon, an English psychologist who had been studying and writing about reading difficulties since the early 1930s and was regarded in England and abroad as a leading authority on the subject.[48] Vernon concluded there was "no evidence" substantiating the frequency of congenital word-blindness "among backward readers in general; but it is unlikely that [it] constitute[s] more than a small portion even of severe cases of reading disability." She strongly criticized Hinshelwood's and Orton's theories of reading disabilities and ended her review of research on "innate causes of disability" with the comment that "the investigations which have been cited give no clear evidence as to the existence of any innate organic condition which causes reading disability, except perhaps in a minority of cases." She summarily dismissed the concept of dyslexia by relegating the only discussion of it to a footnote on page three: Since its hypothesis [of cortical dysfunction] "cannot at present be accepted," she wrote, "the term 'dyslexic' will not be employed in this book." Another college text published the same year disposed of Hinshelwood's theory as one "without credibility in the opinion of most authorities" and "not of value to students of reading deficiencies."[49] Orton got off somewhat better. In the two pages devoted to him in this 449-page book, the authors allowed that his and related work was at best "equivocal." In short, from Hinshelwood's time until the 1960s the body of learning-disabilities research, writing, and instruction lay dead—or, as one observer delicately put it, in "relative quiescence"—for most educators and other professionals who worked with children's academic problems.[50]

Before the 1960s, the area of learning disabilities was not constituted as a field. It consisted of a small number of researchers who had worked in the backwaters of education and psychology and who had had very little impact on either of those fields. In the mid-1960s, LD rose meteorically in the schools and the professions, and its partisans presented it as a field that had already had its own history, experts, and special techniques. LD could explain the seemingly unexplainable—and would have long ago—had the explanation been given credence those many years. As the editors of a book on education and the brain commented, "By the early 1960's, the neurosciences had begun to have considerable impact on the diagnosis and treatment of children who have severe difficulty in learning academic skills."[51] By the end of the decade, children began to be classified as learning disabled, federal funds were appropriated for LD curricula, an array of tests and remedial materials were devised and published, parents' groups were organized, LD graduate-school programs were opened, the number of journal articles and books on the subject multiplied, a profusion of LD research projects commenced, and pharmaceutical companies promoted and profited from drugs for the learning disabled—in all, learning disabilities had suddenly became a growth industry.

This is not to say that since the 1960s LD has been an idea ruling autocratically—without opposition. Many professionals in the field have expressed doubt and criticism of LD, stemming from practice and research that contradict neurological explanations. Nonetheless, though a minority has continued to challenge the basic tenets, even if not not always for the same reasons, the neurological view prevails.

First and foremost in explaining the sudden emergence of LD is the "unexpected" and seemingly unexplainable academic failure of many middle-class children (in contrast to the "explainable" failure of many "disadvantaged" children). This failure grew from and contrasted with another aspect of the current social context, the postwar prosperity, which had led middle-class parents to anticipate continued if not improved success for their children. This expectation was fueled by the belief, partly factual and partly ideological, that education would be *the* vehicle for individual success. And the atmosphere of protest in the 1960s led to demands for the reform of many social institutions, particularly the schools. The LD field was significantly shaped by the federal government's attempt to assuage social discontent and by the ways in which social institutions, and especially the schools, "allowed" reform to occur.

The neurological explanation emerged within a particular orientation toward human problems. Parallel to, and inextricably linked with, the rise of the LD interpretation of educational failure in the 1960s were other biological explanations. Arthur Jensen was arguing that IQ differences between blacks and whites were largely genetic; psychosurgery was proposed as a solution to the violent ghetto uprisings, which were said to be caused by a portion of ghetto residents with malfunctioning brains; amphetamines and Ritalin were prescribed as the treatment of choice for hyperactive children; gender differences—the social-leadership role of men and the child-care responsibilities of women—were attributed to different biological dispositions. These and other biological theories on various facets of human nature by Konrad Lorenz, Jose Delgado, Lionel Tiger, Robert Ardrey, Desmond Morris, and others led in the 1970s to "sociobiology," E. O. Wilson's "new synthesis," the discipline that he said would "reformulate the foundations of the social sciences."[52]

Other popular explanations for social problems such as poor health, poor housing, poverty, and social inequality blamed something within the individuals affected by them. William Ryan characterized these kinds of interpretations as "blaming the victim."[53] Biological reductionism and victim-blaming both have histories that began long before the 1960s. And they both share the view that the makeup and fate of individuals and groups can be explained by—can be reduced to—the properties of those individuals and groups. They find that social circumstances have at most only a minimal influence on individuals and groups. Critiques of these kinds of interpretations have shown that rather than being scientific and objective, they are pseudoscientific; that, consciously or not, they serve to misdirect attention from the need for fundamental social changes; and that they picture social organizations, institutions, and social power as requiring only mere adjustments. Biological reductionism and victim-blaming "encourage" individuals and groups to accept and make the best of their destiny.[54]

This kind of encouragement sometimes contradicts the advice given to the learning disabled. Judging from appearances, it often seems that LD organizations and professionals in no way accept an attitude of "making the best of a given destiny" since they organize around research projects, obtain funds, and establish special schools. However, saying that the correct program can help one circumvent and even overcome LD is still an implicit acceptance and even a reinforcement of the basic tenet of biological, individual-centered causation. When individuals "overcome," they are said, to use C. Wright Mills's distinction, to have overcome their own individual "troubles." And they implicitly "prove" that the "troubles of individuals are independent of social structural causation."[55] The biological starting point leaves only remediation, and certainly no real solution to what is described as LD. Most LD children are never helped to circumvent or overcome their academic difficulties, and thus most achieve no more than their "given destiny."

The biological explanation is by definition a form of blaming the victim, but one important distinction needs to be made from the start. Despite the argument that they are for everyone's good, some approaches are obviously so mean-spirited that it is difficult to imagine that anyone except the nastiest among us would really support them, such as the wholesale removal of brain tissue from the aggressive and violent called for by psychosurgery. Other explanations are essentially just as mean-spirited but present a more good-natured or reasonable appearance. An example of this type is sex-related differences in brain hemisphere function that are said to underlie women's inferior mathematical and spatial abilities and superior linguistic ability; another is genetically based differences in IQ test scores that require different educational programs. In both these instances, recognizing and acting on the differences can ultimately be beneficial for those with inferior or superior abilities. For example, although most women are less likely than men to succeed at mathematics or architecture, this does not mean that women are dumb, any more than men who might avoid trying to build on their own cognitive limitations. It merely means that if women know their respective cognitive abilities, they can pursue vocations in which, say, their linguistic skills could be maximized—for instance, by becoming executive secretaries for architects. Similarly with inherent IQ differences. Knowing children's mental abilities is necessary for schools to provide programs to meet their individual needs—that is, "gifted" classes for some and special education for many.

LD has a comparably caring face. People in the field are not out to harm children. They sincerely want to help provide the best education and guarantee personal development of children whose deficits, if untreated, would lead to painful, frustrating, unfulfilled lives. In fact, thanks to a great extent to dedicated, hard-working practitioners, the pervasive attitude of "passive acceptance"[56] toward the learning disabled and their poor academic achievement can be overcome, and some LD children do improve their reading and succeed in school. Caring practice and benevolent appearance make LD difficult to criticize because the field unites the Truth with the Good, so that questioning the former is consonant with an attack on the latter.

Within these and other conditions, LD did emerge as a "progressive" program, like many other reform programs of the time intended to rectify a problem advocacy groups had placed in the social foreground. But again, like many other reform programs, it misconstrued both the problem and its solution—thereby perpetuating the problem, while strongly encouraging social cohesion, stability, and hope. (It also justified social partitioning.) However, LD was not an ideology descending from above, forced on the duped and helpless. Rather, it ascended, through active social agents and institutions that had a logic of their own, an appearance of exemplary democracy and social progress in action, a motivation of concern and good intention, and a desire to achieve a "harmony of interests" among all concerned. But then the hard-working activists were transformed into allies of the very forces and conditions primarily responsible for the problem. This continued alliance to the social conditions responsible for the learning disabilities typifies one of the more pernicious elements of victimization—the victims themselves participate.

Toward an Alternative LD Theory

Criticism of LD runs parallel with some criticism of psychology for focusing on the individual without taking into account the interactions and relationships that contribute to the individual's development. For example, cognitive psychology, to which LD is closely associated, has been criticized for being overwhelmingly concerned with mental activity and "inner events" while disregarding social reality. Even psychological interpretations that claim to be "interactionist" still concentrate on the personal apprehension of social circumstances, considering them "relatively passive" and "waiting to be assimilated."[57]

Alternatives to conventional psychological theories that attempt to explain the complex interrelationship between the individual (including his or her biology) and social conditions have often been discussed and outlined in broad theoretical strokes, but they have remained at a rudimentary level. As authors Richard Lewontin, Steven Rose, and Leon Kamin observed in their criticism of biological determinism, we are still at a humble beginning in constructing an alternative interpretation:

> We are at a severe disadvantage. Unlike the biological determinists who have simple, even simplistic, views of the bases and forms of human existence, we do not pretend to know what is a correct description of all human societies. . . . But we do not stop our analysis by simply throwing up our hands and saying that it is all too complicated for analysis. Instead, we want to propose an alternative world view. It provides a framework for an analysis of complex systems that does not murder to dissect, but that maintains the full richness of interaction that inheres in the system of relationships.[58]

In keeping with this direction, the study of LD can be presented in a way that begins to take into account more than the countless minutiae of lab research, more than the personal accounts of struggles with LD, and more than the environmental influences in the creation of LD. The study can identify a complex microsystem, a wide web of forces and relations spanning the gamut of the personal to the social, thereby advancing an LD theory that includes the more technical aspects of learning dysfunctions. Some of the disadvantage that Lewontin, Rose, and Kamin felt in proposing an "alternative world view" could be lessened if we began to understand the complex LD microsystem itself and worked toward applying that understanding to a general psychological theory of the relationships and interactions between the individual and social conditions.

2

Perceptual and Attention Deficits

In reviewing an extensive body of research, I will start with the more familiar, less technical, and generally older explanations of the causes of learning disabilities and move on to the more rarefied, technical, and generally more recent explanations, such as those using new technology for examining the brain. This chapter examines perceptual-deficit and then attention-deficit explanations. The latter, though less well known, are related to the first group: some attention deficits are thought actually to be perceptual deficits, and vice versa.

Reversals

It is common for many beginning readers to reverse letters and certain words, and they usually stop by the time they reach the third-grade level. The reading-disabled child, however, is said to experience extensive and persistent reversals. Through the early 1970s, nearly a half-century after Orton first wrote about strephosymbolia, his emphasis on the diagnostic significance of letter and word reversals, though modified, had remained a consistent canon. "Genetic dyslexic boys," wrote one major figure in the field, "have a tendency to reverse the order of letters in a word or reorganize them in such a way that they spell a different word."[1] Minimal brain dysfunction syndrome (MBD), seen as the cause of learning disabilities, revealed itself through "frequent perceptual reversals in reading and in writing letters and numbers."[2] A handbook on LD explained that the neurologically impaired learning-disabled child "will often enter the school system with . . . a visual perceptual set which makes him confuse 13 and B, and which makes him see b as d and p as q, etc."[3] As these statements as well as examples in the previous chapter show, perceptual dysfunction and particularly reversals have perhaps been seen as the most common problem of the learning disabled.

The topic of reversals is therefore a good place to begin testing the evidence substantiating the neurological thesis on which the LD field is built. Even if that thesis cannot be proved, is there enough evidence to suggest that it is probably correct?

Those who until the mid-1970s still held to Orton's basic ideas unfortunately paid little or no attention to one plain truth: those ideas were only beliefs. Through no more than repeated assertion, though, his theory took on the authority of proven fact. The extent to which this had occurred was made clear in a paper published in 1970, just when those authorities quoted at the beginning of this chapter were proclaiming what dyslexics "have" and describing with certainty what they will do with respect to reversals. This paper noted that "the significance of reversals in dyslexia is unknown because the reversal phenomenon itself has not been studied systematically and a number of *preliminary* questions have not been fully answered."[4] Two of those preliminary questions were simply extraordinary: professional confidence aside, it was not known how frequently and consistently reversals occur in beginning readers or whether reversals made up a constant proportion of all errors.

More than a few authorities were no doubt surprised to learn, after taking the time to study the frequency of reversals, that the "symptom" accounted for only a small proportion of errors made by reading-disabled children. Reversals accounted for 25 percent of the misread letters, whereas "other consonant" errors (for example *rat* for *raw*, *trap* for *tap*) made up 32 percent, and vowel errors *(pig* for *peg)* were responsible for 43 percent of misread letters.

Although Orton had distinguished between two kinds of reversal problems, letter-sequence errors (*was* for *saw*) and letter-orientation errors *(d* or *p* for *b),* he and his followers assumed that both were manifestations of the same cerebral dysfunction. However, the one study that approached reversals in a systematic, quantitative way found that these two kinds of reversal errors were wholly uncorrelated—that is, the frequency with which a child might have one kind of reversal error was unrelated to the frequency of the other. Therefore, contrary to Orton's thesis, "no support whatever [was found] for supposing that they [the two kinds of reversals] have a common cause." Moreover, and perhaps most important, the study also concluded that the two kinds of reversals were unrelated to a child's reading ability.

Another study went even further.[5] A comparison of normal and disabled readers demonstrated that both groups experienced about the same number of letter and word reversals, with normal readers making 20 percent letter-reversal and 7 percent word-reversal errors; while the respective percentages for disabled readers were 22 percent and 5 percent. These similarities held through nine years of age, the turning point at which continued reversal errors was thought to portend certain reading doom. Yet a third study found no correlation between the percentages of reversal errors made on a variety of tests and reading levels. In fact, of the two children with the highest number of reversal errors, one was a normal reader (at about grade level) and the other a so-called good reader (one to two years above grade level).[6]

The truth is that reversal errors by both normal and disabled readers can be more consistently explained by a lack of adequate instruction than by any organic deficiencies. Evidence for this conclusion comes from a series of studies, conducted from 1958 to the mid-1970s, that demonstrated "that even 4 and 5 year old children" could be taught to discriminate between reversed letters (such as *b* and *d* or *p* and *q*) and to comprehend the spatial relationships inherent in these reversals (such as left/right and up/down). The studies showed that the discrimination necessary to avoid reversals was a "learned cognitive skill"—in other words, an ability children needed to be taught. Reviewers of this research had concluded: "The assumption that letter reversals were related to [Orton's theory of] confused lateral dominance is accepted as a fact by many educators although its veracity has never been established empirically." In fact, reversals had been found to be "relatively trivial and easily corrected errors, not . . . indicators of internal pathology or serious reading problems that must be remediated with special perceptual training materials."[7] Of course, it is quite possible that studies relying on statistical correlation would fail to identify LD children with genuine neurological impairments because if there were only a small number of these children in an experimental group the overall differences would not be "statistically significant." However, that just proves the point: at most, pathology could be blamed for reversals in no more than a very small number of the learning disabled.

Still, "relatively trivial and easily corrected" though the errors may be, some LD experts continued to see *b,* where the facts clearly indicated *d.* Consider the following. A 1979 pamphlet published by the National Institute of Mental Health pictures a nice-looking boy, about ten years old, and asks: "Why does he read SAW for WAS?" "Can't he see the difference between b and d?" Under the heading, "Who Is This Child?" the answers are given: "This is the child who at school age reads on for no, writes 41 for 14, p for d or q for b, and can't remember the sequence of letters that make up a word." Further he is described as a "child with a disorder" who, in contrast to children with intact nervous systems, suffers from what "a doctor would say" is "neurological immaturity or minimal brain dysfunction."[8]

In a 1985 report aired over three mornings on NBC's *Today Show,* the words *DOG* and *GOD* are flashed under the heading, "Perception." The interviewer asks an LD expert to explain the graphic, which is meant to illustrate that the dyslexic child "sees things just the opposite." "That has to do with sequencing, or reversal problems, difficulty with left and right," the specialist replies. "That's a very typical problem."[9] A 1983 article describing a "ninety-minute procedure" for the "identification of dyslexia" recommends that specialists "check for evidence of . . . reversals of letters or letter-order."[10]

The history of reversals raises issues discernible in all areas of the neurological explanation. Here I mention two and will return to them as I continue to examine LD research and practice. The first pertains to the influence of scientific information on the field. Notwithstanding the many specialists who now recognize that reversals are not what they were once said to be, a considerable number continue to write about and accept this undocumented theory as fact and use it for actually diagnosing children as learning disabled. This process has become a pattern for LD authorities and practitioners. Are they simply unaware of the latest scientific findings? To some extent they are, but a more accurate interpretation would be that proponents of the LD thesis have tended to emphasize those scientific "findings" that support it and to disregard research that does not. Contradictory research has influenced the field and has helped many in it to abandon the predominant view, but most have resisted accepting such research until it becomes scientifically untenable to do so. (As should be clear by now, some cling to the view even beyond that point.) Most important, supporters of the neurological explanation often finally accept opposing research only when another neurological explanation has been devised, one that acknowledges the rejected belief as a scientific correction and a movement forward for the field in the same direction.

A second issue raised by reversals concerns the value of critiquing an LD explanation now generally rejected. In my insistent review of a tainted history, am I beating a dead horse? In *Social Amnesia,* Russell Jacoby discusses "society's repression of remembrance [of] society's own past."[11] Forgetting our past lets us hold on to illusions about the meaning of the present. Amnesia pervades the LD field with pernicious consequences, due to a virtually complete absence of any historical account (except for a few mythical histories). Previous social processes, intentions, and known malpractices are seldom explored or used to measure current work. Amnesia allows the field to march from one hypothesis to another, without questioning whether it is working toward a true explanation or only justifying an old, unproved one.

■●▲ Perception

Reversals are only the most well-publicized of numerous perceptual deficits that have long figured prominently in LD explanations. Deficit-oriented theories propose that these reading problems are actually caused by perceptual deficits which are themselves caused by neurological dysfunctions. Thus mediating biological mechanisms impede learning. The learning disabled are not said to have sensory problems—they can see and hear satisfactorily—but something else prevents them from processing linguistic and some nonlinguistic material as normal children do. They may be unable to distinguish between forms of similar words, to associate words or parts of words with their sounds, or to link either in the eye or in the ear a sequence of word parts to construct a word.

Researchers have scrambled perceptual relationships in every way imaginable. In addition to being analyzed in isolation, different perceptual modes have been studied in the following combinations: visual-auditory, auditory-visual, visual-visual, auditory-auditory, visual-spatial, visual/spatial-visual/spatial, visual/auditory-visual/auditory, among others. When other factors of children's literacy activities are taken into account, such as the motor control necessary for writing and spelling, the lines for investigating processing defects become still more crossed. In order to study these combinations, researchers have created many tasks which children have now been fiddling with for decades. They might be asked to decide whether visual or auditory stimuli are the same (can they distinguish between "sit" and "sat"), or to match sound patterns to dot patterns (for example, would two finger taps with two seconds between each best correspond to: . . , . / . , or . . . ?).[12]

With the blossoming of these combinations, a group of perceptual-deficit theories has sprouted up to match. The more straightforward ones relate to deficits in a single perceptual mode. For more than one mode, there are theories of intersensory-association deficits. A child may be unable to associate letters with sounds (visual-auditory or visual/visual-auditory/auditory) or sounds with letters (auditory-visual or auditory/auditory-visual/visual). Figure-ground (or pattern) perception theories might be used to explain that the child cannot read because he or she cannot visually distinguish patterns from complex backgrounds, and thus has trouble identifying, analyzing, and reading word patterns. There is also a theory that dyslexics cannot serialize information either by sound or by sight, for example, being unable to perceive a sequence of sounds in a word or words in a sentence.

From the 1930s onward, many perceptual tests have been developed and marketed for use with groups ranging from LD school children to adults with brain injuries. These include: the Bender Visual-Motor Gestalt Test, the Motor-Free Test of Visual Perception, the Wepman Test of Auditory Discrimination, and, by no means least, the Lamb-Chop Test of Direction Sense, which uses a figure in the shape of a lamb chop to test spatial perception. In addition to the tests themselves, a large number of perceptual instruments have been created for research.[13]

A critical difficulty with this research is devising a test to evaluate perception only. In one auditory-perception test, for example, children are asked to listen to a word and then change it by either adding, deleting, or replacing portions of it. For example, children are told: "Say 'meat'; now say it again, but don't say /t/." Or, "Say it again but instead of /m/ say /s/." Is this a test of "auditory-perceptual skills" alone? Consider the answers. Children responding to these directions are most likely to get a correct answer if they know the word; know its spelling; have learned to distinguish long, double-vowel sounds from short, single-vowel ones; and are familiar enough with the word to be able to recognize and manipulate the three-part construction (consonant, vowel, consonant).

While the results from such a test might lead to the conclusion that disabled readers do not perceive print the same way that good readers do, that would still not prove that perceptual differences (perceiving words differently) are due to perceptual deficits. Take another example. Because good readers almost by definition have more reading knowledge, when they look at the word *remarkable,* they are likely, both auditorily and visually, to perceive the word in three sections, because they know that *re* is a prefix and *able* is a suffix. Poor readers, on the other hand, are likely to organize the units according to patterns that vary in their minds as they make one attempt or another. At one time they might read the *k* as associated with the *ar* and, at another, with *ab*, thereby alternately reading the "small words" within the larger one as *ark* or *cab*. Thus, while likely to read the word in four sections instead of three, the poor reader may also have to contend with various pairings making up those divisions, depending on how he or she has unsuccessfully "sounded out" the word at a particular moment.

Visual-auditory association will vary as well. Good readers will associate the prefix and suffix with fairly consistent sounds, and the central *ar*, while appearing as a visual pattern, will also indicate a distinct vowel sound, as in *car* or *bar*, not the short-vowel sound of *cat* or *bat*. Because the latter vowel sound is learned early in reading instruction poor readers are likely to try it first. Similarly, they are likely to sound out *le* as *lee*. A study of these perceptual tests bore out the importance of reading ability. It found that there is a higher correlation between tests scores of reading ability and word recognition than between scores for word-recognition and either auditory- or visual-perception tests.[14]

As with LD research in general, recent perceptual-deficit studies have shown a tendency to make the most out of the least. One study, for instance, reports that disabled readers have significant perceptual deficiencies compared to normal readers.[15] Children were given six tests to check several facets of auditory-visual perception. Of thirty-six correlations made between problems with perception and reading achievement, sixteen were statistically significant. On the face of it, that would appear to be strong evidence that such a connection exists. However, an examination of the correlations raises considerable doubt.

Each test consisted of twenty items. For five of the tests, the normal readers had average scores of twelve or thirteen correct, or about 63 percent, and the LD children scored between nine and eleven, or about 53 percent correct. Both groups scored higher on the sixth test, but the relative levels remained about the same. In addition, for each test there was a fair amount of overlap between the groups, with LD children sometimes scoring higher than normal children. Thus, while the normal readers did better than the LD group, they still missed a considerable percentage of the items (about 37 percent), sometimes did worse than LD children, and in all made enough errors to suggest that they themselves might have perceptual problems. However, the study did not even faintly suggest such an interpretation. The standard for normal perception became 37 percent, because the children who made that percentage of errors were normal readers. Conversely, answering incorrectly 47 percent or more immediately branded LD children as having dysfunctional perception. Why? No reason was given other than the implied one that the LD children in the study achieved this percentage of errors. It is important to examine why the LD children did not do as well as others on these tests, but the tautology underpinning the conclusions does nothing to explain the differences. The use of this kind of numerology in interpreting perceptual experiments is not uncommon.[16]

In an extensive review of perceptual deficit theories, researcher Frank Vellutino has argued that where perceptual deficits have appeared to distinguish disabled and normal readers, other factors—such as problem-solving ability, motivation, reading ability, or language skills—were actually responsible for the differences.[17] Several of Vellutino's own studies illustrate this interpretation. One used Hebrew letters and words with three groups of children: poor readers, good readers who did not know Hebrew, and a third group of children learning the language.[18] Vellutino assumed that using a language familiar to only one group would allow for a clearer distinction between purely visual perceptual ability and other linguistic skills. When asked to write the Hebrew letters and words from memory, the first two groups achieved the same level of recall. Neither group performed as well as the children who were learning Hebrew, whose superior performance was attributed to their familiarity with the language and, more specifically, with the letter associations. This jibes with the experience of anyone who has studied a foreign language and observed how much easier it is to recognize letters and spell words when one can name the letters and pronounce the words. (This is especially true if the language is very different from one's native tongue, as, say, the Cyrillic alphabet used for Slavic languages would be for English speakers.)[19]

From this and other experiments, Vellutino concluded that the "perceptual errors" were in fact "linguistic intrusion errors." In other words, both good and poor readers perceive words correctly but good readers know the names of the words and the poor readers do not. The real cause of dyslexia, Vellutino proposed, was linguistic, not perceptual, deficits—problems identifying word sounds, parts, or meanings. In the next chapter I will discuss what these linguistic deficits are and how they have been interpreted by Vellutino and others.

After various people over a half-century had investigated and diagnosed perceptual deficits in the reading disabled, Vellutino undertook a comprehensive review of the relevant literature. He traced a history which moves like a climb over a mountain range. Theories of perceptual dysfunction had been proposed and tested, and eventually been disproven and replaced by theories with seemingly superior interpretations of the problem, and those in turn had also been rejected over time. Systematically going through each and every explanation, Vellutino concluded that in spite of all this very considerable effort, the perceptual-deficit research had not explained why dyslexics had trouble learning to read:

> Having reviewed most of the important studies of the past ten to fifteen years, I can say with some degree of assurance that there is no conclusive evidence to support the intersensory deficit explanation of reading disability. The theory can be questioned on both empirical and theoretical grounds, and in neither context does it fare very well.[20]

Vellutino's critique of perceptual-deficit theories has been echoed by others. In a recent review of LD explanations, an author who had previously published papers suggesting that perceptual deficits caused reading problems, apparently reassessed and reinterpreted the data of his previous work, which he and a coauthor cited along with other studies:

> It has been found that the relationship of perceptual abilities (visual and auditory) to academic achievement is of insufficient magnitude to validate the assumption that perceptual skills underlie academic learning.
>
> LD children do not exhibit greater difficulty than normal children in ability to integrate one modality function with another modality function (intersensory integration, cross modal perception, intermodal transfer).
>
> Evidence suggests that although LD children may exhibit perceptual deficiencies, reading ability is not related to the degree of perceptual deficiency.[21]

Group relationships of "insufficient magnitude" do not, of course, mean that no children suffer from significant perceptual deficits. However, a relationship between those deficits and reading problems is clearly quite rare.

Although critiques of perceptual-deficit explanations have been put forward since the late 1960s and have the support of many in the LD field, they have had little effect on school practice. Forty-three states include perceptual deficits within their definition of LD, and a good portion of LD testing at the local school-district level focuses on these deficits.[22] Only twelve states include the category in their criteria for identifying children as learning disabled, however, but there is no contradiction in this, especially when one considers the frequent use of perceptual tests in diagnosis at the local level. It appears that practitioners include perceptual deficits as part of their LD definition, evaluate children with perceptual tests, and discuss perceptual problems in evaluations, but because of the criticism of the perceptual-deficit diagnosis in recent years, the actual term is not used in formal identification.

In this area of research, perceptual functioning has generally been explained as something determined by the individual's abilities and frame of mind. Few have considered the specific effects of interpersonal relationships on perceptual development. One study that did so arrived at results that promised interesting new avenues of investigation, while highlighting the constrained framework of most perceptual-deficit studies.[23] College students majoring in special education participated in a study they were told was to measure visual-motor coordination in normal and learning-disabled children. The college students were taught to use a testing device consisting of four limb controls (foot pedals like car accelerators and hand levers) that a person would try to manipulate to match lights flashing for each limb. (The device had been used in space research to measure deterioration in visual-motor coordination after stress, exposure to drugs, and various environmental conditions.)

The college students then taught fourth-grade children to use it, explaining that they were studying "how well their eyes, hands, and feet worked together."[24] All the children were selected at random from classrooms of "normal" students; none had ever been diagnosed as learning disabled or was in a special-education program. However, the college students were told that half of them were learning disabled. Different colored scoring sheets (green for the learning-disabled children, white for the normal) were used to heighten the college students' awareness of the children's labels. When the children's performance was tabulated, subjectively by the college students' records and objectively by a scoring mechanism in the device, both tabulations showed that the supposedly learning-disabled girls performed significantly worse than normal girls; the learning-disabled boys also performed worse than the normal boys, although their differences were not considered statistically significant. Thus, the learning-disabled children were not simply perceived as doing worse than normal children; their perceptual-motor performance—objectively measured—was worse. To some degree, then, they actually performed as relatively disabled.

Exactly why this happened was not investigated, but it is clear that the instructional interactions varied according to how the children were grouped and affected the test results. The primary value of this experiment, then, is less in its specifics (for example, why the girls showed greater differences, and what are the effects of labeling) than in its suggestion that subtleties in instructional relationships can influence perceptual abilities and "create" perceptual dysfunction.

The failure of perceptual-deficit research to validate its own hypothesis can be attributed in large part to the reasoning behind it. The logic runs like this: A researcher observes children's reading activities—how they learn the sounds of letters and letter combinations—and identifies a perceptual process, say, visual-auditory association. The process can then be isolated—not just labeled but actually "extracted" and demonstrated with an instrument. Consequently, the individual's performance on that instrument must be a measure of the applicable perceptual process. In this manner, the instrument *related to* the perceptual function is transformed into a *test of* that function, and the complex factors involved in the task (such as knowledge, motivation, confidence, problem-solving ability) are disregarded.

Missing from this reasoning is the recognition that reading activity is not additive—that is, that there is not visual-auditory functioning *and* memory *and* self-confidence *and* instructional method *and* interpersonal relationships *and* motivation, and so on. Merely because each of these can be conceptually abstracted from human activity, it does not mean that they exist independently and can be studied and measured in pure form, separate from other ingredients thought to be removable *parts* of the activity. Nor does it mean that evaluations of these separate parts can explain how each one works.

■•▲ Eye Movements

One perceptual-deficit theory holds that reading-disabled children move their eyes in abnormal ways, due to a cerebral dysfunction, and this interferes with their perception of reading material. Although this theory is fundamentally related to perceptual-deficit explanations previously discussed, it will be examined separately because of its distinct character. Because (for the sighted) reading is a heavily visual activity, this hypothesis appears reasonable. Anyone who has worked with poor readers has observed how they appear to read in a jerky, jumpy way, as if their eyes were focusing erratically all around the words. Researchers have pursued the association of eye movements and reading ability for many years, at least as far back as 1879, when Emile Javal ingeniously studied whether people read letter-by-letter, a popular assumption at that time. He discovered that readers actually glance at meaningful units and move their eyes quickly along lines of print.[25] Since the late 1950s, there seems to have been a consensus that excessive visual fixations, frequent regressions (right-to-left eye movements made during reading), and other eye movements often found among disabled readers are a symptom and not a cause of poor reading. This conclusion is still argued today. For example, a recent summary of eye-movement research by an ophthalmologist who is a proponent of the concept of dyslexia once again repeated: "it was the degree of [reading] comprehension that produces the type of ocular movement," not the other way around.[26]

It would seem reasonable to conclude, given such discussions in the literature, that the issue had been laid to rest. But not so. An important axiom of the LD field is that no biological explanation ever dies or fades away. Like Antaeus, just when the explanation seems to have been flung to the ground for the last time, it bounces back with renewed vigor, challenging once again. In this spirit, the effort to document the causal role of faulty eye movements arising from neurological deficits continues. In one of the most recent efforts, George Pavlidis, a major proponent of abnormal-eye-movement explanations, poses the following rhetorical questions in the titles of two papers: "Do eye movements hold the key to dyslexia?" and, "How can dyslexia be objectively diagnosed?"[27] The answer to the first question is yes; the answer to the second is, With an eye-movement test.

Pavlidis published experiments and discussed unpublished ones in which he recorded and analyzed the eye-movement patterns of dyslexics, backward readers, and normal children in several ways, such as by the number and size of saccades (the movement of the eye as it jumps from one fixation point to another), fixations, and regressions. Explaining his research methods, he emphasized that he was looking for a way to diagnose dyslexia "objectively." He correctly observed that LD research has constantly faced a problem studying dyslexics because a comparison of disabled and normal learners obviously requires a differentiation between the two groups in the first place. Also required is a differentiation of the learning disabled—whose problems are presumed to be of neurological origin—from poor learners—whose problems can be explained by exclusionary factors, such as social circumstances or emotional problems. Pavlidis has pointed out that unless these distinctions are made before research tests are administered, it is impossible to know which of the group's characteristics are related to the results. Thus Pavlidis has stressed the rigor with which his studies initially differentiated dyslexics, poor readers, and normal readers.

Regrettably, he gives no evidence that this care was actually observed in practice. Beyond outlining a fairly inclusive list of exclusionary criteria, nowhere in his published work is there a description of the method used to determine how a child met criteria such as having "adequate motivation to read," "no lack of educational opportunities," and "no overt emotional problems prior to commencing reading."[28] This is no worse than what other LD researchers have done, but it is also no better.

Regardless, somehow these judgments were made and the goal of finding an objective measure of dyslexia was pursued. In his first experiments, Pavlidis compared eye movements of suspected dyslexics, poor readers, and good readers and found the dyslexics significantly different on all measures. For example, dyslexics had a greater number of eye movements, a greater number of forward eye movements and regressions, and longer fixation times.[29] (The eye movements of the poor and the normal readers were essentially comparable.) The results for the dyslexics were the same whether they read easy or hard material, suggesting that their erratic eye movements stemmed from an inherent dysfunction not dependent on the level of the writing. On the other hand, poor and normal readers showed erratic eye movements only when the reading materials became difficult.

These results led Pavlidis to hypothesize that, since the eye-movement problems were symptoms of an inherent deficit in sequencing, the dyslexics should show sequencing problems in a nonreading task requiring similar sequencing abilities. The task devised was to visually track a series of lights that flashed one at a time. Lights were used because they "constitute a universal cross-cultural stimulus . . . completely free of all environmental and intellectual factors."[30] The hypothesis was confirmed when the eye movements of the three groups were found to be virtually the same as those in the previous experiments. Thus, it seemed, if dyslexics experienced erratic eye movements irrespective of whether they were looking at reading material, there must be a "constitutional disability involved in dyslexia."[31]

The history of the LD field seems dotted by such remarkable findings, with researchers emerging from their labs barely able to contain a cry of "Eureka!" This new research seemed especially exciting because it claimed to have discovered what others had always missed. Eye-movement studies published around the same time put Pavlidis's work in strong relief because, like most previous research, they did *not* report that dyslexics and normal readers had different saccadic eye movements.[32] The differences they did find were attributed to dissimilar problem-solving strategies or to dissimilar attention, not to underlying pathology in the learning disabled.[33]

Pavlidis's research attracted professional and media attention and earned him a nomination for the award of the International Reading

Association and a life fellowship from the International Academy for Research in Learning Disabilities. The reported findings also caught the eye of other researchers, who set about to replicate this "key to dyslexia."[34]

The first replication study designed a nonreading task similar to Pavlidis's, using a row of lights that flashed sequentially from left to right and then back.[35] The study selected dyslexics according to conventional exclusionary criteria and examined them according to measures similar to Pavlidis's. However, the researchers found that the eye movements of the dyslexic group were essentially the same as the normal readers. Thus they concluded that their study provided "no support for the notion that eye-movements recorded from a sequential lights test provide a firm basis for the objective discrimination of dyslexics from controls."

In the same issue of the *British Journal of Psychology* in which this study was published, Pavlidis responded that it was not surprising the respective results differed, because the investigations used fundamentally different approaches in subject selection and experimental method. I do not believe his criticisms repudiated the conclusion of the new research, but I will not assess them in the main body of this book because they were even more convincingly refuted by other replication studies that followed.[36]

Two of the studies, for example, listed subject-selection criteria as thorough as Pavlidis's and provided more information than he had about the method used to determine whether or not the children met those criteria.[37] (Of course, these studies were better only relatively speaking; the selection methods by themselves are less than satisfactory.) Except for using an illuminated spot on a screen instead of flashing lights, these studies closely followed Pavlidis's research design. Not only did they fail to distinguish between dyslexics and normal readers on several measures of eye movement, one exception was quite unexpected:

> . . . the control children *made slightly more* saccades than the dyslexic group during the task whereas Pavlidis found that his reading disabled children made more saccades than his control population. On the average, Pavlidis' control group made only seven saccades in his task, while the reading disabled group made 26. This is a difference of over 300%; our subjects showed a difference of only 10% and *in the opposite direction.*[38]

There was also considerable overlap in the number of eye movements of dyslexics and normal readers—quite different from Pavlidis's report that no overlap was found in the total number of eye movements made during the sequential tracking task. The differences here and in other replication studies led to the conclusion that "Pavlidis' finding is exceptional and results from factors other than dyslexia."[39] Exactly what these other "factors" were, the researchers did not say. Other replication studies, undertaken "to replicate Pavlidis's methods in all possible detail," also failed to find any eye movement differences between dyslexic and normal children.[40]

This fusillade did not deter Pavlidis. In a review article titled, "Eye Movements in Dyslexia," published in the *Journal of Learning Disabilities,* he quickly passed over the research that contradicted his own, saying again, as in his earlier reply, that differing results were attributable to different criteria for subject selection and different experimental techniques (such as the timing and spacing of the lights).[41] However, Pavlidis's latest response went further than before, stating that his findings "have been supported by other studies in Europe and the United States." These supportive studies are not discussed in the article but they are described in the bibliography. One is an "informal presentation" at the British Psychological Society's International Conference on Dyslexia in 1982. Apparently this presentation was so informal that afterward it was neither written nor published, judging from the note following the citation, which reads: "Also, personal communication April, 1984." The other two sources said to support Pavlidis's research are cited as "prepublication" manuscripts, both from Czechoslovakia.

The majority of the thirteen pages of one of these manuscripts consists of a general discussion of various speculations about eye movements and reading disabilities, and in the entire paper only two sentences appear to deal specifically with findings on the relationship between eye movements and dyslexia. Under a subsection titled, "Eye Movements and School Performance," these two sentences read:

> Children [who] were examined on their first attendance at the elementary school and in whom a retarded development of eye movements was observed had, in the middle and at the end of the first year, *generally* a worse performance. On the other hand, children in whom a normal pattern of eye movement was found showed *generally* also a better performance.[42]

Except for noting that the latter correlation was very significant, no other information is provided: nothing on whether dyslexia was synonymous with "worse" school performance, nothing about the number or percentage of students who had erratic eye movements, no comparison of the groups' eye movements. Exactly how eye movements were "generally" associated with dyslexia is also not stated. In any case, even if these summary sentences were taken at face value, they would not provide much support for Pavlidis's position. "Generally" can only be taken to mean that a certain number of low academic performers had erratic eye movements but others did not. In Pavlidis's papers, of course, the dyslexics were said to have overwhelmingly anomalous eye movements.[43]

■●▲ Attention

LD explanations take different forms. Sometimes they are like Antaeus, at other times like Hydra. An explanation will rise and later will be rejected, but only to be replaced. Some LD researchers who have rejected the perceptual explanation of LD have replaced it with "attention." For example, a perceptual disorder might be said actually to reflect an attention disorder, perhaps a selective attention disorder that prevents a child from selecting the important parts of language to focus on when learning to read. Another attention explanation substituting for a perceptual-deficit explanation might be that a child has an attention-span dysfunction (cannot attend to a task for the time required to learn or do it), which causes perceptual difficulties. For example, a child cannot hear a short-vowel sound in a word because he or she does not sustain attention long enough to perceive it.

Attention deficit has become the "official" medical category for diagnosing LD. The American Psychiatric Association's 1980 *Diagnostic and Statistical Manual of Mental Disorders* is the manual from which "mental disorders" are diagnosed.[44] It designates "attention deficit disorder" as an official category for classifying children.[45] The term replaces previously popular ones that had been criticized for being nebulous and undiagnosable. Attention deficit disorder, said to be the most common symptom of the nebulous and undiagnosable terms, was selected both as chief symptom and as name for the category because it was thought to be a behavioral and more objective description of the elusive condition. In the words of the manual:

> In the past a variety of names have been attached to this disorder, including . . . Hyperactive Child Syndrome, Minimal Brain Damage, Minimal Brain Dysfunction, Minimal Cerebral Dysfunction, and Minor Cerebral Dysfunction. In this manual, Attention Deficit is the name given to this disorder, since attentional difficulties are prominent and virtually always present among children with these diagnoses.[46]

Intent on even greater precision, the authors of *DSM III* concluded that an attention deficit disorder did not necessarily include hyperactivity. Therefore, "this disorder" was divided into two subcategories: attention deficit disorder "with hyperactivity" and "without hyperactivity." Because we are discussing LD, I will omit addressing hyperactivity. But for all of this new precision, the authors only exercised more artfulness than accuracy in a tangled logic by which the notion of neurological dysfunction remained active and only the words changed. If the condition cannot be described by symptoms, the reasoning seemed to go, then one or more symptoms supposedly manifesting this previously undiagnosable "condition" could be used as the name of the condition. Simply put, *DSM III* used new terms to refer to the same old terms and conditions.

The description of a child with an attention deficit disorder (with or without hyperactivity) is as vague and preposterous as that of minimal brain dysfunction, a concept I will say more about later in the book. A child with the "essential features" of the disorder "often fails to finish things he or she starts; often doesn't seem to listen; has difficulty concentrating on school work; often acts before thinking; frequently calls out in class." Not surprisingly, even those who believe there is such a condition as an attention deficit disorder agree that it "is not well-defined" and that a meaningful classification system has yet to be developed "so that you're studying kids with the same problems, not just those who won't sit still in class."[47]

Attention deficit disorder is different from other LD classifications in that it is both educational and medical. The medical use of the diagnosis, whether it is called attention deficit disorder or one of the earlier terms, has been the official basis for treating this "disorder" with drugs, mostly Ritalin. Consequently, if the diagnosis is faulty, prescribing the drugs becomes questionable. However, for those who prescribe drugs to children diagnosed as having an attention deficit disorder, poor definitions and a classification system with questionable grounds has not hampered their practice any more than it did when the "disorder" was called something else.

Exactly what the biological basis of an attention deficit might be and how it might cause LD has been depicted in various ways. One explanation is that attention deficits are caused by a dysfunction of the reticular system of the brain, a portion that plays a major role in the brain's general activation and arousal level; another, that the learning disabled do not have general arousal problems but problems of focused arousal, possibly occurring because of neurotransmitter dysfunctions; a third, that the attention deficit is due to a problem of shifting from one brain hemisphere to the other while attending to a task.[48]

These and other biological explanations of "attention" display several key problems. While it would seem that learning-disabled children have more attention difficulties than other children, not all attention researchers can agree even on this point.[49] For example, in a study of several facets of attention (such as selective attention, distractibility, and sustained attention), researchers observed children in a series of laboratory tests requiring them to respond in various ways to attention tasks using letters and symbols.[50] Making 232 observations per child failed to find differences in attention between normal and learning-disabled children. Attention behavior observed for the same children in their regular or special-education classrooms also produced the same results: 1,328 observations of different kinds of attention for each child failed to differentiate the learning-disabled from the normal children.

Conclusions that the learning disabled have attention deficits have been derived largely from one line of research, which is concerned with children's ability to filter out extraneous information. Typically, a research project of this kind asks children to concentrate on and respond to a primary (central) task mixed with extraneous (incidental) information that the child must filter out—for example, remembering cards picturing one kind of category (animals) among cards that have pictures of several categories (animals, household objects, tools). Measurements of how much is remembered about the primary task and about the extraneous information presumably tells researchers something about the selective attention of children and their ability to filter out irrelevant information. This and similar attention-deficit research has been criticized in several respects. The most severe criticism of this so-called central-incidental learning challenges the very validity of the task for uncovering attention differences in learning-disabled children. Several studies using the approach have not found that learning-disabled children are more distracted by incidental information than normal learners.[51] The inevitable conclusion from the literature is that one of the primary research methods for establishing attention deficits in the learning disabled has serious limitations, may be totally invalid, and seems unable even to differentiate disabled from normal learners.[52] In addition to seriously questioning the extent of attentional deficits among the learning disabled—even where an association between classroom attention problems and reading disabilities has been found—some researchers have been reluctant to conclude that the former plays a causal role.[53]

A fundamental weakness of this research is the difficulty of knowing what exactly attention deficits are. Is the so-called deficit due to overall lethargy, an inability to sustain attention, an inability to select the right thing to concentrate on, a problem focusing too narrowly within the area requiring attention, or an inability to filter out unnecessary information?[54] Furthermore, attention-deficit tasks such as central-incidence learning are not pure measures of attention because they also involve motivation, memory, problem-solving strategies, and verbal abilities.[55] A number of studies have also identified many distinct ingredients in "attention" and emphasized the difficulty of singling out and determining the relationship of the ingredients to LD. One study that dealt with motivation—a factor always lurking behind a child's response to any task—illustrates this difficulty. In this experiment motivation was tied to money.[56] Learning-disabled children were rewarded with from one to three cents for each item they remembered in a task using ten cards. With a three-cent reward the children remembered an average of 7.56 cards; for a one-cent reward their average recollection was 3.81 cards. Similar results were found for other money arrangements. These findings were interpreted as demonstrating that LD children possessed the necessary processes and strategies for attending to and solving tasks but found it more difficult than normal learners to execute them—doing so "apparently takes a high degree of payoff."[57] Other research has found even more directly what appears to be implied in many studies, that experience with a task strongly influences a child's ability to pay attention.[58]

Research has also been unable to show that attention deficits are symptoms of cerebral dysfunction. Few studies have actually attempted to look directly at brain functioning associated with attention. One study that did used electroencephalograph (EEG) recordings to study possible neuropsychological correlates. First, auditory attention was examined through the use of tone "pips" (or beeps) played through a headset. In one part of the study, normal and disabled readers had to listen for a particular "signal" pip among pips of different tones; when they heard it, they were to press a button. In the other part, the children heard numerous pips in one ear but had to ignore them while they attended to the pips in the other ear, among which they had to listen for a signal pip. On hearing it, they again were to press a button. These tests provided a measurement of selective attention (how many times the pips were identified) and sustained attention (how long the children could continue listening for the pips). Measurement scores for both tasks were not significantly different for the disabled and the normal reading groups.[59]

While the children were doing these tests, electrical waves were recorded from several areas of their brain. In only one area, a portion of the parietal lobe, was there a significant difference found between the groups. However, from this single difference the investigators did not conclude that there was any kind of organic attention problem.

Rather, they theorized, it might reflect differences in information processing and problem solving, with the reading-disabled group perhaps processing information less efficiently and effectively. In any event, this speculation was congruent with the researchers' general conclusion that the overall brain wave and behavioral similarities provide "no evidence for dysfunctions of sustained or selective attention in children whose primary problem is a reading disability."[60]

Research more directly related to classroom teaching has shed light on the purported association between attention deficits and neurological deficits, and on the effect of instruction on attention. A group of children were identified as learning disabled on the basis of poor perceptual-motor test scores and by their display of a "positive sign of choreiform movement" (irregular, involuntary jerky movements), a sign taken by neurologists to indicate "a problem in neurological integrity" in children eight years or older.[61]

The mispronunciation of basic spelling patterns, such as *ai, ee, ea, oi,* and *oy,* was used as a basis for studying selective attention. One group of children was given direct instruction on these patterns through a program designed to promote selective attention. The teaching method involved no unusual techniques; it was merely an organized and consistent system readily available in reading-instruction books and presumably similar to the instruction a trained teacher would use in beginning reading. It was the kind of instruction these children should have received in normal teaching, since these vowel patterns are so basic to reading. This "selective-attention" group was taught by undergraduate students who were trained to use the instructional procedures but who had no previous teaching experience.

A second group was taught individually or in small groups by reading specialists and special-education teachers and received more than twice the amount of reading instruction as the first group. The curriculum was not prescribed, but the study presumed that the trained teachers would provide capable basic-reading instruction.

When the two groups were tested following the instructional period, the selective-attention group was able to identify significantly more words containing these basic literacy patterns than the children in the second group. The respective tests scores were approximately 85 percent to 35 percent correct.

There are a few important conclusions to note about this study. The first is the contrast between the children's presumed achievement potential, as judged by initial diagnostic tests, and their actual achievement when they were instructed systematically. Poor performance on the perceptual-motor tests and a display of a "positive sign of choreiform movement" suggest, according to conventional LD wisdom, that the children "may have been unable to acquire the kinds of strategies needed to complete these vowel pattern tasks because of poor neurological development or integrity."[62] However, this was not the case for the children who received organized instruction. It appears that in spite of what the diagnostic tests were supposed to have disclosed—such as abilities to organize and pay attention—they revealed nothing about the children's neurological makeup.

Second, and probably the most remarkable part of this study, the procedure for attending to and learning the basic vowel patterns was not systematically taught in the second group as part of the regular instruction provided by the reading specialists and special-education teachers. Too much cannot be said about how normal reading instruction for poor readers needs to include direct teaching of these basic spelling patterns. Aside from the obvious implication that this instructional omission for the second group might have contributed in the very creation of LD, it also suggests the necessity of probing beyond appearance in assessing the exclusionary criteria of "normal instruction" and "instructional opportunity."

In the last few years, among some who have been studying attention, there has been an unacknowledged shift away from the concern with whether attention was "the underlying process involved in learning disabilities" and more toward concentrating on the practical issue of how to get learning disabled children to continue to pay attention.[63] By itself, research on finding ways to enhance attention is of course laudable. The shift to this emphasis, however, also implies that, among those studying the problem, there is less inclination at present to attribute attention differences to an "internal processing deficit."[64]

3

■●▲

Language Deficits, Memory Deficits, and LD Subtypes

In the last chapter we saw that the rejection of one neurological LD explanation often simply meant its replacement by another. For professionals committed to finding a disability inside the child, a sequence of exchange is reasonable, perhaps even to be expected, as they track the genesis of LD. For others, the sequence is reminiscent of e.e. cummings's description of his Uncle Sol's labors to achieve a productive farm: "the chickens/ate the vegetables so/my Uncle Sol had a/chicken farm till the/skunks ate the chickens when/my Uncle Sol/had a skunk farm but/the skunks caught cold and/died and so . . ."[1] When Uncle Sol died and finally had a worm farm, this proved to cummings that "nobody loses all the time."

Following the trail of successive LD explanations, this chapter will discuss two more recent neurological-dysfunction theories, language deficits and "subtypes," both of which have followed earlier perceptual-deficit explanations. Many experts today think that because most learning-disabled children have problems with *language* material, language-processing deficits of neurological origin are the source of their problems. Subtype theories, which have gained adherents within the past decade, reject all *single* explanations for LD, while maintaining that each factor (for example, perception, language, attention) may play a part. As the name implies, the idea is to identify unique combinations of factors involved in the creation of the disability. Within the discourse of the field, language and subtypes are considered to be competing, polar explanations, the former a single (or "unitary") interpretation; the latter, multifarious.[2] As I hope to show, they have more in common than many of their respective supporters would like to think. I will also comment on memory deficits, a cognitive process said to be closely related to language, subtype, and other LD explanations.

■●▲ Language

The language-deficit explanation holds that though learning-disabled children perceive language as normal children do, they do not understand or use it the same way. This perception-language distinction may be clarified by an analogy to a "chemistry deficit": A "chemistry disabled" person would be able to perceive letters and symbols but would have difficulty associating them with names of chemicals, deriving a substance's name from a symbol sequence, or understanding the relationships in and meaning of a chemical formula. This deficit would not be due to a lack of exposure to the subject. The person would have been taught but could not learn because of a neurological dysfunction that kept him or her from understanding chemistry terminology, an impediment that through a superficial observation might seem "perceptual" in nature.

As a whole, learning-disabled children do poorly on language tests and appear to have various language difficulties. They use fewer words in sentences; use fewer complex sentences and, therefore, less sophisticated syntax; provide less information in sentences; are slower naming (identifying) words; and make more grammatical errors.[3] These difficulties with linguistic expression are the kinds of "surface manifestations" that suggest that language deficits are the sole cause of dyslexia—a "single-deficit" explanation.[4] The deficits are considered to be severe, making it unlikely that dyslexics will "ever catch up with normal readers."[5]

Although an array of language deficits has been identified in the learning disabled, there is disagreement about the nature of the deficits. Authorities have argued about whether the learning disabled have an overall linguistic deficit or one in a specific area; about whether some deficits are actually secondary to other, primary language deficits; and about the extent to which a particular deficit interferes with the acquisition of reading skills.[6]

Phonological and Phonetic Deficits

In recent years, phonological and phonetic deficits have been considered by many, if not most, LD language authorities to be the language deficits that most clearly distinguish disabled from normal readers.[7] As one put it, disabled readers are "relatively insensitive to the phonemic structure of both spoken and printed language."[8]

Phonological deficits refer to a lack of awareness of or skill with phonemes, the smallest sound units of language (such as *b* in *bad*). These deficits include hearing phonemes at the beginning, middle, or end of words; and combining phonemes to make words. Phonetic deficits refer to a lack of skills in associating sounds with written symbols (letters alone or combined, as in *sh*). Even though the skills are formally distinct, their amalgamation is considered necessary for learning to read. Distinguishing among phonemic sounds, relating phonemic sounds to written symbols, segmenting words phonemically, and blending phonemic segments together are problems commonly found in disabled readers.[9] Specialists have concluded that phonological deficits not only can impede reading development but, because they occur at the basic level of language, can also create higher level—syntactic and semantic—language disorders.[10]

Overall, most LD language specialists have identified phonological and phonetic problems as the chief deficits in the learning disabled and have published more research on these than on any other language deficit.[11] In keeping with this direction and emphasis, my discussion here will be concerned largely with studies of these deficits.

What do phonological and phonetic deficits mean in terms of the LD thesis? Anyone who has worked with disabled readers knows that they do not comprehend the "sounds" of letters and letter combinations, and have difficulty stringing them together and sounding-out words, among other difficulties. Can these problems, however, be attributed to neurological deficits in the majority of learning-disabled children? Among the best research for answering these questions is the type discussed in the previous chapter, which both identifies deficits and *uses instruction* to remediate them.

One such study was done in Oxford.[12] A group of four- and five-year-old children listened to three or four words at a time, all but one of which shared a common phoneme, and afterward was asked to detect the odd word. (An example of a phoneme shared in the first sound of the word is *hill-pig-pin; lot-cot-hat-pot* is a series that might have been used in this test, with three of the words sharing a phoneme in the middle portion.) A correlation was found between children's ability to categorize sounds and their reading and spelling achievement four years later.

The finding suggested a connection between phonological skills and learning to read but did not reveal if the ability to categorize sounds was the reason. To answer the question, the researchers chose sixty-five children from among those with low test scores and divided them into four groups: two groups received "intensive training in categorizing sounds."[13] Group one, with the use of pictures of familiar objects, was taught that words shared common beginning, middle, and end sounds. Group two was taken one step further; the children received explicit sound-letter training for learning to associate the common sounds with plastic letters (the letter *h* for *hen, hat, horse,* or the letter *n* for the end sounds in *hen* and *man*). Each child was seen individually for forty ten-minute sessions, once a week, over two school years. Group three was instructed in mental categorization, but not in phonemic sounds as the first two groups were. The same pictures were used, but the group was taught to classify them into object categories (for example, hen and pig are both farm animals). Group four received no instruction at all.

When the groups were tested at about eight years of age, group two, the one instructed directly on sound-letter correspondence, was reading and spelling *at approximately age level;* the first group, the one taught to associate sounds with pictures but not letters, was slightly below age level in reading and considerably below age level in spelling; the group taught to categorize by objects ranked third in achievement and slightly further below the latter group in both subjects; and the fourth group, having had no preschool instruction, was reading and spelling very poorly, a year behind group two in reading and two years behind in spelling.

The instructional effects described here have been reported in other research. For example, four-year-olds were instructed to segment and synthesize (blend) words of two and three syllables.[14] After thirteen weeks of instruction, five days a week, ten minutes each day, these children had dramatically higher reading-test scores than children engaged in reading related activities but not in this specialized learning. On a word test, the group instructed in word segmenting and synthesizing pronounced correctly 73 percent of the words, whereas the other group achieved only 3.3 percent. Although the study did not identify any of the four-year-olds as learning disabled, it did assess children's pre-instruction abilities and noted "that children who were poorest in word analysis-synthesis skill showed the most improvement."[15] Other studies on the effect of instruction have reported similar improvement in LD children's reading and language skills.[16]

Several conclusions may be drawn from these studies. First, the ability to analyze words phonetically does play a causal role, if not necessarily the only one, in reading development. Second, preschool instruction in this skill can improve grade-school reading abilities. Third, children who have difficulty with phonemic analysis in the preschool years can learn how to do it. A recent review on phonology and learning to read states: "There is now much evidence that . . . phonological [abilities] . . . can be taught at all ages with significant success. Moreover, there is increasing evidence that such phonological instruction has beneficial effects on . . . reading [development]."[17] Fourth, phonemic analysis is not something inevitably acquired through neurological development and thus its absence is not likely to signify a neurological deficit.

It is notable how little time and effort appear to have been needed to help preschool children with phonological deficits so that they could benefit from later reading instruction. In the Oxford study, for example, the twenty sessions a year, each lasting ten minutes, can hardly be called intensive. Furthermore, as with the study discussed at the end of the previous chapter, no magical methods were used; rather, the training systematically presented sound-symbol and sound-categorization techniques (except for use of the plastic letters) similar to those commonly advised in reading texts which any trained teacher would be likely to emphasize in initial instruction. A brief "informal observation" in one of the reports on a successful "phonemic-awareness" program in kindergarten suggests that teachers themselves might require more training to teach basic reading: "More surprising [than the difficulty some children had with phonemes] was the difficulty for some teachers to conceptually handle the phoneme as distinct from the letter name."[18]

These studies lend no support to the neurological thesis and, as the investigators who did the Oxford study concluded, "show how specific *experiences* which a child has before he goes to school may affect his progress once he gets there."[19] Another group of researchers, also stressing that phonetic awareness does not arise spontaneously but through experience, recommended that educators assume children have the cognitive capacity to learn it.[20] Similar advice was given by a researcher who cautioned against assuming "that word-analysis-synthesis skill development is largely maturationally determined and, therefore, not modifiable by controlled instructional experiences."[21] Even a major proponent of language-deficit explanations, who suggested that language disorders underlying dyslexia might be a "constitutional deficit," acknowledged that this may not be true for all dyslexics, since it is "entirely possible that reading deficiencies in even the most severely impaired poor readers are the cumulative by-product of grossly inadequate experience in the critical skills areas."[22]

Despite conjectures that language deficits might be caused by neurological problems, little research on language deficits has attempted to verify these conjectures experimentally.[23] This omission was reflected in the observation by an editor of a journal's special issue on dyslexia that on the whole supported a language-deficit interpretation. All the authors in the issue, she noted, "restrict themselves to *psychological* factors, and do not venture into the underlying neurological factors and their possible origins in genetic or other organic causes."[24] ("Psychological factors" refers to facets of language thinking, such as phonological awareness, language memory, and sentence comprehension.)

Although phonological skills have been demonstrated to have some direct bearing on reading ability and preschool development of these skills has been recognized as very important, it is unclear whether children need to have phonological skills before entering school. The answer seems to be, "Yes, if children continue to be taught as they presently are taught, but no, if instruction is changed."

Teachers often erroneously assume that children entering school have "prerequisite" reading skills developed as part of preschool maturation. Thus they may begin an important facet of reading instruction at least one critical step beyond where they should. Serious learning problems can occur if a reading structure is built without a foundation in beginning reading instruction, as the following study illustrates.[25] Two groups of four-years-olds were chosen for instruction in phonemic blending: one group was proficient in verbally segmenting syllables (being able to say parts of a syllable), and the other was not. This instruction consisted of teaching the children to associate sounds with letterlike forms and then blend the forms together into words (this corresponds to conventional phonics instruction of stringing letters and their sounds to make words). Only the group able to segment spoken syllables into phonemes was able to benefit from the blending instruction.[26]

Although much research has emphasized that the real problem reading-disabled children bring to school is language deficits, the studies reported here imply that there's a different reason some children develop disabilities. These children have "deficits" in learning certain reading skills because they simply have no experience with them and because schools, erroneously assuming children should already have these skills, do not teach them.

Preschool phonemic abilities then do affect later reading development. Conventional instruction that does not recognize this can thus be far more responsible for a child's reading problems than any "deficits" he or she might bring to the classroom. Schools should make phonemic instruction standard, and not just assume all first-graders are competent in this area. In any case, there is no logical reason to teach foundational skills to children before first grade; what four- and five-year-olds can learn, six- and seven-year-olds can learn as well, if not more easily.

To summarize the LD research on language reviewed so far: Most of the work has been on phonemic deficits; phonemic skills are strongly correlated with reading development; instruction in phonemic skills appears to be successful; despite hypotheses of neurological deficits underlying phonemic problems, the hypothesis is unproved and unwarranted because research has concentrated more on psychological description rather than on neurological causation, and has identified learning and experience as key factors in phonemic skill development.

What has all of this contributed to knowledge about reading disabilities? Without denigrating some of the better research on instructional methods for children with language deficits, and refinements made in teaching phonemic skills, this body of work has not moved beyond earlier erroneous LD explanations.[27] When examined as a whole, this forefront of the long LD march, with its emphasis on the role of phonemic skills, has done little more than rediscover that "phonics" is important in learning to read. The advice given teachers in a basal reader series published in 1866 is an example of how far back this insight goes:

> children must be practically taught the various sounds of the language, and their combinations. To give effectiveness to this power, sufficient practice must be had to produce correct *habits*. Daily practice on the "Phonics Chart" or on some combinations of sounds as hereafter presented, will accomplish the purpose. . . . In using the "Phonics Chart" (consonants and vowels shown alone and in combination) the sounds *only* are to be uttered. Let them be given with great force and energy.[28]

For over a century phonics has been considered essential for reading development, even though the argument has swung back and forth over whether reading should be taught by sight-word recognition or by phonics.[29] In light of this historic pendulum, the LD field's alightment on phonemic deficits is reminiscent of Yogi Berra's remark after learning he had been fired as manager of the New York Yankees, the thirteenth managerial change in eleven years, and that Billy Martin was returning to manage the team for the fourth time. Said Yogi, "It was like déjà vu all over again."

Naming

Few studies have directly addressed the assumption that neurological dysfunctions underlie language deficits. Prominent among them, frequently cited, and generally well-regarded in papers on the problem are studies concluding that neurologically based language deficits are manifested in learning disabled children's ability in "naming" objects.[30] "Naming" research does just that; it asks children to name things. In a seminal series of such studies, dyslexics and normal readers were shown and asked to name drawings of objects (such as a book, a shoe). Compared with normal readers, the dyslexics named fewer, took longer to name them, and made different kinds of errors when trying to name unfamiliar objects. This research was derived from earlier research with war veterans who had become dysphasic (acquired language impairment) through missile injuries.[31] The dyslexics' responses were found to be similar in a number of respects to those of veterans with injuries in the left brain hemisphere, the hemisphere more actively involved in language processing. Using the vets as a reference group, the dyslexia researchers concluded that dyslexics "resemble dysphasics in that they have linguistic retrieval problems."[32] The researchers repeated this conclusion in subsequent reports on similar object-naming tests.[33]

The object naming constructed in the original research was derived from a word list (the Thorndike-Lorge list) compiled according to the frequency with which words are used in school texts (from more than a hundred occurrences per million words down to one per three million words). From the list, the names of twenty-six objects were chosen that were "evenly spread throughout the whole frequency range." The words were divided into seven frequency groups, and pictures were drawn of each object (book, chair, and shoe were in the group of most frequently occurring words; metronome, gyroscope, and xylophone were the least frequently occurring). The researchers hoped the test would assist in diagnosing dysphasic patients—whose special difficulty in naming objects had long been known—by providing quantitative, normative measurements of naming ability.[34]

Both dyslexics and normal children correctly named about the same number of objects in the first four word-frequency categories.[35] Only the fifth category revealed a significant difference in performance: the normal children identified 69 percent and the dyslexics 48 percent of the objects (microscope, dice, anvil, horseshoe, octopus, and bagpipe). Both groups did quite poorly with the sixth group (tuning fork, stethoscope, syringe), with similar scores of 37 percent correct for normals and 33 percent for dyslexics. The researchers could not draw any conclusions on the respective scores of 22 percent and 10 percent for the seventh group because they were too low.

Another method of analyzing correct responses was tabulating the mean and median number of objects identified correctly out of the total twenty-six. For reasons that are not explained, these averages were given only for the normal children; however, I was able to calculate them for the dyslexics from a graph of the distribution of scores and found no significant group differences.[36]

To sum up the figures reviewed so far, only one frequency group, the fifth, significantly differentiated normals and dyslexics. For the overall average number of objects named, differences were minimal. Measures of the time taken to name an object also showed few differences. Group response times were virtually the same for the first four categories. Category five showed a bit more of a difference, with the normals' average response time about 2.2 seconds and the dyslexics' 2.5, a difference which was not significant. Again, to sum up, neither for objects correctly identified nor for the speed with which they were identified were there any significant differences.

The third and last analysis was for three categories of errors made when trying unsuccessfully to identify an object. These categories were derived from the study on veterans, and one category seemed to distinguish both adult dysphasics and dyslexics. This was "circumlocutions"—trying to identify an object in a roundabout way (such as responding to "stethoscope" as "a thing the doctor uses to listen to your heart"). Dyslexics made 41 percent such errors (never correctly naming the object) and the controls, 30 percent.[37] A comparison of these percentages with figures for the veterans' research shows that veterans with left-hemisphere damage made 71.6 percent circumlocutions and a normal group of adult veterans made 51.1 percent. Thus both normal and dyslexic children had an error rate below that of normal adults in the original research and considerably below that of dysphasics.[38]

What logical conclusion might one draw from these findings? The dyslexics and normal children named objects equally well for all but one of seven categories; the average total number of objects identified correctly was about the same for both groups; so too was the response time for naming objects; and the circumlocution errors made by the dyslexics were fewer than that of normal adults (and not that different from the 30 percent made by normal children). For the researchers, these findings warranted the following conclusion: "Since this test of confrontation naming has proved a reasonably sensitive technique for measuring residual dysphasia in adults, it appears justifiable to regard the dyslexic children as subtly dysphasic."[39] Happily for the normal children, the "justifiable" interpretation was not extended to them; their errors merited a different construction: "In terms of pictured objects which proved most difficult for the normal children to name, *sociocultural factors* (rather than developmental psycholinguistic factors) may be most important."[40] Why the same was not said for the dyslexics who had difficulty identifying an anvil, a microscope, or a bagpipe, the researchers did not explain.

Aside from its empirical deficiencies, the study is impaired conceptually in its use of the adult reference group. By measuring the behavior of one group against another, and by assuming similar behavior necessarily infers similar (dysfunctional) biological makeup, Hinshelwood's erroneous logic is continued.[41] For example, suppose the pictures of the objects had been shown to adults with severe mental problems or to adults who had not slept for several days. What would similar test scores of these groups and dyslexics mean? Obviously comparable test scores can occur in more than one way, making unjustifiable any conclusions about analogous causes from analogous scores.

In fact, the fundamental conclusion about causation in these studies is exactly the opposite of what it should be. When looking at acquired reading and language problems for analogous neurological causes of dyslexia, those who make this comparison focus on brain lesions. In doing so, they identify the lesions as the primary cause and disregard the causes of the brain damage. However, the primary immediate cause for the veterans' naming problems was brain damage that befell them in military conflicts. If the question were asked, "How can we prevent brain damage in veterans that impairs the naming of objects?" a good answer would be that we create a world that had no wars. Similar experiential causes, often beyond an individual's control, can be found in other brain-damaged adults: accidents, occupational injuries, stress, and improper nutrition (causing strokes). Obviously, profound brain damage is the biological cause of whatever reading or language problems ensue. However, if these acquired reading and language disabilities are drawn on to develop a theory of LD, the patent extrapolation from the analogy would be that social interactions can produce neurological dysfunctions that in turn can produce behavioral changes. This analogy is pertinent to my discussion in chapter nine of actual neurological dysfunction in learning disabled children. There I will propose that even for the small portion of LD children whose learning is impeded because of neurological dysfunctions, it does not follow, as LD definitions claim, that the dysfunction is "intrinsic" and may be found within the child.

This investigation of naming deficits was the beginning of a number of studies and papers on the subject by these researchers and others.[42]

The studies have added to the argument that dyslexics have a neurological naming dysfunction not restricted to linguistic material alone, because they are said to be slower than average readers in naming colors, digits, objects, and letters. However, these studies, too, have fundamental flaws, similar to those noted for other LD investigations. For example, they do not account for numerous influences that could affect naming, such as concentration and motivation. Consequently they fail to identify the source of the errors. Concerning the last criticism, some authorities have pointed to the ambiguous correlation between name-retrieval speed and reading, and have suggested that better reading ability might be the cause of better naming speed because good readers have had more practice developing efficient naming of symbolic stimuli.[43]

The Source of Language Deficits

A question remaining in this discussion is, "Where do these language deficits come from?" As I have said, my analysis assumes that while the majority of children identified as LD do not have neurological complications, a very small number of them do. In later chapters I will discuss more fully possible sources of language difficulties for both these groups. I will briefly review here a language-development study pertaining to difficulties in children who do not have neurological complications. This research illustrates the experiential complexity that can account for diverse language development, a complexity most LD research has never considered.

Both the language and intellectual growth of 193 children was followed from infancy until they were four years old.[44] That age is especially relevant to our discussion because it is when LD phonological deficits have been observed. Therefore, research able to identify any correlates of language disabilities at that age, even if not phonological ones, could shed some light on language deficits.

The children came from families that were "fairly well educated and economically well-off" and in which most of the parents were married. The researchers stressed that this was a socially and physically "healthy, working- and middle-class sample." When LD researchers consider exclusionary criteria for selecting learning disabled children, these "healthy" families are the kinds customarily ruled out as a primary cause of the disabilities. Unlike most, this study went beyond a surface assessment and looked into family life and parent-child relationships in a complex context (which it called ecological variables) to learn whether any factors would predict intellectual and language function in the preschool years. The study found that many did.

For example, development of poor receptive and expressive language—language abilities that would meet LD criteria—was associated with a number of factors, among them: parental educational level; stress on families; spouse and social support for the mother (whether she felt she had enough emotional support from her husband, and whether both parents shared similar concerns); the quality of parent-infant interaction; the degree of stimulation at home; the mother's effectiveness in teaching her children (whether there were sufficient positive messages and few negative ones). These qualities of family life were strongly bound up with many personal and social influences, including: financial strains, health, gender roles, life satisfaction or alienation, life opportunities available to the parents, social support provided by relatives of the family. A less careful probe into the class status of this "relatively healthy, well-developing sample of children" would not have revealed the family and environmental factors that contributed to the children's language skill difficulties.

Moreover, neither single factors nor interactive patterns uniformly accounted for differences in language ability. Rather, the differences were associated with various factors and interactions. In one instance, language deficits were caused by a significant event that changed the child's life, coupled with a lack of social support within the family and ensuing poor interaction between the parents and the child. In another, the problem grew from a poor mother-infant interaction combined with a home environment of low stimulation. In yet another instance, it could have been associated with the mother's low educational level. Similar associations were found for intellectual development, but I will restrict my comments to language, our present topic.

It is important to emphasize again a point the authors stress: on the surface these were normal, healthy families, and only by looking below that were strengths and strains in "ecological variables"—and their association with deficient language abilities—perceptible. As we shall see later in this book, research has established that family dynamics can contribute to language difficulties and LD. (I do not mean to imply that either mothers, parents, or families can be identified as *the* causes of LD.) This present study indicates clearly the complex but discoverable experiential influences that can produce language deficits.

The investigators conclude that there are no magic bullets—no simple explanations—for different levels of language achievement. When compared to the field's neurological explanations of language deficits, to language research that remains at the "psychological level," and to the facile dismissal of family and other social influences in almost every study, this conclusion is not only good advice—it should be a dictum written on the LD laboratory wall.

Memory

My discussion of memory problems in the learning disabled will be brief because of the general view in the field that memory difficulties are a manifestation of other deficits and are not the primary causes of LD.

Many researchers have concluded that differences in memory performance are "a reflection of different processing, or encoding, operations being applied to information, rather than to different 'capacities' of various memory storage systems."[45] Or, simply put, learning-disabled children have problems remembering things not because of a general inability to hold information in their heads or from insufficient memory room but because of the way they process and store information. The LD explanation for memory deficits might be compared to storing food in a freezer: the freezer works fine and has lots of space, but the food will keep and will be easy to get out only if it is wrapped properly and organized well within the freezer. Processing here means the strategies used to memorize information, such as: "rehearsal (repeating items over and over), elaboration (thinking of verbal or visual associations), clustering items by meaningful relationships, or proper apportionment of study time by using the study-test-study method."[46]

Not all researchers believe that faulty strategies cause memory problems; they argue instead that strategy deficits might be secondary to an "unavailability of appropriate information in long-term memory."[47] In this view, it is difficult to remember something if not enough is known about it already. To use the freezer analogy again, if a person is nonplused about wrapping and storing a few pieces of still-warm lasagna, the primary problem might not be "strategy" (knowing how cool the pieces should be so the sauce and cheese do not leak out; knowing whether to wrap each piece separately or all together; knowing whether to use aluminum foil or plastic wrap); the primary problem could be one of having to draw on a memory base built solely of experience on storing food in plastic containers. In this long-term memory formulation, because reading-disabled children are less likely than normal readers to have information related to reading, they are more likely to perform poorly on memory tasks associated with reading. Moreover, if abilities acquired through reading foster better memorization in a reading-related task, then "reading difficulties could be said to cause the memory problem, rather than the other way around."[48]

Some specialists have pointed to language deficits, not problem-solving strategy or long-term information storage, as the primary causes of memory problems.[49] Although language deficits encompass strategy and long-term information deficits, the emphasis on language in this line of analysis reflects various theories about the difficulties disabled readers have processing verbal information, particularly phonological information.[50]

Because strategy and language seem inextricably connected, a number of researchers have proposed that "there is a reasonable amount of evidence indicating that poor readers may display inferior short-term memory performance due to deficits in *both* strategic planning and phonological processing."[51] Other factors believed to affect memory of the learning disabled are attention, distraction, and motivation.[52]

Overall, memory problems are not seen as a primary cause of learning disabilities or as caused themselves by neurological deficits. Where the latter association has been suggested, a primary deficit such as language is considered to be an intermediary factor between the neurological deficit and memory. However, since neurological deficits have not been shown to underlie the primary causes I have reviewed, and since strategy deficits involved in memory problems have not been shown to be more than experiential deficiencies, we must continue to look elsewhere for support of the LD neurological thesis.

■●▲ Subtypes

Even some proponents of the neurological explanations would acknowledge the fruitlessness of the search so far described for a single cause of LD, though perhaps not for the reasons I have given. They have criticized the research for trying to identify a single cause above all others, and thereby overlooking the multiplicity of LD causes—a multiplicity of "subtypes" in a heterogeneous LD population. Failure to document single explanations, say subtyping proponents, is thus not surprising. For example, studies of language disabilities could not be expected to find statistically significant group differences between normal and LD children because only a proportion of the LD population suffers language deficits. Some children might have visual perception problems, others auditory perception problems, and still others a mixture of problems. A full neurological subtyping assessment requires measures of "motor and psychomotor abilities, tactile-kinesthetic-perceptual skills, visual-perceptual and visual-spatial abilities, receptive, mediational, and expressive language capacities" and higher-order thinking.[53]

Thus, the subtyping analysis, which is entrenched in the field, contains a condemnation of decades of previous work and practice and only supports my argument that there's little evidence to prove the LD thesis. One such condemnation of single (unitary) deficit explanations comes from a leader of subtyping analysis. In the preface to a selection of papers said to "reflect recent advances in the exploration of the parameters and implications of the subtypal analysis," he wrote:

> Claims that learning disabilities in children are caused by, result from, or are reflections of more basic attentional, mnestic [memory], linguistic, or perceptual deficiencies abound in the literature in this area. In *most* cases, unfortunately, these "unitary deficit" views are defended in a manner that can be best characterized as narrow, insular, . . . argumentative . . . and self-serving, myopic rationale[s].[54]

This objective appraisal of other explanations provides a fitting start for an examination of what should be comprehensive, rational, and clear-sighted research on subtypes.

Discussions about different kinds of learning disabilities go back many years. However, the current work on subtypes as a specific kind of analysis began around the mid-1970s with a few research papers describing discrete LD subgroups.[55] After this, subtyping attracted more specialists, other research and writings were published, and this mode of classification now holds a place among LD explanations.

People in the remedial educational field have always been concerned with differences in and subcategories of the cause and character of children's reading problems. The nature of the child and his or her life, the child's particular reading and academic profile, and the remediation tailored to a child's specific needs were the subject of graduate reading courses long before LD became popular (even though the principles were not necessarily put into practice in the public schools). What distinguishes this orientation from subtype analysis is that the latter, even though it eschews unitary explanations, shares the same LD thesis, only adding some diversity: "children who exhibit learning problems may do so for a *variety* of brain-related reasons."[56]

At face value, this statement may seem unarguable: surely all human activity, all learning, all learning disabilities, are "brain-related." In neuropsychological parlance, however, the phrase means that brain functioning is the cause of the phenomena, not simply that the brain is integrally involved. Formally, subtype proponents do not deny there are other causes, but when subtyping learning disabled children, they will give lip service to other causes and then move in a single direction, as formulated in the following research "expectations":

> it was expected that the subtypes derived from this analysis would be clinically meaningful and interpretable on the basis of previously demonstrated relationships between neuropsychological measures and the functional integrity of the brain.[57]

In other words, test results were meant to reveal brain dysfunctions that had already been identified. Another example of the subtype interpretation's closed-mindedness comes from the paper "Socio-Emotional Disturbances of Learning Disabled Children," written by the authors of the study cited above. They theorized that "central processing deficiencies can lead to both learning disabilities and socio-emotional disturbances."[58] Though subtype literature contains rare cautionary recommendations to "be wary of inferences alluding to brain abnormalities based on . . . preliminary, unvalidated behavioral subtypes,"[59] on the whole, subtyping research continues to serve the same LD pie, while only trying to slice it differently.

Environmental explanations in subtyping, as in unitary research, are dismissed in short order. For example, one study observed that although "it is difficult to prove conclusively" that experiences of one kind or another do not produce reading disability, "we must be satisfied for the present with the indirect evidence that the disorder occurs even under what appear to be the most favorable environmental circumstances."[60] Presumably, this "indirect evidence" came from the single-cause interpretations of LD that I and subtype proponents themselves have criticized. The study drew on a "detailed developmental, social, academic, and medical history" which identified children who "conformed to the usual criteria of reading disabilities" and who did not have "severe emotional problems" or "marked environmental handicaps."[61] However, some remarks about the families of the children suggest that the research was nonchalant in at least a few details. First, the authors noted "there was a family history of reading disability" in forty-five of the eighty-eight reading-disabled children, a percentage that "probably underestimated the actual incidence of family history, as some parents seemed unwilling to admit problems in other family members."[62] Later they say that findings in an earlier, related study by one of the researchers showed "no evidence of inadequate home . . . opportunity, and, *in most cases, a family history of reading disability.*"[63]

The researchers have little or nothing to say about the fact that many of the parents "seemed unwilling to admit problems in other family members." But this unwillingness could have been a sign that the domestic environment was not as supportive as it should have been and might have contributed to the reading difficulty. Particularly lost seems to be the following contradiction: If the reading problems were a benign issue between spouses and between parents and children, why wouldn't the parents readily identify who had those troubles? The answer of course is that, instead of being benign, the problems might have been a source of embarrassment for the individuals who experienced them. Consider the research circumstances: parents discussing family reading problems with professionals who certainly must have expressed concern about the affected children and the families. Surely in this situation the parents should have been less reticent about family reading problems than they might otherwise have been. Yet, despite the sympathetic and supportive circumstances, it appears that many would not reveal family "secrets" and that, during the "extensive interviews," the investigators left those secrets unexplored. Still, the researchers had no doubt about their conclusion: though more than half of the families admitted having reading problems, and another portion seemed to have problems but were unwilling to admit them, no emotional or environmental handicaps were found in the children.

As I have said, family relationships and reading disabilities will be discussed more fully later in the book. For now, it is sufficient to say that these families seem to have been inexplicably exempt from the extensively observed and discussed social and psychological problems of adults with reading difficulties and from the influence these problems have on parenting and family relationships.[64] If they were indeed exempt, the researchers came upon a group of adult poor readers truly dissimilar to any found in adult-education research and practice.

As might be imagined, identifying subgroups from the mountain of data gathered in most subtype studies is not an easy task. Computers are helpful but can sort only to a certain extent, unfortunately some distance from the completely objective sorting researchers would like to achieve. When additional sorting is required, decisions about children who are not neatly classified fall back to the researchers who, try as they might, are unable to avoid considerable arbitrariness and untidy subtypes. For example, often a child's test scores contain patterns for more than one subtype, potentially justifying placement in more than one subgroup. One research team devised a special method to deal with this problem: "once a subject was assigned to a cluster [subgroup], that individual could not be reassigned to another cluster, even if a greater similarity to the other subjects was found."[65]

Added to the difficulties in identifying distinct subtypes is the finding that subtypes have not been consistent over time and ages. For example, in one study 28 percent of the learning-disabled children aged nine and ten made up one subtype category, but the percentage of children in the category decreased by age, falling to 6 percent for thirteen- to fourteen-year-olds.[66] Conversely, one subgroup had no children aged nine to ten, but the subgroup percentage increased to 37 percent at ages thirteen and fourteen. This study was cross-sectional—that is, studied different age groups at the same time. Other, longitudinal research found similar inconsistencies, concluding that "ability patterns were not stable over time" and "in some instances, the patterns changed considerably within individual subtypes."[67]

One of the most comprehensive subtype studies to date is detailed in an entire book on the subject, and it provides a kind of summary of just how uninformative the data on subtype research is.[68] The following is an example of the analyses found in the study. Seeking a relationship between reading subtypes and scores on thirty-seven neuropsychological tests, the investigators concluded that one subgroup "scored below the other types" on several tests. This is a seemingly important finding, until the average scores said to differentiate the groups are examined.[69] Then, the phrase "scored below" displays a bit of linguistic ingenuity. On one such test, the Peabody picture vocabulary test, the groups scored 105, 94, and 99, with 100 as the normal average. Thus, while there were differences, the 94 for the group that "scored below" was not very far below the score of another group and was still within the normal range.

The Knox cubes test of visual attention, in which the examiner touches a row of blocks in a different order on each trial and then asks the child to match the sequence, produced subgroup scores of 120, 109, and 123. As with the Peabody, the normal average was 100. Thus, the group that "scored below" was not very far below the others and was slightly above average.

The finger tapping test, in which a child taps a mechanical or electrical counter as fast as possible with each index finger in ten-second trials, showed the following subgroup score differences: 54, 49, and 54 for the dominant hand and 52, 48, and 54 for the other. The differences among groups were said to be statistically significant, but it is obvious from the numbers that the differences were not striking. Moreover, when the investigators used an analysis involving "more stringent criteria of reading disability," the statistically significant differences disappeared among the subgroups for the dominant hand,

and only one score remained statistically significant for the nondominant hand.

There were test-score differences between subgroups in the verbal portion of the Wechsler intelligence test, but as the researchers had observed in an earlier part of the book, low scores on these tests "were probably due to a poor fund of general information rather than to a primary linguistic deficit (i.e., poor performance may not have been due to an inherent inability for verbal expression, but to the secondary effects of not being able to read and to acquire knowledge)."[70]

Given these findings, it is bewildering that the following summary was made about this subgroup: "a number of asymmetries in dominant hand performance along with relatively poor verbal concept formation skills and relatively poor auditory and visual attention-memory span were consistent with an interpretation of left hemisphere dysfunction."[71] In a later summary of these results, one of the investigators stated that this group was "most likely to have cerebral dysfunction, with their particular deficiency on verbal tests suggesting possible left-hemisphere involvement."[72] Similar "relatively poor performance" of the other subgroups merited analogous interpretations.[73] Such boldness in espying neurological dysfunctions is not limited to this subtype study alone.[74]

A conceptual error seen in LD research previously discussed is implicit as well in subtype research. In this case, investigators assume that subtyping by neuropsychological test performance will necessarily reveal the cause of the LD subtypes. Even if the tests did measure neuropsychological integrity, however, this conclusion is false. To illustrate this, I will use an example from weight lifting. It shows that, even in physical activities, errors can occur in identifying biological substrates as causes.

Suppose weight lifters were divided into subgroups according to the weight they lifted. And suppose the physiological differences among the groups were examined in an effort to explain strength differences. The research might find that the better lifters had greater muscle density, stronger tendons, and slower lactic-acid buildup (which causes fatigue in the muscles). Analysis of subtypes of poor lifters might become quite sophisticated in identifying subtypes of lifters with fatigue deficiencies, others with fibrous-tissue deficiencies, and others with mixed fatigue and fibrous deficiencies. From these findings the conclusions might be drawn that the physiological factors *caused* the differences in performance. The error in doing so would be that, by themselves, these factors could only be said to be related to differences in performances, not necessarily to have caused them. A more thorough examination might reveal that greater motivation and discipline to train regularly and to work out harder and harder had produced denser muscles and more efficient lactic-acid dispersal. Or, those two factors might have been equal among the groups but coaching vastly different, with the good lifters having received proper training routines and the poor lifters having received haphazard routines, some of which might be generally bad, others satisfactory for improving one lift but not another.

A social-psychological analysis such as this would begin to explain more correctly the causes of respective subtype performance. However, a full explication would go still further, accounting for physiological, psychological, behavioral, and social interrelationships and interactions. Good coaching and motivation might lead to different kinds of routines and more rigorous training, but the physiological changes that underlie, so to speak, different kinds of performance would play an interactive part. Thus the development of better physiological functioning would reinforce the lifter's adherence to the coach's guidance and reward his or her self-discipline and motivation. An analysis of this kind does not deny there are physiological differences among the groups; it only demonstrates that, if physiological functioning alone were examined, lifting differences could never be explained accurately.

An overriding question remains concerning the nature of the relationship between subtype groupings and learning disabilities. If a group of learning-disabled children is divided into subtypes, do the subtypes correlate with patterns of learning disabilities, such as scores on reading and spelling tests? The longitudinal study already mentioned found no correlation between subtype analysis and children's scores on reading and spelling for two of the three subtypes.[75] Similarly, another study, after dividing disabled readers into six subgroups according to scores on language and perceptual tests, found that dissimilar subgroups had similar reading abilities, thereby evincing no obvious connection between the two sets of scores.[76] The researchers concluded there remained "a need to determine whether the different patterns of language and perceptual deficits found in this study are associated with different reading consequences. Specifically, is there a relationship between pattern of deficit and type of reading difficulty?"[77]

The massive subtype study using thirty-seven neuropsychological tests found essentially the same relationship between test scores for the three reading subgroups: no differences were reported among the reading subgroups for most of the neuropsychological subtests; where differences were found, their meaning was not clear or especially significant. Perhaps because of personal reflection, professional criticism, or both, the primary investigator of the study acknowledged this failure two years after the work had been published. The research, he said, did "not find that each pattern of reading skill deficit was associated with a unique pattern of nonreading (language and neuropsychological) deficit."[78] One year after that, after again saying that the research "failed to find definite connections between reading and nonreading deficits," he offered this appraisal of the "current status of subtype research": "There is no indication that we are beginning to arrive at agreement as to the 'real' subtypes of reading disability."[79]

In all, Sir Walter Scott's description of the scholarship of Cosmo Comyne Bradwardine, Esq., may be applied to subtyping explanations of LD: his "learning was more diffuse than accurate."[80]

4

■●▲

Technology and the Identification of Neurological Deficits

Several years ago a popular TV show featured an air force test pilot who had been at the point of death following a plane crash. The program began with a scene of his tattered body lying on an operating table while engineer-surgeons rebuilt his body parts. A background voice (presumably that of a biocrat imploring his superiors prior to the operation) was heard saying something like, "We have the technology. We can make him stronger, faster. We can improve his hearing and sight . . ." And so, thanks to the new technology, not only was the pilot resuscitated but, as a "bionic man," he was indeed made better than ever. The program glorified contemporary fantasies about "high-tech" solutions. Do high-tech and increasingly sophisticated aids employed in dyslexia research provide anything resembling a "bionic" answer for learning disabilities?

In the previous two chapters I discussed research that used children's behavioral and cognitive problems for analyzing and documenting the neurological dysfunctions believed to underpin those problems. As I tried to show, this approach led to many unsatisfactory inferences being made about brain dysfunction. Many LD proponents believe this problem has been mostly solved by the "brain research technologies . . . now being used to search for signs that distinguish the central nervous systems of learning-disabled individuals from those of others."[1] These new technologies are seen to allow either more direct study of, or at least more tenable inferences about, the brain. In a criticism similar to that leveled against the bulk of LD work up to now, professionals laud the "significant advances" made possible by this new technology, while reproving critics of the neurological thesis for disregarding this research and basing "much of their criticism on seriously outdated views of the psychological and neurological literature."[2] Researchers have used these technological approaches in different ways. Sometimes the technological know-how has been applied within an LD theory; at other times it has been used to look for brain differences between disabled and normal groups of learners to devise an LD explanation. This chapter will review the up-to-date LD technologies regarded as the most promising for identifying the neurological basis of LD.[3]

■●▲ Laterality

Samuel Orton's proposition, in the 1920s, that dyslexics fail to establish brain-hemisphere dominance for language has inspired researchers, right up to the present time, to try to confirm it. Assuming that the brain's "mixed dominance" would be manifested in assorted body dominances, investigators spent much time looking to see if there were inconsistencies in an individual's use of limbs and sensory organs that would provide evidence for Orton's central concept. Handedness was examined by having children write, use scissors, deal cards; footedness, by hopping on one foot, kicking a ball; eyedness, by looking through a kaleidoscope or a rifle sight; and earedness, by having children turn their head upon hearing a sound directly behind them or by asking them to listen with one ear to the ticking of a watch. By observing behavior in these and similar tasks, the investigators hoped to determine if dominance for the control of a particular limb or sensory organ had been established in the opposite (ipsilateral) brain hemisphere. For years, evidence of mixed dominance in dyslexics (a child might be right-handed but left-footed) had led to the inference that their hemispheric language dominance was incomplete. Nonetheless, to make an overlong story short, the theory of mixed dominance, as judged through such behavioral tests, has been tested almost from the time Orton proposed it, but never confirmed.[4]

In spite of this Orton's influence has remained strong, barely diminished if at all by the subsequent rejection of his theory of strephosymbolia. Still ascendant is its core: reading disability is biological in origin and is caused by a failure of the respective brain hemispheres to establish correct functioning and interaction. Most of the technologies discussed in this chapter have been influenced by Orton's principles. The first two I call medium-hard, because in reflecting brain functioning, they stand somewhere between many of the "softer" methods (such as paper-and-pencil or orally administered tests) and the "hard" technologies that study the brain (such as the CAT scan).

Dichotic Listening

In dichotic-listening experiments, pairs of sounds are presented simultaneously, with one sound entering each ear. Dichotic listening began to be applied to LD when researchers discovered that normal people perceive linguistic sounds more readily through the right ear. This "right-ear advantage" has been explained by the left hemisphere's superiority for processing linguistic information. In contrast, the left ear has been thought to be relatively disadvantaged in this regard because the hemisphere it is directly connected to is not the one predominantly involved in linguistic processing. From this reasoning it would presumably follow that any dichotic listening irregularities in disabled learners would reflect differences in hemispheric functioning.

Dichotic-listening studies have used fairly similar methods. A person wears a pair of headphones and listens to digits or short syllables, usually presented in segments of about three digits or syllables at a time emanating from each headphone. Often the person is asked to recall the digits or syllables; sometimes he or she is cued beforehand to attend to a particular ear. Results often are compiled by tallying the numbers and syllables recalled for each ear, or by calculating the ratio of right- over left-ear scores.

A decade or so of these experiments has brought this approach through the cycle we have seen before. First, data is reported showing that normal learners have a greater right-ear advantage. Then follows the gradual demise of the conclusions drawn from the data, brought about by a succession of studies that fail to confirm the previous report.[5] Some researchers have suggested there might be an association between ear scores and subgroups, but this has not been validated any more than the first comparison.[6] Others have proposed that differences in dichotic listening between younger and older disabled readers indicates "prima facie evidence" that the development of cerebral functions in the left hemisphere are delayed in disabled readers.[7] However, further research suggests that language lateralization occurs early in life and does not mature over time, as developmental-lag theorists suggest. For example, one study found a right-ear superiority in three-, four-, and five-year-old children. Other research failed to find changes (i.e., further development) in laterality in children between the ages of three and twelve.[8] Dichotic-listening research has also been criticized for being weak conceptually.[9]

Besides these findings, there is still the question of what might account for differences in auditory asymmetry. Some new answers for this came from a study that found the extent of right-ear advantage depended on which ear the children were asked to attend to first during the test. The researchers observed: "If persistent lateral biases can be generated so readily in the laboratory, one must wonder what adventitious biases the subject is bringing with him or her into the laboratory."[10] This and other work has found that dichotic-listening scores can reflect numerous circumstances and conditions. The scores can be influenced by the manner in which children attend to the task, such as whether children's motivation or boredom affects their attention. Another influence can be the children's abilities, such as their understanding of the nature of the task or their problem-solving strategies.[11] A third influence can be the organization of the environment within which the experiment is conducted, such as where the experimenter is positioned in the room.[12]

In sum, particular dichotic-listening scores do not appear to be manifestations of "some fixed, structural attribute of the brain."[13] Recent discussions have emphasized the failure of these studies to buttress Orton's general theory. One group of investigators concluded: "there was no evidence to support previous studies which claimed the dyslexic population was less lateralized for left hemisphere speech functioning than normal readers."[14] In a similar vein, although with slightly more of a qualification, two other researchers stated that the dichotic-listening studies demonstrate "little support" for the hypothesis that LD is caused by "incomplete lateralization which directly affects intellectual or cognitive processes."[15]

Visual Half-Field

The second medium-hard technology that has been used for exploring Orton's general principle tests vision and is derived from the relationship between sight and brain hemispheres. The image of the right visual field (the right half of the area one is looking at) is registered on the left half of the retina of each eye, which in turn is neurally connected to the left hemisphere of the brain. Similarly, the image of the left visual field is connected to the right hemisphere. As with dichotic listening, research has found that linguistic material is perceived better in the right visual field than in the left. This conclusion has led researchers to use "visual-half-field" techniques to test if differences exist between disabled and normal learners in hemispheric functioning.

Visual-half-field research usually requires a person to look straight ahead toward a fixed point while linguistic stimuli, such as words or consonant-vowel combinations, are presented either on one or both sides of the visual field. The stimuli are presented rapidly to evoke an immediate image and to prevent the person from scanning them. To help ensure that the person looks straight ahead, so that the lateral images fall within the proper visual half-fields, a dot and then a dash or plus sign are projected at the center of the screen. The person has to report which symbol is being shown, and thus must focus on the center of the field.

Orton's theory appeared at first to have found some support here, with some research finding laterality differences between good and disabled readers. On the whole, however, as I shall discuss shortly, visual-half-field research has led the LD field to another dead end.[16] Nonetheless, some of it is worth a close look because it provides further evidence of pervasive and compromised patterns in LD research.

Sometimes dyslexics cannot win. Comparing the interpretations in two investigations indicates that whatever scores they achieve, they are always assumed to have failed the test. When in one study, normal readers had higher visual-half-field scores on the right than on the left, the results were seen as expressions of normal hemispheric processing. However, in the other study, when dyslexics obtained this right-left differential, it was taken to be evidence of a processing deficit in the right hemisphere.[17]

Elsewhere, based on the average group scores of visual-half-field tasks, dyslexics were said to be "inordinately impaired" relative to other reading groups, possibly with a "deficit of left hemisphere visual association area function."[18] From the group scores, this appears to be a reasonable conclusion. However, analyzing individual scores offers a different interpretation because most of the dyslexics and normal readers had the same or similar scores, and two normal readers had scores that could be interpreted as evidence of a deficit of the left hemisphere. Thus, only because of three abnormally high scores by normal readers did that group appear to have done appreciably better. Of course, the method of calculation also avoids an obvious question: How did normal readers learn to read when they had patterns similar to those of the dyslexics?

The above contradictions are what two reviewers of the literature had in mind when they observed that the models of laterality are so numerous that any hypothesis testing is precluded. Examples are dominant right-hemisphere spatial ability; slow left-hemisphere language ability; bilateral representation of linguistic and spatial abilities in the right, left, or both hemispheres; and problems of interhemispheric communication. In some cases a number of such models have been used to explain the same data; in others, each model has appeared to sit on its own fiefdom of data that other models are at a loss to explain.[19]

Visual-half-field studies illustrate yet again how the construction of a task can influence measures thought to reflect fixed neurological functioning. Results have differed depending on whether the stimuli are letters or words, whether they are presented unilaterally or bilaterally, whether they are printed in one type-face or another, whether the central focus point is verbal (a word or number digit) or nonverbal (a shape), whether the stimuli are repeated or are always new, whether the experimental instructions and methods vary, whether linguistic stimuli are preceded by linguistic or nonlinguistic stimuli, whether the amount and spacing of the stimuli vary, whether a person has to remember linguistic material while responding to a visual-half-field test, or whether a person has to determine if bilateral stimuli are the same or different.[20] Language effects are particularly interesting with respect to LD because abstract nouns and verbs appear to produce a superiority in the right visual half-field.[21] Consequently, poor readers—who are likely to have more difficulty with abstract nouns and verbs than with concrete nouns—would be likely to have reduced right-half-field scores, and fewer differences between right and left scores. Thus, these and other kinds of test constructions alone can change left- or right-visual-half-field scores or eliminate any asymmetry between the scores.[22]

Overall, criticisms of visual-half-field research, as with dichotic-listening, have concluded that "the data from most of the existing studies are uninterpretable." As such, it was "unwise" to assume that visual-half-field scores indicated cerebral asymmetry.[23]

Finally, an important observation made about visual-half-field research is also pertinent to other work on learning disabilities. While researchers are "always looking for differences in lateral asymmetries between normal and poor readers," the entire point of the research is likely to be that there are not any. However, instead of viewing this as a failure, the similarities should be accepted as "useful background information" and the group differences should be looked for elsewhere.[24]

EEG

Of the "hard" technological tools in LD research, the EEG has been in use the longest, and for quite a while it appeared as though by itself it might have won the day, providing technological documentation of neurological deficits in the learning disabled. A paper in 1949 reported an ample 75 percent of EEG abnormalities in a group of dyslexic children. Research the following year reported a dip to 59 percent, but the percentage picked up in the next decade, soaring to 88 percent in the early 1960s and peaking in the mid-1960s at an astronomical 95 percent.[25]

Then, something must have happened, because the percentages began to decline. Perhaps more stringent research methods were used. Perhaps researchers began to fear having to defend almost implausible figures. Or perhaps it was a 1967 review that concluded that for detecting LD brain dysfunctions the EEG was not the outstanding diagnostic tool that people had once thought:

> The EEG appears to be regarded with more awe than it deserves. It is not very reliable, and there are many technical problems in its use with children, yet our electronic age, with its admiration for gadgets and the paucity of knowledge in the behavioral sciences, lends to this instrument a certain mystique. . . . The influence of the EEG among educators may possibly be due to the inundation of the literature with poorly done papers describing children with supposed minimal brain damage.[26]

The same year, one study reported finding 62 percent EEG abnormalities in learning-disabled children. This was still a substantial percentage of course, but in relation to previous figures, and in retrospect, it foretold that EEG abnormalities in the learning disabled were about to hit the skids. The 1960s ended with a decline to 50 percent and the 1970s opened with 37 percent. By 1973, reported EEG abnormalities in the learning disabled had fallen to 32 percent.[27]

Toward the end of the 1970s there was strong doubt that any significant EEG abnormalities could be found in the learning disabled. Replication studies done "blindly," unlike the studies that had reported high percentages of abnormalities, failed to find differences between normal and disabled groups. When children were grouped for a variety of behavioral and psychological problems, their EEGs proved to be indistinguishable from one another. Furthermore, changes occurred in standards of EEG abnormality. There had been a number of EEG results considered abnormal and found in high proportion in children with various behavior problems; with further research, however, the results were reconsidered and judged to be normal or of questionable clinical use.[28]

Recent reviews leave no question that not only have the initial high percentages of EEG abnormalities disappeared but, in the words of one reviewer (and proponent of the LD neurological thesis), the "clinical EEG has *not* been established as a correlate of dyslexia" and the research could be "interpreted as showing the *absence* of EEG abnormalities among dyslexics."[29] More recently, two reviewers apparently frustrated over a futile search for neurological abnormalities acknowledged, "*Somewhat disappointingly,* a lack of positive correlation between degree of reading retardation and the extent of EEG abnormalities has been the rule."[30] And a year later, another strong believer in the "neurobiological correlates of reading disorders" said, "Over the years, various claims have been made about the significance of non-seizure patterns in the EEG of educationally handicapped students. There is little support for these claims, and in individual instances the routine EEG is neither a measurement of intelligence nor a predictor of reading achievement."[31]

What is the lesson of this history? As with other discarded interpretations, the LD field has treated the demise of the EEG as a problem of the "science" of the procedure—one of poor subject selection, lack of "blind" methodology, inadequate control groups—not as another demonstration of the invalidity of the LD thesis. This reading of the history is especially bolstered by new technology, which I will discuss shortly, that has made the EEG a more sophisticated and valuable tool for studying brain structure and function. It has made "straightforward" EEG analysis—putting electrodes on the scalp and recording electrical activity—appear to be a rudimentary stage in LD scientific development. And so the revisionism continues. Previous EEG research becomes veiled, depicted as "earlier" work not as technically advanced as what's happening now. There is no need to question why researchers did the work they did, what effect the earlier erroneous claims might have had on children, or whether those studies revealed anything endemic to the LD enterprise. No one seems concerned that up to the late 1970s, authoritative publications listed the EEG among the ten most frequently recommended diagnostic tests for LD.[32]

Neurometrics

In his popular 1979 book *The Brain: The Last Frontier,* and in an excerpt in *Psychology Today,* neurologist Richard Restak argued that neurometric research, a new form of EEG analysis, could "confirm the presence of electrophysiological variables that provide 97 percent accuracy in discriminating between normal and learning disabled children."[33] Once again LD's scientific struggle appeared to have accomplished its goal. Neurometrics claimed a diagnostic accuracy two percentage points higher than any of the earlier EEG studies. All that was left was for researchers to hone neurometrics' precision so that they could identify the 3 percent who had slipped past the test.

Neurometrics is a diagnostic method by which a computer analyzes large amounts of EEG data obtained in an "evoked potentials" procedure.[34] Evoked potentials (or responses) are voltage changes (potentials) of the brain "evoked" by presenting a person with various stimuli. When a person is shown an object, its image passes from the retina to the visual area of the cerebral cortex. There, evoked by the image, neurons processing the information generate potentials, which can be picked up by electrodes placed on the scalp over the visual cortex.[35] Neurometrics is but one kind of evoked-potential research; I will discuss others in the next section of this chapter.

The neurometric battery introduces various clicks, flashes, taps, music, geometric forms, and other sensory stimuli to see what changes in electrical activity are evoked in various areas of the brain. The idea was to establish brain-function norms for groups with various problems against which an individual could be compared diagnostically. One of the groups was the learning disabled.

E. Roy John, the developer of neurometric testing, described his LD research in a book devoted to the subject. It is a peculiar book because, while making exceptional claims for the power of neurometrics, the book itself criticizes the neurometric research on which the claims are founded. For example, one assessment was made of fifty learning-disabled children who had been referred to a neuropsychology clinic. The LD diagnosis came not from the researchers but from psychologists, pediatricians, neurologists, or psychiatrists who wanted the clinic "to establish whether an organic basis for an apparent learning disability could be found." John himself criticized the research as suffering "from a severe shortcoming: No objective assessment of learning disability was obtained."

Despite the lack of "independent confirmation of LD" and the possibility the group might have been heterogeneous or have included some neurologically normal children, the neurometric diagnosis found one or more abnormal EEG features in all but one of the fifty children. This demonstrated the unusual diagnostic ability of neurometrics over other methods because many of the children "had previously been judged as normal on the basis of conventional neurological or EEG examinations." Neurometrics' superiority led John to anticipate that "neurometric methods might provide objective signs of brain dysfunction in many of the millions of children with learning disabilities who do not seem organically impaired with conventional means of assessment."[36]

We have seen this logic before: How do we know this potentially heterogeneous group was "organically impaired"? Because the neurometric analysis determined this. How do we know the analysis was correct? Because neurometric analysis can diagnose organic impairment. How do we know the group was learning disabled? Because the learning disabled have organic impairments and neurometrics can diagnose them. How do we know only one child was normal? Because neurometrics analyzed organic impairment in every child but that one. How do we know they were organically impaired . . .

Since John sounded so optimistic about the future of neurometrics the reader might think that criticism of the circular reasoning is mine. It is his. I simply outlined it, as the following quote will disclose:

> Since the functional significance of [neurometric] measures has not yet been established, it would not be legitimate to assert that any child with some measure significantly deviant from the average value has thereby been identified as learning disabled. The measure cannot be assumed a priori to be relevant to brain processes involved in learning. . . . Tautological implications can only be avoided by correlating [neurometric] measures with an independent and valid measure of learning impairment of organic origin.[37]

This sounds like a fair self-criticism and a recognition of future requirements. Yet, the conclusions two pages later give one the feeling of being in the middle of a game of intellectual leapfrog miraculously played by one player. The results of the research, said John, show neurometric "measures are extremely sensitive indices of brain dysfunction in children with learning disabilities, and clear differences exist between carefully defined subgroups of learning disabled children."[38]

Never made clear is where these conclusions came from. In a paper published in *Science,* a journal of the American Association for the Advancement of Science, John and his associates discussed a study of 533 children who came from a school for educationally handicapped children.[39] Presumably, this massive study supported neurometrics. High discriminating power was reported for the test battery, but there was no discussion of the children's characteristics or how they were diagnosed as learning disabled.[40] In short, like other neurometric research, this study did not move beyond, to use John's words, its "tautological implications."

Currently, discussion of neurometrics is strikingly absent in LD books and articles supporting the neurological deficit thesis.[41] As for Restak, his latest book, published in 1984, discusses LD and dyslexia, but it too says not a word about neurometrics.[42]

Evoked Potentials

Evoked-potential methods have made a number of invaluable contributions to medical diagnosis. The technique has been used to differentiate "organic disorders from psychogenic ones" and to identify brain areas active in sensory functioning when "perceptual tests are impractical or unreliable (as they are with infants)."[43] They have diagnosed hearing impairments in infants whose mothers had been infected by rubella during pregnancy and have detected and located brain tumors in auditory areas of the brain. Given this success in examining brain function, is there reason to expect that "evoked-potential methods will be employed routinely to examine child patients with diseases of the central nervous system . . . such as . . . 'minimal brain damage' and disorders of learning?"[44]

Orton's theory of a "failure of hemisphere specialization" found another voice in an evoked-potential study. After finding that normal readers had a higher left-over-right brain hemisphere activity than disabled readers, it concluded that "unless the activity of one hemisphere is suppressed, competing information ensuing from the interaction between both hemispheres may result in delays and misidentifications" in reading.[45]

However, in evoked-potential research the now-familiar cycle reappears. Subsequent research has failed to replicate earlier reports of evoked-response differences in dyslexics.[46] For example, the finding that "right hemispheric amplitudes were *greater* than those in the left hemisphere" for *both* dyslexics and normal readers led to the understated conclusion that evoked-potential brain-wave asymmetry in the left and right hemispheres by itself "may not be a reliable correlate of dyslexia."[47] Similar studies done since the early 1970s have demonstrated that, like dichotic-listening and visual-half-field research, evoked-potential measures are strongly dependent on an individual's attention, motivation, emotional response to the task, and problem-solving skills.[48]

Even when the latter conclusion is considered problematic, some investigators have admittedly been perplexed trying to interpret a "chicken and egg" conundrum. Finding themselves unable to obtain data that would allow their study to define the connection asserted by the title of their paper, "Event-Related Brain Potentials Differentiate Normal and Disabled Readers," a group of researchers decided:

> The specific cause of these [evoked] response pattern differences between normal and disabled readers is unclear at this time. . . . Whether these findings are directly related to the etiology of reading disabilities or whether they are a secondary result of poor reading due to other causal factors has not been determined at this time.[49]

This uncertainty was expressed in another study where group differences were thought to reflect possible neurological differences or to "be due in part to the way in which the subjects perform the reading tasks."[50] Even though a conclusion about correlation could not be reached, these investigators appeared to lean toward an experiential and problem-solving interpretation. They speculated that when both groups read easy and then hard passages, brain-wave changes in the left hemisphere were due to the increased difficulty of the words. They speculated further that evoked-potential differences were attributable to different facets of attention, such as "monitoring or scanning" the flashing lights and "pips" used as "background events." Even though the children were instructed not to pay attention to these lights, they did; consequently, attentional differences produced differences in evoked responses.[51]

As a summary of evoked potential research concluded: "results thus far have been inconsistent and frequently confusing."[52]

BEAM Scans

As I have mentioned, in Richard Restak's 1984 book, his discussion of dyslexia and learning disabilities contains not a word about neurometric diagnosis and its high diagnostic hit rate. This omission did not mean LD was now considered impervious to technological diagnosis. Rather, as readers of *The Brain* were told, the diagnostic means lay elsewhere, in "brain electrical activity mapping." These BEAM scans convert EEG information into a color-coded map of the parts of the brain activated during certain tasks, such as listening to a story, listening to music, or remembering abstract figures. This technique, Restak reported, could correctly diagnose dyslexia "80 to 90 percent of the time."[53] Along with this pronouncement, readers were treated to a full-page comparison of multi-colored BEAM scans of the brains of a dyslexic and a normal reader.[54]

When BEAM has been discussed in LD literature, two studies—and only two studies—are cited. Despite cautionary recommendations that "very few subjects" were used in the studies and that "the large number of statistical tests performed on this small sample makes conclusions based on statistical significance tenuous,"[55] enthusiasm for the two studies has not been dampened for many inside and outside the LD field.

The studies made BEAM scans for silent reading and other tasks, such as those just mentioned, and found group differences not only in language areas of the brain but in the frontal lobes. These differences, concluded the researchers, established "these particular measurements as powerful descriptors of aberrant physiology in dyslexics."[56]

Alpha waves are high electric waves (eight to thirteen cycles per second) produced by the brain during relaxed states; they are produced, for example, in meditation and cultivated in relaxation-biofeedback training. In this study, the consistently greater amount of alpha waves in the dyslexics' frontal lobes was interpreted as possibly signifying "relative underactivation of frontal systems in dyslexic as compared to control boys."[57] This interpretation was based on the view of "many investigators" who believed that "relative increases in alpha represented relative inactivity or 'idling' of the underlying cortex . . . conversely, decreases in alpha activity" represented "cortical activation."[58]

This could be an accurate interpretation, of course, but other explanations besides "aberrant physiology" are also plausible. The frontal lobes play a central role "in the regulation of vigilance and in the control of the most complex forms of man's goal-linked activity."[59] When presented with a complex task, a person's "increased attention arouses changes in the electrical activity in the brain." These changes include the depression of alpha rhythms and an increase in amplitude of faster brain waves. Hence, the absence of these changes could simply mean that someone was not paying attention to a task. The researchers were correct in saying that the "increased alpha anteriorly may signify underactivation of frontal systems in dyslexic as compared to control boys," but this would not mean, as they assumed, that the frontal system was underactivated because of pathology.[60] Rather, the children's responses to the task might have been underactivated.[61] Furthermore, other investigations have failed to find alpha wave differences between disabled and normal readers during reading.[62]

BEAM findings of amplitude differences in regions of the brain active in reading were similar to those in the EEG and evoked-potential studies I have discussed. This is to be expected, since BEAM is derived from both EEG and evoked responses and is "nothing more than a way of enhancing the amount of information available on a standard

EEG."[63] As such, BEAM is subject to the same criticism as these studies, in addition to my criticism that it has confused correlation with causation.

CAT Scan

Our evaluation of LD research has traced a path that has moved closer and closer to the brain itself in the search for the cause of LD. We come now to a means for studying the brains of the learning disabled that is more direct than any procedure or instrument discussed thus far. Computerized axial tomography, known as the CAT scan, is a useful technology for diagnosing certain brain diseases. In brief, a CAT scanner rotates around a person's head and emits X-ray beams directed through the head. The radiation is absorbed in brain tissue according the tissue's density and state of health or disease in various areas. After passing through the brain, the beam is converted into electronic signals and transmitted to a computer that creates visual projections of the brain in layers and from various angles. Understandably, the LD field has considered the CAT scan excellent for comparing the size and shape of the brains of disabled and normal readers.

Some evidence of structural brain asymmetry in dyslexics has been reported. In the general population, CAT scans have found that the rear portion of the left hemisphere tends to be slightly wider than the right. In normal people there is a high percentage of asymmetry in the planum temporale, the upper surface of the posterior temporal lobe, a lobe involved in language processing, such as analyzing and synthesizing speech sounds, naming objects, and recalling words. For example, in approximately 65 percent of autopsied adults, the surface area of the planum temporale was found to be larger on the left; for 11 percent it is larger on the right; and the two areas are approximately equal in 24 percent.[64] These difference were not found in dyslexics, for whom a CAT-scan study reported a larger right-surface area in 42 percent of the dyslexics examined (ten of twenty-four). Along with the reverse asymmetry, the ten had lower verbal IQs and a greater incidence of delayed speech than the remaining fourteen dyslexics.[65] From these findings the researchers hypothesized that brain structure differences preventing normal development of brain functioning in language-related areas might cause dyslexia. In a manner consistent with Orton, they proposed that dyslexia might be characterized by a "mismatch between hemispheric specialization for language and structural asymmmetry of the hemispheres."[66] Another paper two years later by two members of this study group described similar asymmetries for the same percentage of learning-disabled persons (twenty-two of fifty-three).[67] This research was soon cited in texts and articles as "convincing" evidence "that cerebral asymmetries may be related to functional problems in reading and learning."[68]

Significantly, the second report contained two hairline cracks in its theoretical edifice. One was a number of qualifying statements not found in the first paper, such as, "Our studies thus far have shown only correlations, not necessarily cause-effect relationships."[69] The other was an addendum stating that "since final acceptance of this manuscript," a member of the original research group had "encountered difficulty replicating her previously reported distribution of cerebral asymmetry in the general population."[70] In retrospect, these relatively tepid remarks about the meaning and validity of asymmetry set the stage for the LD studies with CAT scans that were to follow.

A year after the second paper was published, a replication study appeared. Using identical measurement procedures this study failed to find an "increased frequency of reversed occipital asymmetry with reading disability reported by others." Reversed asymmetry was found in only 12 percent of the dyslexics, a percentage similar to that found in normal readers in the first studies. Furthermore, no relationship was found between the "posterior width of the hemispheres" and either verbal IQ scores, delayed acquisition of speech, or reading problems.[71]

Corresponding judgments may be found in other studies of structural cerebral abnormalities in learning-disabled children. One concluded that most LD children "evaluated with computed tomography can be expected to have normal scans" and therefore "computed tomography of the brain does not appear to be a necessary screening procedure" in evaluating them.[72] Another study—coauthored by one of the researchers who originally found symmetry differences in dyslexics—reaffirmed this with the finding that the learning disabled "can be expected to have normal scans."[73] Here again, replication studies failed to confirm original findings. Why did this occur?

One major explanation lies in the issue of "blind" analysis, and the bias that can encourage investigators to "find" what they are looking for in an "abnormal" group. To understand the potential for this with CAT scans, a word about the technique is necessary. The visual projection of the brain's structure in a CAT scan can be enhanced by using a contrast solution, commonly an iodine dye injected into a vein in the hand or arm. However, except when researchers expect to find a pathology, the solution is seldom used in children because of its potential side effects, including allergic reactions (hives and itching), severe tightness and shortness of breath, and, in rare instances, even death.

These possible consequences outweigh any anticipated findings. But omitting the solution creates technical difficulties for professionals reading the CAT scans, and has influenced the outcomes of the research.

This is clear in a replication study summarized above that found that in sixteen dyslexics "no dominant hemisphere could be established" due to the difficulty in interpreting brain structure "without contrast injection." The researchers concluded that

> the inability to establish a [structurally] dominant cerebral hemisphere by scanning should not be construed as being secondary to reversed cerebral dominance or lack of cerebral dominance, but it is probably secondary to scanning technique and the difficulty in identifying the interhemispheric fissure without contrast injection.[74]

Quite simply, the researchers could not determine clearly where one hemisphere ended and the other began. Since other researchers did not use contrasting dye, presumably they too would have had similar trouble accurately discerning brain structure.

A more graphic illustration of the problems with interpreting CAT scans comes from another replication study in which two radiologists independently interpreted CAT scans of twenty-five children diagnosed as "neurologically impaired learning disabled."[75] The study did not use a blind methodology—the radiologists knew the children had been classified as LD—and did not mix in scans of normal learners. However, unlike other LD CAT scan research, it focused specifically on the extent of agreement between separate interpretations. Asked to decide whether the scans were normal or abnormal, the radiologists were agreed for only twelve of the twenty-five cases.[76] The other thirteen were judged slightly abnormal or borderline atrophic by one radiologist and normal by another. Of the twelve upon which they concurred, seven were judged to have normal scans and five, slightly abnormal.

Even granting the considerable disagreement, the five "slightly abnormal" scans could be considered a large percentage of twenty-five dyslexics and suggest that the method is fairly useful. However, other evidence in the study raises doubt about this conclusion and further shows the difficulty of determining the relative size of brain areas in LD children through CAT scans. The researchers noted that one or both radiologists judged twelve of the children to have abnormally sized ventricles (left and right brain cavities). But additional comparison with independent figures revealed that the ventrical size of all but one of the children, *"even four of the five considered concordantly abnormal by radiologists,"* were within the normal range.[77]

Dissected Dyslexic Brains

In every approach discussed thus far, the search for abnormal brains has been restricted by one common problem: no one has been able to study the LD brains themselves, to inspect, measure, evaluate the brains *sans* skulls, so to speak. Not yet, that is, with live brains. We come now to second best.

The autopsy of the brain of one dead dyslexic in the late 1960s was a unique study for LD research.[78] In recent years, autopsies of dyslexics' brains have been undertaken as a formal, ongoing, institutional research project through a brain-donor program. Not surprisingly, the project was developed by and remains under the auspices of the research division of the Orton Dyslexia Society.[79] The project's first subject, autopsied in the late 1970s, was a twenty-year-old man who had originally been diagnosed as dyslexic in elementary school and whose diagnosis had been reconfirmed in several periodic evaluations up to the age of nineteen.[80] Though the young man had been evaluated as normally intelligent, his reading level had not gone beyond the fourth grade. At eighteen he began training in sheet-metal work, became a talented metal sculptor, and at twenty obtained his first paying job. Tragically, six days after beginning work, he "died suddenly as the result of an accidental fall from a great height."[81] The cause of death was "multiple internal injuries producing massive bleeding" but miraculously, and fortunately for the researchers, the fall had not affected the portion of the body of interest to the researchers: "At autopsy the brain showed no evidence of trauma or other gross abnormalities."[82]

The method for studying the brain "is known as cytoarchitectonics, or simply, cell architecture, and involves the sectioning of the brain into 3000–4000 sections. Selected sections are then stained and microscopically examined for cellular differences."[83] Several cellular abnormalities were found in the left cerebral hemisphere. In the left temporal lobe, which is active in auditory functioning, researchers identified ectopias (cells out of place) and dysplasias (abnormal tissue forms), particularly polymicrogyria (numerous small, abnormal convolutions). Milder forms of abnormal tissue development were found in other parts of the left hemisphere. In contrast, the right hemisphere and the remainder of the brain appeared normal. These abnormalities appeared to "implicate dysfunction of language-related areas in the brains of patients with developmental dyslexia and suggest that focal disorders of cortical development may underlie some cases of specific learning disability."[84]

The neurologists observed that cell abnormalities found throughout the left hemisphere were essentially identical to those found in the brains of epileptics. Insightful though this was, it was not surprising, because the young man happened to have had "frank epilepsy" and required medication (Dilantin) to control his seizures![85] The researchers acknowledged that this medical condition limited any interpretation of the findings. Because the young man was both dyslexic and epileptic it was impossible to tell "whether or not the anatomical findings have any causative relationship to the clinical findings—much less whether the malformation is responsible for the seizure disorder, the learning disability, both, or neither."[86]

Polymicrogyria have long been documented in epileptics.[87] The dysplasias too, as the researchers noted, "were essentially identical" to those found in "surgical specimens of brain removed for control of epilepsy."[88] Furthermore, the investigators were uncertain what the morphological findings might mean because the "focal polymicrogyrias and mild dysplasias [in the general population] probably do not occur with enough frequency to explain the high prevalence of developmental reading disabilities."[89] In all, these abnormalities could readily have been explained in terms of epilepsy without ever bringing in dyslexia. (The same was true for a twelve-year-old boy whose brain was autopsied after he died of a massive brain hemorrhage. His symptoms, such as "blackouts"—during which on more than one occasion he completely lost his vision without losing consciousness—suggested to the investigators that he was epileptic.)[90]

In addition to cellular abnormalities, the Orton investigators also reported a "lack of asymmetry in the size of the planum temporale on the two sides," similar to that reported for CAT scans.[91] However, Albert Galaburda and Thomas Kemper did not make much of this because, "since symmetry in the extent of planum can occur in as many as 24 percent of normal individuals, this [symmetry of the autopsied brain] is not likely to represent an abnormality."[92]

It is worthwhile noting that subsequent discussions of the first case, by Galaburda and by others, have not mentioned the young man's "frank epilepsy" and the medication used to control his seizures, or the investigators' uncertainty in interpreting the cellular findings because of the relationship between the kinds of abnormalities found and epilepsy. These discussions, then, present the "findings" more conclusively than they are portrayed in the original paper.[93] Regardless of intent, the effect has been to enhance the evidence for the biological cause of dyslexia.

Three other dyslexic brains recently described by Galaburda and his associates have also been reported to have symmetry of the planum temporale. Since, as I have mentioned, this symmetry occurs in approximately a quarter of the general population, most of whom learn to read, it is difficult to understand how "the presence of symmetrical plana is a sufficient condition for dyslexia."[94] However, the primary reason they conclude that brain abnormalities underlie dyslexia is the finding of cellular abnormalities (ectopias, dysplasias, polymicrogyria) in dissimilar patterns in each of the brains.[95]

There are two difficulties in assessing these findings. It is hard to know whether all the individuals actually were dyslexic and whether other physical conditions, such as in the case of the epileptic, were pertinent. Concerning the first difficulty, one of the autopsied brains was from a German man who "just prior to his death had completed the requirements for the postgraduate degree of doctor of engineering."[96] Although he was supposedly diagnosed as dyslexic at an early age, a table, "Results of Reading and Intelligence Testing," presents *no* information about his reading abilities or any objective test results.[97] Although the brief case summary states that "the school psychologist provided very careful histories," the only test information provided by the report is for spelling, for which at the age of fourteen he was said to have spelled at a 3.5 grade level.[98] How was this determined? A footnote explains: "Results of an informal spelling test. Tutor said '. . . performance was like that of children in the third grade.' "[99] No more test information is given for this "medical engineer Ph.D."[100] Presumably by way of suggesting a hereditary connection, the case summary adds that the man had "a mathematically talented father who was almost certainly an undiagnosed dyslexic."[101] How and why this was thought to be so is not explained.

Thus, there is no evidence in the case sketch that the man was dyslexic, other than an informal spelling test. The autopsy also provides no basis for the diagnosis except through the tautology that if he were not dyslexic he would not have had the cellular abnormalities. Given his educational achievement, there is in fact good evidence to think he might have been a perfectly normal reader. If we assume that this was the case, what might the cellular abnormalities signify? Galaburda has no answer.

In this study, unusual medical histories of the so-called dyslexics contributed to the difficulty of determining the meaning of the autopsy findings. The Ph.D. died at the age of thirty-two from a massive brain hemorrhage; no further information is provided because "the official medical record is somewhat sketchy."[102] Another case was a fourteen-year-old boy who died suddenly of heart disease—"acute myocarditis, and it was presumed that an arrhythmia was the cause of death."[103] The final case was a twenty-year-old man who died in an auto accident. At fourteen he had fallen "from an eight-foot wall and sustained a linear fracture" on the left side of his head, which subsequently caused daytime drowsiness and some EEG abnormalities over the right hemisphere.

In summation, we have four dyslexics, one who was an epileptic, one with a fractured skull, another who died at fourteen of heart problems, and a fourth who died of a brain hemorrhage but not before getting a Ph.D. in medical engineering. Galaburda and his colleagues say that "the lesions seen in these brains represent developmental anomalies acquired some time before birth, probably during the middle of gestation, a time that coincides with peak rates of neuronal migration from the germinal [neurons] of the cerebral cortex."[104] Nonetheless, for three of the four cases, the abnormalities could have been solely associated with their unusual medical problems. The cellular abnormalities the researchers described have been found to have a number of possible causes, including circulatory problems, infections, syphilis, or anoxia.[105] The researchers note that cellular abnormalities are "frequently seen in routine postmortem examinations" and mention one study that found them in 30 percent of a "population of derelicts" with a "high rate of congenital anomalies." Thus, the abnormalities found in the four presumed dyslexics could either have been caused by biological factors not centered in the brain (such as the circulatory problems that led to the fatal heart disease and brain hemorrhage) or, as in the case of the epileptic, could have been neurological but had nothing to do with dyslexia.

Another possible assumption is that the cell abnormalities caused both the medical and the reading problems. To draw this interpretation, however, much more information is required than the brief case descriptions provide. Did these individuals meet exclusionary criteria of dyslexia? Can their reading problems be reasonably explained through experiential factors or through medical factors, such as a long-term childhood illness? If, for example, none of them meet dyslexia criteria, how would we account for the coincidental findings reported in the four consecutive cases above without resorting to circular reasoning?

The research Galaburda and his colleagues performed in the Laboratory for the Study of the Biological Foundations of Dyslexia has only recently been reported. Certainly, if the history of LD has anything to teach—with its recurrent exuberant claims of new findings and the subsequent replication studies that repudiate the initial claims and often reveal gross methodological errors and tendentiousness—it is that one must proceed cautiously and wait for additional evidence. One commentator, who advised that these findings of cellular abnormalities "should be interpreted with extreme caution" and that there was a "need to know much more about Galaburda's patients," pointed out that the autopsy research had not yet shown that the sensorimotor functions involved were associated with cellular abnormalities: "Thus, one cannot speak of the 'reading center' of the brain, or even of a 'dyslexic brain,' which only means a 'brain that reads with difficulty.' One must discover which of the sensory or motor subroutines were affected by the abnormal cellular migrations, for it is the subroutines that go together to make reading possible."[106]

LD autopsy research presents unusual replication problems.[107] Locating a dyslexic's brain is difficult for most researchers, and I believe the Orton Dyslexia Society's brain-donor program is the only one of its kind. Additionally, the equipment necessary for storing, sectioning, and examining the brains is not readily available to most LD researchers. At present, and perhaps for a long time to come, the unusual requirements of this research will make replication and verification difficult. However, Sandra Witelson and Marc Colonnier have been studying the brain of a sixty-year-old dyslexic man since 1985 and report preliminary findings at variance with Galaburda and his associates. Their work is part of a larger study of normal brains. Most of the individuals could read, but this man, after being unable to read a consent form, was diagnosed as dyslexic. Some histological findings were described by Witelson as "atypical" compared to other brains autopsied for the study. At this time in her research, however, she did not consider them necessarily "abnormal" on the basis of neuropathological examination. Most importantly with regard to Galaburda's findings, autopsy of those regions Witelson and Colonnier have studied has revealed neither dysplasias, polymicrogyria, nor ectopias.[108]

■●▲ Conclusion

The sum of this indefatigable "deficit-driven" research using newer and newer technologies has been a failure to substantiate the LD explanation.[109] However, in light of this outcome, a point made earlier should be restated here. The overwhelming failure of these technical approaches to provide validation has still not quashed the researchers' hope, which is sustained by the very few individuals found with true neurological dysfunctions—the genuinely learning disabled. However, though these individuals may turn up in "LD" groups, their numbers are never significant enough to validate the LD explanation—once more suggesting that they represent quite a small portion of the great hordes who are said to be learning disabled.

5

■ ● ▲

Drugs and LD Explanations

> The most effective single treatment for minimal brain dysfunction is medication. . . . Stimulant drug treatment is, when effective, one of the most striking effective physical treatments in psychiatry, comparable, perhaps, only to electroconvulsive therapy in treatment of serious endogenous depression.[1]

So wrote Paul H. Wender, a physician and a leading researcher of minimal brain dysfunction—the syndrome until recently said to cause LD—and a leading proponent of drug treatments. Drugs have a twofold function in LD explanations: they are used both to help validate the existence of a biological cause and to treat the condition. "The slowing down of the child," Wender said, referring to the reduction of hyperactivity, was "the least remarkable effect" of drug treatment. Of "greater importance, [and] of considerably greater interest," was its "effect on complex psychological functioning." By taking stimulant drugs—primarily amphetamines (Benzedrine and Dexedrine) and methylphenidate (Ritalin)—"children may display more mature cognitive . . . functions than they have ever shown."[2]

■●▲ Ritalin

Wender's hosanna was but one in a chorus from professionals who, from the mid-1930s onward, argued that drugs not only reduced hyperactivity but also improved academic achievement. And that the drugs did more than merely calm children, improve their attention, and make them more receptive to teaching. Yes, Wender said, they actually enhanced the cognitive processes. Professionals cited "growing reports of vastly improved behavior and better academic performance in many cases following the uses of medication."[3] Academic productivity and grades improved, as did performance on laboratory and psychological tests "that measure important components of the learning process such as sustained attention and short-term memory."[4] These fervid accounts of children's responsiveness to the drugs lent proof to the claim that the very effectiveness of the drugs on brain actions implied neurological dysfunction. Children responded, Wender proposed, because the drugs were "operating at a point relatively close to the origin of the etiological chain," probably at the level of the neurotransmitters.[5] This reasoning has a now-familiar construction: if a drug "improves" a problem thought to occur from a brain dysfunction, that demonstrates that a brain dysfunction is the source of the problem. Based on "growing reports" of drug success, professionals were heartily encouraged to prescribe the drugs, especially Ritalin, for minimal brain dysfunction (MBD) and its symptoms, hyperactivity and LD.[6] Standing atop professional support (and through various means cultivating it) were the drug companies promoting their products.[7]

According to IMS America, a pharmaceutical data-collection firm, approximately 396,000 prescriptions for Ritalin were written by private physicians for children examined in their offices in 1972.[8] The number climbed to 480,760 by 1974, then jumped to 608,660 the following year. In 1976, perhaps because of a good deal of widely publicized criticism of the drug, the number dropped to approximately 422,000. This decrease might suggest that Ritalin was being prescribed more cautiously, but when the figures are compared with the total number of prescriptions filled by pharmacies, a different picture emerges. For example, in a one-year period during 1972–73, pharmacists filled 623,000 prescriptions for Ritalin; for the first ten months of 1977 the figure was 1,463,000, with a projected annual total of approximately 1,800,000. The figures therefore indicate that while the number of children for whom Ritalin was prescribed for the *first* time was approximately the same in 1972 and 1977 and even declined from 1975 to 1978, the total number of youngsters taking Ritalin increased during the five-year period. The difficulty obtaining data prevents a thorough analysis of the number of children on Ritalin. For example, not included in calculations are prescriptions written in clinics or the size of prescriptions (whether the prescription was for one month or one year).

Even without this information, however, it is clear that the number of youngsters on Ritalin during this time was sizable. One independent researcher's recent estimate of children taking stimulant drugs, usually Ritalin, puts the number at between 300,000 and 600,000.[9] By another account, it is up to 700,000.[10] A representative of CIBA, the company that manufactures the drug, told me that in 1985 Ritalin was prescribed to treat attentional deficit disorder in up to 500,000 children. This number was likely to increase, I was told, because marketing research has concluded that an increasing number of children are being diagnosed as having that disorder.

Given the history of the field's other claims, no one should be surprised to learn that the statements about the beneficial effects of drugs on the "origin of the etiological chain" that caused LD were totally without foundation. First, as discussed in chapter two, MBD—a term used to describe the biological basis of LD and a medical category used to prescribe Ritalin—came under continued criticism and in 1980 was eventually excised from the third edition of the Diagnostic and Statistical Manual of Mental Disorders because of its totally ambiguous definition. A task force had attempted to make the definition more precise but had ended up with a list of ninety-nine of its most prevalent "symptoms," among which were: hyperactivity, perceptual-motor impairments, general coordination deficits, attention disorders, impulsivity, memory disorders, general awkwardness, slowness in finishing work, quick fatigue, social boldness and aggression, extreme sensitivity to others, impaired ability to make decisions, and, the primary symptom, LD. Also in the inventory were neurological soft signs which range from mixed laterality to poor muscle tone. As you might expect, the ambiguity of this "basket" definition led to studies that failed to distinguish the condition from normal children on the basis of those symptoms. Even when neurologists tried to use soft signs to reach differential diagnoses, the results were the same.[11]

The failure of the term "MBD" to describe manifestations of the biological basis of LD betrayed the shaky foundation on which the prescription of Ritalin rested. In fact, "Ritalin" was written on hundreds of thousands of prescription pads not because research supported administering the drug but because there was in the air an *"impression"* from laboratory studies that it facilitated cognition.[12] Several remarkable findings contradicting this impression were reported in an important 1978 review of both short- and long-term studies on the use of stimulant drugs with children who were hyperactive and learning disabled.[13] Few studies had been done over three decades, from 1940 to the mid-1970s, to determine how stimulant drugs influenced learning. Of a total of seventeen studies, almost all had been poorly designed and controlled, and eleven were short-term studies of between two weeks and three months. Worst of all for drug advocates, whether the studies were short- or long-term, whether they met basic scientific criteria or not, all the conclusions converged: "stimulant drugs have little, if any, impact on . . . long-term academic outcome." Their major effect seemed to be an "improvement in classroom manageability."[14] The 1978 review obviously had little implicit praise for the members of the medical and psychological community who had treated LD children with drugs, but even less to their credit was the fact that the review was not news. Its critique only elaborated conclusions of other reviews published in the preceding twelve years.[15]

The continued failure to find evidence to support the use of Ritalin and other stimulant drugs for LD required drug advocates and drug companies to retrench.[16] Of course, they now said—dropping the claim about drug effects on the dysfunctional neurology underpinning cognition—stimulant drugs could not be expected to improve academic skills because drugs cannot replace instruction; they can only provide a basis for academic growth by improving attention and classroom behavior. Given this revised explanation, researchers naturally wondered whether this sound educational basis could be established without drugs. They compared the benefit of Ritalin alone, educational intervention alone, and their combined use in improving academic performance in hyperactive LD children, and again drug advocates could not hold the line: educational intervention alone was found to be as successful or superior to any program using Ritalin.[17]

Some still questioned whether hyperactivity by itself could be helped by Ritalin. The few studies that investigated this found at best dubious benefits from Ritalin in treating hyperactivity, emotional adjustment, or social interaction. For example, parents' and teachers' assessments of a child's hyperactivity were often conflicting; when they were not, little was ascertained about the child's overall well-being other than that he or she had become more docile, compliant, and manageable when treated with the drug.[18] Now, of course, Ritalin is prescribed for attention deficit disorder rather than for hyperactivity. This revision further weakens claims about the use of Ritalin because, as we have discussed, studies have demonstrated that behavioral interventions alone have successfully eliminated attention problems and improved academic performance.

Finally, even CIBA pharmaceutical company has acknowledged the lack of evidence to support the use of Ritalin for an extended period of time. In a recent product information release on the drug, under the heading of "Warnings," the company stated: "Sufficient data on the safety and efficacy of long-term use of Ritalin in children are not yet available."[19]

In all, support never existed for the claim that Ritalin aided in locating and treating a biologically based condition, reduced learning disabilities or hyperactivity alone, or provided any extra benefits when used in combination with nondrug methods. However, none of this sufficiently deterred CIBA from promoting the drug or physicians from prescribing it.[20]

In his presidential address to the clinical experimental-behavioral science section of the American Psychological Association, K. Daniel O'Leary estimated that the potential market for LD-hyperactivity drugs is 5 percent of all children in elementary school.[21] No one except the companies knows how much profit has been accrued from the drugs, but there is little question that it is considerable. Ritalin has been among the top two hundred drugs prescribed in the U.S., which together account for 70.3 percent of the total number of prescriptions.[22] Over the years other pharmaceutical companies have tried to compete for the potential market and profits, but CIBA's Ritalin has remained preeminent. Whether this will continue remains to be seen. With the failure of any study to show that Ritalin contributes to improvements in learning-disabled children's reading and academic achievement, the market is wide open for a drug that will accomplish this, or give the appearance of accomplishing this.

■●▲ Piracetam

At least one drug is now rising to claim to do what others cannot. Its name is Piracetam, and its manufacturer would like it to be used for dyslexia. As a protocol for research funded by the manufacturer explains, successful instructional methods for treating dyslexics do not exist, and even if they did, many schools would not have the personnel to implement them. Also, "available drug therapies appear to be inadequate from the standpoint of efficacy and safety." Given these educational and pharmaceutical conditions, "the benefit of safe and effective drug therapy to aid in the treatment of dyslexia is obvious."[23]

Developed by the UCB pharmaceutical company in Brussels, Piracetam is said to have "a direct positive effect upon the higher mental functions" and to enhance learning and memory.[24] Classified as a nootropic drug (from *noös,* "mind," plus *trepein,* "turn, toward"), Piracetam is believed to activate cell neurotransmission, thereby improving messages from one nerve cell to another. However, this is merely speculation, because its exact action remains unknown. Piracetam differs from Ritalin in that it is said to improve mental and language abilities among the general population and in special groups representing a wide range of neurological and psychiatric conditions. In addition to dyslexics, these special groups include epileptic, brain-injured, and geriatric patients, and children classified as mentally retarded and speech disordered. This distinction aside, there remains an essential shared rationale for their use: both drugs are said to treat LD's very cause, which resides in the brain.

Exactly how significantly Piracetam enhances mental functioning is more uncertain than UCB will acknowledge because the effects of the drug appear to be confined largely to limited gains in rote learning. For example, in a study asking college students to memorize a list of nine words, more words were retained with Piracetam than with a placebo, even though group differentiation for this task was not especially noteworthy: the placebo group increased its mean number of words learned from 4.92 to 5.63 (0.7 improvement); the Piracetam group gained from 5.04 to 6.21 (1.2 improvement). Giving the college students Piracetam, therefore, enabled them to attain an average increase of half a word over what they would have learned using placebos.[25]

Before I review the studies on Piracetam and dyslexia in particular, I should clarify their purpose. Most of the studies in the United States have not been disinterested scientific explorations of hypothetical Piracetam effects. Rather they have been funded by UCB with the intention of obtaining the approval of the Federal Drug Administration to market the drug as a pharmacological treatment for dyslexia. I am not saying that the researchers have consciously skewed their work toward that purpose. I do maintain, though, and UCB would not deny this, that managerial supervision by an industry consultant and strict protocol guidelines have both been imposed by the company, not in the interests of objective research but in order to document the drug's efficacy for ultimate FDA approval.[26]

In spite of UCB funding and company priorities, the results of tests to date give UCB very little ground for optimism. A glow of success appeared with a neuropsychologist's initial judgment that ten of fourteen learning-disabled children had improved "with Piracetam on tests of memory, attention span, concentration, and eye-hand coordination." However, the glow quickly dimmed when this subjective judgment was compared with the children's failure to demonstrate improved scores on objective neuropsychological tests of learning, memory, attention span, and reaction time.[27]

A similar dimming is evident in a different kind of comparison, this time between the published report and the original manuscript of an English study of forty-six dyslexic boys.[28] While the manuscript reported equal improvement for the Piracetam and placebo groups in reading comprehension, the Piracetam group was reported as having greater increases in tests of reading accuracy (reading the words of a story correctly) and reading rate.[29] In reading rate, the Piracetam scores were especially significant because they were "almost twice that of the placebo group." The manuscript concluded: "both speed of reading and actual reading ability improve" with Piracetam. Apparently reading comprehension was not considered part of "actual reading ability."

The same results were *not* reported in the published discussion of the study that appeared in the *Journal of Learning Disabilities.* Here, the results for rate and accuracy appeared, but the comprehension test results were lost somewhere between drafts, so that it appeared from the article that the study had not tested reading comprehension! Found between drafts, however, was an additional test, for word identification.[30] This addition was fortunate for UCB because the test showed statistically significant improvement for the Piracetam but not for the placebo group. Why this test was never mentioned in the original manuscript version is not clear.

The manuscript also contained the results of a spelling test and several measures to determine if Piracetam had an effect on the left hemisphere. There were no group differences for any of these tests.[31] Inexplicably, these outcomes, like the results of the comprehension tests, never found their way into the published version of the research. Of course, omitting them reduced both the number of similar Piracetam and placebo scores and the number of negative conclusions to be drawn about the beneficial effect of Piracetam on dyslexia and left-hemisphere functioning.

As a step toward obtaining FDA approval, UCB funded and coordinated a large-scale research project on Piracetam and dyslexia at six U.S. sites, both at universities and at children's hospitals.[32] Clear margins of Piracetam-over-placebo improvement for the 257 reading-disabled boys who participated in the project appeared to be limited to reading rate (for Piracetam, words-per-minute change was 80 to 87; for placebo, 79.2 to 82.4). Group gains were approximately equal on tests of reading accuracy, reading comprehension, spelling, syllabication, word-naming, and digit span.

Researchers at each site undertook a special project of their own, but these produced only limited additional outcomes.[33] For example, at one site, performance on tests of auditory and visual perception did not differ for Piracetam.[34] At another, differences in evoked responses from an EEG test were interpreted to mean that Piracetam improved the processing of verbal stimuli—but this interpretation was not supported by the children's actual performance on verbal tasks. Whether using Piracetam or placebo, they had the same rate of errors.[35] There is no question that for the overall group, the consistent failure to show greater reading-comprehension gains with Piracetam indicates that the drug does not enhance thinking ability in literacy tests. Equally apparent is the failure to demonstrate with Piracetam that dyslexia is caused by brain dysfunction.

Nonetheless, the researchers concluded that Piracetam might contribute to reading improvement. They reasoned that even though significant changes were not found for reading accuracy and comprehension, improvement in reading speed could help dyslexics meet classroom demands that require students to complete work within a given period of time. The inverse relationship of reading speed to reading accuracy and comprehension in dyslexics often meant academic failure because

> they do not complete the material required . . . or are both slow and inaccurate. Comprehension of material actually read is usually fairly good and the discrepancy between poor rate (or accuracy) and relatively good comprehension is often a significant key for diagnosing a child as being dyslexic. As with most children, a dyslexic child may slow the reading rate and improve accuracy and comprehension or may increase the rate and sacrifice accuracy and comprehension.[36]

Therefore, the reasoning goes, a dyslexic child having to work within classroom constraints could benefit from Piracetam because it would improve reading rate without interfering with accuracy and comprehension.

We can assess the soundness of this conclusion by using the aforementioned reading-rate improvements of 7.0 words per minute for the Piracetam group and of 3.2 for the placebo group. The investigators, using a statistical crystal ball composed of an "analysis of covariance, baseline covariate, adjusted mean differences, and one-tailed and two-tailed tests of significance," interpreted these "data" as "significant." However, when simple arithmetic, real life, and common sense are brought to the analysis of the groups' numbers, the rate differences become trivial, the recommendations absurd. If the Piracetam group read at the drug-improved rate of 87 wpm and the placebo group read at their worst (nonplacebo) rate of 79.2 wpm, for each minute of reading the Piracetam dyslexics would read eight words more. At the end of ten minutes of straight reading, the Piracetam dyslexics would have read 870 words and the non-Piracetam dyslexics 790 words—the latter group would thus need one more minute to catch up. The profound impact of Piracetam on timesaving is unmistakable: better to give Piracetam than to modify instruction to accommodate children who comprehend as well as their peers but need a little extra time to do so.

Piracetam's efficacy is not the only issue, of course; its side effects are another concern. No short-term side effects have been reported in the dyslexia studies, but the long-term side effects are unknown.[37] Proponents argue that possible long-term side effects must be weighed against the long-term effects of poor teaching and its damage to a student's intellectual potential and self-esteem. If society were to accommodate itself to the "dyslexic's difficulty . . . with the symbolic system of communication presented by society," drugs like Piracetam would not be needed. However, since "it is very unlikely that society will change" and "in fact is reluctant to even recognize the problem," the question is, "do we let suffering continue for years, when methods may be available to help?"[38] All that was missing from this emotional appeal was a quotation from the Bible: "Suffer the little children to come unto me. . . ."

As I have said, marketing Piracetam is the ultimate reason UCB is funding investigations in the United States. Regrettably for the company, that desire may not be theirs alone. Apparently a few years ago UCB made the Piracetam formula known to other pharmaceutical companies, which then went ahead and developed analogs of the drug. These companies have not yet published research on these, but this research may be under way. When I asked a UCB representative how far along the company was in obtaining FDA approval, I was told that the information could not be divulged. The reticence is understandable: only by guarding one's moves is there any hope of being the first to walk through the golden FDA gateway to that 5 percent of all elementary-school children.

■●▲ Motion-Sickness Drugs

In the waiting room of the Medical Dyslexic Treatment Center in Great Neck, New York, were seven families anxious to have their dyslexic children evaluated. Among the "spillover crowd" in the building's cafeteria sat many who had made appointments up to a year in advance and had come from throughout the United States and from overseas. Parents interviewed by a newspaper reporter said they were "willing, even eager" to pay the $500 fee for the "diagnostic-treatment evaluation" and were prepared to have their children take medication that might be prescribed for as long as six years.[39]

The diagnosis and medication offered at the center is based principally on the work of Dr. Harold N. Levinson, founder and director of the clinic and associate professor of clinical psychiatry at the New York University Medical Center. A brochure states that "75% of individuals will have a favorable therapeutic response to various combinations of medications." A caveat adds: "favorable response will vary from mild to dramatic, and is thus far not predictable." (The brochure also advises that the $500 fee "must be paid at the time of the examination.")

Levinson's LD explanation is a biological one, but it differs from others in that it places the cause in a part of the brain other than the cortex.[40] The popularity of his explanation and therapy is indicated by the considerable sales of his two books and by the considerable media attention he has received. He has appeared on the *Phil Donahue Show* and the *Today Show* and has been featured in articles in the *New York Times, Philadelphia Inquirer, Detroit News, McCall's,* and *Family Weekly.*[41]

Levinson's explanation is included in this chapter partly because it uses drugs to validate a biological explanation of dyslexia. His explanation is also discussed here because its popularity, and the many who seek out his treatment for their children or for themselves, exemplify how desperation induces people to accept uncritically even the most unfounded LD explanations, especially those that involve drug use. There are other specialists who have lucrative clinical practices which offer diagnoses and claim to treat learning-disabled children; Levinson is among the most successful and is certainly the most visible, due to the massive popularity of his books and his wide media exposure.

As I said, Levinson's theory runs counter to the dominant neurological explanation that identifies the cortex, the outer layer of the brain, as the area where dyslexia originates. He maintains that the entire history of research of dyslexia offers little evidence of cortical dysfunction. He offers instead the cerebellum, a structure located below the cortex in the middle, rear part of the brain, which coordinates fine movement and muscular coordination.

Levinson has a singular interpretation of the field's insistent and misguided diagnosis, calling it cortical dyslexic scientific neurosis.[42] He takes the long view, seeing this "neurosis" as a response to evolutionary events that contradict humanity's view of itself and, specifically, LD professionals' view of themselves. What he's talking about is the development of the cerebellum prior to that of the cortex, a sequence that left humans with an animal "cerebellar subcortical heritage" that strongly determines their mental and linguistic functions. Humanity in general and LD professionals in particular, when faced with this heritage, prefer to think of themselves as conscious, thinking beings, and therefore respond with a "defensive megalomania" and "narcissism," and are thrown into a "phylogenetic identity crisis" and "defensive subcortical or cerebellar denial."[43] In other words, because cerebellar functions were part of our earlier, primordial crawling, walking, and "nonthinking" period of evolution, contemporary humans, trumpeting their intelligence over that of earlier forms of human life, deny that nonthinking processes, primitive in origin, could determine their mental and linguistic functions. To accept this influence would, for many in the LD field, contradict their identity as evolutionarily advanced beings. Hence, the misinterpretation of the causes of dyslexia.

If this explanation makes one's head orbit, it is no accident. Levinson views his study of dyslexia as much more than a scientific inquiry; it has been, to use his words, a "scientific 'space shuttle' " probing the inner mental worlds, analogous to "America's remarkable space program" that "probes the cosmos" and provides those on earth a "cosmic perspective."[44]

Levinson's space craft is almost impregnable. Critics are dismissed for not facing up to the animals they are—for not recognizing that their criticism comes from the "emotional roots underlying their scientific 'cortical facades' " and from their "unconscious resistance" to acknowledging the influence of the primitive parts of their brains.[45]

Levinson's theory is essentially a variation of the "eye fixation" explanation of dyslexia. The causal sequence begins with a dysfunction of the inner ear's vestibular system and of the cerebellum, the portion of the brain to which the vestibular system is connected. In general, the cerebellum and vestibular system help maintain visual and auditory coordination, directionality, balance, and spatial orientation. A dysfunctional cerebellum would be unable to guide and control eye movements, especially the focus needed for reading. The result of faulty eye movements, Levinson has concluded, may be dyslexia.

Levinson has found an abundance of cerebellar-vestibular (c-v) dysfunctions among dyslexics. In 115 New York City schoolchildren referred for "neuropsychiatric testing in an attempt to explore their apparent 'refractory response' to special education procedures," he identified the dysfunction in 97 percent of them.[46] To document further the validity of the diagnosis, he randomly selected twenty-two of the children and referred them to two neurologists for blind evaluations. All but one child, reported Levinson, had c-v signs; in fifteen, a clear c-v dysfunction was identified. The major signs were clumsy or awkward coordination, difficulty with fine muscle coordination, immature and distorted drawings, poor letter formation and spacing (graphomotor incoordination), and impaired successive movements of fingers. Other signs were difficulty hopping, throwing, catching, and kicking; and slurring of speech.

Oddly, among those who thought these were not particularly significant indices were the two neurologists. Apparently, Levinson maintained that the neurologists had found c-v dysfunction, but the two themselves repudiated this interpretation of their diagnosis. Levinson acknowledged this in a discussion of criticism of his views. Nonetheless, the space capsule was kept intact. Recounting how the two refuted "the inference drawn from their work-ups," Levinson tolerantly recognized that their "cerebellar denial should have been anticipated, for it was . . . consistent with the traditionally rooted cortical perspectives of dyslexia."[47]

Electronystagmographic caloric testing (ENG), a common c-v evaluation method, has also been employed to support his theory. The test uses warm and cool water or air to stimulate the vestibular system and to produce nystagmus (a rapid involuntary oscillation of the eyeball), an indication of c-v dysfunction. Explaining his eye-fixation theory further, Levinson proposes that nystagmus "secondarily scrambles the visual output," thereby interfering with the ability of the intact cerebral cortex to interpret print.[48] In his study of the New York City schoolchildren, Levinson referred seventy-five of them to seven different medical centers for blind ENG testing. He reported that 90 percent were found to have some ENG abnormalities suggestive of a c-v dysfunction.

One might expect Levinson to conclude that there is a greater incidence of nystagmus in disabled readers. Surprisingly, he does not even claim that nystagmus is correlated with reading disability! In a 1975 discussion of his work at a meeting of the Orton Dyslexia Society, one participant cited a personal study in which nystagmus was found in 20 percent of *both* disabled and normal readers. Levinson replied that the finding, rather than disproving the association, actually demonstrated an essential, and heretofore overlooked, characteristic of dyslexics: many of them "compensate" and learn to read without necessarily ever exhibiting reading difficulty. Thus, he was not surprised to learn that someone had found an equal distribution of nystagmus in the two groups; the normal reading group included "reading-score compensated dyslexics." Furthermore, Levinson continued, not all poor readers are dyslexic. In the discussant's study, the only true dyslexics were the 20 percent of poor readers with nystagmus. More will be said about "compensation" in a moment. For now I will merely point out the obvious: Levinson's reply left that participant and any other critic without a space station to stand on.

Central in Levinson's work is his effort to validate the theory of c-v origins by demonstrating the therapeutic value of drugs. The primary drugs he uses are the anti-motion-sickness medications Antivert, Marezine, Dramamine, Benadryl, Phenergan, Thransderm-Scop, and Atarax. In addition, Levinson's armamentarium includes the psychostimulants Ritalin and Cylert; the amphetamine Dexedrine; and the antidepressants Tofranil and Elavil. He also prescribes vitamins.

In one set of experiments, Levinson tried to demonstrate that the drugs improve ENG response and performance in an eye-tracking test. However, not only did he fail to show drug improvement for either outcome, he even found that performance on eye-tracking tests did not differentiate normal readers from dyslexics.[49] As always, Levinson was undaunted. Lack of "pharmacologic correlations" did not mean he should discontinue prescribing drugs or abandon the view that dyslexia was of c-v origin. Confronting the scientific juncture head on, he "had the courage to invoke Einstein's famous tongue-in-cheek remark, 'If the facts do not fit the theory, then the facts are wrong.' "[50]

Using "compensation" as a key concept, Levinson totally redefined the definition of dyslexia. He concluded that dyslexia was a c-v dysfunction with varying symptoms such as perceptual, balance, coordination, behavioral, and psychiatric problems, but among which reading and learning disabilities might not be present. Dyslexia had to be regarded as a condition independent of reading scores because, as he had explained at the Orton meeting, when dyslexics did not demonstrate reading problems, it was because they had compensated for their disability and learned to read.[51]

Regardless of experimental outcomes, which he admits have failed to validate "a solution to the riddle of dyslexia," Levinson feels his clinical results have justified the use of drugs, especially anti-motion-sickness drugs, as "fine-tuners" of c-v functioning.[52] For over ten years he has "treated many thousands of dyslexic children and adults with medications" and reports having had positive responses "approximately 75 to 80 percent of the time."[53] Levinson's alleged accomplishments through medication are as extensive as his definition of dyslexia. Evidence of these successes come in the form of case descriptions illustrating "typical therapeutic responses." However, although case studies have made an important contribution to the development of psychology, medicine, and other fields, Levinson's case studies offer meager substantiation of his claims. For example, he cites testimony that a seventeen-year-old boy improved his writing when he began taking Dramamine and Ritalin, but the case sketch contains only an oblique hint of a reading problem and any improvement: "When driving, Stan noticed he was reading the signs on the parkway faster and clearer. . . . This could be because of greater familiarity."[54] A sixteen-year-old girl said, "Upon taking Marezine . . . my reading speed increased at a rate beyond that which I could comprehend." She also tried Dimetapp and Antivert but found they had no effect. The case description contains no other information about reading changes. Marezine and Ritalin apparently helped a sixteen-year-old boy take a greater interest in school and improve his grades, but here too the case sketch provides no information about reading problems or reading improvement. Other cases discuss the use of anti-motion medicine with "dyslexic" patients who had clear c-v signs but who read normally. Levinson included these cases as examples of dyslexia because, he said—employing the escape-hatch logic of his theory—the patients' normal reading demonstrated that they had "compensated" for their dyslexia.

These reports are typical of the scant information about reading problems and improvement found in all of Levinson's "dyslexia" case studies. Absent is more detailed, basic information, such as the extent to which the individuals were reading disabled, or reading levels before and after the use of medication. Also absent is the requirement that a case demonstrate reading problems at all.[55]

Support for Levinson's explanation has come from independent studies, but all have had serious methodological deficiencies,[56] the chief of which has been the use of the Southern California Postrotary Nystagmus test, not considered to be a valid test of vestibular function.[57] Levinson seems not to regard these and similar studies as supportive of his views because none is cited in his books.

Other studies of Levinson's theory have used both caloric stimulation and a "rotation" method which consists of rotating a person seated in a chair in absolute darkness (thereby avoiding confusion of visual and vestibular stimulation) in both clockwise and counterclockwise directions. Unlike caloric stimulation, which Levinson used, the rotation method affords adequate control over stimulus intensity and does not cause discomfort or nausea in patients. Rotation affects both the vestibular system, which is sensitive to angular rotation of the head, and the cerebellum, which plays a role in posture and spatial orientation. This method produces eye movements with nystagmus patterns that can be recorded by electrodes placed around the eyes and measured.[58] Rotation has been found to compare favorably with caloric testing as a diagnostic method, a conclusion with which Levinson agrees.[59]

The research results of both methods may be summarized in the words of one investigator: "there is no support for the notion that LD children suffer from vestibular dysfunction."[60] (None of the investigators has addressed Levinson's compensation explanation.) In addition, critics have observed that Levinson's theory is exceedingly speculative because "the role of the vestibular system in the higher cortical functions required for academic performance is not known, nor is it immediately obvious."[61] For example, "extensive cerebellar lesions have not been shown to produce cognitive disorders or, specifically, dyslexia."[62] Speculation is legitimate in science, critics have remarked, but Levinson constantly leaps "from *if* to *it is true* and writes . . . as though his view of the cerebellum is fact."[63]

Meanwhile, spillover crowds wait for treatment.

6

■ ● ▲

Genes, Gender, and the "Affliction of Geniuses"

Through the preceding chapters, I have discussed explanations that identify biological dysfunctions as the cause of learning disabilities, but not what might create these dysfunctions in the first place. This final chapter in my review discusses two prominent causal interpretations. Of these, the first and major one centers on genetics, whose role is explored through three different types of studies—family, twin, and linkage analyses. This last is a type of family analysis but will be considered separately because of its special methodology. The second causal interpretation argues that the learning disabilities of boys stem from the sex-determined differences in their brain makeup. Because far more boys than girls have severe reading disabilities, it is not surprising that this interpretation is prominent in the field. It is of course a kind of inheritance theory, but I present it separately because proponents of sex-difference explanations assume that these differences are inherited, even if inheritance has not been demonstrated, and concentrate on the learning differences they perceive as being associated with biological sex-differences. Finally, I will discuss the "men of eminence" literature. Although these biographical accounts are used to illustrate rather than prove the LD thesis, the considerable attention they have received in the professional press and mass media has contributed to assumptions about the validity of the thesis, as well as to a romanticization of learning disabilities.

■●▲ Genetics

Family Studies

From Hinshelwood on, LD has been considered to be a hereditary condition. As discussed in chapter one, LD has been defined as an "intrinsic neurological dysfunction." Exactly what the "intrinsic" nature of LD is has never been established by the field. Some have suggested it occurs in prenatal development, but the most common assumption is that it is genetic in origin. For McDonald Critchley, former president of the World Federation of Neurology, dyslexia is entirely inherited. At the National Conference on Dyslexia in 1966, he explained, "Dyslexia is a genetically determined constitutional disorder. This is extremely important, because it means that . . . dyslexia arises independently of environmental factors."[1] A somewhat more cautious estimate, but considerable nonetheless, came from Alexander Bannatyne, an LD expert whose diagnostic and remedial approaches have been widely published and researched. Bannatyne proposed that a specific type of genetically derived dyslexia probably exists in "the majority of the learning disabled population as a whole."[2] Even with hedging and qualification, the implication has been clear: "there are some reasons for believing that reading disability can be genetically determined."[3] Outside the professional literature, heredity has also been identified as the LD wellspring. For example, Eileen Simpson states in her autobiographical account of her "victory over dyslexia" that an estimated 25 million Americans may have a "neurophysiological flaw" in their brain's ability to process language, a flaw which "seems to have little to do with cultural, emotional, or family circumstances" and is "probably inherited."[4]

There is a sensible component to genetic explanations, particularly if you accept the principle of neurological dysfunction. If LD comes not from "circumstances" but from an individual's biology, and if it also runs in families, why not expect the problem to originate in the genes? Though supporting evidence has amassed over the years, I will review only a few recent pieces of research; their techniques are as good as or better than those of earlier studies.[5]

There are three family studies prominent in LD literature dealing with genetics and reading disabilities. The first found high percentages of reading problems in disabled readers and their parents and siblings.[6] Using the logic of exclusionary criteria, Joan Finnuci and her colleagues concluded that the problem had a genetic basis. It was "improbable," they said, that the aggregation of reading problems within families was

> the result of factors in the family environment. All the families, including those with an affected parent, were greatly concerned about their children's reading disability, recognized the value of learning to read, and sought help for their children at one of the special schools. Furthermore, the differences in reading ability within families are not merely differences of degree. Very good readers and very poor readers exist side by side in sibships [sibling relationships], in contrast to what would be expected if a child were copying the behavior of older sibs.[7]

The second investigation studied "unexpected reading failure" in 108 middle-class children. Judging from the respective public and private schools the children attended, there were no "obvious reasons" for their reading problems.[8] From the group, researchers Jean Symmes and Judith Rapoport eliminated fifty-four children who failed to meet the selection criteria of the study: their "reading problems" could have been explained by other factors such as emotional, family, motivational, or sensory problems. I qualify the term "reading problems" because, contrary to the schools' assessments, the investigators found that some of the children were actually good readers.

As in Finucci's study, genetics appeared to play a role in the reading problems, chiefly because the disability of the remaining fifty-four children could not be attributed to family relationships. In fact, both parents and children seemed to have "positive mental health":

> With almost no exceptions, these children were considered easy, pleasant children to raise; often they were considered more relaxed than other siblings free of learning problems. The bulk of the sample impressed the clinicians who saw them with their maintenance of stability and smooth social functioning. . . . Parents seemed to have a solid basis of other satisfactions from these children.[9]

Good family mental health plus "the high incidence of reading difficulties" predominantly in males in the families suggested "the possibility of a genetic explanation being relevant to this group."[10]

A third study, by far the most thorough one to date, was conducted by the Institute of Behavioral Genetics, in Boulder, Colorado.[11] The Colorado Family Reading Study, as it was called, sought to identify familial patterns in reading-disabled children by administering a battery of achievement, perceptual-motor, and neurological functioning tests to disabled readers, normal readers, and their parents and siblings. To sum up a heap of data, the disabled readers and their relatives had considerably worse test scores than their normal counterparts, and this was seen to signify a substantial hereditary influence in reading disability.

All three of these studies concluded that LD was inherited. All three also disregarded family and educational experiences, saying they had no significant bearing on the reading disabilities. To judge the validity of their conclusions, I will take a look at the experiential factors that were thought to be so unimportant.

The studies all recruited the learning-disabled children from local schools. However, the schools were merely a source for "subjects," and any contribution they might have made to the creation of the children's reading disabilities was unexplored. Clearly, Symmes and Rapoport should have thought to explore those schools from which some reading-disabled children were found to have been referred for "no obvious reason." The investigators apparently were not struck by two discoveries they made when examining the children with standard techniques available to the schools. First, the causes of reading failure became quite obvious in half the children; second, some children were reading at grade level, an accomplishment the schools didn't realize. Amazingly, these discrepancies did not evoke a single question about how well the schools had evaluated, understood, and instructed the children.

Nor did the researchers think anything was amiss either in the teachers' behavior or in the parents' description of teacher behavior. The study has little to say about the report that "parents had defended their children from the teacher's frequent complaint that 'he doesn't apply himself,'" and had supported their children "in the face of critical appraisal from the school system."[12] Assuming from the mistaken referrals that the parents' accounts had been accurate, what might be inferred from the teachers' frequent complaints and erroneous criticisms? Certainly, as reported in the study, the teachers did not appear to have been understanding, attentive, sympathetic, or supportive; rather, at least from the parents' perspective, they were impatient, rigid, and annoyed. It is possible that an alternative hypothesis implicating the schools would have been incorrect and that "unexpected reading failure" should have been explained by another hypothesis that the investigators also failed to consider. Perhaps the teachers were right to conclude that the children disliked academic work, were uninterested in learning to read, and, in spite of their intact egos, were persistently indifferent to instruction. Since we do not have more information, there is little value in speculating further about the meaning of the incorrect referrals and the teachers' behavior. But these issues suggest that other explanations besides "unexpected" reading disability should at least have been explored.

The influence of family relationships also receives short shrift in the studies. The Colorado study did not mention them; the other two studies did, but their arguments and interpretations demonstrated either a meager understanding of family influence or a bias toward excluding all factors that might undermine conclusions about inheritance. The Finnuci study observed that not all children in each family were poor readers, "in contrast to what would be expected" from copying behavior.[13] This statement, presented as evidence that the reading problems did not emanate from the family environment, might have been correct if children were indeed "copies" of their parents and older siblings. However—and it is incredible that the point should have to be made—although family influence is strong, its effect is not a simple linear and mechanical reproduction between generations and age groups. Complex family dynamics may affect the personality, abilities, and mental health of family members in diverse ways, producing both similarities as well as stark differences in psychological stability and educational achievement. Why should diversity have surprised the investigators? How could psychologists and educators have expected to find clones among the children in these families?

If we return to the Symmes and Rapoport study, which described school criticism of the problem readers, we see another example of inadequate analysis of family influence: the failure to determine how accurate the parental reports were. If the schools did not act as the parents reported, this finding should have raised several questions about the families' possible contribution to the children's problems: Why were the parents needlessly defensive and protective of their children? Were parents projecting their own guilt about their role in their children's academic achievement? These are the kinds of questions that might have emerged had the research been less narrow.

We must also address the comments in that study about the good mental health of the disabled readers, who were often "more relaxed than other siblings" and whose "maintenance of stability and smooth social functioning" impressed the researchers.[14] On the surface, this stability and sociability may seem impressive; yet in the face of the reported complaints from the schools and the apparent antagonism between some parents and teachers, how was it possible for the children not to have been troubled by their own school problems? Why were the children "relaxed," and indeed was it psychologically healthy for the children not to have been bothered by their difficulties? Given the complexities of both familial and school interrelationships, could the children have been receiving some kind of satisfaction from their reading difficulties? Again, these questions are only meant to point out the superficial treatment of issues other than "genetic" ones.

The Colorado study restricted its examination of family influence to a comparison of the scores of a perceptual and neurological test battery. This line of investigation led only to two banal conclusions: that the scores demonstrated familial patterns in reading disability; and that "familial resemblance is necessary, but not sufficient, evidence for genetic influence."[15]

Researchers in these and other family studies had hoped to identify intergenerational patterns of reading problems that would reveal particular modes of genetic transmission. To date, this mode of analysis has led to the rejection of a number of models. Unfortunately they have only been replaced by little more than speculation and additional hypotheses. Conclusions in the Colorado study encapsulate the conclusions of all these investigations: Neither autosomal dominant inheritance, autosomal recessive inheritance, nor any other "single-gene model was found to account adequately for the transmission of reading disability" within the families.[16] The investigators theorized that "perhaps a more complex genetic model . . . is needed to explain familial resemblance with respect to learning disability."[17] Perhaps these intergenerational patterns prove nothing about inherited learning disability, and what is needed is to drop this fruitless approach.[18]

Twin Studies

Comparisons of identical (monozygotic) twins with fraternal (dizygotic) twins have also been used to document that reading problems are inherited. The idea is that if the experiences of identical and fraternal twins can be established to be essentially equal, a greater concordance of a characteristic between identical than between fraternal twins could be attributed to genetics (identical twins have identical genes and fraternal twins share roughly 50 percent of theirs). As with the family studies, I will review more recent investigations that duplicate the results of earlier studies and are, in sample size and methodology, as good as or better than earlier ones.[19]

The Louisville twin study was a major investigation of over 300 pairs of twins followed from infancy into school years. Among preadolescent twins, one report of this work described higher within-pair correlations of academic achievement and reading ability for identical than for fraternal twins. This led the researchers to infer that academic and reading achievement have some "hereditary component."[20] Another report investigated twins with academic problems. From the 440 children of school age, forty-six (twenty-eight males, eighteen females) were selected from thirty-two pairs of twins "solely on the basis of the children having been identified by teachers or guidance counselors as showing poor academic performance." Of those forty-six, fifteen were concordant pairs (both were reported to be doing poorly academically), of which thirteen pairs were identical and two pairs same-sex fraternal. The remaining twins came from sixteen discordant pairs (only one child was reported to have academic problems). Of these children, four were identical twins, eight same-sex fraternal, and four opposite-sex. The likelihood of both twins having academic problems was markedly increased if the pair were identical. Their concordance of academic problems was significantly larger than same-sex fraternal and larger still compared with all fraternal twins. The investigators again concluded that these results "suggest genetic influence on the underlying [intellectual] processes."[21]

In another study of reading problems in twins, club organizations for mothers of twins were used to identify 338 pairs of same-sex twins ranging in age from eight to eighteen. Of these 676 children, ninety-seven (14.5 percent) had a "history of reading disability," and reading problems occurred in as many identical as fraternal twins (14 percent and 14.9 percent, respectively). However, the concordance of reading problems was significantly different: "84 percent of the affected identical twins were concordant, compared with 29 percent of the fraternal twins."[22]

Although I could raise a number of questions about methodology here, I won't dispute the conclusion that the rate of concordance is higher for identical twins. An examination of twin studies in general shows that identical twins are more concordant than fraternal twins on innumerable traits, many of which will be discussed below, and there is no reason that shouldn't have been so in this instance. The important question is: Are these differences attributable to inheritance? An affirmative conclusion rests, as I have said, on the assumption that the experiences of the identical and fraternal twins are basically equivalent. Because the studies assumed this equivalence and therefore did not assess experiential influence, it is necessary to look elsewhere to determine if the assumption is valid.

The most extensive and detailed twin study to date examined 850 sets of same-sex twins who, in their junior year of high school, took the National Merit Scholarship Qualifying Test (NMSQT).[23] Identical twins showed higher concordance rates for a multitude of traits. However, unless one reinvokes the nineteenth-century "unit-character" theory—the concept of unitary traits, or "unit characters," as discrete particles of hereditary information—it is evident that experience better explains many concordance differences among twins. For example, identical twins were more alike on the the following personal characteristics: making a good impression, sense of well-being, self-acceptance, sociability, responsibility, and desire for status. They also shared career aspirations more frequently, aspiring to join the military, become a crime fighter, go into construction work, become a stage director, and so forth. An analysis of clusters of characteristics revealed that identical twins also had a greater concordance of personal and social ideals. While the cause of differences for other traits was not as clear, a considerable number were more easily accounted for by experience than by genetics, raising strong doubts about the assumed similar treatment and experience.

An analogous appraisal may be made of the greater number of similar scores identical twins made on the NMSQT subtests (English usage, mathematics, social studies, natural science, and vocabulary). It is implausible to attribute this variance to inherited brain dysfunction in any of the fraternal twins because the differences here are not between underachievers and achievers; presumably all applicants, by virtue of their confidence in taking this high-level academic test, were cognitively competent. Could it be that the identical twins shared genes that predetermined their ability in vocabulary, natural science, and other subjects? Or can these differences between identical and fraternal twins be reasonably accounted for by the fact that the former had more similar educational experiences? The identical twins were more likely to have had the same teachers, to study together, and to spend similar lengths of time reading at home. This shared reading interest is especially instructive. Since it is not related to ability, it suggests that experiential influences shaped the identical twins' similar desire to read and, presumably, their comparable academic performance.

Other evidence for an experiential explanation of greater similarities between identical twins comes from a separate analysis of the NMSQT data by Leon Kamin.[24] In the earlier study, the researchers had concluded that "the greater similarity of our identical twins' experiences . . . cannot plausibly account for more than a small fraction of their greater observed similarity on the ability variables."[25] Kamin challenged this judgment by reanalyzing the data and comparing the twins according to reported differences in treatment. "For 225 of 502 identical pairs, the parent indicated that she or he tried to treat the twins 'exactly the same.' " Kamin's analysis revealed that the "within-pair variance [of the NMSQT total score] of identical twins treated 'exactly the same' was significantly less than that of identical twins *not* treated exactly the same."[26]

In an additional analysis of sex differences, Kamin observed that in a section on IQ variance, one of the coauthors of the first study had found that within fraternal twins—but not identical twins—female pairs reported significantly more similar experience than males. There is no reported difference between male and female pairs of identical twins.[27] Thus, assuming that different experience leads to different IQs, one would expect not only that the IQ scores of identical twins should be more alike than those of male fraternal twins, but also that female fraternal twins should be more alike than male fraternal twins. In an analysis of thirteen IQ studies, Kamin demonstrated that, as predicted by an experiential model, ten of the studies showed that within-pair variance of male fraternal twins was significantly greater than that of female fraternal twins. Only in the remaining three studies were there no significant differences.

Applying these sex differences to his separate analysis of the NMSQT study, Kamin was able to reject the authors' conclusion that on the whole the differences between sexes in experience or treatment were not great. By pooling zygosities (putting the identical and fraternal twins in one group) and analyzing the variance between sexes, Kamin found that in fact female pairs did have more in common, not only dressing more alike and spending more time together but also studying together more, having more of the same friends, and having a shorter maximum length of separation. In each case, female twins had more similar experiences than males. To the question, "Were female fraternal twins more concordant than male fraternal twins in their NMSQT scores?" Kamin answered, "Almost but not quite," because "though the within-pair variances differed in the expected direction," the differences fell slightly short of being statistically significant.[28] "This marginal failure of prediction," Kamin concluded, "seems more than offset by the ten previously cited cases in which the expected difference was detected."

The NMSQT and IQ findings give little support for conclusions about the inheritance of reading and academic problems. While strictly speaking these conclusions are not disproven, a genetic interpretation remains at least ambiguous. At worst, the NMSQT and IQ data, particularly as reanalyzed by Kamin, indicate how superficial research on reading disability in twins has been. The assumed similarity of experience between identical and fraternal twins has been accepted as a given, without evidence, and without even the recognition that the assumption might be unwarranted.[29]

Linkage Analysis

Linkage analysis is the newest and by far the most technically complex method of genetic research on LD.[30] To understand linkage analysis, one must first know a few things about genetics. The closer two genes on a chromosome are located to each other, the more frequently they will be inherited together. Conversely, genes located farther apart on the same or on separate chromosomes are more likely to be transmitted to the offspring in random combinations. Linkage analysis tries to determine if, among families having a common trait, linked genes are passed from one generation to the next by more than chance. When that can be determined, the genes are said to have played a part in the development of a given trait.

The genetic field's limited knowledge of the identification and location of genes prevents linkage analysis from actually surveying genes that might be associated with a trait (at present, approximate positions are known for about 450 of an estimated 100,000 genes). What is scientifically available is an indirect method in which known genes (for example, those related to blood groups and red-cell enzymes) are compared to see how frequently they appear among families having a common trait. Taking this information, a computer program performs a linkage analysis said to estimate the probability that two genes are closely linked together on the same chromosome. There is then said to be the same probability that, on the chromosome where the known genes are, linked genes related to the trait will also be found: "if a trait can be shown to be linked to a known gene . . . the trait is [assumed to be] influenced by a major gene on the same chromosome."[31] This means, of course, that if families of dyslexics demonstrate the same linkage, the disability is said to have a genetic cause.[32]

The probability of linkage is expressed as a "lod" score, which is the *log* of the *odds* of likelihood of linkage. A lod score greater than 3 has generally been considered sufficient to establish linkage; a lod score less than −2 refutes linkage. A total lod score greater than 3 is roughly equivalent to a significance level of 0.001, that is, to a one in a thousand chance that the two genes would be linked within the families studied.

Members of an ongoing project analyzing linkage in reading disability have recently reported the results of work with a growing number of families. The initial portion of the project selected eight families in which, from pedigree analysis, "specific reading disability appeared to be inherited in an autosomal dominant fashion."[33] This selection process assumed that in families with a trait transmitted through an autosomal dominant gene, the linked genes responsible for the trait could be identified. And identified they were: on chromosome 15 strong evidence was found for "a gene playing a major etiologic role in one form of reading disability."[34] Since this first report, the project has added eight other families and has done further linkage analyses, which will be included in my discussion.

A fundamental conceptual problem in this mode of research is the classification of "reading disability" as a trait. Strictly speaking, reading disability simply means an individual cannot read; as we have seen in our review of LD explanations, the assumption of a biological cause for this activity (behavior) remains unproved. Consequently, reading disability cannot a priori be considered a genetically fixed "trait" as the term is defined in genetics:

> To count as a trait, a property of an organism must be under genetic control. And it is far from obvious when one describes a property how accessible to genetic control it is. . . . If we start from arbitrarily chosen behaviors, even if they are of selective and ecological significance, we have no real basis for supposing that these behaviors are traits.[35]

This is one reason an association between reading disability and a known gene would not demonstrate a causal relationship. Another is the failure of linkage analysis to determine that reading disability is the only "trait" that could be ascribed to the families. By arbitrarily picking out one type of behavior and disregarding any others, the studies leave unresolved the question of whether the "gene" could be the cause of other family "traits." Suppose, for example, thinking about and purchasing pizza on Sunday evenings was a predominant behavior among the families. Nothing in the logic of linkage analysis prevents the conclusion that an identified gene common to the families causes this cognitive activity and behavior. The example is absurd, of course, but it is no more arbitrary than identifying "reading disability" as *the* common trait.

Aside from the conceptual problems in linkage analysis, further reason for mistrust lies in its very method of searching for and identifying genes. Even in tracking *known* genes common to a population, the best linkage analysis can do is to claim to have found an association, or lack of one, between known genes and a behavioral "trait." However, the known genes themselves are associated with something other than the behavioral "trait" the analyses are concerned with. Thus, finding a commonality of known genes in a population has limited meaning because linkage analysis can only *assume* that the commonality indicates that somewhere in the vicinity of the known genes are unidentified genes also common to the families.

Turning again to the linkage studies of families with reading disabilities, we find that the lod score for the first eight families was 3.241, a score above the 3.0 said to represent statistically significant evidence of linkage. These numbers seem to reveal something important until the individual scores embedded in the cumulative score are examined. Then the data become a little less convincing.

The lod score of one of the eight families was 2.237, a score of almost all the logarithmic value needed to obtain a lod of 3. In contrast, two of the eight families had negative lod scores of −0.126 and −1.076. Except for one score of 0.766, the other family scores were quite low: 0.215, 0.215, 0.465, and 0.465. In other words, one of the eight families alone obtained a nearly "significant" lod score, and it accounted for almost the entire score of all the families. Hence, even within the assumptions of the study, evidence of a common gene linkage among the eight families is meager.

The researchers' eagerness to find linkage can be seen clearly in their interpretation of the large negative lod score of −1.076. After acknowledging that the score "could indicate nonlinkage," they immediately retook the little ground they appeared to have yielded. "The distinct possibility remains," they decided upon reconsideration, "that this family may have a different type of dyslexia, *with the locus being on another chromosome.*"[36] Why this possibility was distinct was not explained.[37]

Evidence of a reading-disability gene was weakened further when additional families were added to the analysis. With two more families, the recalculated lod score dropped to 2.488. One of the families had a considerable negative score of −0.887, the other a low score of 0.214. When six more families brought the total number to sixteen, half of the entire sample of families had negative lod scores and the cumulative lod score again fell below 3, this time time to −2.690, suggesting no linkage at all. Of those families with positive scores, only the one with the high lod score in the original study clearly suggested linkage.

The lod-score analysis of the sixteen families used a different linkage program from that of the first study, and some data are still being collected on the families. Therefore, future reports will probably contain lod scores somewhat different from those cited here. Regardless, it is unlikely that these changes will influence the overall disintegration of evidence for a gene on chromosome 15 underlying reading disability.

Sex

In the United States, Canada, Japan, and France, more boys appear to have reading problems than girls do. However, the pattern of sex ratios has not been consistent among countries. For example, boys as a group have been found to be better readers in England, Nigeria, India, and West Germany. These differences appear to be due to many factors, including the societal differences in educating boys and girls and the differences among studies in defining and assessing reading disability. Nonetheless, given these factors, in most countries boys appear to have more severe reading disabilities, by a ratio of about three or four to one.[38] This difference has been the starting point from which some researchers have looked for and uncovered a biological cause of dyslexia in boys.

The most comprehensive presentation of a sex-differences explanation of dyslexia is in Diane McGuinness's book, *When Children Don't Learn.*[39] In explaining the cause of dyslexia, McGuinness emphasizes the neurological differences between the sexes, differences that are the basis of *two* kinds of learning disabilities: one is in reading, which boys suffer from, the other in mathematics, which afflicts girls. According to McGuinness, girls seldom become dyslexic because their superior verbal ability enables them to benefit from reading instruction. Unfortunately for boys, their relatively inferior verbal ability often prevents them from learning to read. Conversely, boys have superior cognitive skills necessary for mathematics and the physical sciences; girls often lack them, as is unmistakable in their serious "inability to visualize spatial relations."[40] These differences explain why girls do worse in mathematics and are "underrepresented in those branches of the physical sciences that rely heavily on higher mathematics, such as physics and engineering."[41]

For McGuinness, the two kinds of learning disabilities arise not from biological sex differences alone but from the interaction of these differences and the failure of schools and society to recognize them. As a result, socially important expectations have been created concerning the particular abilities boys and girls are supposed to have. Boys who are unable to meet these expectations are penalized and labeled dyslexic. Girls escape this penalty and label, but only fortuitously: "if schools taught mechanics rather than reading, the remedial classes would have a higher proportion of girls instead of boys."[42] One solution to the sexual differential in abilities would be to have "two sets of norms for achievement test scores, one for boys and one for girls."[43]

In keeping with my focus on reading disabilities, I will discuss only that half of McGuinness's theory. The design of her theory is integral to assessing its content. It is not based on direct evidence of sex differences in verbal abilities and a connection to reading achievement. Rather, her theory rests on studies that purport to show sex differences in language and verbal abilities and on other studies that specify the skills required for reading. McGuinness connects the conclusions of the two kinds of studies and argues that the inferior verbal abilities found in males are those which have been shown to be necessary for learning to read.

McGuinness holds that language functions are organized differently in the sexes, giving females an advantage both in language development and in being more protected or "buffered" so that their language abilities are "far more difficult to disrupt." A centerpiece in McGuinness's evidence comes from research on aphasia (acquired disturbance of language functions), especially the research of Doreen Kimura. Kimura reported that "irrespective of the extent and type of brain damage, men were more likely to suffer from various forms of aphasia than women," particularly when the damage was in the left hemisphere, and that aphasia was "caused by a wider area of tissue damage in males than in females."[44] The research also indicated that "the two hemispheres are organized differently in males and females":

> Males suffered from language-related deficits with lesions in either the front or the back portion of the left hemisphere. Females were far less likely to suffer permanent disability from lesions to the posterior parts of the left hemisphere, the region considered to be the "classical language area." . . . [Verbal tasks] are affected by damage in either hemisphere in females but are affected only by left-hemisphere damage in males.[45]

The conclusion that this research is evidence of sex differences in brain organization is not shared by Andrew Kertesz, a researcher on aphasia who has pointedly challenged Kimura's finding. In a study of stroke victims, Kertesz found aphasia in a greater proportion of *females* (52 of 61, for 85 percent) than males (68 of 118 for 57 percent).[46] Furthermore, he reports, on an aphasia test the results were

> not suggestive of any sex differences in cerebral organization. In fact, from the point of view of any hypothesized bilaterality for females, the data indicate a slight tendency for females to be somewhat *more affected* than males on reading, naming and comprehension and overall AQ [aphasia quotient], although the results in no case approach significance. Only the writing scores suggest greater impairment for males. The [statistical difference] however is far too small to consider this difference very seriously.[47]

Kertesz also formulated a taxonomy of alexias (acquired reading disabilities) based on test scores. Alexia was divided into several syndromes, such as sentence alexia (poor comprehension of sentences but a good ability to read words and letters); global alexia (all aspects of reading severely affected); and diffuse alexia (all aspects moderately affected). Again, the results indicated "an even distribution between the sexes."[48]

Kertesz also analyzed the sex distribution of alexia in fourteen stroke studies by other researchers and in his own study of stroke victims in two Canadian hospitals. This research did not reveal significant differences between males and females. Kertesz observed that although males may appear to have alexia more often, this is only because they suffer more strokes.

In a recent study of 128 aphasic patients (70 male and 58 female), Kertesz and and his colleague, Thomas Benke, found additional evidence to contradict Kimura's claims.[49] Using more rigorous methods than Kimura had for locating and categorizing lesions, and for determining the extent and kind of aphasia, Kertesz and Benke found "no significant sex differences in interhemispheric organization of language function." Concerning Kimura's specific claims, they found "no anatomical or physiological evidence to indicate that the anterior regions in females subserve functions that are carried out by posterior areas in males."

The evidence McGuinness cites to support her theory that females are more "buffered" against language disruption comes from research on brain stimulation prior to surgery. She correctly states that the stimulation disrupted language ability over a wider region of tissue in men than in women. However, she neglects to add that the investigators emphasized that their findings were preliminary and required "several cautionary notes."[50] Especially pertinent to McGuinness's theory was the caveat that "the considerable individual variability among patients must be stressed." That is, the overlap among males and females obviated any conclusions about identifiable sex differences of brain areas related to the task used to assess language ability! McGuinness also quotes dichotic-listening and related research as evidence for sex differences in brain laterality, but this research is as unconvincing as the laterality research I have already reviewed.[51]

McGuinness also draws on various studies dealing directly with sex differences in language abilities. Unfortunately for her argument, many of these contain data and conclusions totally opposite to her depiction of them. Under the heading "Sex Differences in Reading-related Skills," McGuinness discusses a study using the Illinois Test of

Psycholinguistic Abilities with British four-year-olds. She states that "girls were found to be accelerated" on several language tests.[52] A comparison of McGuinness's summary and the actual report suggests that somewhere along the way the data were transformed. Girls did do better on two language subtests of auditory-verbal comprehension, but their scores were *not* statistically significant. Moreover, no sex differences were found on three other similar tests. Nor were there sex differences on other subtests or on the total score of the nine subtests. Along with that data, McGuinness failed to mention the investigators' summary of the different scores by sex on the Illinois test: "It will be apparent that these are largely insignificant."[53]

Another study McGuinness cites is an eight-year study of London children that she says reported the appearance of "a reliable sex effect . . . by about twelve to eighteen months" and a "correlation between early language development in girls and later verbal and intellectual ability. No such relationship was found for boys."[54] This summary is accurate, but it is derived through fancy correlational footwork that does not convey the substance of the research. All the above correlation means is that at twelve to eighteen months, a particular aspect of language development in girls appeared to predict their future verbal and intelligence test scores. It does *not* mean the study found that the future scores of those girls were higher than the boys'.

A closer look at this longitudinal study clearly reveals her error. Of the large number of tests taken by the children, only one, a speech test administered when the children were eighteen months old, showed a significant difference in favor of girls. McGuinness says nothing about other tests—of vocabulary, language comprehension, language maturity (length and complexity of sentences), enunciation, vocalization, vocal communicativeness, and reading—administered when the children were three, five, seven, and eight years old. Why? The answer undoubtedly lies in the original investigator's conclusion that except for the girls' speech quotient at eighteen months, "none of the other sex differences, either between means or between variances, is significant."[55] Restating this in terms of McGuinness's thesis, not only were there no language differences between boys and girls from three years of age onward, most important, on a reading test administered at seven years, boys and girls were reading at exactly the same level. When these sex similarities are compared to McGuinness's account of the "correlation" between early and later development, we see that the research that contradicted her argument was not cited.[56]

McGuinness similarly misinterprets research showing superior verbal abilities in girls at about two and a half years. Her facts are correct but misleading within the larger picture of child development. As the authors of an extensive review on sex differences concluded: "If girls do have an early advantage with respect to . . . aspects of language development, it is short-lived. At about 3 the boys catch up, and in most population groups the two sexes perform very similarly until adolescence."[57]

If her discussion of a study of almost 40,000 junior-high-school students is not exactly misleading, perhaps it could be described as leading us only so far. She accurately reports the study's finding that boys had superior math scores. However, while thoroughly describing those findings (reproducing a table of math scores from the study), she fails to mention that the same study found "no important difference in verbal ability" between males and females.[58]

McGuinness proposes that boys have superior visual skills. She also believes that girls have superior auditory skills, which underlie their greater desire for social interaction, which in turn enhances their verbal abilities. The major reviews on the topics do not support these positions.[59]

Some sex differences in verbal ability do emerge, but not until around the age of eleven. This of course means that during the first three or four years of beginning reading—the period when most reading disability appears—there are no verbal differences between the sexes. Whatever significant verbal differences might emerge at a relatively late age in childhood could not be construed as a sign that the poorer verbal abilities of the boys caused their dyslexia. This kind of falling off the edge at age eleven was not what McGuinness had in mind when she postulated that early sex differences in verbal abilities produced dyslexia in boys.

Furthermore, three reanalyses of the data on verbal skills after age eleven have determined that sex differences are small, accounting "for only about 1% of the variance in verbal ability."[60] There were such broad differences within one sex and so many overlapping scores that the significance of average group differences was reduced drastically. In the words of one of these reports: "If all we know about a child is a child's sex, we know next to nothing about the child's verbal ability."[61]

A fourth reanalysis concluded that sex differences in all cognitive areas were greater than the estimates in the earlier three studies. However, the dissenters added an important observation: the magnitude of sex differences was associated with the years the studies were published. Thus, "In all four areas of cognitive skills, including the three areas showing male superiority, as years went by, females gained in cognitive skill relative to males."[62] These critics were unable to determine what accounted for the gains (again, past the age of eleven), but they could say that "whatever the reason, in these studies females appear to be gaining in cognitive skills relative to males *rather faster than the gene can travel!*"[63]

Some work has been done on sex differences within the reading-disabled population. One study worth noting began with the assumption "that there should be fairly marked sex differences among children who are retarded readers on at least some measures known to be sensitive to the integrity of the cerebral hemispheres."[64] Contrary to this expectation, however, boys and girls performed equally on measures of perceptual, psychomotor, linguistic, and concept-formation abilities, thereby suggesting no differences in the brains of male and female disabled readers in the early school years. Another study also found few cognitive and language differences. Where they were found, in verbal ability and abstract thinking, the differences favored boys, not girls.[65]

McGuinness's failure to substantiate her theory of reading disabilities in boys and her omission of contradictory evidence is paralleled in her theory of mathematics disabilities in girls. Because I have been using reading disabilities as representative of LD as a whole, I will leave the reader to pursue the criticism by others of the purported mathematical inferiority of females.[66]

LD Men of Eminence

Leaping from the minutiae of the LD scientific literature to the broad, often poetic accounts of the "men of eminence" who are said to have been learning disabled may seem frivolous. But these famous achievers must be discussed because they play a part in the neurological explanation. Men of eminence are used to illustrate how a neurological dysfunction can adversely affect learning ability even in extraordinary and often brilliant people. Had the biographical accounts not been used in this way in the professional literature, in textbooks, and in popular articles written by professionals, I would not analyze this segment of the LD literature.

These accounts have also become the popular image of the LD affliction, as evidenced by discussion in magazines from *Psychology Today* to *People,* in TV specials on LD, and in advertisements. Stories of men like Einstein and Edison have contributed to a greater public acceptance of LD diagnosis because they lessen the stigma and promote an aura of romanticism toward what has been referred to as the "affliction of geniuses."

To surmount the decidedly male orientation in the eminence

theory—featured afflicted geniuses include President Wilson, General Patton, Don Mattingly, and Yeats—I will discuss two eminent men and one eminent woman.

Einstein

In LD lore it is believed that Einstein's parents and teachers considered him to be a mentally slow child, as shown by his failure to talk until he was four and to read until he was nine. At twelve he was "brilliant in mathematics and physics but had no gift for languages." Perhaps this is why he had to take his college entrance examinations twice before passing them. He was unable to find steady employment after graduation, and his loss of three teaching positions during two years "might have been due in part to language disability."[67] Thus goes the LD account of the specific disability in an otherwise brilliant mind. Now, compare this interpretation with that found in Ronald W. Clark's comprehensive biography of Einstein.[68]

Clark's description of Einstein's relatively late speech development and his parents' fear "that he might be subnormal" parallels the LD portrayal of Einstein as a child.[69] However, the similarity ends there. Clark pointedly considered the LD interpretation that Einstein was learning disabled and rejected it as a "special pleading" on behalf of the men-of-eminence theory. "Far more plausible," concluded Clark, "is the simpler situation suggested by Einstein's son Hans Albert, who says that his father was withdrawn from the world even as a boy."[70] Whether one accepts this interpretation, other information helps us to judge Einstein's language abilities after he began to speak. While he might not have learned to read until he was nine, at twelve he was reading physics books. At thirteen, after reading the *Critique of Pure Reason* and the works of other philosophers, Einstein adopted Kant as his favorite author. About this time he also read Darwin.

Clark also disagrees with the LD view that Einstein's difficulties in school emanated from within the child. His problems appeared to stem not from a language disability but from his hatred of the authoritarian, disciplinarian Prussian character of the schools he attended. Einstein recalled, "The teachers in the elementary school appeared to me like sergeants and in the Gymnasium the teachers were like lieutenants."[71] Most of the teachers in the Gymnasium, Einstein said, encouraged "academic *Kadavergehorsamkeit* (the obedience of the corpse) that was required among troops in the Imperial Prussian Army."[72]

True, Einstein did not pass the college exam the first time he took it. However, aside from his having been sixteen, two years below the usual age one took the exam, the plain fact was he did not study for it. His father wanted his son to follow a technical occupation, a decision Einstein found difficult to confront directly. Consequently, as he later admitted, he avoided following the "unbearable" path of a "practical profession" by not preparing himself for the entrance test.[73] As Clark puts it: "Thus although the horse had now been brought to the water in Zurich nothing could make him drink."

After graduating from the university, Einstein had difficulty finding a post mainly because his independent, intellectually rebellious nature made him, in his own words, "a pariah" in the academic community. One professor told him, "You have one fault; one can't tell you anything." Einstein went through three jobs in a short time, but not because of a language disability. His first job was as a *temporary* research assistant, the second as a *temporary* replacement for a professor who had to serve a two-month term in the army. Clark remarks that it is "difficult to discover but easy to imagine" why Einstein held his third job, as a teacher in a boarding school, for only a few months: "Einstein's ideas of minimum routine and minimum discipline were very different from those of his employer."

In all, by comparing the cursory account of Einstein's language disability in the LD literature with a full biographical discussion of his life, we see that Einstein, like many if not most LD children, did have learning difficulties. He had "language problems" early in life and school problems later on. Nonetheless, the comparison illustrates that an understanding of learning problems must go beyond the surface of the problems, contrary to the reductionist interpretations made in the eminence literature. Doing so, as Clark demonstrates, shows that categorizing Einstein as learning disabled and identifying his language difficulties as seminal to his school problems is another instance of LD mistaken identity.

Edison

LD lore holds that Edison was deemed "defective at birth," was later taken out of school and taught at home, and that many of his relatives thought he was abnormal. He was a poor speller, had appalling grammar and syntax, and "surely at 19, with his intelligence" and "after years of individual tutoring, would have acquired much greater language facility had he not had a definite disability in learning to read, spell, and write."[74]

Compare this interpretation with other biographical accounts. Because Edison had been a sickly child, his formal education was delayed until he was eight and a half. Young Edison was "continually plaguing his parents and neighbors with questions of the why- and how-type" and upon enrolling in a one-room school "he proved to be completely incompatible with the methods used in conventional education at that time."[75] The school was run by the Reverend Engle, who taught by rote, a method to which Tom could not adhere. Frequently finding his student "inattentive and unruly," the Reverend swished his cane and terrified the boy.[76] After a few weeks, young Edison ran away from the school:

> It appears to have been by mutual agreement. . . . The schoolmaster felt the child was too stupid to learn, his mother decided she wanted to teach him herself, and the father was either having financial difficulty or was reluctant to pay the small school fee.[77]

Tom's mother, "realizing that Tom had unusual reasoning powers," ignored the ABC approach and began at once to read world history and the classics to him. He became fascinated by these books, "was inspired to read them himself," and "within a year he was a rapid reader and had included science in this sphere of interest."[78] When he attended another private school at the age of eleven, he ran into trouble because he was a nuisance during reading lessons. However, the problem was not that Tom was a poor reader but that he became annoyed with having to share the text with other children. Tom, *"a rapid reader,* had no patience with his classmates."[79] He was thought "abnormal" at this time because he was mischievous.[80] Friends of the family suggested that "Tom's mind might be too active for his body and advised his parents "not to let him read so many books."[81] Edison finally left school at age twelve partly because of his behavior and partly because a succession of illnesses caused repeated absences from school. There is no evidence that a learning disability had anything to do with his departure.

Edison went to work, a course not unusual for twelve-year-olds at that time: "only the larger cities had a high school, and enrollment beyond the sixth grade consisted mostly of the offspring of the well-to-do."[82] For the next few years he worked long hours on the railroad hawking newspapers and sundries, and, after the age of fifteen, producing and selling his own newspaper. Whatever problems in spelling, grammar, or syntax he had should be viewed in light of the excessively long hours he worked and his having terminated his formal education at the age of twelve. He did continue to read, however, and at eighteen, apparently because he was "fond of reading turgid novels," was nicknamed Victor Hugo.[83]

Once more we see that the exclusionary influences ignored in the LD field's discussion of Edison can contribute to an explanation of his learning and school difficulties. Edison, at the beginning of his schooling, did seem to have had a "learning disability"—namely, he was not learning. It is clear, however, that his poor health contributed to this, as well as the clash between his inquisitiveness and the intellectual constraints of the school, an experience analogous to Einstein's. Though he did have problems in school because he was mischievous and exhibited behavior undesirable by any standard, the conclusion that he might have been "abnormal" was based on problems in his social behavior, not in his mental abilities. Unable to conform to and benefit from instruction early in his schooling, he was in the process of becoming "learning disabled." Had Edison remained in school, with the same kind of instruction and with the same kinds of constraints, he might have become permanently learning disabled even though he was a bright youngster. Fortunately, his mother gave him a second opportunity to learn.

Whatever residual literacy limitations might have remained during his life can be accounted for by social-class influences that restricted the schooling available to Edison and simultaneously made child labor "opportunities" readily available. Once again, we see an illustration both of how LD can possibly be created by complex social conditions and interactions and how any explanation of LD must include a thorough analysis of these conditions and relationships.

Eileen Simpson

While Eileen Simpson is not usually listed among the eminently afflicted in the LD literature, she has nonetheless gained a degree of prominence as both a writer and a psychologist, and her self-ascribed dyslexia and its relationship to her later achievements certainly duplicate the "failure-success" pattern of the men of eminence.[84]

In her autobiography, Simpson describes early literacy problems and LD symptoms such as reversals, problems with right-left directionality, and sound-sight word-association errors. She laments that throughout her childhood and adolescence she never knew these educational problems were due to an identifiable disorder. Not until she was twenty-two was her condition diagnosed, and then not by a psychologist or reading specialist but by a poet, John Berryman, whom she later married. Berryman had heard of dyslexia because a brilliant student of his had bizarre spelling problems and was being helped by an "Orton-trained remedial teacher." Berryman became familiar with

Orton's work and his writing on dyslexia and, after receiving a note from Simpson with several misspelled words, concluded that her errors were not ordinary spelling errors but symptoms of dyslexia. Simpson was never formally evaluated, but as a psychologist familiar with the professional literature on dyslexia she later confirmed for herself Berryman's initial appraisal: her problem stemmed from a minimal brain dysfunction that had "little to do with cultural, emotional or family circumstances."[85] Considering the description of her symptoms, there is little reason to think that an independent diagnosis by an LD specialist would not have reached the same conclusion.

Do the circumstances of her life support this interpretation? Judging by her definition of dyslexia and by her failure to connect her life circumstances to her literacy difficulties, Simpson appears to believe that the following events described in her autobiography could not account for her dyslexia. When she was two months old her mother died; when she was five years old, her father died. Simpson had a large family, but no relatives offered to adopt her after his death, *which occurred about the time she was to begin school.* Consequently, she was sent to a boarding school run by nuns. She remained there through second grade, and attended a nonsectarian school for the next year. At that time an aunt did adopt her, and from then on Simpson attended school in Manhattan. Simpson describes a childhood spent daydreaming about what life would have been had her "indulgent father" not died when he was only thirty.

As a child, Simpson was continuously ill. She had annual bouts of pneumonia, accompanied one winter by a high fever the doctor could not bring down. In kindergarten her "annual respiratory infection" traveled to her ears, making her feel as though her head were going to burst. Rushed to a hospital, a radical mastoidectomy was performed on her right ear. More than once during these years the old family doctor thought she "was a goner." In boarding school she received extreme unction three times, and the directing nun decided that a child this sickly was not likely to live too long.[86]

Her early schooling, by any standard, can only be described as horrendous. The following example illustrates its flavor:

> When formal lessons in penmanship began in first grade, the preference I showed for using my left hand, which heretofore no one had commented on, distressed the first-grade teacher. It was as if Mother Serafina had discovered in me a moral flaw. Each time she caught me with the pencil in my "bad" hand, she put it into the "good" one. I would have made the change to please her had I not been delighted with my left-handed skill in making letters and dismayed at my right-handed squiggles.[87]

When Simpson was unable to copy clearly with her right hand a letter written on the blackboard, Mother Serafina made her copy it over and over late into the day.[88]

The biographic accounts of these and other eminent people—whether, like Rodin[89] and Hans Christian Andersen,[90] they came from poor families or, like Rockefeller,[91] Patton,[92] Wilson,[93] and Yeats,[94] they came from educated and financially sound families, or even whether they were deplorable "dyslexics" like Lee Harvey Oswald[95]—offer illustrations of the complicated experiences and social interactions that better explain the learning and school difficulties these individuals encountered. They grew up within families and social settings, had experiences both unique to themselves and in common with other people, were enmeshed in class and cultural relationships, were the object of actions and in turn responded to them, made decisions and took actions, and so on. Each individual had some special, personal configuration of factors that could have accounted for a learning disability. But patterns of external factors can be identified that may have contributed to the difficulties these eminent persons faced. For example, one of many general themes running through these biographies is a disparity between children's imagination and interests and the intellectual and creative constraints the schools put on them. Another is the complicated family relationships that may have profoundly affected the children's academic careers.

■●▲ Conclusion

This chapter ends my critique of the major LD neurological explanations. In trying to be exhaustive but not exhausting, I have not covered all the biological explanations of LD. Some explanations, such as maturational lag theories, are very similar to those previously discussed—studies supporting them are rife with methodological and conceptual problems; initial research favoring biological explanations have not been replicated. A review would simply repeat criticisms I have already made.[96] Peripheral explanations, such as a chiropractic "breakthrough" that recommends cranial manipulation to correct central nervous system disorganization, have laid claim to a successful mode of treatment but without substantive evidence that can be evaluated.[97]

We can now draw some general conclusions about the nature of the considerable body of research reviewed. This summary will be presented at the start of the next chapter, where I will also begin to discuss an alternative interpretation of LD. The summary, both a general criticism of the LD research and an extrapolation of the insights embedded in that research, provides a starting point for surmounting the LD neurological explanation.

7

■ ● ▲

Families, Children, and Learning: An Overview of the Theory of Interactivity

Among Cecile Opron's series of oceanside scenes is a painting of the water extending horizontally in the background and a boardwalk extending immediately before it, closer to the viewer; parallel to the boardwalk is an asphalt road. Vertically, stretching forth almost from the viewer, is a white-striped walkway leading across the road and boardwalk to the ocean. While the walkway is inviting, where it intersects the road are ominous traffic lights, each painted black, and each hanging from long armatures. There are no cars on the road, yet the mute traffic lights offer no way of knowing when crossing the road would be safe. Rather than helping, the lights prevent one from ever going to the end of the inviting walkway and reaching the ocean.

The LD neurological theory is the social scientific counterpart of Opron's artistic vision. The theory is meant to take us closer to the LD child, so that we can understand why he or she does not learn. At first glance the theory that the disability is within the child is reasonable and appealing, offering a direct way for understanding the child. A more and more precise understanding of the function of neurological processes is considered the key for unraveling LD mysteries; neurological functioning is seen as the concrete basis on which LD science is and will continue to be built. The theory's researchers believe that the more refined the methods for understanding fundamental neurology become and the more accurately neurological functioning can be dissected into discrete and associated processes, the better dysfunctional learning will be understood. A predominant aim of this research is to interpret the results of instruments and tests said to reveal neurological functioning and cognition. Correspondingly, developing new instruments, tests, and procedures to do the job better is a major preoccupation of LD researchers.

However, when we explore the theory and its research, as we have in the preceding review, and understand them not just as individual theories but as an ensemble, it becomes clear how impenetrable a barrier they place between us and the child in question. Hinshelwood's spirit is pervasive, biological reductionism abounds, all but biological explanations are disregarded, causation is confused with correlation, logic is frequently contorted, circular reasoning is prevalent, statistics, numbers, and other data are manipulated to demonstrate "proof," convenient explanations are substituted for complex analyses, bias constantly skews conclusions, and at times calculated distortions appear to underlie "findings." No matter whether brain structure and activity were inferred, pictured, or mapped; whether the brain was directly examined; or whether drugs were used to influence brain activity, no body of evidence has confirmed—and much of it has repudiated—the many neurological-deficit interpretations. Nonetheless, every explanation reviewed here continues to have its adherents, who regard the claims as though they were supported by factual evidence.

An a priori method has been standard in most of this research. The LD child is assumed to be neurologically impaired, the tests are designed (and assumed) to measure neurological impairment, and test score differences have been assumed to be indices of neurological impairment. Using this method, researchers have failed to determine what the tests actually measure or to recognize that this failure invalidates their conclusion that certain test scores reveal neurological impairment. For example, most of the studies reviewed here assert that the experimental task a researcher concocts corresponds with the way the subject goes about it. With this as the starting point, the subject's actual response to the task—which we have seen can be shaped by motivation, prior learning, and other factors—is not regarded as an issue for investigation even though it may in fact be the central issue.

Ever more sophisticated technical means have been used to study the LD child, but these have not brought the field any closer to validating the neurological hypothesis. Although this technology has been heralded for leading research beyond "seriously outdated views," it has led us further from understanding the disability by reinforcing the undocumented view that the problem is located within the brain and by raising barriers through which only certain experts are said to be able to pass.

And this research has been considered "scientific": as one explanation or set of explanations is rejected for another, this is taken as movement toward a richer understanding of the assumed neurological disorder. Even earlier spurious work that made absurd claims is usually said to have had merely a technical problem of poor research methodology or unsophisticated instruments. By concentrating on current empirical work thought to be in the scientific vanguard, researchers have ignored the historical processes, intentions, and misrepresentations in the development of LD work. Russell Jacoby's observation about "social amnesia"—that through a selective amnesia, the present is allowed to maintain its illusions—applies to the theory and practice of the LD field.

Proponents of the neurological thesis have failed to see that a primary reason the research has not provided an understanding of the learning-disabled child is that the theory itself has "disabled" most of this research. The neurological theory is not only a theory but also a research agenda, a guide for organizing experiments that simultaneously pursue and "validate" the theory through a reductionist agenda that strongly prescribes and proscribes what should be attended to and examined. The theory that learning disabilities are a consequence of the child's brain and mental processes carries with it a methodology in which brain structure and function are considered to be the primary, and usually the only, causal influences that need to be examined. By focusing on "compact causal" biological explanations,[1] this methodology encourages us not to consider interpersonal interactions, social relationships, and experiences—the "exclusionary factors" the LD field so readily dismisses.

This disregard is found not only within the LD field but within a concordant orientation common to psychology and education, the chief disciplines to which the LD field is allied. In criticizing this orientation in psychology, Urie Bronfenbrenner observed that it is almost commonplace "to assert that human development is a product of interaction between the growing human organism and its environment."[2] Nonetheless, he continued, although this is a proposition with which "none would take issue, and that few would regard as in any way remarkable, let alone revolutionary, in its scientific implications," he considered himself as one of the few who did regard it as remarkable and potentially revolutionary. Despite the field's lip service to the proposition, Bronfenbrenner observed, there was a striking contrast and a marked asymmetry in psychology between this interactive principle and the frequency in research to focus on the properties of the person, giving only rudimentary attention to the environment and the interaction between the two.[3] In a similar vein, the Soviet psychologist A. N. Leontiev, criticizing those who believe psychological and neurological processes can be understood in isolation from the social world, reformulated an amusing remark by Marx:

> Like St. Sancho, who naively believed that with a blow of steel we will chop out fire that is hidden in rock and was derided by Marx, the psychologist-metaphysician thinks that the psyche can be extracted from the subject himself, from his head. Like Sancho, he does not suspect . . . [that] the sparks are the interaction of the rock and the steel.[4]

Ironically, evidence that social relationships and experiences are the missing dimensions required to explain the cognitive "sparks" of the learning disabled—evidence that can be used to negate and transcend the reductionist and determinist neurological thesis—may be found embedded in the same research that has attempted to validate the LD thesis.

In general, LD researchers have been devoted almost exclusively to studying the "products" of learning; very little attention has been given to the processes that brought about those products. Seldom have the administration and results of tests been carefully evaluated vis-à-vis the learner as an entire person. A few researchers have looked at what the child was *doing* while responding to tests, not just his or her scores. Another approach, sometimes tied to an examination of process, has used intervention to try to change a child's learning and test activity. By varying conditions, experience, and interactions, these studies brought about changes that went beyond a mere appraisal of an experimental product (test results) and began to explore how and why the product evolved.

Reversals—thought to be a common symptom of dyslexia and said to be a manifestation of mixed dominance—were found to be "relatively trivial" and easily correctable with instruction. "Perceptual" deficits were explained through a youngster's "nonperceptual" qualities of problem-solving ability, motivation, self-confidence, reading ability, or language skills.

In several experiments, an instructor's preconception and teaching created learning difficulties. Recall the experiment in which college students taught children how to use a device involving visual-motor coordination. As documented by objective measurements, subtle differences in the instructional relationship had divergent influences on the perceptual abilities of two groups of children, creating poorer perceptual skills in normal children identified as "learning disabled" than in normal children identified as normal. Family studies on the inheritance of reading disability contained evidence suggesting that school professionals' diagnostic skills were deficient. In one investigation of children who had been diagnosed as having "unexplained" reading disabilities, researchers found that some of their difficulties was readily explained by obvious reasons—such as emotional, motivational, or family problems—and that other children were actually reading at grade level.

Researchers initially concerned with validating the neurological origin of attention deficits appear to have abandoned these efforts and now focus on interventions that resolve attention problems. Some of the successful approaches include strategies that address a child's low motivation and increase the student's awareness of his or her own attention level during instruction. The study by Ronald Shworm on the effect systematic and unsystematic teaching can have on selective attention to vowel sounds and combinations illustrates how much influence a teacher's ability and instructional relationships can have on attention.

In language studies, phonological and phonetic-skill deficits were identified as the chief deficit in learning-disabled children. Instead of finding that these skills arise spontaneously and intuitively, research suggested that they develop through experience. Other research has found that instruction has rather easily remediated deficiencies in these language skills, without need of extraordinary methods. Furthermore, some educators employed in language studies lacked the instructional knowledge necessary to teach phonetic and phonological skills. Yet more research found that others did not always teach these skills in the early grades.

Dichotic-listening experiments revealed that experience, attention, and the construction of the test situation could strongly determine performance. Laterality differences varied with circumstances and did not reflect fixed brain properties. Researchers emphasized that laterality changes could be readily generated within the laboratory and were related to experience and skills.

Results differed in visual-half-field research according to the nature of the test construction, instructions, and stimuli. Examples of the latter were abstract nouns and verbs, which produced higher left-hemisphere activity than concrete nouns did, thereby demonstrating that reading ability (better readers read more abstract nouns than disabled readers) can determine laterality activity.

Similarly, evoked-potential tests were not measures of fixed cerebral processing. Instead, they were strongly affected by the children's attention, emotions, attitude, experience, and problem-solving ability in the experimental situation. One example was the finding that evoked-potential results were related to children's decisions about how they would comply with the directions. In BEAM analysis, differences in brain activity could be interpreted as caused by attention and arousal.

Taken together, this collection of findings reveals that despite LD researchers' almost exclusive concentration on children's minds and on test results, the fact that children are *entire* persons in interactive relationships still managed to find its way into some explanations. Most researchers have resisted these "incursions," but a few no doubt allowed this penetration of the neurological surface because they have recognized both the vacuity of the thesis and the need to look beyond children's minds to explain test results.

The test results that contradict the prevailing explanation are scattered among the LD research and can only be melded into an interpretation that is far from complete. Still, in combination these insights are the rudiments of an inchoate alternative interpretation that suggests that complex individual attributes and social interrelationships are the starting point of many learning disabilities. Among the characteristics that influenced children's test performance were learned academic and problem-solving abilities, various prior experiences, interest, motivation, emotions, self-confidence, and attitudes; other powerful "external" influences included teachers' ability, the dynamics of instructional interrelationships, and organization and construction of a test situation.

We may further conclude that in trying to understand how and why test products evolved, learning must not be seen as an additive process: it is not comprised of the distinct factors of memory plus interpersonal relationships plus visual-auditory processes plus neurological functioning plus instruction. Rather, in the creation of learning failure, each "influence" involved is integrally bound and interactive with all others. Just because each influence can be conceptually abstracted from human interactivity does not mean that they can or should be separated from their contexts in the effort to understand LD. Doing so will distort not only that particular influence but the interactivity as a whole.

This is not to say that even one set of influences can simply be substituted for neurological ones in imitation of the LD neurological paradigm. Other factors do not operate as unidirectional determinants of an individual's cognitive makeup. Instead, the scattering of research findings discloses a complexity of potential causes whose influence varies with intricate interactivity. They also reveal that, as part of the interactivity, individuals do not passively receive influences but actively respond to and in turn change the situation. Thus, to restate an essential point, an interactivity theory of LD does not just substitute another set of determinist factors for neurological ones; it encompasses both neurological differences and neurological dysfunctions.

With respect to neurological functioning, it is well to rephrase an important observation made about visual-half-field research that applies to an alternative theory of LD. Researchers have looked almost exclusively for neurological dysfunction in the learning disabled. Most of the neurological differences found between disabled and normal learners may be regarded as nonpathological biological conditions that are part of the overall interactivity and are not causal conditions. This conclusion does not invalidate the assumption that some genuine neurological dysfunctions do exist among a small number of LD children. However, the most salient conclusion of the research, as I have stated, has been and is likely to continue to be that there are many neurological differences but few neurological dysfunctions. These findings do not constitute a research failure but serve as a useful starting point for a reinterpretation of the LD problem and for a redirection of the research.

▪●▲ Introducing an Alternative

It is important to restate at the start an essential point: We must understand the cause of LD not just as a scientific question but, more important, in order to establish a way to give learning-disabled children the help they require and to prevent LD from occurring in other children. At the beginning of my review I stated that the neurological-deficit theory was a legitimate hypothesis for researchers to pursue. I hope I have now demonstrated that the mountain of research, in failing to substantiate the explanations, has failed as well to provide a rationale for LD programs that diagnose and treat children. Furthermore, the neurological-deficit theory fails to account for evidence within its own research that points away from biological, reductionist explanations. So long as researchers and practitioners continue to look at the LD problem from a flawed perspective—as a fundamentally biological problem created within the child—there seems to be no reason to expect that what is being sought will ever be found.

In formulating an alternative theory—what I have termed an interactivity theory—I must address one issue at the outset. When we abandon an explanation that for decades has been the primary formulation for research, an alternative theory will almost certainly carry limited evidence, at least initially. This limitation is almost a given in the progress toward acceptance of theories of greater explanatory promise than those older but still inadequate ones that have received the most empirical attention. However, evidential limitations alone should not prevent the adoption of a new working theory; if they did, science would be victim of a lamentable Catch-22 and the generation of alternative theories would virtually be terminated.

In discussing the generation of new theories, sociologist Robert Nisbet distinguishes between the "logic of discovery"—the reasoning acceptable for uncovering new ways of looking at a phenomenon—and the "logic of demonstration"—the reasoning required for showing that the new approach is valid. Nisbet rightly criticizes social scientists who maintain that the road to the first is through obedience to the rules of the second. For Nisbet, "only intellectual drouth and barrenness can result from that misconception."[5]

Consider also the dialectical nature of social-science theories, which are not simply isolated views of a phenomenon. Rather, an "expressed" social-science theory contains what may be called "foil" theories that vie against it and compete for explanatory hegemony. For example, when Thomas Malthus argued and presented evidence against governmental aid to the poor on grounds that Nature decreed their poverty, he was trying not only to promote and validate his "expressed" theory but also to refute the "foil" theory that class and the inequitable distribution of wealth cause poverty. Each effort to validate the expressed theory is at the same time an effort to falsify foil theories. If the reasoning and evidence in support of the expressed theory are meager or absent, and cannot account for evidence that continues to emerge in support of a foil theory, then the expressed theory—in this instance the LD neurological theory—is increasingly falsified while the foil theory—that the interactions of "exclusionary factors" must be reintegrated into the explanation—is strengthened.[6]

The working theory of interactivity I discuss attempts to be comprehensive first by interweaving numerous social and personal activities and interactions, and second by integrating an individual's biological functioning within these interactions. Since this has not been attempted before in published LD research, it is important that we not use the positivist criterion—that an alternative theory is "valid" only if proof can be immediately mustered—for judging it. My beginning interactivity theory will require new methods to account for the complexity of relationships and to test its validity, and will deal with the totality of learning difficulties—not just those portions that easily lend themselves to laboratory verification. Thus I am consciously proceeding on the assumption that "the great harm of the present consecration of method [demanding immediate objective verification], is that it persuades [one] that a small idea [even if] abundantly verified is worth more than a large idea still insusceptible to textbook techniques of verification."[7] On the other hand, though my evidence does not "abundantly verify" the alternative theory, it is substantial enough to support the use of the interactivity theory as a working model for understanding children's learning difficulties.

"Interactivity" Defined

Before "interactivity" can be defined, the concept "interaction" must be discussed. In psychology and education, *interaction* is commonly used to refer to relationships between or among individuals, or between individuals and situations—say, between a parent and a child or between a student and classroom instruction. For example, the guiding hypothesis of one LD research institute is that "the academic failure experienced by learning disabled children *results from* an interaction between the way they process information and the information processing demands of the instructional methods in use in their classrooms" (emphasis added).[8] Another interaction approach holds that the reading process consists of an interaction between the reader, the different kinds of information in the material (such as semantic, syntactic, letter relationships, word sequence information), and the general context in which the material is read.[9] Many interaction approaches in psychology also display, to use once more Bronfenbrenner's phrasing, a "marked asymmetry" that focuses "on the properties of the person." The asymmetry of these interactionist paradigms lies in considering the environment to be only a passive context for the active subject who, when learning, "interacts" and extracts from the environment what is required for learning growth. An example of this conception is Piaget's work, which, as Jerome Bruner has observed, depicts the growing child as interacting but nonetheless virtually alone, basically as a problem solver.[10] *Interaction* is also used to describe relationships within an individual, as between emotions and thinking or between neurology and language ability. We will recall that in subtype studies, the interaction was within the child: the child's neurology, language, and reading ability.

Many of the influences, developments, and transformations denoted by *interaction* in the above models are important in beginning to explain LD, but if these elements themselves are fully explained, the deficiencies of the use of the term become evident. If, for example, in an instructional interaction between a teacher and a child, the child fails to learn, the *cause* of the child's academic performance must be explored by looking at but also beyond the immediate teacher-child interaction to other interactions that might not be readily apparent. The experiences that might have led the teacher to instruct as he or she does must be considered. It is necessary, too, to know about the school itself, and specifically the school's influence on classroom instruction and relationships. We must also identify (as well as we can) the economic, social, political, and cultural forces that affect the school, the child, and the teacher. Finally, we have to assess the learning-disabled child's biological functioning and how that has worked on other elements in the interactions.

An *interactivity* theory of LD combines the concepts interaction and activity. Interaction emphasizes processes, relationships, and transformations, but insufficiently denotes activity. Activity emphasizes events and active persons, including the makeup of persons (such as neurology, language and reading abilities, motivation), but insufficiently denotes interaction. Interactivity, in combining the concepts, denotes the numerous and complex activities and interactions that comprise the creation, sustenance, remediation, and prevention of learning disabilities. The concept of interactivity is not an environmental or behavioral interpretation of LD: as described here, those influences that interact with a person are not external ones that simply etch their mark on the mind; nor is there a similar etching on groups or members of social institutions involved in the interactivity. Interactivity is also different from many cognitive approaches: at all times the interactivity involves active persons who are affected and changed by and in turn affect and change circumstances.

The interactivity theory should not be interpreted as a potpourri of random elements. Although interactivity has many combinations, a basic assumption of the theory is that broad social, economic, political, and cultural influences, which are not always immediately apparent, are fundamental to the creation or prevention of LD. This does not mean that these broad influences by themselves "determine" LD; it does mean that they are inseparable from all activities and interactions that are a part of LD.

I will begin by addressing the chief conundrum posed in LD neurological theory: How and why could a child from a middle-class family, with presumed middle-class advantages and presumably no obvious emotional or educational disadvantages, develop a learning disability? Without question, children in other social classes and circumstances have been identified as learning disabled. However, I will continue to concentrate on the typical LD research child to ensure that my discussion of interactivity theory pertains to the same population with which neurological theory has been concerned. Moreover, if the interactivity theory can be applied in explaining the learning disabilities and neurological functioning of middle-class children, which do not seem to be explained by the children's conditions and experiences, then the theory should be even more applicable in explaining the learning problems and neurological functioning of children from other groups whose conditions and experiences can more obviously interfere with learning progress.

Family

Recent investigations of children's cognitive development within middle-class families have essentially studied the presumed picture-perfect home life desired in LD research. One investigation, for example, studied families of middle socioeconomic status, mostly white, mostly married, almost all of whom had fathers who were employed full-time.[11] All the parents had graduated from high school and about 60 percent had gone to college, with a sizable portion having completed college and even postgraduate work. The children, whose cognitive development was followed through their first four years, were free of overt neurological and visual abnormalities.

Unfortunately, the picture of ideal families providing ideal conditions to facilitate cognitive development did not extend beyond these outward characteristics. Home environment, parental interaction, and cognitive stimulation varied among these families and was associated with differences and deficiencies in cognitive development among the children. These varying experiences and interactions included: the amount of time per day spent reading to a child; the mother's responsiveness to a child; the variety of stimulation resulting from toys and games (particularly educational ones), reading materials, and manipulable items; stimulation of academic (educational) behavior; expressions of parental pride, affection, and warmth; the number of times the child was taken out of the home, either to visit neighbors or on longer trips; enhancement of skills in a variety of child-training categories, such as social, self-help, language, and motor skills; and modeling and encouragement of social maturity.[12]

Other research looking at specific interactions between parents and children in middle-class families found an association between cognitive development and frequency of parental responsiveness to a child's verbalization, parental use of nonverbal responses to a child's verbalizations, parental interactions with the child involving the use of questions, parental affect in interactions, the time a parent took to respond to a child, encouragement of a child's vocalizations, and parental praise of a child's actions.[13] Parental involvement in these interactions and activities was found to be crucial in cognitive growth, with extremes in either direction—parents either uninvolved or overly intrusive—harmful in cognitive development.[14] While none of these interactions and activities by themselves determined cognitive development, various combinations were found to shape cognition significantly. In some instances, considerable stimulation might have been responsible for promoting cognitive growth even though affection and warmth were minimal. In other instances, cognitive growth was found to have occurred through affection, warmth, and encouragement that nurtured interaction with adults even though educational toys and other tools were lacking. Cognitive growth might have resulted from a child becoming self-motivated and self-directed through interaction with objects and a corresponding diminishing reliance on adults for motivation and direction.

These studies of middle-class children's cognition are important for an interactivity theory of LD, even though they do not deal directly with children identified as learning disabled. Other work has specifically examined families of learning-disabled children; one such study of three families began with the intention of studying parents who contributed to their learning-disabled children's "social-skill development."[15] All of the children were having problems with peers at the time of the study, and the investigator, Doreen Kronick, chose these particular families because of the support they seemed to offer the children. Kronick's choices were well-considered: she had been familiar with the families through organizations for learning-disabled children and their parents. One family had "appeared warm and caring," another "had demonstrated impressive communication skills and awareness of their feelings"; the third was different in that the parents appeared to have "needs of their own which appeared to conflict with those of their child's," but this family "also appeared to have some strengths, such as a degree of mutual affection and common goals."[16] Overall, the families were chosen because Kronick "did not want to contaminate [her] findings with pathology that predated the emergence of the learning disability." As she said about one family:

> [The family] is one that presents itself to the world as [possessing] impressive communication skills, ability to examine its mistakes, flexibility in dealing with problems, and an environment that is conducive to [their learning-disabled child's] learning conceptual skills, which is the reason that I chose them for my sample.[17]

In view of her initial knowledge of the parents and children, Kronick was especially surprised by discoveries she made once she came to know them better.[18] In her desire to avoid contaminating her findings with family pathology that existed prior to the onset of the learning disabilities, her research took an unexpected turn, as the following conclusion explains:

> Though I am not particularly Freudian, I was struck by the ongoing nature of the problems the families demonstrated. Most of the parents in the study had felt a profound lack of nurturing as children and so, in turn, were crippled in their ability to nurture their offspring, notwithstanding their desire to be more adequate parents than their own had been. I felt a strong urge to entitle this book *The Sins of the Fathers.*[19]

It is worthwhile to quote some of her descriptions directly to appreciate what she meant by the parents' having felt "a profound lack of nurturing as children":

> Manny and Sheila came from backgrounds in which their mothers were chronically ill and there was considerable discord and lack of nurturing in both homes. Sheila spent her preschool years in boarding schools. As a young child Manny was strapped and left alone. Both sets of parents were unable to cope with expressions of hostility. When Manny displayed anger, he was strapped . . . whenever he played baseball, as soon as he was called to bat he was fetched to work in the house. If he failed to comply, he was so badly beaten that he "never forgot it."[20]

These beginnings continued into adulthood. Both parents had "extensive feelings of inadequacy"; Manny's family "used to call him 'dummy' "; "his brothers feel he is the family failure"; "Manny's family did not value education and did not support his efforts to obtain a secondary school education"; "both spouses avoid interaction with one another." Kronick reported numerous instances in which Manny and Sheila duplicated with their children the child-rearing practices that had befallen them. The family itself was "profoundly disorganized" in "routine, money, and use of time"; Sheila observed: "Structure just isn't our style."

A second family was said to be difficult

> to describe because many games were being played simultaneously and many mixed messages were being conveyed. . . . When I was observing this family, so much simultaneous pathology was demonstrated that I was incredulous at the time. . . . I have known few parents who so consistently arrange to mess things up for their children. . . . However well Gordie [the learning-disabled child] has learned the family games, the family has not provided the kinds of learning that would enable him to interact effectively with his peers. As a matter of fact, he uses behaviors learned within the family on the peer group, and these serve him poorly . . . one cannot help but conjecture that his disability may have emerged to serve a scapegoat function.[21]

Family problems and dynamics in the third family were equally severe for its children. You can glean a sense of this in the following observation: "She [the mother] also may need to have nonachieving children as confirmation that worthless people such as herself and her husband are incapable of producing worthy offspring."[22]

These are observations about families Kronick selected because she had known them and felt they had certain strengths that should have aided the social development of their learning-disabled children. Her closer look forced her to change the conventional views she had held about LD:

> When I began this study, I had a strong bias toward the "nature" side of the "nature-nurture" controversy in terms of the etiology of learning disabilities, particularly since I have two learning-disabled children. It was my opinion that learning-disabled children, by virtue of their deficits in social decoding and encoding and their rigidity, transform intact families into less intact ones. I intended, using this thesis, to begin to study the effects of these secondary behaviors on the child's social learning. However, after observing all three families, it became apparent to me that they all represent primary pathology, some of which had to precede the advent of the learning-disabled child. . . . The learning disabilities of the children in this sample may be related totally or in part to lack of nurturing. Since three of the six parents feel that they were not nurtured as children, they have little nurturing experience to bring to parenting and have such pressing needs of their own that they may have been unable to nurture any child.[23]

I will say more about this study shortly, but first I want to describe related research by family therapists who worked with families of reading-disabled boys.[24] "In the initial interview," the therapists reported, "we were often greeted by a cheerful, cooperative, 'all-American' family whose members were striving to attain their ideal of 'togetherness' and were sure that they had no problems apart from the boy's retardation in reading."[25] Attempting to understand reading problems apparently resistant to remediation, the therapists closely examined the child's role within the family. After a few interviews, they found that the initial presentation of a family as TV sit-com perfect broke down to reveal that it had numerous problems in stability and that its very survival as a unit appeared to depend on continuation of the child's problems.

Many parents, insecure about their own intellectual abilities, nurtured a "dumb" child in order to aggrandize their own mental competence. Or, a child might have found satisfaction in playing the disabled role because it offered a relationship with the parents, or a sense of power over their lives; all of these were lost when the child's reading improved.[26]

Furthermore, reading improvement brought disastrous results to the family. Members showed signs of mental illness, even psychosis; parents obstinately denied the child's progress; parents increased their quarreling; physical fights occurred; parents neglected their families; parents punished the child drastically for misbehavior they had previously ignored; other children in the family failed in school, thereby filling the "problem" child's vacated role. In short, the child's reading retardation was required for the family's stability, and family members had an "investment in perpetuating the symptom and, indeed, engage[d] in activities that reinforce[d] it."[27] These relationships had not been readily apparent because "family teamwork protects the family's secrets."[28]

The clinical observations of the Israeli psychologist Reuven Feuerstein are similar to those just described. Discussing how hard it was to help children with learning disabilities, Feuerstein noted that instructional intervention was sometimes impossible because the family resisted, primarily the parents, whose belief that their child was cognitively impaired "formed the basis for the status quo and an equilibrium in the family constellation that [could not] easily be renounced."[29]

Feuerstein described several cases where a lack of "mediated learning experiences" appeared to be instrumental in the development of cognitive problems in children of middle-class families. One instance was a boy named Roger, whose parents and teachers thought he was mentally retarded. Feuerstein reflected wistfully that when he first evaluated the boy he had not yet thought that youngsters from "privileged socioeconomic conditions" could have acquired learning problems; instead he suspected the condition had "an endogenous basis, such as mental disorder, retardation, or organicity."[30] Further study of Roger, whose parents were both "academically trained," revealed that the seemingly more plausible hypothesis was incorrect. Instead,

> a special set of circumstances and a condition unique to this family had obstructed the communication patterns within the family. Communication with the children was limited to the necessary minimum. . . . Roger was highly resistant to his parents' attempts to mediate their world to him; by association, he rejected anything concerning learning.[31]

With these insights, Feuerstein was able to help the youngster overcome his "mentally handicapped" status and eventually achieve an "advanced academic university degree."[32]

In the development of the interactivity theory of LD, these family studies provide evidence that by looking beyond the surface of family relationships, numerous combinations of both subtle and overt mediations, interactions, and activities will be found that adversely affect children's cognitive development and strongly contribute to the creation of learning disabilities. Parents play a major role in mediating cognitive development; however, the child is an active participant who does not simply and solely reflect the extent and quality of parental mediation. General patterns of influence are discernible, but for any individual, combinations of determinants play themselves out in varied and complicated ways. LD research on the neurological-deficit thesis is correct in assuming that the "ideal" middle-class family should provide proper nurturing for cognitive growth, but it has neglected—and this a focus of the interactivity theory—the gap between the support a child needs and what he or she actually receives. The specific ways in which family relationships are involved in the creation of learning disabilities remain to be determined. Because the research above concerning middle-class home environments (not specifically on LD families) was limited to children's school years, there is no way to know the precise influence the various levels of cognitive development had on learning during the elementary grades. In developing an interactivity theory of LD, these and similar issues on the relationship between preschool cognition and elementary-school academic success will need further study.

Having proposed a connection between family relationships and LD, it does not automatically follow that family relationships cause LD. Social influences are deeply involved as well, and this hypothesis can only have meaning if the family as an institution can be understood in that broader context. For example, the findings that mothers do not always respond sufficiently to a child's verbalizations, that parents may duplicate the injurious child-rearing practices by which they themselves were raised, or that parents harmfully enmesh a child in their marital disputes tell nothing about why these relationships and influences occur. Unless that more fundamental question is addressed, there is no hope of ever getting to the etiology of the family experiences and relationships that affect children's cognitive development and can cause LD.

Family research has found that mothers hold the primary responsibility for a child's cognitive development. In middle-class nuclear families, fathers help out, but the division of labor leaves women in the roles of housewife and mother writ large. These roles are demanding, and make up more than a full-time job; they may become inordinately complex and unending for a working mother. These responsibilities did not occur "naturally." They have developed historically within wider social conditions and, like the family as a whole and the role of husband-father, have always been very much shaped by the conditions under which this society makes them work.

In addition to mediating development of cognitive abilities, women also feed, clothe, and care for their children as well as socialize them "for their roles in the work world and the society as a whole."[33] As mothers, women help children learn to desire, to achieve, to be acceptably submissive, and to develop "specific personality characteristics and interpersonal capacities" that in adult life become appropriate for various kinds of work.[34] Women are also expected to resuscitate and nurture their working husbands, physically, psychologically, and emotionally. Women play the role of the family's " 'social-emotional' leader," the one who provides the necessary "tension-managing and stabilizing of the husband/father," so that he may participate in the "extradomestic work world."[35] Integral with their activity as mothers and wives, and adding to their responsibilities, women play the role of the family's primary consumer, a role "importantly interwined . . . and absolutely necessary for . . . the economy."[36]

Despite a greater number of appliances and gadgets, women today spend as much time doing housework as they did at the beginning of the century and even during colonial times.[37] After World War II, millions of U.S. families moved to the suburbs, to individual households, and the benefits of technology in housekeeping. However, the technology carried an unexpected price. Husband and wife "discovered that the technological systems . . . simply would not function unless someone . . . (surely mother) . . . stayed home to operate them."[38] A study in the mid-1960s found that full-time homemakers averaged about "fifty-six hours a week doing housework compared to the average fifty-two hour work week of the counterparts in the 1920s." That is but one of many investigations that document the continued great amount of time women have spent doing housework.[39]

These responsibilities have been made more onerous by the extensive isolation that suburban life spawned. Unlike earlier times when town life and extended families allowed women more contact with other adults and relief from their motherly roles, today's suburban mothers and children are often confined, with no relief. Women may have no adult contact for days at a time. "Even if facilities exist, such as playgrounds or mother and toddler clubs, they necessitate a special expedition which requires planning and preparation."[40] In all, women have responsibilities to the family that are essential to the survival of the larger social, political, and economic arrangements, responsibilities that are not only considerable but inordinate.

Many of the contradictions of traditional family roles may only fester as unresolved frustrations. Simone de Beauvoir observed, "Most women simultaneously demand and detest their feminine condition; they live it through in a state of resentment"; and there are parallels for men as well.[41] Studies of families with LD children describe mothers frustrated with the role of housewife and feeling the stress of trying to work and nurture, fathers working long hours to maintain a desired level of material life, and parents dissatisfied with their lives and feeling worthless and insecure about their abilities.

Fathers, by default, generally have fewer prescribed responsibilities for children's cognitive development. Thus, they usually do a poorer job than mothers in nurturing this growth. In fact, in many families they hinder their child's cognitive development. The tension of daily work life can detract from their relationships as husband and father. Nonetheless, when "blame" for a child's poor cognitive development is assigned, women usually get the most of it because historically this development has been their responsibility. Correlations have been found between what mothers do and their children's cognitive development; therefore it seems to follow—and social norms confirm—that mothers are responsible when "their job" is not done well.[42]

So, on top of parents' "skills," personal characteristics, and lingering troubles from their own youth, these many household responsibilities may strongly contribute to the mother's failure to provide adequate cognitive nurturance. However, I want to emphasize that even under the most economically and emotionally secure conditions, these responsibilities—shaped through broader social relationships—are so numerous and complex that they alone can be sufficient to hinder her ability to nurture her child's cognitive development. And though women are usually caught in this bind, if the gender roles were reversed, men would fail just as often.[43]

Thus the nuclear family does not seem to fulfill its obligation to larger social forces, insofar as it fails to provide all children with satisfactory cognitive development. In the real world, however, all children do not need to have satisfactory cognitive development that will translate into school and work success, because economic production does not require these successes for all members of the work force. In fact, it would be difficult to rationalize divisions in the work force if all its members achieved the social success associated with superior early cognitive development. A discussion of this social need for failure is beyond the scope of this book. Suffice it to say here that differences in cognitive development are not a larger social conspiracy. Rather, they arise from the interactivity among individuals, family, school, and the wider social order. They are accepted and no effort is made to reduce them because they ultimately fit in well with the social arrangements in which they occur.

Social and economic factors shape families, mothers-wives, and fathers-husbands, but this does not mean that families and their members are simply repositories of these wider influences and relationships that reproduce the social order.[44] Contradictions and resistance within families, and between families and broader social formations—as evidenced by the development of contemporary feminism, the changes in family life many women have demanded and opted for, and the disintegration of the model nuclear family ("working" husband and "nonworking" housewife)—illustrate that families are more than "empty space" filled at the behest of ruling interests.[45]

This discussion has been limited primarily to middle-class nuclear families. When we add to this an analysis of the cognitive development of children whose parents are divorced or unemployed, or whose mother runs the household alone, we see even more graphically the strains that can impede a parent's ability and opportunity to nurture cognitive growth. In many families, parents cannot provide nearly the amount of support for their children that society and family members themselves expect. This deficiency, the circumstances which allow it to occur, and the relationship of nurturance to hindered cognitive development are primary focuses of the interactivity theory of LD.

If families are involved to some extent in the creation of learning disabilities, it is clear that to eliminate the sources of the problem, current family life must not be accepted as a given. The interactivity theory then is also concerned with how parents' lives can be fundamentally improved so that they can better nurture their children's cognitive development. Developmental psychologists have on the whole concentrated on changing the interaction between parents and children as the way to strengthen this development. Programs have been developed to help parents "parent" better, but they are not enough. With their "how to" emphasis on stimulating children's development and no corresponding attention to changing the forces that deleteriously shape family life and keep adults unsatisfied, these kinds of programs can help to some extent, but will never be more than patchwork solutions.

In the next chapter, I will show that even if a child does not have the benefit of optimal family interactions and activities before entering school, he or she may still avoid learning disabilities. Conversely, if this wealthy environment was a part of the child's preschool experience, educational success is still not guaranteed.

8

Schools and Schooling in Interactivity

Right after completing four years of college I began teaching sixth and seventh grade. Like most people beginning in the field, I was filled with ideals and optimism. Three years later I left teaching, disillusioned. Whenever I have talked about those years I have said, "I loved the kids but couldn't stand the school systems." (I taught in two.) Unfortunately, loving the kids was not enough to make me feel good about teaching. I think I was at least an above-average teacher who tried to do a good job, and frequently succeeded, but I became increasingly aware that I was not doing the job I wanted to do, particularly with the youngsters who were having academic troubles. The reasons were complex. First, despite my competence and good intentions, I did not have the instructional skills I needed. Second, the school system required that I devote much of my time to nonteaching assignments and paperwork, so that during the week these tasks constantly infringed on my teaching time. Third, my teaching was influenced by an implicit school policy: if children were not learning, teachers should teach them as well as possible, but the students were not expected to learn past their school-assessed potential. Looking at my colleagues, I saw a mixture of teaching commitment and abilities, but neither the teachers nor the administrators ever expressed doubts about the schools' assumptions about students and their commitment to educate all the students. Fourth, by the time the students reached me in sixth grade, a significant number of the low achievers had given up on themselves. These influences—my ability, other demands on my time, the school's tacit policy, and the student's "resistance"—led me to begin doing what other teachers did. I became a "realist" and did the best I could, teaching students to do the best they could. While the school systems were quite satisfied with the compromised "best" I did, and equally satisfied with the same from everyone else, I felt frustrated with my accomplishments and with those of the school. I finally concluded that schools were not great places in which to teach or, for many children, in which to learn.

The dissatisfaction I experienced continues to be felt among teachers. Recently, after teaching a course titled "Teaching Under Pressure," Herbert Kohl wrote:

> The members of the class teach in public, private and parochial elementary and secondary schools. What they have in common is a feeling that they are workers under pressure and that the conditions of their work are out of their control. They feel themselves unable to engage in the craft, art and profession of teaching and unable to propose solutions for themselves or their schools.[1]

These teachers, more so perhaps than others, are conscious of many of the conditions that prevent them and their colleagues from doing the job they would like to. Sadly for many children, these are the school conditions in which they must learn: school organization, and often teachers themselves, establish children's limited "ability" and "potential" early, ordaining the narrow channels of their academic careers. The teachers can be, in effect, victims of the system's limitations along with their students.

The interactivity theory posits that classroom interactions and the experiences of children even from stable middle-class homes can make them poor learners and readers. As is true at home for these children, "micro" interactions and experiences in school are not separate from other social phenomena but are related to and shaped by forces outside the schools. Consequently, both the immediate instructional relationships as well as relationships to these other forces must be elucidated if the children's learning and reading failure are to be explained. We will begin our discussion with an outline of schools and their broader contexts.

Schools and Society

Like families, schools are formed within society and reflect society's organization, hierarchical power relationships, and economic forms of productions.[2] Jean Anyon examined classroom "work tasks and interaction in five elementary schools in contrasting social class communities" categorized by jobs and incomes as either working-class, middle-class, or affluent professional.[3] For schools in each of these communities, Anyon found that classroom work and relationships reflected the types of occupations members of the respective communities were likely to hold. In middle-class schools, work is perfunctory and minimally creative; "work is getting the right answer," usually from a textbook and in a workbook; work is figuring out and following directions within prescribed alternatives:

> the work tasks and relationships are appropriate for a future relationship to capital that is bureaucratic. Their school work is appropriate for white-collar working-class and middle-class jobs in the supportive institutions of United States society. In these jobs one does the paperwork, the technical work, the sales and the social service in the private and state bureaucracies. Such work does not usually demand that one be creative, and one is not often rewarded for critical analysis of the system. One is rewarded, rather, for knowing the answers to the questions one is asked for, for knowing where and how to find the answers, and for knowing which form, regulation, technique, or procedure is correct.[4]

A stratified society means that whether through birth, fortune, or environment, some (a few) are on the top, some in the middle, and some at the bottom. Though this is an inequitable arrangement, in the eyes of many people it is a natural order. Stratification finds its way not only into school systems and schools as whole institutions but also into classrooms, where it shapes the roles of teachers and students and the relationships between them. As people who have grown up in a given society, teachers and other school personnel bring to their jobs views from that society: views about stratification and others influenced by social stratification; views about how life is ordered and run, such as how one behaves in various relationships, how intelligent people comport themselves, and how the sexes differ. Teachers' actions too are consonant with those views, which are often the mainstream ideas outside the classroom.

The classroom situation is similar in many ways to production of both goods and services. As in most employment situations, prescribed rules of behavior govern both employees and their managers (who are in turn employees).[5] Teachers, as classroom managers, expect what all managers expect, that their employees will adhere to these rules. They must also bring special abilities to the job. Even when job training is available or when an employee has learned the job himself or herself—even if it's an entry-level position—a modicum of physical and mental abilities is necessary. So too for children entering school. Thus, as on the job, academic success depends both on ability and obedience. Unluckily for the child, the similarity ends there. An adult in the workaday world who performs poorly may face the ultimatum "Shape up or ship out" and have to look for work elsewhere. As limited as those options are for most working people, children usually have no alternative, since it seldom happens that a child who has done poorly in one school will be able to attend another. Confronted with their own continued failure to learn, and their own powerlessness, an alternative for many children who do not shape up is to find ways to "ship out" within the school, ranging from passive to aggressive responses to instruction. For those students who can transfer, whose parents can afford private or parochial schools, the alternatives will likely offer minimal, if any, amelioration. Private school practice does not offer a dramatic departure from public school practice. And school records will have preceded the student, thus setting initial expectations for the child, who in turn will find it difficult to leave former school experiences behind.

School personnel by and large reflect society's assumption that success is stratified, and thus they are also likely to expect that it is the destiny of some children to end up at the bottom. Schools can also reflect society's notion of "scarcity"—that high measures of success are available only to a few. Colin Greer has observed about schools: "The assumption that there must always be losers . . . is deeply ingrained in them."[6] Although they are generally optimistic about children's possibilities, their belief "that there must always be losers" also makes them "realistic." "Realistic" acceptance of school failure is "the educational equivalent of definitions of full employment that accept high levels of unemployment as tolerable."[7]

School personnel want all children to do well; they do not want children to fail. But when children do poorly academically, the failure accords with other kinds of failure. In an employment situation, if an employee fails to perform a job properly, usually management does not cry "Mea maxima culpa." Similarly, it is understandable that schools would be reluctant to blame themselves for children's educational failure.

■●▲ School Expectations and Learning Success

With this outline, we can now examine some of the more common classroom scenarios in which the middle-class child can become a poor learner and reader. Several important findings from the research I have discussed are useful here. Recall from the LD research on language that children differ in their phonemic and phonological competence when they begin school, and that researchers have concluded that these children may become learning disabled because they lack the requisite skills for beginning reading. Recall too that the research on specific, basic phonics skills requisite for reading found that trained teachers in school classrooms did not always teach these skills. As is the case for employment, the requirements for the reading "job" in schools appear to be fixed, and those who succeed appear to be those who have the required entry-level skills.

How do the children obtain these skills? Recall that those children who, in relation to their peers, had been deficient in these skills were able to learn them when the skills were taught directly and properly at a preschool age and certainly could have learned them more easily in early grammar-school years. These conclusions correspond with findings that early environment did not play a singular and determinant role in future cognitive development. If cognitive growth were poor because of early experiences, later experiences and interventions could change it.

When all these findings are put together, we see that schools do, but ideally need not, resemble economic employment. True, children may lack "entry-level skills," but this may not be the source of their reading disability. Their "insufficient" phonemic and phonological skills may not be, as many LD researchers believe, a consequence of the "natural" acquisition of linguistic skills. Rather, the research indicates, children are more likely to have insufficient skills because they have not had the necessary mediating experiences for learning them. If so, schools, and some educational and psychological researchers, have misunderstood the reasons for the difference between what children know and should know, and have had unjustifiable expectations about the ability all children should have acquired prior to beginning-reading instruction. Consequently, the methods for teaching beginning reading have erred in failing to accommodate children's entry-level abilities.

I have focused on phonological skills, but this area is only one of several in which unjustified expectations may occur. For example, some children might enter school not yet skilled in bridging between preschool language that has always been contextual (related to the present and past contexts of their lives) and early school reading, which is decidedly decontextual (for example, reading words in isolation, using workbooks whose sentences are based on skills rather than content). Children might fail to make this bridge on their own because they have not had previous reading experience with parental mediations to help them become familiar with various facets of reading language and with books whose stories are distinct from the children's own lives. However, in beginning-reading instruction, failure to make the bridge from contextualized oral language to "decontextualized" reading language might be a consequence of omitting direct instruction on how to make that bridge, on the assumption that children can make it themselves.[8]

Thus, the actual contradiction that can contribute to a learning and reading disability may be between the school's erroneous expectations (and thus methods) and children's acquisition of prerequisite abilities developed through interactions and experiences mediated primarily within the family. Because all parents are not able to help their children attain the prerequisite abilities the schools expect, and because the schools do not modify their expectations for each student, the children's learning and reading are likely to suffer. And if children are judged to be lacking the "necessary" abilities, it is because schools have established a curriculum that begins at a level higher than it should. As I said in chapter three, by beginning instruction a critical step or two beyond where it should, and by not considering and not providing the mediating experiences that will enable children to acquire basic abilities for reading, a learning and reading disability may occur from the outset of school reading instruction because the children are not able to benefit from that instruction. This initial failure may become compounded by many other factors, such as a child's concomitant lack of self-confidence and motivation and by a teacher's giving increasingly more attention and time to "better" students.

If the family difficulties discussed in the previous chapter were eliminated, children might be more likely to have the prerequisites that would enable them to benefit from conventional reading instruction. Because many children lack these prerequisites, proper teaching that accommodates children's various cognitive abilities is much more challenging and complex. Schools have the added burden of dealing with many cognitive outcomes of a variety of detrimental influences. Fortunately, although accommodating for cognitive differences among children is difficult, it is not insurmountable. Again, the research suggests that the prerequisite abilities that help children learn to read can be acquired through proper instruction. The issue of why schools and teachers have inadequately recognized and accommodated for prerequisite differences will be further addressed, but first it should be said that the problem of how to work with children of various cognitive abilities is not simply an instructional one. To be effective, as I suggested at the beginning of this chapter, teachers must struggle against influences within the larger educational and social context that limit the extent to which they can instruct well. Many of these influences are the same ones that have contributed to the parenting problems that helped create children's cognitive inequalities.

■●▲ Classrooms and Educational Outcomes

LD research has spent meager effort examining the connections between schools, classroom instruction, and LD. Fortunately, other research is available that can contribute to an interactivity theory. It comes from the literature on academic failure of children from non-middle-class backgrounds, and it contains insights that can be extended to explain the educational experience of many middle-class learning-disabled children.

One of these studies concerns differences in academic achievement and IQ test scores among first-grade children. The children were not learning disabled as the term is conventionally defined but were from impoverished socioeconomic backgrounds and went to a school where the student body as a whole had poor academic-achievement records; the school itself had "a reputation among teachers as the most difficult school under its particular board."[9] The study compared the success of children of substantially similar backgrounds who had been randomly placed in each of the classrooms of three first-grade teachers who had taught at the school for many years.

The researchers found that although family status and conditions were related to academic success, the effect of teacher influence was quite strong. Using reading achievement as the primary measure of educational achievement, the children in the class of one teacher (Miss A) were found to be 64 percent high achievers, compared to 28 percent for the other first-grade classes. Conversely, Miss A had 7 percent low achievers compared to 28 percent in the others. Furthermore, the average academic achievement of children from Miss A's class remained consistently higher throughout their elementary school years. Similar differences were found in scores on IQ tests, tests which can be considered to represent learned information and learned cognitive abilities associated with school learning. The varying levels of educational success found in the three classrooms, each of which had a mixture of similar students, shows that preschool background and the cognitive abilities children bring to school need not determine their academic success.

Exactly what occurred within Miss A's classroom to enable so many of her students to do well academically is not clear from the research. The investigators note that a reporter who did an in-depth story on Miss A and her pupils found that her attitude was, "It did not matter what background or abilities the beginning pupil had; there was no way that the pupil was not going to read by the end of first grade."[10] Miss A imbued her students with self-confidence and an appreciation of the importance of schooling. Hard work was one of the keys to her success with students: for children who were slow learners, Miss A devoted extra hours.

Explaining the children's varying levels of educational success requires a close examination of classroom interactivity, but the study reveals that one must also look beyond the classroom, to an implicit school policy of indifference. Miss A had significantly more high achievers than other teachers, but the school appeared to care little about the relative lack of success of the students in the other classes that had been taught by other teachers for decades. Thus, even though the school administrators had a standard by which they could have judged teaching success, they did not intervene or take corrective measures to change less effective instruction and less favorable student outcomes. Given this policy of "acceptance," which translated into the expectation that a proportion of students would fail, Miss A's colleagues appeared to have been doing an acceptable and normal job. Like the stratification of society as whole, students were expected to distribute themselves along a continuum; in this school, no doubt more were expected to find themselves at the lower end. In contradistinction, Miss A's success, while indicative of the impact teacher intervention could have, remained hers alone. Had she been much less successful, less would have been just as acceptable. Thus is life ordered. The school's acquiescence to differences in classroom rates of success and failure suggests that teachers—while being the immediate mediators, and while possibly sharing the social views of those above them—cannot be seen as the only or even primary mediators determining a child's success. Also involved are other school personnel whose outlooks and actions stem from beliefs about the limited degree to which teachers can successfully instruct all students and the limited degree to which students can succeed.[11]

Applying the study to the learning disabled from middle-class families, we may expect that children who come to school without the "necessary" cognitive prerequisites, but who are capable of learning, might fail to learn because the classroom instruction is inadequate for them. In the study, the other two classes nevertheless had many students who learned to read at or above grade level. Therefore, one may assume that teachers who are quite capable in many respects will frequently provide less-than-adequate instruction to children who do not learn with the "normal" mode of teaching. When this happens, schools will not consider the instruction to be insufficient; rather, the insufficiency will be identified within the children who fail. The implicit outlook, expectations, and practice of classroom instruction and school policy are strongly bound together, and reflect the views in the wider society. On the other hand, teachers and other school personnel are not puppets. Miss A's teaching reflected an orientation and practice contrary to that of the school as a whole. These limiting expectations and practices may be overcome, and the interactivity explanation must consider how this can happen in order to identify not only why children fail academically but also why they succeed.

■•▲ Classroom Interactivity and Educational Outcomes

A shortcoming of the above study is its failure to examine classroom interactivity so that any of the actual interactions and experiences that might have caused learning failure—and success—are revealed. The following study made just that kind of examination.

Ray Rist observed one class of children from kindergarten through second grade in a school situated in a poor, predominantly black neighborhood.[12] He found that on the eighth day of school the kindergarten teacher grouped the children according to her judgment of their "ability" and, for instruction, assigned the groups to different tables in the classroom. During her few days of contact with the children she had observed them but not tested them; nor did she have any other test information from the school or other sources. Rist explored the criteria for the teacher's selection and found that the following characteristics had constituted the basis for differentiating the children: interactional behavior (the children's assertiveness and confidence), language (their talkativeness and use of "school language"), physical appearance (dress, body odor, blackness), and social background. In other words, judgments about "ability" were determined by how children handled themselves in the classroom, *appeared* to be competent, knew how to elicit teacher attention, and how they stood in the social strata. Subsequent interactions between the teacher and the "ability" groups were influenced by these conclusions and produced distinctly different educational experiences, cognition, school behavior, and achievement for the respective groups. When asked about her criteria for differentiating the children, the teacher expressed conviction that she had appraised the children objectively, was well-intentioned, and taught without bias. To Rist she seemed genuinely unconscious of how she behaved dissimilarly with the groups.

After the initial categorization, children were not simply passive recipients of unequal treatment; they participated actively with the teacher to produce their own academic outcomes. For her part, the teacher did not simply convey "messages" to the children; she actively engaged the children in an instructional process that contributed to shaping and producing the academic outcomes. As the children progressed from kindergarten to second grade, those who had been judged as having the least potential, and were taught accordingly, internalized that appraisal and in turn responded increasingly as learning-disabled youngsters. For example, they had considerable difficulty with sound-symbol correspondence, auditory comprehension and memory, right-left directionality, and reading comprehension. Conversely, those the teacher thought had greater academic potential reacted correspondingly. As was true for the children in the Miss A study, the academic-achievement levels established when the children entered school persisted in subsequent grades.

Several of Rist's findings parallel the Miss A research and are equally applicable to the interactivity theory of LD. First, noncognitive factors affected the interaction between children and teachers, set in motion classroom activity, both instructional and noninstructional, and created a learning disability. Second, once again classrooms reflected wider social stratification both in structure and attitude. The classes from kindergarten through second grade were stratified initially by *assumed* learning capacity when the children began school and afterward, as they progressed, by school-*created* academic achievement and underachievement. The teachers and other school personnel considered the stratification to be a consequence of the children's ability, not of instructional and school practice. Also applicable to the interactivity theory was the third finding, again similar to the Miss A research, that the teachers were not generally bad teachers. Many of the children learned to read and did well in other subjects. Possibly, as the professor of one of my reading courses once said,

"Children learn to read in spite of what we do," but it is more likely, as Rist proposes, that the teachers had skills that became available only to certain children as a result of student-teacher interactions based on factors besides children's learning capacities. Fourth, children actively participated in the creation of their own learning and academic failure. By acting in accordance to the way in which they had been acted upon, children not only became victims of school practice but also participated in their own victimization. A fifth aspect of the research useful for explaining LD is the crucial influence of children's experience and learning activity in the initial grades. These early events appear to affect numerous factors, from children's acquisition of basic skills to school classifications that contribute to the perpetuation of their academic success or failure. Thus, early experiences, while initially unique for each student, become antecedents for a systemic structure and systemic relationships that regulate learning and academic achievement.

■●▲ Closer Examinations of Classroom Interactivity

The Rist study discloses that an explanation of the creation of LD requires detailed examination of classroom interactivity. Some of this detail is provided in other studies that have looked at teaching methods and communication and at how children are required to behave and learn in classrooms.

Traditional classrooms mainly require students to "do as they are told." That phrase sometimes denotes a harsh command; here, however, this is not its primary meaning. Doing as one is told in the classroom describes the "normal," relatively passive mode of learning in middle-class classrooms, by which children are guided by an adult whose authority remains dominant. Children are required to approach a task primarily as the adult has defined it and to attend to it for a length of time the adult has decided. Teachers teach an established curriculum to students who are required to learn it in the manner in which they are "required" to learn it. As we saw in the cases of Einstein and Edison, children do not always find this a joyous experience.

I should also say that teaching an established curriculum in prescribed ways may not be any more joyous for the teacher than for the student. One educator observed that, like most factory workers, most students and teachers "do their chores without real enthusiasm or authentic involvement; the system makes it impossible for most of them to care much about the work itself most of the time."[13] Given existing practice, the teacher's task, in Paulo Freire's words:

> is to "fill" the students with the content of [the teacher's] narration. . . . [It] turns them into "containers," into "receptacles" to be "filled" by the teacher. The more completely he fills the receptacles, the better a teacher he is. The more meekly the receptacles permit themselves to be filled the better students they are. . . . Education thus becomes an act of depositing, in which the students are the depositories and the teacher is the depositor.[14]

Since the early 1900s research on teaching practices in the U.S. have documented that this instructional mode pervades classrooms nationwide. In a recent study in which over a thousand elementary and secondary classrooms were observed, Kenneth Sirotnik described a pervasive teacher-student interaction:

> in the elementary classes observed, we estimate that, on the average, just under 3 percent of the instructional time that the teacher spent interacting with students involved corrective feedback (with or without guidance). At the secondary level, this estimate is less than 2 percent. . . . Providing corrective feedback in combination with additional information designed to help students understand and correct their mistakes is almost nonexistent. . . . Thus, one of the most touted pedagogical features of classroom instruction—immediate corrective feedback—rarely occurs in our sample of classrooms.[15]

The study also found that teachers gave students little reinforcement of any kind, "whether in the form of specific task-related acknowledgement and praise or general support and encouragement."[16]

Where feedback is involved, the method is frequently a didactic form in which a child responded to a teacher-initiated inquiry that forced the child to focus on the information the teacher thought important, leaving the child in the role of respondent, not active participant.[17] An example is as follows:

> Teacher: *What was the color of Jack's coat?*
> Student: *Blue.*
> Teacher: *Good.*

Children do learn even through this frequently used form, with its narrow, imposed roles. Researchers on this discourse structure, after failing to locate an analogue of it outside of school, concluded that the "form does not appear often in natural speech—there is something peculiarly 'teacherly' about it."[18]

The commonality of teaching methods and teacher-student interactions in classroom after classroom makes evident that the sameness is not merely a matter of individual or collective choice. Rather, as the teachers in Herbert Kohl's course complain, teachers too are objects of systemic influences that make them middle-managers whose power resides in a prescribed workplace structure, within constrained modes of "proper" instruction. Formal training, hierarchical parallels in the classroom, and school policy (ideology) are among the many systemic forces that produce a standard form of instruction.

Research specific to reading instruction reported instructional patterns similar to those found in studies of instruction in general.[19] Dolores Durkin found that third-graders observed during a reading period spent approximately 28 percent of the time listening to instruction, 33 percent of the time writing, usually in commercially prepared workbooks and instructional materials, and only 13 percent of the time reading, either orally or silently. Ensuring that children were learning to read became a secondary consideration:

> In all the observed rooms, completing assignments and getting right answers seemed much more significant than concerns like "Do the children understand this?" and "Will what I'm assigning contribute to reading ability?" Lack of attention to the second concern must have been exceedingly common because a large number of assignments had little or no significance to reading.

In this study, teachers were concerned—even with disabled readers—that reading lessons leave enough time for children "to complete written assignments (regardless of their value)," as is apparent from the following illustration of a teacher's work with a low reading group:

> What she was doing (attending to new words, discussing the meaning of some, posing questions about the story that was to be read) seemed essential. Nonetheless, she rushed. Why she hurried was explained with her own comment: "I want all of you to get 2 workbook pages done by 10 o'clock." And while the children completed them, the teacher just waited. Waiting while a class worked on assignments was common in the observed classroom.[20]

Furthermore, supporting the analysis made earlier in this chapter of teacher expectations and instruction of "entry-level" language skills was the finding that in the reading period very little time was spent teaching reading comprehension and even less teaching phonics, word-analysis skills, or vocabulary. Among third-graders observed during reading classes, *no* phonics instruction was taught.

A few years ago, a former colleague of mine returned from a day of classroom observation and, sinking into her desk chair, said, "I had forgotten how *boring* schools were!" Boring, indeed, and much more so for a child who is trying to learn to read but who spends only a small portion of each reading period reading; receives insufficient instruction in reading comprehension, phonics, or vocabulary; gets little or no feedback that explains the mistakes he or she makes; interacts with a teacher who gives little or no praise; does unimaginative and often irrelevant "instructional" work; and does what he or she is told. For middle-class children as well as others, the difficulty many of them have learning to read should not be surprising.

Researchers who have studied the compliant, "recipient learner" role demanded of students have called it the student role.[21] It has strong gender effects because boys and girls as groups differ in the way they acquiesce to it. These effects are a variation of a scenario in the Rist study in which noncognitive factors set in motion interactions that influenced learning outcomes. Studies at the elementary-school level have found that "boys are more active" and more likely to have conduct problems and that girls are more likely to assume the student role and to be more "teacher-oriented." Boys in the early grades are likely to be "sex-stereotyped in their behaviors and interests . . . to be more disruptive and aggressive . . . to be more active and to have a shorter attention span . . . to show less emotional maturity . . . to be more peer-oriented and less adult-oriented [and] to be more independent and less likely to seek help or approval."[22]

The socialization of males requires them to strike two contradictory attitudes at the same time if they are to be successful students. They must achieve a balance between "male qualities," which can underlie independent, creative, or aggressive actions required by society, and conformity to institutions and rules, which society also requires. In adult life, examples in which this balance is struck are military personnel, who are at the same time aggressive, even "creative," and extreme conformists; university or industrial researchers, who are "independent" and creative but who also adhere to and never question the professional or commercial frame of reference in which they work; and anyone who exhibits qualities of strength, pride, self-confidence, and individualism in the service of a blind nationalism and unquestioning conformity. It is a very important phenomenon with far-reaching educational and social consequences that schools are the first formal institutions in which males are required to strike this balance. For a boy who does not do so, who does not take on the student role, the price may be high. It could be a reading disability.

The research suggests that teachers interact with students according to how they take on the student role. Teachers base their responses not on a student's gender but on his or her activity; since boys behave less in accord with behavioral requirements of the student role, however, teachers treat boys and girls differently, being more negative with boys. This negativity is likely to be expressed in instructional mediation in various ways, such as teachers being more critical of boys' efforts and giving them less time and less help.

An investigation of second-grade classrooms studied teacher-student interaction in reading and mathematics instruction. Analysis of videotapes of "teacher instructional behavior" showed that

> there are specific, identifiable teacher behaviors that are differentially applied depending on the sex of the student and the subject being taught. Teachers make more academic contacts with girls than boys in reading and fewer with girls in math. A greater percentage of the contacts that are directed to girls are academic. They spend more of their instructional time with girls in reading and boys in math.[23]

These differences were associated with academic outcome: "although there were no differences in initial abilities, sex differences were found in end-of-year achievement in reading."[24]

When they find contradictions in the research on teacher behavior toward boys and girls, reviewers have generally explained them by noting how the studies concentrate on preschool and kindergarten, where differential treatment has been acknowledged. Thus, they propose, "early discrimination against boys [who do not conform] produces lower levels of expectations and performance that persist in later life, even in the absence [and indeed reversal] of discrimination against males."[25]

Having said this, the reviewers then point out that an explanation based on differential gender treatment cannot simultaneously account for performance differences by gender in reading and math. If boys generally did not assume the student role, and teachers reacted negatively to them, why would they do better than girls in math? To explain the differences, the reviewers cite a "feminization hypothesis" which suggests "that teachers and students view certain subject areas as feminine and others as masculine" and "that they act accordingly" with gender-defined expectations and motivation.[26] Based on studies of teachers' differential behavior toward students presumed to be "bright" or "dull," the reviewers conclude:

> it seems reasonable to hypothesize that teachers will respond differently to those they presume to be able and likely to read well than to those presumed less able or less likely to do so. If teachers expect more girls to fall in the first category and more boys to fall in the second, then it is possible that they behave toward boys and girls in a manner that turns their expectations into self-fulfilling prophecies.[27]

Another explanation of gender differences in reading achievement postulates that U.S. teachers have gender-influenced teaching styles, with female teachers showing more affection, which "may serve girls more effectively than boys" in early grades.[28] For example, a study that examined the interaction of gender and social class reported that "high socioeconomic status boys achieved best in classrooms that were low in warmth, whereas high socioeconomic status girls did best in classrooms that were high in warmth."[29]

The reviewers concluded that although research did not conclusively demonstrate the superiority of any of these explanations, they could all be considered credible hypotheses which alone or in combination with other socially based causes could explain gender differences in reading achievement. "Certainly," the reviewers maintained, "there is no logical reason why the same outcome cannot be produced by different causal processes in different contexts."[30]

The scenarios discussed here illustrate how children with adequate learning abilities may become enmeshed in an interactivity that is initially generated by noncognitive influences but that itself subsequently generates learning disabilities. These scenarios could help explain why endless LD research has found a multitude of differences in learning-ability test scores between learning-disabled and normal children and why groups of children appear to have more neurological differences than dysfunctions.

The preceding scenarios are examples of LD that could be created within the school. However, I would also propose that for some learning-disabled children whose problems are created outside of the schools, little if anything could be done within the schools to eliminate the LD. For example, the studies of "LD families" discussed in the last chapter suggest that some children may be ensnared in unhealthy family interactivity that damages their learning, emotions, motivation, and self-confidence. In these instances, even with the best instructional conditions, the children's problems might be beyond the point where effective teaching could be expected to succeed.

■●▲ A More Detailed Look at Instructional Interactivity

The above research underlines the necessity for scrutinizing the content of classroom interactivity in order to understand exactly how children may become learning disabled. In this chapter's progression of studies, the following examination is still more detailed. As a case study, it is presented less as evidence of the merit of an interactivity theory (even though case studies have contributed to the progress of psychology and other scientific fields) and more as a guide to the kind of interactivities revealed in detailed examinations of instruction, interactivities which have been lost in traditional LD research and require new methodologies to assess. This examination makes clear that unless instruction is meticulously explored, nothing unusual may appear to be going on during instruction because covert, fleeting exchanges rather than overt misteaching and mislearning may characterize the interactivity.

The study focused on a segment of a video-taped lesson between an LD clinician and a client in a program for adults with severe learning and literacy problems.[31] Although the instructional segment involves an adult, the significance of its interactivity is equally pertinent to children's learning.

At the time of instruction, John was thirty-seven, a generally intelligent, married man who had begun adult education as a virtual nonreader. When asked to write the alphabet he omitted twelve letters and could read only at a first-grade level. The LD specialist who had referred him to the program had diagnosed him as dyslexic.

The instructional segment to be discussed here was a phonics lesson in which John learned to read words containing an *ee* combination, as a first step in reading words with long vowels. We can easily imagine a somewhat comparable situation in a grammar school in which a youngster would be trying to learn the same skill. A commonplace facet of reading instruction was chosen for the analysis because it is relatively straightforward, compared with, say, story interpretation. As with most instruction, John's learning achievement was not a consistently positive or negative linear development but was a sequence of understandings and misunderstandings. The sequence and its bearing on the issue of how LD might be created in the classroom can be traced by examining some of John's errors and the clinician's responses to them. These were the key interactions and critical junctures in the session.

The first error occurred near the beginning of the lesson when, having explained the basic principle of the long-vowel sound, the clinician asked John to decode the word *deep*.

John responded, "The word is 'dip.' But I think I know that word more from memory."

The clinician next wrote the word *feel,* which John identified as *fell,* then as *fill.* Following this, the clinician went into further detail about the long *e,* using *deep* as an example. At the conclusion, the clinician asked, "What's the word?"

J: *E . . . eep . . . deep.*
C: *You remember what you said the word was?*
J: *Dip.*

In the interchange, John was not told he had read the two words incorrectly; rather, his responses were momentarily accepted. Postponing recognition until he could correct himself avoided a failing response and any possible negative effect on his confidence and self-esteem, which in turn could have affected his cognition, and perhaps impeded learning momentum. In this way his own error was used as a starting point, a pretest, and the self-correction confirmed his cognitive growth and demonstrated an ability to learn. It also made John feel like not merely a passive recipient of information but an active learner.

Feel was the next word they reexamined. The clinician said, "Let's look at this word. . . . How many vowels are in the word?"

J: *Two.*
C: *Are the vowels together? . . . Take it one step at a time. What's the vowel sound?*
J: *E . . . eep.*
C: *There's an "l" at the end . . .*
J: *Lee, lit, leet . . .* (laughs)
C: *I'll tell you, it's not uncommon for someone just working on reading to have trouble with the "l" ending. Let me make this [ending] a "t" and you'll see . . . What's the word?*
J: *Eet, feet.*

Perhaps the foremost question about this interchange is whether John's responses should be interpreted as symptomatic of a learning disability. His errors—substituting consonants (*t* for *l*) and a short vowel sound for a long one *(lit),* and reversing the letter sequence *(lee)*—appear to be problems of visual perception, visual-auditory association, and sequencing. However, once one looks beyond the surface of these LD "symptoms," another interpretation is possible, which focuses on the learning interactivity and accounts for both John's learned abilities and the clinician's actions.

The clinician made an error by using a word with an *l*-ending as one of the first practice words, because beginning readers indeed often have difficulty with this kind of word. The letter *l* is pronounced with a short vowel sound at the beginning *(eh, ehl),* rather than with a consonant sound, as found in the initial pronunciation of other letters such as *t* or *p.* Because this short-vowel sound does not blend with the preceding long-vowel sound in a word such as *feel,* the beginning reader commonly flings out guesses in an effort to read the word. In

John's case the process appears to have been something like this: He silently read the word; had trouble fitting the long vowel *(ee)* with the short vowel *(ehl);* and attempted various solutions, such as unconsciously substituting a final consonant that could have blended with the medial long-vowel sound *(eet),* positioning the *l* in the word's letter sequence where pronunciation of its sound might have been more manageable *(lee),* and deriving a short sound for the long-*e*–short-*e* sequence he was trying to synthesize.

John's sequence of *eet, feet* demonstrated that when he was able to blend the medial vowel sound with the terminal consonant, he could for the first time concentrate without distraction on the initial consonant and then correctly decode the word. Another factor to be accounted for in this learning interaction is the clinician's response to the error. Attributing the difficulty to the developmental process common to beginning readers, and not to John's particular mental abilities, diffused John's frustration. Had the clinician not recognized his own error and persevered in trying to have John decode the word, both John and the clinician undoubtedly would have become more frustrated, resulting in poorer learning and poorer teaching. Explaining away the error as a common one among beginning readers involved a communicative sublevel because it conveyed the clinician's professional experience. John responded to both the explanation and the clinician's professional competence by rapidly decoding the word *feet.*

A person brings to educational situations a set of abilities and a frame of mind that create an opening for learning. What the student will learn is also contingent on instructional mediation that is not only manifest—helping a student understand a phonics principle, for example, or responding to the student's feelings—but also unstated, occurring at a communicative sublevel. Concerning various kinds and levels of communication, Lev Vygotsky has written:

> Behind every thought there is an affective-volitional tendency . . . understanding of another's thought is possible only when we understand its affective-volitional basis. . . . To understand another's speech, it is not sufficient to understand his words—we must understand his thought. But even that is not enough—we must also know its motivation.[32]

Some of the affective-volitional sublevels of communication can express intentions, such as the intention to instruct and the intention to learn; or emotional and mental states, such as a student's fears and inhibitions; or attitudes, such as a teacher's confident and encouraging manner.

Leontiev distinguishes between two kinds of meanings: "significance" and "personal sense."[33] Significance is meaning in its independent, objective existence, as it has been developed in society. But this significance is only one part of the "double life" that meanings have. In their "second life, meanings are individualized and subjectivized."[34] Using the system of letter grades as an example, Leontiev explains: one side is its objective significance, a letter signifying a level of accomplishment on a scale with others' grades; on the other side is the personal sense, perhaps "a step (or obstacle) on the way toward a chosen profession, or as a means of winning approval in the eyes of those around" the student.[35]

The *meaning* of an educational event, its significance and personal sense, then, is a central question. Meaning, motives, and goals that appear to be inherent in a task, as I noted in the review of LD research, cannot be assumed to be those constructed by a student or teacher; rather, they are areas for extensive investigation. In the interchange with John, the significance of his failing to identify terminal-*l* words was that he did not have the ability to blend sequentially certain symbol-sound correspondences. But the personal sense for the clinician and for John might have been entirely different. For the clinician, it might have demonstrated an inherent and perhaps unremediable "auditory sequencing disability." John's personal sense of the error might have been that it was another illustration that he was dumb (a term he used to describe himself). Either or both personal senses of the event could have produced a disastrous turn in instruction and learning.

A question about the instructional segment remaining to be answered is how the problem of decoding terminal-*l* words was solved. The clinician and John continued working with words that did not have a terminal *l* until John had successfully applied the long-vowel principle to a considerable number of words. Terminal-*l* words were then reintroduced and John was able to decode them better but still with some difficulty. Through insight and visual-verbal adjustment, John began to stretch the long-vowel sound so that it overcame any interference that might have arisen when blending it with a terminal *l*. For example, he had difficulty decoding *heel* until he articulated the word as "Ee . . . eeeeeeeeel . . . *heel!*" By exaggerating the intensity and length of the long vowel, he could blend the medial and terminal sounds and correctly connect them to the initial sound. It appears that John was able to devise this tactic because of an instructional dialectic: the clinician provided him with knowledge and skill, a body of words to practice on, and mediation that fostered a positive momentum; John, in turn, used what was provided to participate as an active learner and problem-solver.

Responses and interactions can be identified in which cognition could have developed differently and perhaps have been impeded, as when John made errors and when the clinician introduced a task which John was not yet prepared to solve. These situations indicate that in instruction there are "divarications"—junctures where one direction leads to continued successful learning, another to learner frustration, problems, and even failure. These junctures may be created by any number of elements, such as a teacher's abilities, other pressures within a classroom situation, or a student's understanding or misunderstanding of the rules of an instructional situation. A teacher could make a student feel intellectually inept in numerous ways, as if, for example, the clinician had hinted that John could not learn because of deficits he had brought to the session. More often than not, when learning difficulties similar to those in this instructional interchange are manifested in public-school classrooms, educators are likely to interpret them as symptomatic of the learner's dysfunctional cognition, rather than as part of instructional interactivity. As has been suggested, even when a divarication is initially created by the learner, and even more so when it is not, other elements such as instructional mediation have to be taken into account before the junction can be understood. It should be emphasized that mediation appropriate at one junction—for example, not immediately informing John of the errors he had made—might be inappropriate in another, depending on the learner himself or herself.[36]

The phonics interchange also illustrates the necessity for recognizing the inextricable relationship between learning and cognitive development, a relationship to which Vygotsky gave special attention. He hypothesized that there was unity, but not identity, between the learning and cognitive processes. The relationship was not unidirectional in one way or the other: learning advanced cognitive development and vice versa.

■●▲ Learning and Cognitive Development

Vygotsky distinguished between cognitive development as "determined by [a person's] independent problem solving [ability] and his or her level of potential development as determined through [the process of] problem solving under adult guidance or in collaboration with a more capable peer." The difference between these two abilities he called the zone of proximal development. Vygotsky criticized psychologists who, by limiting assessment to cognitive development, assumed that "only those things that children [or adults] can do on their own are indicative" of cognitive abilities. For example, if in the course of testing a person were offered leading questions or were assisted in any way to arrive at a correct solution to a problem, that answer would not be regarded as indicative of the person's cognitive development. Vygotsky notes: "Even the profoundest thinkers never questioned this assumption; they never entertained the notion that what children can do with the assistance of another might be in some sense even more indicative of their mental development than what they can do alone."[37] We can see in John's instruction, for example, the limited information about his cognition that would have been available if only his responses to the phonetic problem were appraised and not his responses with the clinician's mediation.

Thus, an instructional error that can contribute to the development of disabled learning is seeing cognitive ability as separate from learning and learning strategy. One cannot say that the cognitive abilities will persist as they are, that learning will simply form "on top of" the cognitive limitations, rather than improve the cognition itself. In Vygotsky's own words, learning does not merely form a "superstructure" over cognitive development.[38]

Because cognitive development is interconnected with learning, new learning through assistance also means growth of new cognitive processes and, consequently, a new zone of proximal development—the "processes that are currently in a state of formation, that are just beginning to mature and develop."[39] We can see that John's achievement of new cognitive processes (more complex processing of sound-symbol correspondences) meant that new mediation was possible and a reassessment of John's new *potential* was necessary because he was now at a new stage of proximal development.[40]

Vygotsky's concept is a necessary part of the interactivity theory but by itself is insufficient. His zone of proximal development assumes that mediated learning can change the level of cognitive development. However, this may not lead to practices that will produce any more cognitive growth than is now achieved in conventional instruction or assessment because it does not suggest how to appraise a situation in which mediated learning is unsuccessful. For example, in the interaction with John, we saw divarications in which learning might have been blocked. When learning is halted, the central question is how to interpret the outcome. Should one conclude that the student has reached his or her potential and cannot go further? Perhaps. But perhaps it is the "mediator" who has obstructed learning and has reached his or her own potential. Perhaps the student does not have the motivation to learn. Thus, the zone of proximal development is a valuable tool, but we still need ways to explore unsuccessful instructional mediations so that the failure is not automatically blamed on the learner's cognitive abilities.

■ ● ▲ Students' Role in Creating LD

As any of the scenarios described in this chapter begin to generate learning failure, children are likely to feel and act more intellectually powerless, and actually participate in the creation and re-creation of their learning disability.[41] The children do not merely accept a label ascribed by others and then acquire the self-concept of being powerless and act accordingly. Rather, in the activity of failing, of being unable to accomplish academic tasks, and in having their activity defined as one exuding intellectual powerlessness, the child becomes powerless. The child does not only begin to act and appear powerless, but actually *is* powerless, particularly when instruction seems persistently insurmountable.[42] Being intellectually powerless means that the individual's actions will display learning-disabled behavior that will lead important overseers, such as teachers and parents, to respond to the child in ways that increase the learning disability.

Being and feeling intellectually powerless may take various other forms. Research by Joseph Torgesen and his colleagues suggests that though learning-disabled children have the cognitive ability to complete academic tasks successfully, their passivity keeps them from spontaneously and efficiently employing learning strategies to accomplish them. Provided the proper mediation, however, disabled children have been able to exercise these dormant abilities.[43] Again, the complexity of unraveling compounded problems in the LD child is evident in the work of researchers who found that failure to use learning strategies does not always differentiate learning-disabled and normal children.[44] Learning-disabled children may learn strategies and still not be able to apply them any better.

Peer relationships in the instructional situation may also involve the child in creating LD. For example, to once more use Leontiev's categories, the significance of reading aloud in a classroom might be in exercising literacy development. However, a child's personal sense of the task may be that he or she will be humiliated before classmates. Thus, the child may respond by attending more to his or her classmates than to the text, or by hurrying through the text, regardless of mistakes made, to end the excruciating task as quickly as possible. The child may refuse to read aloud for fear of making mistakes, may be disruptive, or may find other ways that reflect a desire to avoid the task.[45]

Once begun, the learning-disabling process becomes increasingly intricate and increasingly harder to disentangle. Students may participate in the process by developing qualities and reactions that add to the disability. In many children, lower self-esteem and poor motivation, distractibility, and emotional distress are among the qualities that develop concomitant with a learning disability.[46] Overall, being intellectually powerless makes the cause of LD appear to be within a child.

■●▲ Conclusion

I have laid out a number of scenarios in which children might become learning disabled either through school or nonschool experiences, but they do not by any means describe all the ways in which children may become learning disabled. Nor is the sequence of the scenarios intended to suggest that they occur separately. In an individual's complex activity in the classroom and elsewhere, the scenarios easily and often interact. Stifling behavioral requirements in class might combine with erroneous expectations about a child's language ability. A teacher's negative response might be affected by the student's personal qualities, including physical appearance, which of course are independent of the student's cognitive abilities. In turn, the student's lack of application to an academic task central to the teacher-student interaction might be a consequence of harmful family relationships.

Conversely, the interplay of various factors may keep one or a combination of the scenarios from producing a learning disability. Adverse family relationships and language difficulties may be overcome by a skilled, committed teacher. Confident, motivated children and supportive families may compensate for potentially destructive classroom interactions. Nor will harmful scenarios necessarily harm children. Struggling to learn, resisting influences that impede learning, a child may correctly blame his or her failure on circumstances and bad luck (for example not being placed in Miss A's class). This child may maintain his or her self-esteem and motivation, avoid feeling personally powerless, and remain hopeful for a better (luckier) academic future.

9

■●▲

Reconsidering Neurology

I have concentrated so far on the social experiences and relationships of individuals and groups. Still to be elaborated is how neurological functioning, the kernel of conventional LD theory, fits into the interactivity theory. I will address this issue by exploring the associations of brain functioning, social experiences and relationships, and disabled learning. As was true when I considered other aspects of the interactivity theory, the useful point of departure is the previously discussed LD research.

■●▲ Neurological "Differences"

Most LD research on neurology failed to find differences in brain structure and functioning between LD and normal children. Of those few that did, if we were to eliminate studies of dubious scientific merit (as epitomized by the autopsies of "dyslexic" brains), the neurological differences found in the remaining studies could be explained either by test design, children's knowledge, motivation, attention, or other personal characteristics experiential in origin. In other words, within the constellation of studies, there are scattered findings which, when put together, suggest that the differences in brain functioning do not emanate from within the brains themselves. Rather, the individual's characteristics formed through social activity and relationships, as well as various influences within the test situation itself, either were or could have been interpreted as preceding or being concomitant with brain-functioning differences. These rudimentary insights, embedded in and contradicting the primary conclusions of LD research, provide a direction for understanding neurological functioning in the learning disabled.

Some research supporting this orientation comes from a series of laboratory experiments with rats that showed that divergent experiences can produce divergent changes in brain anatomy and chemistry. Mark Rosenzweig and his colleagues studied rats that lived in enriched environments, containing a variety of objects to play with, and rats that lived in impoverished environments. Autopsy examination of the rats' brains found that the groups differed in several ways. Rats with enriched experiences had a heavier and thicker cerebral cortex, larger cell bodies and nuclei, a larger number of dentritic spines per unit length of dentrite, and larger synaptic junctions than the other rats. Further research confirmed these results and added the important finding that changes were not confined to young rats; changes could occur to the same extent in fully mature rats, although the mature rats required a longer period of enriched experience to show the maximum effect.

Results of research on rats cannot be used to draw conclusions about human learning, of course, but these experiments are worth noting because their results are analogous to the insight buried in LD research: experience can produce brain changes. The rat studies also suggest that brain changes are not necessarily laid down early in life, thereafter to be the foundation on which other learning may or may not develop. Instead, for rats at least, brain changes can be initiated by diverse experiences at different times in life.[1]

Another important set of studies specifically related to LD looked at psychosocial dwarfism, a condition in children characterized by long-term failure of the pituitary gland to secrete growth hormones and by limited physical, intellectual, and behavioral growth.[2] For many years psychosocial dwarfism had been diagnosed as a condition caused by a pituitary insufficiency; later it became clear that pituitary problems were secondary to the actual cause, which was eventually found to be child abuse. Apparently conclusions overrode information directly before clinicians' eyes: though evidence of child abuse had often been quite available in clinical investigations, they had persisted in identifying physiological malfunctions as the causes of psychosocial dwarfism. Before the correct cause was identified, the academic underachievement accompanying the growth delays had frequently been diagnosed as a learning disability that was part of the child's intrinsic dysfunction. In retrospect, the identification of "intrinsic" learning disabilities was of course a pseudoscientific procedure, a "quasineurological diagnosis based on so-called soft neurological signs."[3] Astounding as was the discovery that detrimental intrafamilial relationships can interfere not only with intellectual and behavioral growth but with *physical* growth as well, research also found that the forms of dwarfism could be reversed simply by moving a child into another home, a hospital, or other supportive environment.[4]

This research demonstrates a postulate in the interactivity theory: biological makeup that appears to be or in fact is dysfunctional may be caused not by an inherent breakdown in the organic processes but by exogenous social and psychological conditions which reciprocally interact with biological functioning. For example, abusive parent-child relationships can create an environment of limited experience that in turn may limit intellectual and brain development. This limited development then adversely affects a wider and wider circle of social relationships, especially in school. In its turn the ever-widening circle affects the intellectual and brain development of the child. However, these outcomes need not be permanent: learning and neurological functioning may be changed by changing experiential conditions.

Also contributing to a working interactivity theory is a pilot study that analyzed the respective functioning of the brain hemispheres (brain-hemisphere laterality) in illiterate adults who were learning to read.[5] The purpose of the study, conducted by Leonide Goldstein and myself, was to see if any laterality changes occurred as these adults improved their reading and when they read material of varying difficulty. We sought to clarify further the relationship between laterality and reading and compare that relationship to the claims that dysfunctional laterality is symptomatic of LD. The study also explored whether its methodology would be fruitful for additional investigation. This methodology, unlike that of most research on the neurological thesis, examined laterality as a phenomenon in process: not in relation to conditions viewed as static, such as low reading ability, but to *changes* in individuals, in this instance, reading-ability changes occurring through instructional intervention.

Five adults in the specialized-instruction program I direct were selected for the pilot study because, unlike other participants, most of whom had at least a modicum of reading ability, these five were virtually illiterate when they came to us. On their own they were able to read material of only first- or second-grade level, and by any conventional testing standards would have been diagnosed as severely learning disabled.

In singling out these individuals, we sought to restrict our study to adults whose cerebral laterality was associated with persistent learning failure rather than with the mixtures of success and failure common in the history of program participants who were at relatively higher literacy levels. The study was restricted to five because the instructional mediation for very low levels of literacy requires considerable effort and time to bring about changes.

The five men in the study were between twenty and thirty-eight years of age, intellectually normal (based on Wechsler Adult Intelligence Scale scores), and employed (one had his own business, another worked in a skilled trade, the other three had unskilled but fairly well-paying jobs, such as with a county road department). The study used a computerized analysis of the EEG to measure occipital-lobe activity in the right and left hemispheres. The occipitals are the center of the visual system in the brain, and in reading they are active in the recognition, analysis, and interpretation of written material. The right occipital appears to be responsible primarily for visual-spatial perception and the left, for visual-semantic perception. Computerized EEG analysis calculates the proportion of time a brain area is active relative to another, in this instance determining the relative proportion of time the left and right occipitals were active during a reading task.

The men were first tested shortly after entering the program and were retested one to one and a half years later, when their reading had improved two to four grade levels. The EEG analysis was conducted while they read several different stories without assistance, first silently and then aloud, one at the "independent" reading level, another at the "instructional" level, and a third at the "frustration" level. At the independent level a reader knows almost all the vocabulary and requires no help for comprehension. With instructional-level material, a reader has some difficulty reading alone and needs an instructor for complete word recognition and reading comprehension. Material at the frustration level is much too difficult for the reader, even with instruction. The difficulty of the material at the independent grade level was the same in both the first and second tests, but changed for the next two levels: because the men had improved their reading ability, material that was at the frustration level for the first test became the instructional-level material for the second. Accordingly material at the top level was also made more difficult. Different stories were used for each test.

A control group was not used, for two reasons. First, a comparison of the five adults with good readers would mix the proverbial apples and oranges. Good readers would simply be qualitatively different because they would be likely to bring a totally different set of reading abilities, reading experiences, general and academic knowledge, self-confidence, and emotional associations. Second, the left lateralization of language and reading functioning in normal readers has been amply reported; therefore, we only needed to study how the laterality characteristics of developing adult readers compared to that already described in normal readers.

With independent and instructional material, there was an overall shift toward greater left-occipital activation between the first test and the second, when reading skills had improved. At the independent level, in the first test two adults had greater left activation for both silent and oral reading; in the second test, left activation was greater in four of the five. A similar shift was found for instructional-level reading out loud; however, silent reading results at that level showed a mixed picture for left and right lateralization in both test sessions, with no consistent pattern. At the frustration level, there was little change between the two tests: in both, relatively greater activation remained primarily in the right occipital for silent and oral reading.

Comparing the results of the three reading-level tasks for the group as a whole, there was in both tests more left activation at the first two levels than at the frustration level. In other words, with more manageable reading material there was a tendency toward greater left-occipital activation; with more difficult material, right activation was more likely.

Especially instructive for this analysis is the occipital activation with reading material that had been at the frustration level for the first test and then, because the adults' reading ability had improved, became instructional-level material the second time. In this comparison in which the *same* level of *material* was used for both tests, a decided shift toward greater left activation occurred, especially in silent reading. The most significant percentage shifts of left activation were 14 percent to 67 percent, 9 percent to 51 percent, and 16 percent to 63 percent.

Recall now the relative functions of the occipital lobes: the right appears to be responsible primarily for visual-spatial perception and the left, for visual-semantic perception. Right-left activation is not all there is to reading, of course. The activity is not localized in one hemisphere or brain area; rather, a complex subsystem involving both hemispheres is activated.[6] Nonetheless, not all parts of the system are equal to one another. The following interpretation should clarify this.

When people are first learning to read, the central task for them appears to be figuring out what the words are. Beginning readers will vary their solutions according to the language information they use, but their early attempts to identify a word seem to involve considerable attention to the graphic information—the letters' actual physical appearance—and the sounds associated with it. As demonstrated by the way beginning adult readers often talk about a word they are trying to identify, words at this early stage are almost "palpable" to them, and they seem to think that the tangible deconstruction and reconstruction of a word is the principal method for naming it. Semantic information, used more by advanced readers, is often given less attention by beginning readers, especially with more difficult material. Reading-disabled adults usually have to be taught, and repeatedly reminded, that words convey meaning and that attending to the content of a reading selection is part of the method for reading the words. As beginning readers improve, they pay increasingly less attention to graphic information and more to semantic information. When they become good readers, they can move quickly along lines of print and concentrate almost entirely on understanding what they are reading.

In light of these observations, I believe the activation changes from the first test to the second reflect changes in reading ability and use of language information. Since the words in the independent-level material had become more familiar to these adults by the time of the second test, greater concentration was given to their meaning. Hence the higher left-occipital activation. The same explanation would hold for the changed results with material that had been at the frustration level in the first test but was at the instructional level in the second, when the ability to give greater attention to meaning meant greater left-occipital activation. On the other hand, the consistent right activation when reading at the instructional level in both tests suggests continued use of graphic information in the reading strategy used for this level material. At the frustration level, where the adults seemed to depend primarily on graphic information for this very difficult reading material, right activation was even more evident. The adults appear to have abandoned all hope of understanding the material, trying as best they could to decipher the words by concentrating on their construction.

Thus far only group results have been discussed, but the laterality shifts within individuals are also very revealing. It appears, based on information about the the five adults in the program, that in order to explain laterality patterns we have to consider factors within and outside the immediate act of reading. For example, there is evidence that stress and other emotions had some connection with right-occipital activation. An instance of this was one adult's higher right-occipital activation when reading independent-level material in the *second* test. He was the only adult with this pattern at that level and his laterality pattern was even more surprising when he switched to higher *left* activation upon reading instructional-level material. This occipital change could be interpreted as "mixed laterality" in the traditional LD meaning of that term, but knowledge of this adult's life and emotions leads to another interpretation.

On the day of his second test, this adult had just learned he was to be laid off from work the following week. He did not discuss or express his feelings about this before the test. However, in a discussion later in the day, he revealed this news and his distress. His distress seemed to have had physiological correlates, judging from his EEG data, which showed that when he began the test, the features of the distribution of amplitude in his right hemisphere had a pattern similar to that of depressed patients.[7] This finding agrees with some evidence that the right hemisphere processes various emotions, although the meaning of the association is uncertain at this time.[8] Even though the exact nature of the association in this man was also unclear, some link was evident when he went from independent- to instructional-level material and had fewer EEG signs of depression, indicating perhaps he had become more focused and relaxed. At the same time he showed a switch to more active left-occipital activation.[9] The relationship of emotions, cognition, and right-left hemisphere functioning in this case (and in two other instances in the study) indicates that the processing of an acute emotional state in the right hemisphere impedes the shift of cognitive activation to the left hemisphere, a constraint corresponding perhaps to the commonly observed impediment depression can create in thinking.

An adult who changed activation from right in silent reading to left in oral reading provides another example of the need to consider a variety of influences when interpreting laterality information. Beginning readers, adults and children, usually have a preference for and more skill in oral than silent reading, due mostly to their frequent experience with this mode in beginning instruction. This man's preference for oral reading was stronger than that ordinarily encountered by the clinician who had worked with him and who, in notes, had attributed this preference to the fact that oral reading aided the client in overcoming persistent insecurities about whether he was reading the words correctly. Hearing the words aloud, the clinician's support, and the immediate feedback all helped him recognize words and comprehend meaning. Despite improved reading ability, his insecurities had not abated much at the time of the second test and his laterality shifts between oral and silent reading could be explained in part by his different emotional responses to each reading mode. Generally, other laterality patterns also seemed more understandable when factors directly or indirectly associated with reading were taken into account.

Right-occipital activation may be viewed not as something inherently "bad" or pathological but as heavily reflecting a beginning reader's strategy, which may fall somewhere between astutely using graphic information and unwisely disregarding semantic information. Conversely, left-occipital activity need not be regarded as something necessarily "good" in beginning readers. Heavy emphasis on semantic meaning (as expressed in dominant left-occipital activity) at an early stage may mean that the reader is using an ineffective strategy that relies too much on context and too little on graphic-based analysis. At the instructional level, "mixed" laterality—about equal activation of the right and left occipitals—might indicate effective use of different types of information.

Right- or left-occipital activation appears to be not a fixed organic given that promotes or retards reading but a part of the process, interacting and varying with the person's entire reading activity.[10] This activity includes the person's reading ability and strategies, the difficulty of the text and the mode by which it is read, the instructional method, and the person's special characteristics and emotional status. The complexity associated with the laterality information of these few adults, as a group and as individuals, shows the range of meaning that brain functioning can acquire in the context of the full human experience.

■●▲ Neurological "Dysfunction"

Having emphasized the *conjunctive* relationship of an individual's learning and neurological functioning, I return to a question posed early in the book: Do any learning-disabled people have neurological dysfunctions—the genuine biological abnormalities the LD field has been trying to identify—that can interfere with learning and academic achievement? As already noted, some controversial evidence suggests that a very small portion of children labeled LD do have these kinds of dysfunctions. Although the number is too small for them to make up a prominent group in the volume of LD research reviewed, statistical-correlation studies might have missed identifying them because their small number in an experimental group would not make the entire group's differences statistically significant. However, while recognizing that some children have neurological dysfunctions, the interactivity theory proposes that the presence of these dysfunctions does not correspond to the formal definition of LD—that they are the *cause* of a learning disability. To clarify this proposal, we will examine the evidence that some children have LD neurological dysfunctions and the bearing of this evidence on the issue of causation.

An example of disabling neurological abnormalities appears to be those associated with toxic metals, such as lead and cadmium. Excessive exposure to lead has for a number of years been known to cause neurological damage, severe behavioral disorders, mental retardation, and even death. Recently, amounts of lead that had been thought to be low or moderate have also been linked to cognitive and behavioral problems, suggesting that no amount of lead should be considered to be within tolerated limits.[11] This conclusion has implications for LD, even though the relationship between lead and LD has not been strongly established.

The chief method for studying this relationship has been to collect hair samples from the nape of children's necks. Hair is said to collect trace elements, providing "a continuous record of nutrient mineral status and exposure to heavy metal pollutants."[12] These studies are contradictory. For example, among those that have reported a relationship, methodological problems prevent drawing firm conclusions about the effects of lead. One study that found higher amounts of lead and other toxic metals in learning-disabled than in normal children cautioned that the differences could have been derived from age differences between the two groups.[13] The learning-disabled group was made up of children approximately 1.3 years younger, who therefore were smaller, a concern that is more than methodological nitpicking since concentrations of metals and minerals are known to be higher in younger children and to decrease as children grow older and bigger.[14]

Further hampering conclusions about lead effects is a study that found markedly higher concentrations of lead in the hair of normal children.[15] A study providing an ambiguous picture of the influence of lead on academic achievement found that lead concentration in hair distinguished public-school children on IQ scores, after age, sex, race, and socioeconomic status were controlled for, but did not distinguish them on reading, spelling, or math scores.[16]

On the whole, even in view of all the methodological limitations and inconsistencies of the low-lead research, enough doubt has been cast on the "harmlessness" of being exposed to any levels of lead. In view of the consensus among most investigators in the United States, Britain, and other European countries that "there is no threshold below which exposure to lead is safe," the conclusion may be drawn that "low" levels of lead can impair cognition.[17]

Higher concentrations of cadmium have been also found in the hair of groups of learning-disabled children, and the findings have been similarly inconsistent.[18] For example, in one study "the cadmium levels of the learning disabled group were slightly less than those of the normal group."[19] Between two other studies that found higher cadmium levels in learning-disabled children, one study[20] found cadmium levels in some normal children that were higher than those of the learning-disabled children in the other.[21] Research on cadmium and other factors related to cognitive functioning and academic achievement found that cadmium did seem to cause lower scores on IQ tests, but also offered a mixed picture because one study found no relationship between cadmium and performance on tests for math, spelling, or reading. However, another study by the same researchers concluded that cadmium was related to poor test scores.[22] While in yet another study, a more consistent negative relationship was found between the proportion of refined carbohydrates and cognitive and academic performance. In both studies, however, by far the most powerful predictors of IQ and academic performance were socioeconomic class, race, and age.

Overall, where a relationship between cadmium level and reading ability has been found, it has not been a simple one. Research indicates that cadmium levels interact with certain "nutrients," such as refined carbohydrates, and minerals, such as zinc.[23] Even so, the meaning of these relationships and interactions is disputable. First, there is the question of the accuracy of hair analysis: little information is available on the correlation between the concentrations of specific elements in hair and the concentrations in other organs and tissues.[24] (In rats, for example, hair zinc "has been reported to correlate with bone zinc and zinc in the testes, but not blood, liver, or kidney zinc.")[25] Thus the efficacy of hair analysis is limited.[26] Second, when higher levels of toxic metals are found in learning-disabled groups, does this mean that the metals are affecting brain functioning or that the levels are a manifestation of nutritional deficiencies, which are the actual primary influences on learning? A third consideration is whether both nutrition and metals reflect another factor directly responsible for cognitive and learning problems. Conceivably, for example, the poor nutrition that influences toxic-mineral levels could also be a manifestation of parental failings that include insufficient cognitive stimulation of children. Fourth, exactly how toxicity affects the learning-disabled individual is uncertain. Does toxicity affect certain aspects of cognition or does it produce lethargy and inattention, which in turn affect cognition? Or, are all of these affected by toxicity?

The above questions are not meant to dismiss the likelihood that toxic metals can affect brain functioning and impair learning. The research *implicates* toxic metals as an influence in the learning disabilities of some children; nonetheless, premature and disproportionate conclusions should not be drawn from the research.

The toxic-metals literature also proposes that nutrition has a singular, negative influence on brain functioning. This is another example of how a neurological dysfunction could impede learning. The predominant theory on the relationship between nutrition and LD was developed by Benjamin Feingold, who was a pediatrician and allergist. Though his work is often thought to be solely on hyperactivity (his major book is *Why Your Child Is Hyperactive*), he considered hyperactivity and LD usually linked, and used the shorthand H-LD to denote the linkage in the children he treated.[27] Feingold theorized that food additives, particularly artificial colorings and flavorings, were implicated in the creation of H-LD, as well as in many childhood behavior problems, and he reported that in his clinical practice, up to 75 percent of the H-LD children responded favorably to a prescribed diet free of additives.

Feingold's evidence came from case histories of patients he treated successfully. His book was widely read, and many parents who used the Feingold diet, perhaps with as many as 300,000 children, apparently found it beneficial. However, despite continuous reports of the benefits of nutritional treatment, the results of formal studies on nutrition and H-LD have not supported the extensive claims made by parents and others for nutritional regimens.[28]

The following are some examples of mixed results. In one study, teachers did not judge the Feingold diet to be as effective as parents did. Similarly, direct observation of children's behavior in another study did not support parents' high ratings. Ambiguous results were obtained in studies using a "challenge" method, in which substances are introduced "blind" into a child's diet to determine its effect. Challenging children's diets with food coloring has occasionally had an adverse short-term influence on performance in tests of visual-motor tracking ability and rote learning, but even among research showing some effects on these tests, artificial coloring appeared to have had no influence on many other cognitive measures.

In contrast to these limited successes, improving children's overall nutrition, not eliminating food additives alone, seemed to have significant benefits for performance on intellectual, school achievement, perceptual, and behavioral measures. The investigators, however, cautioned that they could not be certain that the gains had not been "produced by parental enthusiasm" for dietary intervention.[29] Furthermore, megavitamin treatment, another intervention in this investigation, did not help the children's cognition. Elsewhere, conflicting conclusions have been reached on the influence of sugar consumption on hyperactivity and cognition.[30]

These mixed research results have led to varying reviews of the literature on dietary benefits. For example, one critic concluded:

> Based on the available studies, it seems fair to say that no single study has reported a consistent dietary effect. . . . In addition, the positive findings that have been reported . . . have been relatively sporadic and not consistent between studies, and so may be chance findings. . . . Clearly there is no rationale for being an advocate *for* artificial food coloring; these additives serve no function except cosmetic. But concerns regarding their effects on the behavior and learning of children seem to be unwarranted.[31]

More positive conclusions came from an extensive review of the Feingold diet. Posing the question, "Is there anything to Dr. Feingold's hypothesis?" the reviewer answered, "Yes, something—but not much and not consistently."[32] Leaning even more to the yes side of the spectrum was a survey that concluded: an "undetermined proportion of children" improved "on a diet free of artificial colors and flavors, and some children respond[ed] adversely, at least over short time periods, to food dyes."[33]

These conclusions about diet and H-LD are difficult to assess because the research has barely scratched the surface in evaluating the large number of possibly deleterious foods and food ingredients and their interactions. This point was made by Bernard Rimland, an advocate of Feingold's theories, who outlined several reasons the research was not definitive.[34] Overall, fewer than ten artificial colors have been studied, though Feingold had called attention to the more than three thousand food additives that had not been tested for their effects on behavior. Besides food coloring there were flavorings, preservatives, thickeners, and moisteners—all of which Feingold thought should have been investigated. Attempting to establish where the study of these additives should begin, Feingold had recommended in 1975 that the initial studies focus on a few food colors. Following a spate of studies, Feingold protested in 1981:

> I recommended that, in view of the complexity of the problem and the many compounds involved, studies be designed focusing upon the limited list of colors, which lend themselves to better control. This statement is repeatedly distorted by the Nutritional Foundation to imply that I implicate colors as the most important factor. Neither I nor anyone else has the data today to support such a contention.[35]

A second critic of the critics of dietary solution noted that they failed to take into account that some individuals and subpopulations are more susceptible to toxic effects. Thus, in H-LD dietary experiments, the individuals who are more susceptible to food colorings and show mild or "striking" responses, are the very children who demonstrate the harm of one diet and benefits of another.[36]

Even though the research on the association between neurological dysfunctions and learning disabilities is inconsistent and controversial, evidence suggests that a very small portion of the learning disabled might have genuine minimal neurological dysfunctions. The actual number cannot be determined at this time, but it is indisputable that even a small number is consequential. However, while recognizing the likelihood of this association, we still must examine whether the neurological dysfunctions are the *primary* causes of disabled learning. We also need to determine how neurological functioning fits into the interactivity theory of LD.

■●▲ "Different" vs. "Dysfunctional" Neurology

Dysfunctional neurology is defined as an actual brain malfunction associated with learning problems found for example in some studies on poor nutrition and metals. Dysfunctional neurology means that something is definitely *wrong* with the brain. In contrast, different neurology, illustrated by the research on laterality changes in adult illiterates, is one in which the brain is still functioning properly. Here, brain functioning is different as a result of variances in knowledge, personality, emotions, and experience.

Within the interactivity theory of LD, the two categories unite over the issue of causation. The cause of either kind of brain functioning is not ascribed to the individual or, more specifically, the individual's brain. Rather, for both categories, individual social relationships, both direct and indirect, have created the conditions of the brain. Looking at the effects of schooling or family influence, for example, brain "difference" might arise through poor teacher or parent instruction.

Furthermore, if we were to follow the trail beyond the identified causes of brain dysfunction, such as toxic metals or food products, we would find that both brain "differences" and "dysfunctions" share a common source: both are created within social relationships and activities. For example, the primary sources of lead poisoning, a possible cause of LD, are gasoline, solder in food containers, and paint in older homes. Cadmium "contaminates the environment through smelting and refining of zinc and lead ores, recovery of scrap metal, combustion of coal and oil, disposal of sewage sludge and waste plastics, battery wastes, electroplating, and phosphate fertilizer contamination," as well as cigarettes. For children (presumably nonsmokers), the main source of cadmium is "food followed by air then water."[37] Food products containing ingredients that can cause brain dysfunction are to be found everywhere, at home and at school, in stores, and from vending machines.

The government allows the food industries to make and profit from toxic products, despite evidence of the harm they inflict.[38] When brought into focus, however, it is clear that this production backdrop is affected by economic and social, as well as political, factors—all of which ultimately have an impact on the lives and well-being of children.

For most of us it is impossible to live unconnected to this nexus. Families and children, for example, have little real choice about what they eat. Of course they may jump into the "cracks" of food production and try to eat more wholesome, less contaminated food.[39] Still, harmful products remain the standard fare in all food stores, despite new awareness and label inspection. The shelves carry only "the food of our world," those we learned were healthy for us—which we and are reminded of by a steady volley of advertising. Parents generally carry out their responsibility to feed their children with only the knowledge they have acquired within an economic-social system that promotes predominant types of foods and makes available primarily products that support that system. In food consumption, parents play the part of intermediaries between broader economic-industrial forces and the family.

Brain dysfunction does not have to be permanent, any more than brain difference: what was done through socioeconomic and personal interactivity can be undone. At the primary source, a socioeconomic and political shift allowing a change in the control and purpose of industries could totally eliminate the harmful cognitive (and other health) effects of products. Short of this, limited measures are also available, such as individual families improving their nutrition.[40]

■●▲ Conclusion

Most learning-disabled children then have different brains, but some evidence—itself far from conclusive—suggests that a small number of them have dysfunctional brains. The point is that *both* are created through social relationships and activity. Stated another way, both brain difference and brain dysfunction are created within *dysfunctional social relationships and activity.* Social interactivity and the brain functioning associated with them are mutable: a positive change in the former can allow for a positive change in the latter.

Researchers pursuing the cause of LD have tried to filter out, divide up, and chart the features of the learning-disabled brain. Doing so, to rephrase a basic argument in this book, has been like analyzing the wounds of gladiators mauled by lions in the amphitheater to determine the cause of their "disabilities."[41] If a finger were pointed only to the immediate causes of brain dysfunctioning, it would be like blaming the lions and not the empire.

10

■●▲

The Function of the LD Field

As I hope is now clear, the emergence of the LD field in the 1960s and the way in which children have been diagnosed as learning disabled since then has not been a result of a scientific breakthrough. Furthermore, even if the neurologic thesis had been confirmed, this would not have necessarily meant that all problem learners should be classified as learning disabled. Those children said to have a brain dysfunction, or with learning difficulties whose causes were not apparent to psychologists and educators, might simply have had their academic problems and instructional needs described behaviorally ("weak in diphthongs," for example, or "can't read for more than ten minutes at a time"). Nor was it inevitable that the correction of these problems would have necessarily led to the creation of a new educational field. The problems and needs of the children could have been addressed by the staff—perhaps expanded—of existing classrooms and programs.

Most accounts of the rise of the field in the 1960s identify the response of many middle-class parents to their children's "unexplainable" failure to learn in school as a pivotal event in LD history. Parents, with the assistance of professionals, recognized the actual cause of their children's learning problems and demanded that schools address these special disabilities. Schools responded, and a new profession blossomed. I believe that the broadest outlines of this account are correct: first, many middle-class children were indeed having academic learning difficulties; second, the reactions of parents, educators, and other groups were crucial in the creation of LD as a formal school category and as a multidisciplinary profession. However, I propose that the history of the emergence of LD—the formalization of the category, the school practice addressing it, and the arrival of LD as a field—unfolded quite differently.

Careful attention must be paid to two issues in the account. First is the seeming anomaly of the educational problems of many middle-class children. Americans often think of the two decades following World War II as a continuously bountiful era for the middle class. How educational problems could have arisen within these circumstances was indeed a perplexing question that, by the way in which it was asked, implied that the answer had to lie outside of the "obvious" prosperity. However, I propose that the educational problems of these children were quite concordant with new difficulties and disappointments of a considerable portion of the middle class. The second issue concerns the response prompted by pressure from advocacy groups, the school, and the government. Certainly, as the historical accounts suggest, school and governmental policy-makers exhibited a concern for children's needs. Nonetheless, I believe that they did not accept LD because of its intrinsic merit as the best way to solve the children's problems. They embraced it as a reform measure because, unlike other critiques made during the 1960s, it was not a call for fundamental changes in schools and society. Institutions, by making only a few readjustments, were on the whole allowed to continue to function as they had. Although solving problems and making a few readjustments are not always antithetical, in this instance they were.

■●▲ The "Affluent Society"

The story of LD is then embedded in the events of the two decades following World War II. This may seem an odd route into LD, but it's necessary if we are to understand the middle-class circumstances in which LD was identified in the 1960s as an unexpected problem.

The U.S. economy after World War II was marked by unprecedented economic expansion.[1] Flight from urban areas began, and, by the mid-1950s, "the rush to the suburbs and its peripheries had escalated to a gallop."[2] From the end of the war to the mid-1960s approximately 15 million one-family houses were constructed, mostly in the suburbs. Despite an inequitable distribution of wealth in the

U.S., "median family income rose from $3,083 in 1949 to $5,657 in 1959, a rise which, when corrected for inflation, still amounted to a 48 percent" increase.[3] Credit and credit cards were issued in abundance, and installment payments and mortgages became a convenient but also necessary means to the Good Life. Private debt rose in the 1950s from $73 billion to $196 billion.

Up until the 1950s large numbers of people lived either on farms or in cities and the majority identified themselves as blue-collar workers. This also changed during the years following the war, as the number of people employed in manufacturing continually decreased and the number in nonindustrial, white-collar employment such as sales, service, commodity distribution, advertising, and assorted other professions continually increased.[4] All of these changes, and especially the expansion of suburban living, contributed to the emergence of, in the words of Paul Baran and Paul Sweezy,

> the image of American well-being in the years following the Second World War. The suburban house with its electric kitchen and washing machine; multiple bathrooms; rumpus, family, and TV rooms; backyard, front lawn, and two-car garage [became] the symbol and showpiece of America's affluent way of life.[5]

Life in the suburbs did represent a "significant advance in the physical well-being of middle-class families," but, unfortunately, for many families the image of suburban life concealed the reality. Carefree home "ownership" veiled the sizable expenses of long-term mortgages, real-estate taxes, utility bills, and recurring repair costs, all of which claimed "a major share of 'owner's' income." Similarly, as the number of people moving to the suburbs increased, so too did the number of automobiles on the highway. Once a means of rapid and convenient transportation, automobiles became impediments to transportation, causing "increasingly time-consuming, tedious, and nerve-wracking" commuting. Costs and expenditures for automobiles became considerable: when combined, the total amount Americans spent for automobile transportation became "a substantial and increasing part of their personal incomes."[6]

Furthermore, despite the abundance implied in John Kenneth Galbraith's term the "affluent society," there were "qualitative differences between and within suburbs." Being "middle class [might have meant] comfort bordering on opulence; but it [might also have meant] outright poverty, or deprivation that [was] only one step removed from poverty."[7] Economically, and long before the recession that began at the end of the 1960s, the waning of the affluent society was apparent in the increasingly weightier burden many middle-class adults—most of whom were in reality middle-working-class—had to shoulder in trying to achieve or maintain the Good Life. Nevertheless, the image of suburban affluence continued:

> Despite the fact that over half of suburban residents, after the middle fifties at least, were working-class, the idea of the suburbs as the exclusive domain of the upwardly mobile white middle class became widely accepted. The suburban working class . . . became almost invisible in the public consciousness. . . . Instead, what Americans perceived was what Bennett M. Berger in 1960 first called the "suburban myth," an attempt to falsify experience, to render the suburbs as a contented, classless, homogeneous, affluent society.[8]

The strains of suburban life were more than economic. For many families, the search for the Good Life meant transience between suburban homes, rather than the idealized stability. William Whyte's study of a suburban community in the 1950s found that men expected to be transferred by their companies every two or three years. In one year's time 18 percent of the suburban community had moved, a statistic which reflected residence changes for the country as a whole and which frequently meant a move from one region to another.[9]

A graphic index that all was not well with the glorified nuclear suburban family (or with families elsewhere) was the divorce rate. In the mid-1960s the proportion of marriages ending in divorce began to climb drastically, with an increasing number of divorces involving families with children; at the same time the overall number of two-parent families began to decrease. Without question divorces have their positive side in enabling people to terminate stifling, wretched, or abusive relationships. The point for our discussion, however, is that divorces were a sign that flourishing suburban family life had, for many people, become problematic. Other indications of the strains accruing in middle-class life were the rapid widespread use of Valium and Librium, following their introduction in the early 1960s, and especially their disproportionate use by women (taking them at a two-to-one ratio); job-related stress and illness among white-collar workers; the increasing suicide rate among professional-managerial groups; and the alienation and rebellion of the young.[10]

Educational Failure in Suburbia

The lack of fulfillment in middle-class life extended to children's education, which in turn had ramifications for children's futures. The association between a person's years of education and his or her income, documented by social scientists but readily apparent in everyday life, strongly bolstered parents' desire to see their children educated. Unfortunately, as Kenneth Clark said in 1961, summarizing what others had documented, the schools were not providing the needed education that was the key to social betterment.[11] "Our public-school system," Clark concluded, "has rejected its role of facilitating social mobility and has become in fact an instrument of social and economic class distinctions in American society."[12] Clark's emphasis was on the poor and minorities, but the implications of his message were not lost on middle-class parents. These were people who, by and large, expected that their children would be able to live their lives at a middle-class level, at the very least. Hopeful parents did not automatically condone social differences and the schools' promotion of them, but inasmuch as these distinctions existed, they wanted the schools to fulfill their parental aspirations, which, within the social order, meant that the schools would provide further advantages for the middle class. As the 1960s ended, many middle-class parents saw their aspirations and expectations collapse. Representative of the academic problems of middle-class children was the *National Assessment of Educational Progress,* a 1970–71 evaluation of the reading rate and comprehension of students nine, thirteen, and seventeen years old. This span of ages meant that the evaluation assessed the outcome of the reading education of nearly the entire 1960s decade.[13] Children taking the reading tests had to answer five questions for each passage; the assessment divided the answers into two categories, "3 or fewer correct" and "4 or more correct." It did not group the youngsters by social class but did compare the reading-test results by "size-and-type of community" and by "parental education," two indices strongly associated with socioeconomic class.

For nine-year-olds, 15.7 percent living in an "extreme affluent suburb" scored three or fewer correct and 84.3 percent answered four or more correct. Of children living in the "suburban fringe," 22.8 percent had three or fewer correct. Similar outcomes were found in the "parental education" results. Of nine-year-olds whose parents had "graduated high school," 23.4 percent had three or fewer of the five questions correct; among children whose parents had "post high school" education, the percentage dropped to 18 percent, still a substantial number of incorrect answers.

Results for thirteen- and seventeen-year-olds were worse. Of thirteen-year-olds living in an "extremely affluent suburb," 56.3 percent scored three or fewer correct; for those whose parents had a "post high school" education, 46.8 percent had three or fewer correct. The assessment did not discuss exactly how the results translated into reading failure among these groups. Nonetheless, the general findings confirm what many middle-class parents had discovered: their children were encountering academic problems and faced a dismal future.

I have sketched some of the contradictions between the promise and the reality of middle-class life, and have included children's educational failure within it, as a framework for proposing that the *entirety* of middle-class life must be the starting point from which to begin an analysis of the emergence of LD. LD specialists have taken off a slice of the whole—the learning difficulties of middle-class children—and have pondered its "inexplicability." However, when the academic failure of these children, and the role of schools and other social relationships creating the failure, are placed within the array of various disappointments of middle-class dreams, the academic failure is no more inexplicable than failed marriages, personal misery for which tranquilizers were prescribed, heart attacks from job stress, family financial pressures, or lead pollution from the plethora of automobiles. Middle-class children's learning disabilities were not an anomaly—some kind of "fluke," as LD specialists have often concluded; rather, they were part of a larger failure of U.S. middle-class life to achieve post–World War II promises and expectations. Historically, schools had always failed to educate a sizable number of children. Middle-class parents thought or were led to believe that their children would be spared what had been a consistent feature of U.S. schooling. Educational failures had not been eliminated, however, any more than failures had been eliminated in other fundamental areas of U.S. life. The only difference in the 1960s was that in the face of great promises and expectations, many parents were shocked when their children failed to learn in school.

■●▲ The Push to Recognize Educational Failures

Many middle-class adults began struggling with their economic, social, and cultural problems both personally, as in divorce necessitated by marital discontent, and politically, as in feminist consciousness and organizational work necessitated by social inequality. For many parents whose children were doing poorly academically, the struggle became part of the period's widespread social activism. They turned to and on the schools, which they saw as the cause of the academic problems as well as the agencies for rectifying them. Bolstering this activism were large-scale critical studies of education, such as Charles Silberman's *Crisis in the Classroom,*[14] an examination of the "problems that beset American education," as well as scathing personal accounts of classroom and school practice, written by teachers and ex-teachers, including Jonathan Kozol, Herbert Kohl, and James Herndon.[15] Blacks in particular, feeling even more than middle-class white parents the contradictions between the promise of schools and the educational failure of large numbers of their children, demanded desegregated and improved education, and greater control of the schools.[16]

At this historical juncture, many middle-class parents began demanding that schools do more for *their* children. These parents were spurred on by increased social spending, particularly for compensatory education for those youngsters who were identified as socioeconomically deprived. The Elementary and Secondary Education Act of 1965 provided funds for instruction, teacher training, and research for the "disadvantaged." The Job Corps was a vocational and educational program for the same group, and the Adult Education Act of 1965 funded literacy programs, most of which were established in poor, urban areas. These educational programs occupied an important place within the Great Society programs.

Understanding how parents conceptualized their children's needs is an important step toward explaining the emergence of LD. Parents might have, for example, identified systemic social influences on the schools as the basic causes of the inequality of academic achievement, as some radical educational groups had done, and demanded appropriate changes. Or, they could have blamed principals and teachers for ineptly handling their neurologically *normal* children. They might have decided that their children were emotionally disturbed, slow learners, ecologically disabled, or just bored to death by school. There was nothing inevitable about the road to learning disabilities.

In the 1950s and 1960s, small parent groups concerned about their children's school problems began arranging joint parent-professional meetings and conferences with physicians and psychologists who espoused an LD explanation (the term "learning disabilities" did not predominate until 1963, but similar nomenclature up to that year had meant the same thing). The professionals strongly influenced the thinking of the parents who attended these meetings; the meetings sparked a national movement. Local and regional groups were formed, including the Fund for Perceptually Handicapped Children, in Evanston, Illinois, organized in 1957, and the California Association for Neurologically Handicapped Children, organized in 1960.[17] In 1963, the Conference on Exploration into Problems of the Perceptually Handicapped Child, a national conference organized by parent organizations and professionals, voted to form a parents' advocacy organization, the Association for Children with Learning Disabilities. The years following the conference saw several LD professional groups organized and the beginning of the LD field as it is today.

Reviews of this history have portrayed it as an example of democracy in action. Parents (the grass roots) recognized early on what only a few professionals understood, and worked relentlessly to bring about changes in the schools, in federal legislature and funding, and in professional practice. One account explains:

> Parents who were convinced that [early LD] views perceptively described their children welcomed the theories. . . . However, they soon discovered that educators, physicians, and psychologists were generally unaware of the concepts. . . . Many parents, believing the public schools should provide the special education required for their children, organized parent groups for the purpose of convincing schools that these exceptional children were educable and that it was the obligation of the schools to provide appropriate education. As has been typical in the history of special education, the pressure and impetus came from parent groups rather than from educators.[18]

Another interpretation, stressing the unity of parents and professionals, concludes that the work sponsored by both kinds of groups has been a

> valuable means of information and dissemination and catalysts for research, program development, and advocacy through the judicial system. Each organization formed a strong national lobbying group to promote legislative recognition of learning disabilities. Input from over 2,200 parents, professionals, and advocacy groups was involved in [establishing federal legislation that provided] LD identification criteria, diagnostic procedures, and monitoring processes. The presence of a strong national group strengthened state and local affiliates, thereby influencing legislation and practice at the state and local levels.[19]

■●▲ The LD Appeal to Parents

To determine how accurate these assessments are, we need to understand why many middle-class parents were drawn to the learning-disabilities explanation and found it so much more plausible than other analyses. Several interpretations of their motives have been advanced. One is that the term "learning disabilities" extricated parents from "blame," as, for example, the classification "emotionally disturbed" would not have done; second, the term did not carry the stigma of "mildly retarded."[20] Another possible explanation for parents' misguided acceptance of the LD explanation was that they lacked the expertise for evaluating it. Credence in the "scientific" legitimacy of LD was no doubt enhanced by the genuinely valid information about the brain that appeared during the years in which it emerged, such as information on neurotransmitters and brain mechanisms for perception and memory. The wealth of neurological discovery created a context that could have suggested to some that LD was part of a new frontier in science.[21] Furthermore, LD held hope, even considerable promise—in spite of the field's failure to explain how profound neurological problems might be overcome by remediation. The LD field held out reports of academic improvement and a list of illustrious achievers—the men of eminence—who had "overcome" and who stood as monuments embodying children's possibilities and parents' longings.

These and other influences, such as the promotion of LD "information" by drug companies, undoubtedly contributed to the explanation's appeal, but probably the most important influences were the parents' social consciousness and the practical, daily life of middle-class America. Despite their positive motivations, the parents were, like other members of society, victimized by a powerful ideology with long historical roots that blamed individuals, and commonly the biological makeup of individuals and groups, for their own failures.[22] At the time it emerged, LD was only one among many of these victim-blaming and biologically reductionist explanations. Other such explanations maintained that members of the lower social class were there because their biological makeup prevented higher social achievement; humans (particularly men) had an innate propensity for violence and aggression; inheritance accounted for most of the racial differences in IQ; and malfunctioning brains were responsible for numerous emotional states, addictions, and antisocial behaviors (many of which could be remedied with electric brain stimulation, psychosurgery, or electric-convulsive [shock] therapy). The poor were blamed for their poverty and all that went with it—poor health, poor housing, dependence on welfare, and family difficulties; numerous psychological and life problems were explained as individual, biochemical mental illnesses (for which "medication" was frequently the treatment of choice); and the unemployed were blamed for not having the right job skills.[23]

This general orientation for explaining failure has been predominant in the U.S. and in Europe for many years. In a climate filled with such rationalizations, the LD explanation undoubtedly appeared perfectly credible to many parents of children with learning problems.

Supporting the credibility of the LD explanation was the fact that, in many respects, the surface of middle-class life remained intact even while, for many, the suburban dream crumbled. Middle-class parents on the whole were still more affluent than their parents or working-class families. Material advantages fostered the expectation that educational advantages would also accrue for middle-class children.

The expectation was further fueled by the everyday outcome of schooling. Although the content of the education itself and the kinds of persons it fashioned was a leading educational issue of the time, many middle-class children did well within those confines. Hence, the schools appeared to teach middle-class children effectively, and whatever the schools' deficiencies might have been, many parents did not see them as inherent in the schools' practice. Schools did not seem *fundamentally* culpable for the children's failures, and it was credible that many of them had a minimal, inherent deficiency that the schools had failed to recognize and treat. Undoubtedly, further validation of the LD thesis came from the small number of children whose brains and learning were indeed dysfunctional (as the term has been defined in this book) and whose school problems did seem inexplicable except on neurological grounds.

Thus, the conditions and quality of life in which children's learning difficulties were created were simultaneously the very conditions and qualities which made the LD thesis plausible. Partly because middle-class parents failed to recognize this contradiction, they demanded that the schools correct their instructional "deficiencies" by addressing the special needs of learning-disabled children.

■●▲ The Appeal for Schools and Institutions

How did the success of the parents' demand compare with the success of the many other demands made of schools at the time, which were based on equal or stronger criticism of school practice and policy? Each of the other demands also had active supporters, yet when all was said and done, notwithstanding the short-term achievements of many other activist groups, the schools and the powers behind them repelled most of the demands: community groups did not take control of the schools, public-school classrooms did not model themselves after "free school" or Summerhillian environments, universities did not eliminate their corporate and military ties, and schools were not, in

Ivan Illich's term, "disestablished." Certainly other criticisms and demands were not rejected because the evidence supporting them was less valid than evidence for LD. To the contrary, the excellent critical research done at the time on schools and society provided other groups with much stronger evidential support than was available to LD organizations, which in fact had none.

Conceivably, the schools could have rejected LD demands as well. For decades, as I have previously discussed, educators had been concerned with, and reading specialists were trained to provide remediation for, the academic problems of normally intelligent children. True, these professionals had not solved the literacy problems of all children with whom they worked, but in response to LD demands, the schools might for example have expanded and attempted to improve the remedial-reading profession. The schools chose another course, not because of the limited success remedial reading had had but more because its pragmatic approach was narrowly centered on the reading process (I have described its model of reading "interaction"), and therefore it did not adequately address the causation issue raised by LD groups.

By accepting the LD definition and by meeting LD demands, limited as they were, the schools could resolve the causation issue while remaining within the bounds of school practice and theory. LD made "professional sense." Unlike other criticisms of the 1960s, which charged that the schools were classist, racist, authoritarian, hierarchical, and sexist, LD criticism fundamentally protected the schools and the social order to which they are tied. Governmental agencies were willing to back LD, thus enabling schools to respond. Together, schools and governmental institutions could accept criticisms that they had not made and supported provisions to treat learning-disabled children—by making *adjustments.*

From the U.S. Progressive period onward, schools have attempted to respond to social inequality by explicitly trying to cater to "individual differences."[24] Unfortunately, the catering has meant serving different-sized dishes in accordance with what the schools concluded each student or group of students could digest. For example, when large numbers of working-class students entered the schools following the termination of child-labor laws, schools were roundly criticized for their failure to consider the students' individual differences.[25] Schools accepted the criticism, made adjustments, and gave these children the education suited to them: vocational education for the boys, "domestic-science" courses for girls.[26] Scott Sigmon defines the years from around 1920 to 1960 as the "remediation stage" in education. This period saw the growth of school psychology, school counseling, remedial education, and the child-study movement, out of which came sanctioning and "scientific" descriptions of "individual differences which allowed for the development of student classification," usually within tightly bound academic tracks.[27]

Treating individual and group differences meant learning more about their problems, but no one tried to analyze the problems within a context of social relationships. Instead, they explored only parts of the problem, splitting it into a "number of concrete practical ones, for each of which a technological solution [could have been found] without touching" the social system in which it was embedded.[28] For the schools, LD meant understanding another category of child and finding the techniques suitable to the child's improper workings.

Federal legislation and funds gave the LD field the sustenance required to grow. They legitimated the category within the schools, helped establish a set of professional and public assumptions, and heavily influenced the orientation of research. LD programs and services flowered in the public schools. Universities received funds and were encouraged to provide the training and marketable credentials for a growth field. Postgraduate LD training grew from 538 students in thirty universities in 1969 to 2,148 students in forty-seven universities in 1972. And the next year, at least ninety-five universities offered LD courses.[29] A profession was born, but not out of a scientific explanation, which was meager. Rather, as I have said, the explanation prospered because it was consonant with schools' other explanations of learning failure and reinforced rather than challenged fundamental assumptions about educational inequality. Validity was of little importance. The LD explanation only had to make sense within a prevailing institutional approach toward children who failed to learn. Furthermore, when LD criticism and demands are placed within the entire struggle and counterstruggle that began in the 1960s and continues today, the school's incorporation of LD can be seen not as an isolated phenomenon but as part of a wider "conservative restoration" from kindergarten through college, typified by a back-to-basics movement, an emphasis on "quality" more than on equality, a turn away from critical education and toward career training, and the reestablishment of central school boards' authority.[30]

LD was not imposed from below, as historical accounts maintain, nor was it created from above as an ideological means to dupe people and enable schools to maintain their essential properties and reproduce social relationships. The entire process involved an interaction of forces: parents, professionals, researchers, and government officials, all tied together by hierarchical structures. The LD explanation and practice were initiated below, and continued to develop as those in control of social institutions admitted LD into the realm of permissible discourse. Decisions to admit the LD explanation were not conspiratorial. Instead, as I have emphasized, for all groups involved in the emergence of LD the explanation made sense within established school and social theory and practice. If it had not made sense, if it had not been rooted in the material reality of people's lives and had not had a ring of truth, it could not have been used as the ideological tool it turned out to be.

This assessment should not be interpreted as an attempt at degrading the struggles of parents who fought for a better education for their children, or as a suggestion that the response of professionals was a one-sided, crass cooptation and accommodation. If parents did not get everything they wanted for their children, they did obtain more services than had been available before, and which they would not have obtained without a struggle. Many professionals supported the LD explanation primarily because LD funds allowed for expanded programming and because they saw these programs as the best if not the only way for the underachievers to receive the intensive help they required. Not all educators were fully convinced, but they could do little because they too lacked the expertise to confront this formidable explanation. Unfortunately, the best intentions still encouraged—and meager resistance or skeptical acquiescence allowed—the blame for children's school failure to be placed on the children themselves, and as a result, the victory was won, and the war was lost. At least for the time being.

■●▲ LD Practice and Assessment

Given that the LD explanation was incorporated into school practice even though there was no validation, the consequences for children diagnosed and treated for learning disabilities are not difficult to imagine. I will highlight some of them, but to dispel anyone's uncertainty I will begin with the words of a former LD teacher:

> Two years ago, I quit my job as a teacher of children with learning disabilities. I had to. *I no longer believed in learning disabilities.* After having invested several years of my life in getting a Master's degree in learning disabilities and teaching special education classes, I came to the realization that these classes and the whole notion of learning disabilities were basically destructive to children.[31]

The claim that researchers had devised tests that could distinguish learning-disabled children from others contributed to the continued use of these tools in a destructive school process. LD specialists, using tests devised from this research, declared they too had the means to identify LD. However, what investigators had not accomplished in research, LD specialists certainly could not accomplish in school practice. Nearly a decade ago I reviewed the research on the most frequently recommended and used tests in LD assessment in schools and concluded that assertions about their diagnostic power had no basis.[32] Since then, no additional validation research has refuted my conclusion and nothing has interfered with the widespread use of the tests in school diagnosis.[33] New tests have entered the armamentarium of LD professionals, with no more support justifying their use than there had been for the older ones.[34] I will spare the reader a review of the research on all these tests because it would only parallel what I have said about LD tests in earlier chapters.[35]

Instead, I will say a few words about the general use of tests for diagnosing children in the schools. It has become apparent to at least a few LD researchers that in school diagnosis: "It has proven very difficult to translate our conceptual definitions of learning disabilities into assessment procedures that are defensible from either a scientific or practical viewpoint."[36] A research group voiced a similar sentiment in this terse statement: "Most tests currently used in the psychoeducational decision-making process are technically inadequate."[37]

The lack of defensible principles is evident in the exceedingly arbitrary decisions that have surrounded the use of these invalid tests. For several years, the Institute for Research on Learning Disabilities, at the University of Minnesota, has studied LD school practice. One of its conclusions was that children identified as learning disabled and others identified as low achievers but who were not learning disabled could not be "differentiated accurately" by psychometric test scores.[38] For example, comparison of the performance on a battery of psychoeducational tests by children identified by schools as learning disabled and those categorized only as low achievers revealed "considerable similarities . . . in fact, an average of 96% of the scores were within a common range," and "more than half of the scores in the two groups were identical."[39] A related study examined the test scores of fifty-one boys who had been evaluated because of their academic difficulties. School personnel had identified twenty-four as learning disabled. However, examination of the boys' scores on a battery of achievement, perceptual-processing, and various cognitive tests disclosed that the learning-disabled and non-learning-disabled boys differed only on tests of reading and spelling achievement, for which the learning-disabled group had lower scores. Among studies of this kind, the primary characteristic differentiating school-identified learning-disabled and non-learning-disabled low achievers was academic-achievement level, with the learning disabled being even lower achievers than the so-called low achievers.[40] In other words, LD was no more than "a sophisticated term for underachievement."[41] The investigators point out that the argument could be made that the results showed that many of the low achievers actually were learning disabled, and vice versa. The sensible conclusion is that, according to the schools' own LD standards, many children are classified by illusory criteria.[42]

Illusory classification criteria were also apparent in a group of nationwide LD service centers.[43] Federal funds created the Child Service Demonstration Centers, whose purpose was to identify, diagnose, and provide services for learning-disabled students. From 1971 to 1980 ninety-seven of these centers were established, with each state and the Commonwealth of Puerto Rico having at least one. They were required to comply with the "classic definition" of LD as expressed by federal guidelines, which required that a learning-disabled child have average mental ability, lack "other handicapping conditions or clear evidence of cultural deprivation," and demonstrate "some type of psychological process disorder." Of all the centers, only three adhered to these criteria in making diagnoses. The overall impression of the investigators was that even where a psychological-processing disorder was identified, this core of the LD definition remained "secondary in consideration" to academic underachievement, which was in fact the primary criterion for LD classification.

Whether a child is classified as learning disabled is influenced not only by intraschool judgments but also by the vagaries of identification standards among schools, school districts, and states. One study found that a child with a certain set of characteristics might be classified as LD according to criteria within one school but not by the criteria of another.[44] Interviews in fourteen Michigan school districts with school psychologists, LD consultants, and other professionals who participated in diagnosing learning-disabled students found that "except for certain tests which enjoyed popularity, districts did not agree on how to identify specific disabilities."[45] Similar inconsistencies were found across districts in Hawaii.[46] A national sample of 118 LD teachers who described their school districts' criteria for identifying learning-disabled students found variability in criteria among and within states. The survey suggested "that not only is there little national consensus about a definition of learning disabilities, but there is also little agreement as to who should be served by LD services."[47]

The Institute for Research on Learning Disabilities has studied these inconsistencies and misclassifications within schools and the decision-making process of LD classification.[48] The institute analyzed videotapes of meetings of interdisciplinary teams held, as prescribed by federal guidelines, to evaluate children referred usually by classroom teachers for diagnosis and possible LD classification. Team personnel usually included LD specialists, school psychologists, teachers, and school administrators. Researchers found that a teacher's referral strongly determined team decisions: the "teams serve[d] primarily a function of verifying the existence of problems first observed . . . by teachers." The chief assumption of team members appeared to be "that it is their task to find out what is wrong with a student about whom a teacher believes something is wrong, and they use tests in attempts to find problems." If LD was not immediately evident upon testing, more tests were administered in an unflagging search to find the "internal causes" that would explain the child's behavior; "the more mildly handicapped a student was the more tests team members administered." The function of the placement team was not to assess the student independently but to "substantiate the teacher's opinion."[49]

What made a teacher refer a student for an LD evaluation? In most cases, the answer was not that the action was a last resort, after a teacher had worked with a youngster and disconsolately concluded that the student was unable to learn through conventional educational means. A teacher could and often did make a referral without having first attempted to use any modified instructional interventions and without having called on specialists for help. Instead, teachers used the LD classes as a quick fix to remove difficult students from their own classrooms; other, more conscientious teachers saw the LD classes as the best means for students to obtain help unavailable in a regular classroom. These were students "in need of small-group or one-to-one instruction for whom special education seem[ed] to be the only available alternative, even if it [might] not [have been] the most appropriate solution." Thus, not only were the LD classes containers in which to dispose of students requiring unusual but feasible classroom instruction, they were also used for general remedial purposes,

> as evidenced by the practice at some schools of referring all students functioning below grade level. . . . Teachers utilized the only avenue available to obtain additional, small-group instruction. Teachers seemed interested primarily in securing auxiliary services for their students. . . . However, they were reticent to mention overtly the need for one-to-one placements on referral forms, perhaps because this would not be interpreted as a compelling reason to place the student in special education. In effect, then, special education services for mildly handicapped students were redefined as general remedial services—which better met the instructional needs of many students and teachers.[50]

The placement team's impulse to substantiate the teacher's referral, regardless of the motives for the referral, appeared to override test information indicating a student's eligibility for LD services. A considerable amount of information about students was collected, underscoring the supposed importance of test results in decision-making. The researchers, however, found that assessment data were not "used to support or refute eligibility," that team decision-makers used "assessment data to support or justify decisions that [had been] made independently of the data," and that there was "little relationship between . . . the data support [of] eligibility for service and the decision actually made by the team."[51] Also, the "process of seeking consensus" and the tendency to "accentuate similarities in perceptions" fettered any independent examinations by team members of the faulty instruments used in diagnosis or the overall justifiability of the diagnosis.[52]

Special-education placement, especially for ethnic and racial minorities and lower-working-class children, is further demonstration that LD has functioned in the schools quite removed from professional decisions based on valid evidence. From 1976 to 1983 the number of children classified as learning disabled in schools went from approximately 800,000 to 1.8 million. At the same time, the number categorized as mentally retarded decreased from approximately 970,000 to 780,000. These figures suggest, as some research has confirmed, that children who previously might have been classified as mentally retarded were now being classified as learning disabled.[53] If the LD diagnostic instruments had been valid, these figures by themselves would not necessarily demonstrate anything inherently wrong with the diagnosis. It could be argued that more refined assessment techniques could now better differentiate children with marginal neurological dysfunctions. But since we know that the tests had little diagnostic value, the differences appear to represent a classification redirection following criticism of the schools' classification of normal children, particularly black children, as mentally retarded, principally by IQ test scores.

A study of special-education populations in more than fifty Texas schools over an eight-year period beginning in 1970 found that the largest number of youngsters in LD classes were white. This was not surprising, since there were many more whites than blacks or Mexican-Americans in the schools. However, proportionally, blacks were over-represented in LD classes, as were Mexican-Americans.[54] The study also showed a startling inverse relationship between the two categories of "educable mentally retarded" (EMR) and LD for all groups. From 1973 onward, as the number of students in EMR declined, the number in LD classes increased. For the investigator, the LD category allowed discrimination to continue but in a less blatant form:

> It does not take much imagination to infer that there is at least the possibility that when it was no longer socially desirable to place black students in EMR classes, it became convenient to place them in the newly provided LD category. It took about a year to make the changeover, but the resultant proportional differences were maintained. Is it an accident that at about the same time the civil rights movement began to emphasize the moral ills associated with inappropriate placement of minority students in MR classes that the LD category was waiting in the wings ready to receive these very students—under a new guise, but for the same reasons?[55]

The changeover does not mean that the EMR category is no longer discriminatory. Even though the number of blacks in EMR classes has fallen, blacks are still overrepresented.[56]

Overall, figures on ethnic, racial, and class representation are not entirely consistent. For example, an Arizona study found that lower-class Hispanics were more likely to be placed in an LD class than whites.[57] On the other hand, even though Hispanics were overrepresented, LD still remained the classification of choice for white children, with middle-class white children having a proportionate edge over lower-class white children. Also, few middle-class black children were found in any of the LD classes in Arizona. Such inconsistencies may reflect differences in school policy or even differences in parental acceptance of or resistance to the LD label. The investigator of this study hypothesized that parents might have acquiesced to and even encouraged categorizing their children as learning disabled because the LD label is less offensive than EMR.[58]

Nevertheless, research suggests that even though LD began and is still used as a category for middle-class whites, many school systems have found it a useful category for other groups as well. Studies of school districts in California during the 1981–82 school year reported that black and Hispanic students were overrepresented in learning-disability (and mental-retardation) programs and that students from school districts of low socioeconomic status were twice as likely to be placed in LD classes as students from high-socioeconomic districts.[59]

Parents, as individuals, do not seem to have had much to say about these practices. When campaigning to bring LD into the schools, parent groups demanded some voice in educational decision-making concerning their children. LD legislation accordingly required parents to participate in team meetings and approve their decisions. Schools appear to have met the letter but not the spirit of this requirement because parents' participation has been no more than pro forma. The videotapes of team meetings previously discussed show that parents were "not active, informed participants in team decision-making":

> [They] were never asked their understanding of the purpose of the meeting nor their expectations for the meetings. Parents were seldom asked for their perceptions of the problems their youngster was having. (When they were, they were usually asked to verify a problem observed by a team member).[60]

Even though many children have been victims of poor classroom instruction, been erroneously identified as learning disabled, and have had their school careers heavily determined by institutional and political exigencies only remotely connected to their actual cognitive and academic problems, all this might be excused if in the final outcome these children were found to have improved academically. Follow-up studies, however, have documented that these children have fallen progressively behind their peers in basic academic subjects.[61] Certainly there are exceptions to this general conclusion, thanks to those good teachers who in LD classrooms and "resource rooms, regardless of the mystique surrounding the LD specialty, are successful with the very same instructional approaches, materials, and techniques" used "with any other students."[62] But for most LD students, the LD route has led exactly to the place where they began—educational failure.

The LD solutions developed by school personnel have not been founded on sound theory and research that convincingly explain why children fail. Rather, the field ultimately "explains away" failure, avoids responsibility, and limits itself to "the best that can be done" to help children who are failing. Without a proper foundation, school personnel cannot assess children's needs or be critical of the forces and relationships that produce LD and that shape and constrain school practice.

■●▲ The Future of the LD Field

The LD professionals who recognize that the neurological explanation is mostly unfounded have been debating what changes the field should make. If they consider the mythology on which the field has been built, the more harmful effect it has had on children's academic development, and the ways in which it has helped cloak the causes of academic failure, perhaps the proper question is whether the field should continue at all.

The most popular recommendation has been that the field drop its search for neurological causes and establish a new direction by adopting a pragmatic approach to learning problems. In a paper titled "Learning Disability Is for Educators," John McLeod advised eschewing the neurological viewpoint and replacing the term "learning disability" with the less pejorative "underachievement," which would be judged against the achievement of children "of the same age and of the same measured general ability."[63] With "underachievement" precisely defined in terms of a child's manifested educational problems, educators would be able to provide the diagnosis and treatment for the youngster's problems.

Another paper, which admonished, "LD or not LD: That's not the Question!" counseled the field not to "ponder, argue, quibble, and mix about exactly what to call" students who are failing in school, because this "has merely served to sidetrack interest from the bigger, more important question—what do we do with them."[64] If educators were to ask this pragmatic question, the argument continued, they could then pursue answers to such related useful questions as, "What system of service delivery for student's failing in school makes sense?"[65] Along with developing remedial systems, measures could be undertaken to prevent underachievement within the schools. The pragmatic approach puts questions about the nature of the children's educational problems and the best methods for solving them far ahead of questions about causation. In fact, this approach maintains that information about the cause of a child's academic deficiencies are of little if any help to an educator faced with the task of remediating the deficiencies.

The pragmatic approach has a degree of soundness that cannot be ignored. Even if children's academic failure arose from systemic social causes, anyone concerned with students who fail to learn should not ignore the students' immediate needs in their absorption with changing the systemic conditions. Many of the pragmatic proposals would be useful if implemented. Nevertheless, educators and other professionals would do themselves and children a disservice by trying to solve the problems of academic underachievers solely by introducing different programmatic methods into the schools. The central problem of the pragmatic position is that in disregarding the LD field's concern with etiology, it wants to throw out the baby with the bath water. Certainly professionals in the field have been misled, and have misled others, in their search for biological causes of educational problems. They have, however, been correct in recognizing that identifying the causes of academic problems is indispensable for solving them.

Improving referral and decision-making, eliminating invalid tests in diagnosis, identifying children's cognitive abilities, distinguishing their unique characteristics, and determining the instruction best for them are all measures worth implementing, or trying to implement. So too, other pragmatic changes would begin to move schools toward a more enlightened understanding and better instruction of children, such as "implementing intervention strategies and evaluating their effects *before* a student is referred," deemphasizing standardized tests and emphasizing continuous evaluation and monitoring of student performance in the classroom, and disbanding classes organized solely to serve learning-disabled students.[66] However, the LD field is not predicated on the proposition that failure and inequality are built into the schools and into society as a whole, and that learning failure is bound within and shaped by systemic conditions. The best pragmatic intentions would be thwarted, as well as subverted, by educational practices that would inevitably arise to facilitate and justify academic failure.

This revisionist perspective bids the field not disband or choose an exclusively pragmatic course but use a two-pronged approach. LD must develop into a critical field, to examine and contest the social organization, power, practices, and ideology that shape the conditions for educational failure. In doing so, a critical LD field must identify the complex interactivity in which LD is created. The interactivity theory of LD proposes that while various features of an individual (including neurology), groups, and institutions, and social, economic, and cultural forces each have their own characteristics, identity, activity, degree of influence, and interdependencies, at the same time they all combine to create the processes and products of learning and disabled learning. One might think of this interactivity as a "polyphony," a musical term for melodic parts that are both independent and interdependent. The musical lines have an "individual design, each of which retains its identity as a line to some degree," but the music comes from the simultaneous combination of the lines.[67]

According to the interactivity theory, systemic economic, social, and cultural conditions are the principal influences contributing to learning failure. These conditions are not sociological abstractions that can be optionally added to or separated from psychological explanations or analyses of narrower, more limited interactions. Every aspect of learning failure, even an interaction between a student and teacher in the most minute detail of literacy education, is related to these broader conditions.

Qualities and actions of people in relationships and the nature of institutions in which learning failure is created cannot be understood if we only investigate the limited meaning of interaction usually found in education and psychology. A new inquiry must account for the broader conditions in the interactivity that strongly shape institutions, individuals, and narrower relationships. Social-class relationships contribute to the shaping of a myriad of school hierarchical structures, to many school policies, and to the social views of school personnel, which also influence instructional interactions and outcomes. Economic, social, and political conditions directly or indirectly affect neurological functioning and are also the major determinants in the failures of family life, and have shaped the place of women in families, especially their primary responsibility for children's cognitive growth. These influences are overarching: the gender influences that contribute to women's disproportionate role as cognitive nurturers also express themselves in teachers' expectations of appropriate gender behavior and in the respective gender-determined behavior of boys and girls. These systemic conditions create inequalities and failures throughout society. Among these, learning failure is but one problem.

Mediating institutions, which are historically and socially grounded in and integral to the broader organization and hierarchical structure of society, contribute to the creation and "explanations" of learning failure. Schools are embedded in a social and economic organization that shapes their structure and practice. Thus they are constantly balancing between causing and attempting to eliminate learning failure, between fulfilling their purported goals and at the same time "explaining away" learning failure.

The interactivity theory of LD requires a new conception of the field's sphere of interest. LD has shared with other academic disciplines a narrow concentration, a disregard of areas of scholarship thought to be extraneous to it. Sociologist Terence Hopkins has observed that the continued narrowing of vision allows professionals to legitimize ignorance, as expressed in the view, "That subject I can be ignorant about."[68]

For example, researchers in the field known as the "social foundations of education," which encompasses history, sociology, anthropology, economics, and philosophy of education, have done extensive work useful for an interactivity theory of LD. Social foundations has inquired into the social, political, economic, and ideological nature of schools; the relationship of educational stratification to social stratification; the overt and covert agendas of schooling; the difference between schooling and education; the philosophical assumptions of school practice; and the changing nature of schooling in the past century. These and related inquiries have been pursued in an attempt to identify the fundamental characteristics of schooling. Yet LD professionals, exemplifying Hopkins's remarks, have almost totally disregarded all of this work. Using the interactivity theory to interpret the creation of learning failure requires using social-foundations research and other areas of scholarship that go beyond the narrow band of work in psychology and neuropsychology to which the LD field has primarily restricted itself.

Professionals in the field should be partisans, not just researchers and providers of service for educational failures. Partisanship is required because the interests of both children and the professionals who work with them are not in harmony with the interests represented by the structural conditions in which learning failure arises. A graphic example of this antagonism comes from the educational analysis and policy recommendations of conservative groups such as the Heritage Foundation.[69]

On their national agenda are the issues of LD and special education. The groups have cited some of the criticism of LD as evidence for conservative policy proposals—including LD's specious definition and diagnosis, schools relabeling mentally retarded children as learning disabled, teachers referring children to LD classes to minimize teaching effort, and schools classifying children as LD to obtain federal funds. However, this evidence has been cited to demonstrate the failure of special education and to support a call for the *elimination* of federal funds for students with special educational problems.[70] Either children learn in "normal" classrooms, or else, say conservative groups, too bad: "Public schools should not be required to educate those children who cannot, without damaging the main purpose of public education, function in a normal classroom setting."[71] Conservatives do not address what constitutes a "normal classroom" or the resources to educate all children within a classroom. Their sights are on eliminating federal responsibility for children who do not do well in school: "Federal assistance should be seen as the assistance of last resort, not a right."

Conservative recommendations might appear to contradict my previous analysis of the function of LD. Why would they want to eliminate a rationale for one of the many inequalities they regard as an inevitable part of the world. To the contrary, these "no-frills" recommendations simply strip LD of its exterior while remaining true to its core, which is that the individual is at fault for his or her failure. Thus, the fundamental explanation of educational inequality is only more clearly disclosed by the position that schools and government have no responsibility in helping the student overcome academic problems. Their proposals demonstrate what has been true of LD explanations and other explanations and practices based on beliefs about inequality: they arise not from empirical evidence but from a "social philosophy, political ideology, and cultural mythology" associated with a social order and the maintenance of that order.[72] The measures taken to maintain that order are flexible. Sometimes when the social order is pressed, beneficent measures can be wrested from it; when demands on the social order abate, however, the revised measures can be cruel. The measures may differ, but underlying all is the fact that those in control of social organization and institutions permit them to be vehicles in perpetuating inequality in schools and elsewhere. This partisanship on the side of educational inequality mandates that we take up a partisanship to eliminate educational inequality. This must include a change from the special-interest orientation toward middle-class children that has characterized LD organizations. LD organizations must recognize that even though academic failure differs in extent among children and takes particular forms across class, race, and gender, the commonality of the sources and kinds of educational failure calls for the LD field to concern itself with the educational failure of all children.

Addressing, challenging, and trying to change the systemic conditions that are the wellspring of learning failure is a formidable prospect. Teachers working to implement pragmatic recommendations may find that their efforts leave them little time and energy to deal with learning failure in any other way. Action outside the classroom or clinic may appear especially unnecessary to professionals who do improve the academic achievement of the children they work with. To a parent who is struggling unsuccessfully simply to obtain help for her or his *single* child, anything else may seem overwhelming. Professional and LD groups may consider any attention to systemic conditions to be too "political" and beyond the territory of issues they see as their legitimate domain. And for those adults who bear the consequences of educational failure, coping with the literacy and functional problems of each day may seem difficult enough.

Consequently, if the conservative forces do not have their way, better pragmatic answers that help a few more children and offer a bit more satisfaction to those who provide the help may be all that the future holds. Without question, the pragmatic changes would improve current practices and educational outcomes. However, if pragmatism is all that transpires, and the structural forces and relationships in the interactivity that produces educational failure are not addressed, challenged, and changed, the educational "poor" will be with us forever.

Notes

Introduction

1. Because the introduction only briefly summarizes the major arguments and mentions research that will be thoroughly discussed and documented in the extensive discussion to follow, I have omitted footnote citations here.

1 Hinshelwood's Legacy

1. Hinshelwood, J., "Four Cases of Congenital Word-Blindness Occurring in the Same Family," *British Medical Journal,* 1907, vol. 2, pp. 1229–32.

2. Hinshelwood, J., "A Case of Congenital Word-Blindness," *British Medical Journal,* 1904, vol. 2, pp. 1303–07.

3. Hinshelwood's 1896 letter to the editor of the *British Medical Journal* was the first instance in which he made this relationship. It is found throughout his writings thereafter. Hinshelwood had worked with adults with brain lesions who had acquired word-blindness, hence his clinical experience fostered the association. See Hinshelwood, J.: "Word-Blindness and Visual Memory," *Lancet,* 1895, vol. 2, pp. 1564–70; "A Case of 'Word' Without 'Letter' Blindness," *Lancet,* 1898, vol. 1, pp. 422–25; "A Case of Word-Blindness, with Right Homonymous Hemianopsia," *British Medical Journal,* 1904, vol. 2, pp. 1304–07; "The Visual Memory for Words and Figures," *British Medical Journal,* 1896, vol. 2, pp. 1543–44; and *Congenital Word-Blindness* (London: H. K. Lewis & Co., 1917).

4. Hinshelwood's failure to criticize school instruction as responsible in any way for causing reading problems is interesting in light of his occasional remarks on some apparently common school practices, such as the following: "It is a matter of the highest importance to recognize the cause and the true nature of this difficulty in learning to read which is experienced by these children, otherwise they may be *harshly treated as imbeciles or incorrigibles and either neglected or flogged* for a defect for which they are in no wise responsible" (emphasis added; Hinshelwood, J., "Congenital Word-Blindness," *Lancet,* 1900, vol. 1, p. 1508). In Hinshelwood's mind, these methods were apparently not responsible for creating poor reading development and would not have been employed had a child either read well enough or been correctly diagnosed as congenitally word-blind.

Hinshelwood's failure was the beginning of a long line of similar attitudes and omissions by others working with learning-disabled children. A pertinent example here is a direct quote of the above paragraph in the mid-1960s, by Macdonald Critchley, a British neurologist and strong proponent of dyslexia theories, who changed the word "flogged" to "punished," a change which softens the portrayal of schools' conduct (Critchley, M., *The Dyslexic Child* [Springfield, Ill.: Charles C. Thomas, 1964]), p. 7.

Another example of Hinshelwood's awareness that conditions in the schools were less than optimal is this observation: "With the children of the well-to-do, when such a defect [congenital word-blindness] is observed, there will be no difficulty in carrying out the education of the child, but what is the lot of such a child attending one of our *crowded* infant elementary schools? It may be years before the true nature of its defect may be observed" (emphasis added; Hinshelwood, J., "Congenital Word-Blindness, with Reports of Two Cases," *Ophthalmic Review,* 1902, vol. 21, p. 99).

Hinshelwood's mode of analysis can also be seen in a report of two cases that he felt demonstrated that congenital word-blindness was hereditary: he never mentions the parents' occupations or the children's home circumstances (Hinshelwood, J., "Two Cases of Hereditary Congenital Word-Blindness," *British Medical Journal,* 1911, vol. 1, pp. 608–09).

In a discussion of a thirteen-year-old boy who had failed to learn to read through the "look-and-say" method but who made considerable progress after Hinshelwood introduced a "phonics" approach, he concluded that the boy's "progress had been continuous and rapid, much to the surprise of his parents. He . . . had made more progress in the last thirteen months than he had made in the preceding seven years when taught on the 'look and say' principle." Hinshelwood interpreted this change as evidence that the boy was congenitally word-blind, since this kind of child usually had difficulties with the look-and-say method but could make progress with "proper treatment" that took account of their brain defects (Hinshelwood, J., "The Treatment of Word-blindness, Acquired and Congenital," *British Medical Journal,* 1912, vol. 2, pp. 1033–35).

5. For an example from the 1960s see Critchley, M., *The Dyslexic Child,* p. 7.

6. The term "word-blindness" was coined in 1877 (Drew, A. L., "A Neurological Appraisal of Familial Congenital Word-Blindness," *Brain,* 1956, vol. 79, pp. 440–60.). "Congenital word-blindness" first appeared in an 1896 paper by W. Pringle Morgan, an English physician, who discussed a case he had seen in his work with local school children (Morgan, W. P., "A Case of Congenital Word-Blindness," *British Medical Journal,* 1896, vol. 2, p. 1378). Hinshelwood

gave credit to Morgan for reporting the first case of the condition but noted that Morgan's paper followed one that he, Hinshelwood, had published the previous year. With the intention of keeping the record straight at that time and perhaps for a future historical account of who contributed what, Hinshelwood quotes from a letter Morgan sent him: "It was your paper—may I call it your classical paper?—on word-blindness and visual memory . . . which first drew my attention to this subject" (Hinshelwood, 1907, p. 1230). Morgan, following Hinshelwood's discussion, theorized that congenital word-blindness was caused by a defect in the left angular gyrus. In the same paper quoted above, Hinshelwood credits Dr. C. J. Thomas with first suggesting that the problem could be hereditary. His introduction to the discussion of the four brothers made the following connection with Thomas: "The present example . . . is a brilliant confirmation of the correctness of Dr. Thomas's observation" (p. 1230). It is uncertain whether brilliant meant "illuminating" or referred to Hinshelwood's analytical judgment.

During the first decade of the twentieth century, papers on congenital word-blindness were published in Holland, Argentina, Germany, France, and the United States (McCready, E. B., "Defects in the Zone of Language (Word-Deafness and Word-Blindness) and Their Influence in Education and Behavior," *American Journal of Psychology,* 1926, vol. 6, pp. 267–77).

7. Hynd, G. W., and Cohen, M., *Dyslexia: Neuropsychological Theory, Research, and Clinical Differentiation* (N.Y.: Grune & Stratton, 1983), p. 12.

8. Farnham-Diggory, S., *Learning Disabilities: A Psychological Perspective* (Cambridge: Harvard University Press, 1978), pp. 20–21.

9. Strictly speaking, the term "congenital word-blindness" actually had a somewhat longer life. Although after the 1920s it was on the whole replaced by other terms, it continued to appear from time to time. For example, it was used in the 1956 paper "A Neurological Appraisal of Familial Congenital Word-Blindness," by A. L. Drew. In the lead article of a 1968 issue of *Medical Journal of Australia,* titled "Congenital Word Blindness or Specific Developmental Dyslexia: A Review," those two terms were discussed as synonyms for the same condition (Hagger, T. D., vol. 1, pp. 783–89). Slight variations of Hinshelwood's term also appeared, for example, in the 1939 paper "Hereditary Word-Blindness as a Defect of Selective Association," by W. Marshall and J. H. Ferguson (*Journal of Nervous and Mental Disorders,* vol. 89, pp. 164–73).

10. Farnham-Diggory, *Learning Disabilities,* p. 24.

11. Hynd and Cohen, *Dyslexia,* p. 25.

12. U.S. Office of Special Education and Rehabilitative Services, *Seventh Annual Report to Congress on the Implementation of the Education of the Handicapped Act* (Washington, D.C.: U.S. Department of Education, 1985). In 1976–77, approximately 283,000 children were classified as emotionally disturbed and approximately 969,000 as mentally retarded.

13. Shepard, L. A., and Smith, M. L., "An Evaluation of the Identification of Learning Disabled Students in Colorado," *Learning Disabilities Quarterly,* 1983, vol. 6, pp. 115–38.

14. Meier, J. H., "Prevalence and Characteristics of Learning Disabilities Found in Second Grade Children," *Journal of Learning Disabilities,* 1971, vol. 4, pp. 1–16.

15. Gaddes, W. H., "Prevalence Estimates and the Need for Definition of Learning Disabilities," in R. M. Knights and D. J. Bakker, eds., *The Neuropsychology of Learning Disorders: Theoretical Approaches* (Baltimore: University Park Press, 1976), pp. 3–24.

16. *The Orton Dyslexia Society and the Problem of Dyslexia,* pamphlet from the Orton Dyslexia Society (Baltimore, date unavailable).

17. *Understanding Learning Disabilities,* pamphlet from the Foundation for Children with Learning Disabilities, (N.Y.: n.d.). Previous prevalence estimates have ranged from 0 to 2 percent, in a publication of the 1920s, to 10 to 20 percent, in publications in the 1940s and 1950s (see Drew, "A Neurological Appraisal"). The pamphlets from the Orton Dyslexia Society and the Foundation for Children with Learning Disabilities were circulated in 1985.

18. Tarnopol, L., and Tarnopol, M., *Reading Disabilities: An International Perspective* (Baltimore: University Park Press, 1976); also, Gaddes, "Prevalence Estimates," in Knights and Bakker, eds., *Neuropsychology of Learning Disorders.*

19. Drew, "A Neurological Appraisal."

20. Kavale, K. A., and Forness, S. R., "Learning Disability and the History of Science: Paradigm or Paradox?," *Remedial and Special Education,* 1985, vol. 6, pp. 12–23.

21. Hinshelwood's definition of "congenital word-blindness," from his book by that title, was: "A congenital defect occurring in children with otherwise normal and undamaged brains, characterized by a disability in learning so great that it is manifestly due to a pathological condition and where attempts to teach the child by ordinary methods have completely failed."

In a well-researched review of sixty years of work on reading disability, Drew reviewed the definitions in the literature and found one from a Danish publication that he felt was representative of them all: "A reading disturbance which cannot be ascribed to poor intelligence, intellectual and physical immaturity, emotional factors, defects of sense organs, disturbances of articulations and other motor functions, reduced physical vitality, home and school conditions, dialect and other linguistic difficulties" ("A Neurological Appraisal," p. 449).

22. Foreword by W. M. Cruickshank, in Gaddes, W. H., *Learning Disabilities and Brain Function: A Neuropsychological Approach* (N.Y.: Springer-Verlag, 1980). Emphasis in original.

23. Doehring, D. G., Trites, R. L., Patel, P. G., and Fiedorowicz, A. M., *Reading Disabilities: The Interaction of Reading, Language, and Neuropsychological Deficits* (N.Y.: Academic Press, 1981), p. 2.

24. Knights and Bakker, eds., *Neuropsychology of Learning Disorders.*

25. Hynd and Cohen, *Dyslexia,* p. xv. Another example of professional agreement comes from a book by two authors who, at the time of the book's publication, had a "combined total of twenty-five years" involvement in research, diagnosis, and remediation of reading disability: "We share the belief that research on the central nervous system basis of this disorder will yield findings of greatest educational and clinical significance." The book's dedication also provides a sense of the appreciation many contemporary professionals have for the interpretation "early and recent authors have agreed to" and the promise it is said to hold: "[To] those physicians of the late nineteenth and

early twentieth centuries who first recognized the relationship between reading disabilities and brain dysfunction. . . . Those educators, psychologists, physicians and others who have continued to pursue neuropsychological bases of reading even when it was not the popular thing to do. Those children of future generations whose reading skills will be stronger because of research which books such as this can inspire" (Sobotowicz, W. S., and Evans, J. R., *Cortical Dysfunctioning in Children with Specific Reading Disability* [Springfield, Ill.: Charles C Thomas, 1982], pp. v, vii). An additional example, this one more strongly arguing that there is a convergence of recent evidence to support the neurological thesis can be found in *Dyslexia Research and Its Applications to Education:* "The position of those who still doubt the value of the concept of 'dyslexia' seems to us to be rendered particularly uncomfortable not only by the remarkable coherence of the evidence from different disciplines but also by the fact that those working in the same discipline have independently arrived at similar conclusions" (Pavlidis, G. Th., and Miles, T. R., eds., [N.Y.: John Wiley & Sons, 1981], p. xx).

26. National Advisory Committee on Handicapped Children, *Special Education for Handicapped Children* (Washington, D.C.: U.S. Department of Health, Education, and Welfare, 1968), p. 4.

27. Two years before the 1968 definition, a U.S. government task force of the Minimal Brain Dysfunction National Project on Learning Disabilities defined minimal brain dysfunction as referring to "children of near average, average, or above average general intelligence with certain learning or behavior disabilities ranging from mild to severe, which are associated with deviation of function of the central nervous system. These deviations may manifest themselves by various combinations of impairment in perception, conceptualization, language, memory, and control of attention, impulse, or motor function" (Clements, S. D., *Minimal Brain Dysfunction in Children: Terminology and Identification* [Washington, D.C.: U.S. Government Printing Office, 1966], pp. 9–10). The vagueness of this definition, along with the ninety-nine symptoms the task force used to describe the condition, led to the abandonment of "minimal brain dysfunction" as a term, though not as a concept, and contributed to the National Advisory Committee's charge to devise an definition for learning disabilities.

28. Hammill, D. D., Leigh, J. E., McNutt, G., and Larsen, S. C., "A New Definition of Learning Disabilities," *Learning Disabilities Quarterly,* 1981, no. 4, p. 336 (emphasis added). The six organizations were the American Speech-Language-Hearing Association, the Association for Children and Adults with Learning Disabilities, the Council for Learning Disabilities, the Division for Children with Communication Disorders, the International Reading Association, and the Orton Dyslexia Society (formerly the Orton Society).

29. Ibid., pp. 338, 340.

30. Ibid., p. 340 (emphasis added).

31. "ACLD Adopts New Definition of Learning Disabilities," *LD Forum,* 1985, vol. 10, pp. 12–13.

32. "The Learning Disabled," *New York Times,* November 11, 1984, pp. 1, 45–58.

33. Mercer, M., and Liebowitz, M. R., "Solving the Mysteries of the Mind," *Family Circle,* July 21, 1981, pp. 92–136.

34. CBS *Evening News,* September 4, 1985.

35. *Understanding Learning Disabilities,* pamphlet from the Foundation for Children with Learning Disabilities.

36. Thompson, L. J., "Language Disabilities in Men of Eminence," *Journal of Learning Disabilities,* 1971, vol. 4, pp. 39–50.

37. Aaron, P. G., "The Neuropsychology of Developmental Dyslexia," in Malatesha, R. N., and Aaron, eds., *Reading Disorders: Varieties and Treatments* (N.Y.: Academic Press, 1982). This lore is commonly found in college texts on learning disabilities. For example, one leading text states: "There is at present a growing concern for the child with learning disabilities. The enigma of the youngster who has difficulty in learning is, however, not new. Children from all walks of life have experienced such difficulties throughout the years. Indeed, there is evidence that some of the world's most distinguished persons had unusual difficulty in certain aspects of learning." Among those discussed are Edison, Rodin, Wilson, Einstein, and Nelson Rockefeller (Lerner, J. W., *Children with Learning Disabilities* [Boston: Houghton Mifflin, 1976], pp. 2–3).

Another text discusses the dyslexic "men of eminence" in a section titled, "Favorable Outcome Studies" (Smith, C. R., *Learning Disabilities* [Boston: Little, Brown, 1983], pp. 293–94).

A recent book on nutritional help for the learning-disabled child provides the introductory assurance that "the roster of the learning disabled includes such illustrious names as Sir Winston Churchill . . ." (Cott, A., *Dr Cott's Help for Your Learning Disabled Child* [N.Y.: Times Books, 1985], p. 6).

Citation and discussion of dyslexic "men of eminence" can be found in popular writings and in the public information literature of LD organizations (see pamphlets by the Foundation for Children with Learning Disabilities, the Orton Dyslexia Society, and the Association for Children and Adults with Learning Disabilities). TV and radio follow suit. For example, an ad in the *New York Times* for a local New York City news program shows pictures of Edison, Einstein, Patton, and Wilson, with the caption, "A serious learning disability doesn't have to hold a person back." The ad reads, "As children these four men who eventually took their place in history often couldn't keep their place in class. They were children with learning disabilities." Not realizing I would ever need the ad for scholarship, I framed it and hung it over my desk, cutting away the date in the process and thereby preventing a specific citation. My apologies to anyone who wanted to look it up.

The evidence for the theory that these men of eminence were dyslexic will be discussed later in the book.

38. Clarke, L., *Can't Read, Can't Write, Can't Talk Too Good Either* (Baltimore: Penguin, 1974), p. 36.

39. *People,* August 12, 1985, pp. 86–87, in the section "Lookout: A Guide to the Up and Coming." The quotes are from "The Barbarians: Smarter Than They Look?" *Muscle and Fitness,* August 1985, pp. 104–82. Despite their dyslexia, the Barbarians graduated from the University of Rhode Island. I have been unable to find out their major.

40. "The Link . . . Undetected Learning Disabilities and Juvenile Delinquency," *Their World,* 1985, pp. 52–56.

41. Thompson, L. J., "Did Lee Harvey Oswald Have a Specific Language Disability?," *Bulletin of the Orton Society,* 1964, vol. 14, pp. 89–90.

42. Ames, L. B., "Learning Disability: Very Big Around Here," *Research Communications in Psychology, Psychiatry, and Behavior,* 1985, vol. 10, pp. 17–37.

43. Gray, W. S., *Summary of Investigations Related to Reading.* Supplementary Educational Monographs, no. 28 (Chicago: University of Chicago, 1925).

44. Two years earlier, Gray had written a major work on the diagnosis and treatment of remedial-reading cases. Congenital word-blindness was given as one of fourteen possible causes of reading failure. However, in a book replete with detailed case studies of reading problems, he did not provide a single case of congenital word-blindness or dyslexia (a term he used twice). It is likely that Gray considered congenital word-blindness to be rare and not especially important to reading specialists because in subsequent years he showed little regard for it or for other concepts of organically caused reading disability. (Gray, *Remedial Cases in Reading: Their Diagnosis and Treatment,* Supplementary Educational Monographs, no. 22. [Chicago: University of Chicago, 1922]).

45. Geschwind, N., "Why Orton Was Right," *Annals of Dyslexia,* 1982, vol. 32, pp. 13–30. Orton's clinical work, Geschwind mused, exemplified the words of Louis Pasteur: "In the fields of observation, chance favors the prepared mind."

Norman Geschwind was a professor of neurology at the Harvard Medical School and is considered to have been "one of the leading authorities on the organization of the human brain" (Miller, J., *States of Mind* [N.Y.: Pantheon, 1983], p. 119.)

46. Orton, S, "An Impediment to Learning to Read—A Neurological Explanation of the Reading Disability," *School and Society,* 1928, vol. 28, pp. 286–90.

If the notion of "mixed dominance" or "mirrored copies" seems unclear, try the following to comprehend Orton's explanation for what is supposed to take place in the relationship of the right and left hemispheres. Put your left hand in front of you, palm up, point your forefinger straight ahead, thumb pointed to the left, close the other three fingers, and imagine that the forefinger and the thumb form a *d* with the thumb as the "belly" of the letter. Now do the same with your right hand, pointing the thumb toward the right. If, as Orton said, the engram is formed in a mirror image on the opposite side of the brain, the thumb that is the belly of the *d* on the left hand forms a *b* on the right hand. The same "reversal" may be made with your thumb, forefinger, and middle finger. Assign each a letter of the word *was* and see how it comes out *saw* on the other hand.

47. John Dorsey, quoted in Geschwind, "Why Orton Was Right," p. 15.

48. Vernon, M. D., *Backwardness in Reading* (London: Cambridge University Press, 1957).

49. Bond, G. L., and Tinker, M. A., *Reading Difficulties: Their Diagnosis and Correction* (N.Y.: Appleton-Century-Crofts, 1957), p. 99.

50. Aaron, "The Neuropsychology of Developmental Dyslexia."

51. Chall, J. S., and Mirsky, A. F., eds., *Education and the Brain* (Chicago: University of Chicago Press, 1978), p. xi.

52. Wilson, E. O. *Sociobiology: The New Synthesis* (Cambridge: Harvard University Press, 1975).

53. Ryan, W., *Blaming the Victim* (N.Y.: Random House, 1971).

54. For example, see Chorover, S. L., *From Genesis to Genocide* (Cambridge: MIT Press, 1980); Tobach, E., Gianutsos, J., Topoff, H., and Gross, C. G., *The Four Horsemen: Racism, Sexism, Militarism and Social Darwinism* (N.Y.: Behavioral Publications, 1974); and Gould, S. J., *The Mismeasure of Man* (N.Y.: W.W. Norton, 1981).

55. Mills, C. W., *The Sociological Imagination* (N.Y.: Oxford University Press, 1959).

56. Feuerstein, R., *The Dynamic Assessment of Retarded Performers* (Baltimore: University Park Press, 1979), p. 17.

57. Sampson, E. E., "Cognitive Psychology as Ideology," *American Psychologist,* 1981, vol. 36, pp. 730–43.

58. Lewontin, R. C., Rose, S., and Kamin, L., *Not in Our Genes* (N.Y.: Pantheon, 1984), p. 266.

2 Perceptual and Attention Deficits

1. Bannatyne, A, *Language, Reading and Learning Disabilities* (Springfield, Ill.: Charles C. Thomas, 1971), p. 391.

2. Clements, S. D., "Minimal Brain Dysfunction in Children," in Sapir, S. G., and Nitzburg, A.C., eds., *Children with Learning Problems* (N.Y.: Brunner/Mazel, 1973).

3. Spears, C. E., and Weber, R. E., "The Nature of Learning Disabilities," In Weber, ed., *Handbook on Learning Disabilities* (Englewood Cliffs, N.J.: Prentice-Hall, 1974), p. 33.

4. Liberman, I. Y., Shankweiler, D., Orlando, C., Harris, K. S., and Berti, F. B., "Letter Confusions and Reversals of Sequence in the Beginning Reader: Implications for Orton's Theory of Developmental Dyslexia," *Cortex,* 1971, vol. 7, pp. 127–42 (emphasis added).

5. Black, F. W., "Reversal and Rotation Errors by Normal and Retarded Readers," *Perceptual and Motor Skills,* 1973, vol. 36, pp. 895–98.

6. Kaufman, H. S., and Biren, P. L., "Persistent Reversers: Poor Readers, Writers, Spellers?" *Academic Therapy,* 1976–77, vol. 12, pp. 209–17.

7. Moyer, S. B., and Newcomer, P. L. "Reversals in Reading: Diagnosis and Remediation," *Exceptional Children,* 1977, vol. 43, pp. 424–29.

8. "Plain Talk About Children with Learning Disabilities" (Washington, D.C.: U.S. Government Printing Office, 1979).

9. "Today Show," NBC, September 16–18, 1985.

10. White, M., "Identification of Dyslexia: A Ninety-Minute Procedure," *Journal of Learning Disabilities,* 1983, vol. 16, pp. 32–34.

11. Jacoby, R., *Social Amnesia* (Boston: Beacon Press, 1975), p. 5.

12. Other tasks include feeling hidden geometric forms and then matching them to ones that can be seen, or recounting the order in which visual or auditory stimuli have been presented.

13. Additionally, there are the Frostig Developmental Test of Visual Perception, the Illinois Test of Psycholinguistic Abilities, the Purdue Perceptual-

Motor Survey, and the Southern California Figure-Ground Perception Test. Any LD textbook will list, discuss, and recommend a bevy of perceptual tests of far greater number than the sample listed here.

14. Weaver, P.A., and Rosner, J., "Relationships Between Visual and Auditory Perceptual Skills and Comprehension in Students with Learning Disabilities," *Journal of Learning Disabilities,* 1979, vol. 12, pp. 617–19.

15. Hatchette, R. K., and Evans, J. R., "Auditory-Visual and Temporal-Spatial Pattern Matching Performance of Two Types of Learning-disabled Children," *Journal of Learning Disabilities,* 1983, vol. 16, pp. 537–41.

16. A similar example of LD numerology may be found in another study of intersensory integration. Here, disabled and normal readers took four auditory-visual perception tests, each containing twelve items. The respective scores were: 10.2 vs. 10.6, 6.7 vs. 7.7, 8.7 vs. 9.5, and 7.4 vs. 9.2. This meant that three of the scores were differentiated by 0.4, 1.0, and .8, respectively, and only the last score difference of 1.6 (equaling approximately 77 percent vs. 62 percent) gave even a hint of a meaningful difference. As in the previous study, the questions must be asked, Is 77 percent correct normal and 62 percent dysfunctional? If so, on what basis? Neither the similarity of scores for three of the tests nor the problematic significance of the difference in the final one seemed to give the researchers pause as they concluded that the "hypothesis that LD children perform more poorly on intermodal and intramodal matching tasks is supported." Technically they did perform "more poorly," but by itself the term comes to take on a meaning greater than the numerical differences would support. See Zendel, I. H., and Pih, R. O., "Visual and Auditory Matching in Learning Disabled and Normal Children," *Journal of Learning Disabilities,* 1983, vol. 16, pp. 158–60).

17. These influences continue to be ignored in perceptual-deficit research. For example, differences have been reported between disabled and normal readers on both verbal and nonverbal tests, but the meaning of the results are not as apparent as researchers would like to believe (Tallal, P., "Auditory Temporal Perception, Phonics, and Reading Disabilities in Children," *Brain and Language,* 1980, vol. 9, pp. 182–98; Tallal, "Temporal or Phonetic Processing Deficit in Dyslexia? That Is the Question," *Applied Psycholinguistics,* 1984, vol. 5, pp. 167–69). An examination of the children's behavior during the testing showed that, as with earlier studies, problems blamed on perceptual deficits could be interpreted as outcomes of group differences in motivation, problem-solving strategies, attention, self-confidence, or the kind of reading and language abilities I have just discussed.

18. Vellutino, F. R., *Dyslexia* (Cambridge: MIT Press, 1979).

19. In a related experiment, poor and normal readers, between the ages of seven and eleven, were briefly presented different types of verbal and nonverbal stimuli, such as words of varying length *(fly, form, drawn)*, scrambled letters *(gzfs, hbd)*, numbers of varying length *(182, 4328)*, and simple geometric designs. Asked to copy them from memory immediately afterward, poor readers generally performed as well as normal readers. In contrast, poor readers did not perform as well as the normal readers when asked to pronounce the "real words," or, in the case of younger poor readers, when asked to name the letters and numbers. Frequently, poor readers could correctly recall the letter sequence of a given word but mispronounced the word when asked to read it "because they can't name them correctly" (Ibid., p. 178).

20. Ibid., p. 207.

21. Kavale, K. A., and Forness, S. R., "Learning Disability and the History of Science: Paradigm or Paradox?" *Remedial and Special Education,* 1985, vol. 6, pp. 12–23.

22. Perlmutter, B. F., and Parus, M. V., "Identifying Children with Learning Disabilities: Diagnostic Procedures Across School Districts," *Learning Disabilities Quarterly,* 1983, vol. 6, pp. 321–28; Mercer, C. D., Hughes, C., and Mercer, A. R., "Learning Disabilities Definitions Used by State Education Departments," *Learning Disability Quarterly,* 1985, vol. 8, pp. 45–55; German, D., Johnson, B., and Schneider, M., "Learning Disability vs. Reading Disability: A Survey of Practitioners' Diagnostic Populations and Test Instruments," *Learning Disability Quarterly,* 1985, vol. 8, pp. 141–57.

23. Sutherland, J., and Algozzine, B., "The Learning Disabled Label as a Biasing Factor in the Visual Motor Performance of Normal Children," *Journal of Learning Disabilities,* 1979, vol. 12, pp. 17–23.

24. Ibid., p. 19.

25. Javal, E., "Essai sur la Physiologie de la Lecture," *Annales d'oculistique,* 1879, vol. 87, pp. 242–53.

26. For a 1958 discussion of the research see Tinker, M. A., "Recent Studies of Eye Movements in Reading," *Psychological Bulletin,* 1958, vol. 55, pp. 215–31. For a recent discussion see Goldberg, H. K., Shiffman, G. B., and Bender, M., *Dyslexia: Interdisciplinary Approaches to Reading Disabilities* (N.Y.: Grune & Stratton, 1983), pp. 77–78.

27. Pavlidis, G. Th. "Do Eye Movements Hold the Key to Dyslexia?" *Neuropsychologia,* 1981 (a), vol. 19, pp. 57–64; Pavlidis, "How Can Dyslexia Be Objectively Diagnosed?" *Reading,* 1979, vol. 13, pp. 3–15.

28. Pavlidis, "How Can Dyslexia Be Objectively Diagnosed?" and "Sequencing Eye Movements and the Early Objective Diagnosis of Dyslexia," in Pavlidis, and Miles, T. R., eds., *Dyslexia Research and Its Applications to Education* (London: J. Wiley, 1981).

29. An instance of the dyslexics' eye-movement problems was found in their effort to move visually from one line to the next: "Dyslexics were unable to move their eyes accurately from the end of a line to the beginning of the next with one saccade. Instead they broke the return sweep into little saccades, some giving the impression that they were scanning the text from right to left" (Pavlidis, *Dyslexia Research,* 124).

30. Ibid., p. 145.

31. Ibid., p. 153.

32. Leisman, G., and Schwartz, J., "Aetiological Factors in Dyslexia: 1. Saccadic Eye Movement Control," *Perceptual and Motor Skills,* 1978, vol. 47, pp. 403–07; Adler-Grinberg, D., and Stark, L., "Eye Movements, Scanpaths, and Dyslexia," *American Journal of Optometry & Physiological Optics,* 1978, vol. 55, pp. 557–70; Lahey, B. B., Kupfer, D. L., Beggs, V. E., and Landon, D., "Do Learning Disabled Children Exhibit Peripheral Deficits in Selective Attention? An Analysis of Eye Movements During Reading," *Journal of Abnormal Child Psychology,* 1982, vol. 10, pp. 1–10.

33. Lefton, L. A., Lahey, B. B., and Stagg, D. I., "Eye Movements in Reading Disabled and Normal Children: A Study of Systems and Strategies," *Journal of Learning Disabilities,* 1978, vol. 11, pp. 549–58.

34. Pavlidis and Miles, *Dyslexia Research,* book jacket notes. For other comments on media attention see Pollatsek, A., "What Can Eye Movements Tell Us About Dyslexia?" in Rayner, K., ed., *Eye Movements in Reading: Perceptual and Language Processes* (N.Y.: Academic Press, 1983).

35. Stanley, G., Smith, G. A., and Howell, E. A., "Eye-Movements and Sequential Tracking in Dyslexic and Control Children," *British Journal of Psychology,* 1983, vol. 74, pp. 181–87.

36. Among the criticisms of the replication research were several concerning differences in technique. One was that the lights in the replication study were closer together and had different flashing times. A second was that the children in the original study were told the sequence pattern that would occur, but in the replication study they were not. These differences alone, Pavlidis maintained, could have prevented the "manifestation of the erratic eye movements found" in the original studies. There was also a third difference, subject-selection methods.

Pavlidis's criticisms of the technical differences seem weak in view of his earlier observations that persistently emphasized that the erratic eye movements of dsylexics are pervasive and easily identifiable. For example, one paper described dyslexics' behavior before a test while waiting for the recording instruments to be adjusted: "When they were asked to 'hold' their eyes for a few seconds on a light source . . . their eyes were wandering around the point of fixation and blinked considerably after a second or so" (Pavlidis, "Do Eye Movements," p. 60). If dyslexics could not keep their eyes still for even a few seconds, it seems that any technical differences in time and distance between the flashing lights, or similar technical differences, while not exactly replicating the original studies, should not have prevented the manifestation and identification of erratic eye movements so easily recognizable without instrument measures. Furthermore, some procedures that were criticized could easily have been used to draw entirely different conclusions. For example, not telling children in the replication study what the sequence would be might foster more, not fewer, erratic eye movements than in the original studies, where this information was provided.

As for the criteria for selecting dyslexics, those described in the replication study could be interpreted to be essentially the same as those of the original work. It is true that the replication study did not describe the methods used to determine that dyslexics had met the exclusionary criteria but, as I said, neither had Pavlidis (Pavlidis, "Erratic Sequential Eye-Movements in Dyslexics: Comments and Reply to Stanley, et al., *British Journal of Psychology,* 1983, vol. 74, pp. 189–93).

37. Brown, B., Haegerstrom-Portnoy, G., Adams, A. J., Yingling, C. D., Galin, D., Herron, J., and Marcus, M., "Predictive Eye Movements Do Not Discriminate Between Dyslexic and Control Children," *Neuropsychologia,* 1983 (a), vol. 21, pp. 121–28; Brown, Haegerstrom-Portnoy, Yingling, Herron, J., Galin, and Marcus, "Tracking Eye Movements Are Normal in Dyslexic Children," *American Journal of Optometry & Physiological Optics,* 1983 (b), vol. 60, pp. 376–83.

38. Brown, et al., "Predictive Eye Movements," p. 125 (emphasis added).

39. Ibid., p. 126.

40. Using a larger number of dyslexics (thirty-four compared to Pavlidis's twelve), one study found no significant differences between groups for any of

Pavlidis's three major variables: number of saccades, regressions, and fixations (Olson, R. K., Kliegl, R., and Davidson, B. J., "Dyslexics and Normal Readers' Eye Movements," *Journal of Experimental Psychology: Human Perception and Performance,* 1983, vol. 9, pp. 816–25.). The following year another replication study confirmed this conclusion: no differences were found between dyslexic children and normal children in eye movements examined for fixation time, speed of fixation, and other measurements similar to those Pavlidis used (Black, J. L., Collins, W. K., DeRoach, J. N., and Zubrick, S. R., "Dyslexia: Saccadic Eye Movements," *Perceptual and Motor Skills,* 1984, vol. 58, pp. 903–10).

41. Pavlidis, "Eye Movements in Dyslexia: Their Diagnostic Significance," *Journal of Learning Disabilities,* 1985, vol. 18, pp. 42–50.

42. Cizek, O., and Jost, J., "Eye Movements and Development of the Child," unpublished ms., 1984, p. 10 (emphasis added). Pavlidis gives the title as "Eye Movements, Dyslexia and Child Development," but the paper Professor Jost sent me was the one to which Pavlidis referred.

43. I tried, through correspondence, to obtain the other prepublication manuscript. I wrote to Professor Z. Matejcek, a leading researcher on reading disabilities in Czechoslovakia, asking if he could help me obtain copies of the manuscripts. Sometime afterward I received the manuscript discussed here, in English translation, and a letter from one of the authors, Jiri Jost. Neither Matejcek, in a separate letter, nor Jost mentioned the other reported "prepublication manuscript" in their correspondence. Therefore, I again wrote to Czechoslovakia, this time to Jost, asking for help in locating the paper. He replied saying he had contacted an author of the other paper and had asked him to send it to me. More than a year has passed since I received the letter from Professor Jost and since then I have received no manuscript.

44. *Diagnostic and Statistical Manual of Mental Disorders* (Washington, D.C.: American Psychiatric Association, 1980, third edition).

45. Forness, S. R., and Cantwell, D. P., "DSM III Psychiatric Diagnoses and Special Education Categories," *Journal of Special Education,* 1982, vol. 16, pp. 49–63.

46. APA, *Diagnostic and Statistical Manual,* p. 41.

47. "Attention Disorders Need Better Measures and Theory," *APA Monitor,* January 1985, p. 16.

48. Spreen, O., "The Dyslexias: A Discussion of Neurobehavioral Research," in Benton, A. L., and Pearl, D., eds., *Dyslexia: An Appraisal of Current Knowledge* (N.Y.: Oxford University Press, 1978); Sheer, D. E., "Focused Arousal and 40-Hz EEG," in Knights and Bakker, eds., *Neuropsychology of Learning Disorders.*

49. For example, see Vrana, F., and Pihl, R. O., "Selective Attention Deficit in Learning Disabled Children: A Cognitive Interpretation," *Journal of Learning Disabilities,* 1980, vol. 13, pp. 387–91; Deikel, S. M., and Freidman, M. P., "Selective Attention in Children with Learning Disabilities," *Perceptual Motor Skills,* 1976, vol. 42, pp. 675–78; Hallahan, D. P., Kauffman, J. M., and Ball, D. W., "Selective Attention and Cognitive Tempo of Low Achieving and High Achieving Sixth Grade Males," *Perceptual and Motor Skills,* 1973, vol. 36, pp. 579–83; Copeland, A. P., and Reiner, E. M., "The Selective Attention of Learning-Disabled Children: Three Studies," *Journal of Abnormal*

Child Psychology, 1984, vol. 12, pp. 455–70; Tarver, S. G., Hallahan, D. P., Kauffman, J. M., and Ball, D. W., "Verbal Rehearsal and Selective Attention in Children with Learning Disabilities: A Developmental Lag," *Journal of Experimental Child Psychology,* 1976, vol. 22, pp. 375–85.

50. Samuels, S. J., and Miller, N. L., "Failure to Find Attention Differences Between Learning Disabled and Normal Children on Classroom and Laboratory Tasks," *Exceptional Children,* 1985, vol. 51, pp. 358–75.

51. Hallahan, D. P., Gajar, A. H., Cohen, S. B., and Tarver, S. G., "Selective Attention and Locus of Control in Learning Disabled and Normal Children," *Journal of Learning Disabilities,* 1978, vol. 11, pp. 231–36; Pelham, W. E., "Selective Attention Deficits in Poor Readers? Dichotic Listening, Speeded Classification, and Auditory and Visual Central and Incidental Learning Tasks," *Child Development,* 1979, vol. 50, pp. 1050–61.

52. Another criticism of the central-incidental learning research concerns "the extent to which . . . it relates to processes found in the natural learning environment." Central-incidental learning is a narrow piece of attention demanding "focused attention in the presence of intratask distractibility." This might be part of the attention necessary for learning, but, by and large, the attention involved in learning processes such as reading go far beyond it, as do the attention problems teachers generally describe (Fleisher, L. S., Soodak, L. C., and Jelin, M. A., "Selective Attention Deficits in Learning Disabled Children: Analysis of the Data Base," *Exceptional Children,* 1984, vol. 52, pp. 136–41).

53. Sinclair, E., Guthrie, D., and Forness, S. R., "Establishing a Connection Between Severity of Learning Disabilities and Classroom Attention Problems," *Journal of Educational Research,* 1984, vol. 78, pp. 18–21; Hebben, N. A., Whitman, R. D., Milberg, W. P., Andresko, M., and Galpin, R., "Attentional Dysfunction in Poor Readers," *Journal of Learning Disabilities,* 1981, vol. 14, pp. 287–90.

54. Koppell, S., "Testing the Attentional Deficit Notion," *Journal of Learning Disabilities,* 1979, vol. 12, pp. 43–48; Samuels, S. J., and Edwall, G., "The Role of Attention in Reading with Implications for the Learning Disabled Student," *Journal of Learning Disabilities,* 1981, vol. 14, pp. 353–68.

55. Tarver, S. G., Hallahan, D. P., Cohen, S. B., and Kauffman, J. M., "The Development of Visual Selective Attention and Verbal Rehearsal in Learning Disabled Boys," *Journal of Learning Disabilities,* 1977, vol. 10, pp. 491–500; Lovrich, D., and Stamm, J. S., "Event-Related Potential and Behavioral Correlates of Attention in Reading Retardation," *Journal of Clinical Neuropsychology,* 1983, vol. 5, pp. 13–57.

56. Hallahan, D. P., Tarver, S. G., Kauffman, J. M., and Graybeal, N. L., "A Comparison of the Effects of Reinforcement and Response Cost of the Selective Attention of Learning Disabled Children," *Journal of Learning Disabilities,* 1978, vol. 11, pp. 430–38.

57. Ibid., p. 437.

58. For example, one study failed to find a "motivation effect" using a scheme in which children could earn points to buy toys (perhaps not as big a payoff as hard cash!). Regardless of motivation, however, attention performance of learning-disabled children improved the *second* time they were tested. Although the disabled and normal learners did not do equally well in the second session on all attention measures, practice did produce equal responses on some and considerably closed the gap on others. Exactly how "practice" had benefited the learning-disabled youngsters is not certain, but it appears that they might have "learned more efficient methods of performing on these experimental tasks." Some anecdotal observations reported in the study illustrate group differences in strategy and organization and are interesting in ways that go beyond the immediate meaning of the research. Even though the learning-disabled children showed that they understood the task before they were tested the first time, their strategies while taking the test were not the same as those of the normal learners. For instance, the normal learners positioned their hands close to the buttons they had to press. By contrast, many learning disabled did not, while others placed their finger on a particular button and "impulsively" pressed it, thereby making numerous errors (Kistner, J. A., "Attentional Deficits of Learning-Disabled Children: Effects of Rewards and Practice," *Journal of Abnormal Child Psychology,* 1985, vol. 13, pp. 19–31).

59. Lovrich and Stamm, "Event-related potential," pp. 13–37.

60. Ibid., p. 34.

61. Schworm, R. W., "The Effects of the Selective Attention on the Decoding Skills of Children with Learning Disabilities," *Journal of Learning Disabilities,* 1979, vol. 12, pp. 639–44.

62. Ibid., p. 642.

63. Fleisher, Soodak, & Jelin, "Selective Attention Deficits," p. 140.

A common method of encouraging attention has been to have children "self-monitor" their attention while they are engaged in a task. For example, the children listen to a tone, sounded periodically on a tape recorder, that cues them to think about whether they are paying attention when they hear it. They might be asked simply to reply yes or no to themselves, or to write the answer on an attention questionnaire. This method has been shown to increase attention and improve academic work in learning-disabled children and to have had an effect lasting after the training period ended (Hallahan, D. P., and Sapona, R., "Self-Monitoring of Attention with Learning Disabled Children: Past Research and Current Issues," *Journal of Learning Disabilities,* 1983, vol. 16, pp. 616–20).

64. Fleisher, Soodak, and Jelin, "Selective Attention Deficits," p. 140.

3 Language Deficits, Memory Deficits, and LD Subtypes

1. e.e. cummings, "nobody loses all the time," *e.e. cummings: collected poems* (N.Y.: Harcourt, Brace & Co., 1946).

2. Frith, U., "Experimental Approaches to Developmental Dyslexia: An Introduction," *Psychological Research,* 1981, vol. 43, pp. 97–109.

3. Feagans, L., and Short, E. J., "Developmental Differences in the Comprehension and Production of Narratives by Reading-Disabled and Normally Achieving Children," *Child Development,* 1984, vol. 55, pp. 1727–36; Andolina, C., "Syntactic Maturity and Vocabulary Richness of Learning Disabled

Children," *Journal of Learning Disabilities,* 1980, vol. 13, pp. 372–77; Knight-Arest, I., "Communicative Effectiveness of Learning Disabled and Normally Achieving 10- to 13-Year-Old Boys," *Learning Disability Quarterly,* 1984, vol. 7, pp. 237–45; Wiig, E. H., Semel, E. M., and Abele, E., "Perception and Interpretation of Ambiguous Sentences by Learning Disabled Twelve-Year-Olds," *Learning Disability Quarterly,* 1981, vol. 4, pp. 3–12; Wiig, E. H., Becker-Redding, U., and Semel, E. M., "A Cross-Cultural, Cross-Linguistic Comparison of Language Abilities of 7- to 8- and 12- to 13-Year-Old Children with Learning Disabilities," *Journal of Learning Disabilities,* 1983, vol. 16, pp. 576–85; Denckla, M. B., Rudel, R. G., and Broman, M., "Tests That Discriminate Between Dyslexic and Other Learning-Disabled Boys," *Brain and Language,* 1981, vol. 13, pp. 118–29; Vellutino, F. R., "Childhood Dyslexia: A Language Disorder," in Myklebust, H.R., ed., *Progress in Learning Disabilities,* vol. 5 (N.Y.: Grune & Stratton, 1983); Leong, C. K., "Cognitive Processing, Language Awareness, and Reading in Grade 2 and Grade 4 Children," *Contemporary Educational Psychology,* 1984, vol. 9, pp. 369–83; Williams, J. P., "Phonemic Analysis and How It Relates to Reading," *Journal of Learning Disabilities,* 1984, vol. 17, pp. 240–45.

4. Firth, "Experimental Approaches," pp. 102, 106.

5. Olson, R. K., "Disabled Reading Processes and Cognitive Profiles," p. 10, in Gray, D., and Kavanaugh, J., eds., *Biobehavioral Measures of Dyslexia* (Parkton, Md.: York, 1986).

6. For example, see Mann, V. A., Shankweiler, D., and Smith, S. T., "The Association Between Comprehension of Spoken Sentences and Early Reading Ability: The Role of Phonetic Representation," *Journal of Child Language,* 1984, vol. 11, pp. 627–43; Simms, R. B., and Crump, W. D., "Syntactic Development in the Oral Language of Learning Disabled and Normal Students at the Intermediate and Secondary Level," *Learning Disability Quarterly,* 1983, vol. 6, pp. 155–65.

7. Olson, "Disabled Reading Processes," p. 5.

8. Vellutino, *Dyslexia,* p. 304.

9. Baron, J., "Orthographic and Word-Specific Mechanisms in Children's Reading of Words," *Child Development,* 1979, vol. 50, pp. 60–72; Fox, B., and Routh, D. K., "Phonemic Analysis and Severe Reading Disability," *Journal of Psycholinguistic Research,* 1980, vol. 9, pp. 115–19; Helfgott, J. A., "Phonemic Segmentation and Blending Skills of Kindergarten Children: Implications for Beginning Reading Acquisition," *Contemporary Educational Psychology,* 1976, vol. 1, pp. 157–69; Treiman, R., "Onsets and Rimes as Units of Spoken Syllables: Evidence from Children," *Journal of Experimental Child Psychology,* 1985, vol. 39, pp. 161–81; Richardson, E., DiBenedetto, B., and Bradley, C. M., "The Relationship of Sound Blending to Reading Achievement," *Review of Educational Research,* 1977, vol. 47, pp. 319–34; Kochnower, J., Richardson, E., and DiBenedetto, B., "A Comparison of the Phonic Decoding Ability of Normal and Learning Disabled Children," *Journal of Learning Disabilities,* 1983, vol. 16, pp. 348–51; Bradley, L., and Bryant, P. E., "Difficulties in Auditory Organization as a Possible Cause of Reading Backwardness," *Nature,* 1978, vol. 271, pp. 746–47; Manis, F. R., and Morrison, F. J., "Reading Disability: A Deficit in Rule Learning?" in Siegel, L. S., and Morrison, F. J., eds., *Cognitive Development in Atypical Children* (N.Y.: Springer-Verlag, 1985); Stanovich, K. E., "Individual Differences in the Cognitive Processes of

Reading: 1. Word Decoding," *Journal of Learning Disabilities,* 1982, vol. 15, pp. 485–93; Shankweiler, D., Liberman, I. Y., Mark, L. S., Fowler, C. A., and Fischer, F. W., "The Speech Code and Learning to Read," *Journal of Experimental Psychology: Human Learning and Memory,* 1979, vol. 5, pp. 531–45; Godfrey, J. J., Syrdal-Lasky, A. K., Millay, K. K., and Knox, C. M., "Performance of Dyslexic Children on Speech Perception Tests," *Journal of Experimental Child Psychology,* 1981, vol. 32, pp. 401–24; Lundberg, I., Olofsson, A., and Wall, S., "Reading and Spelling Skills in the First School Years, Predicted from Phonemic Awareness Skills in Kindergarten," *Scandinavian Journal of Psychology,* 1980, vol. 21, pp. 159–73.

10. Liberman, I. Y., and Shankweiler, D., "Phonology and the Problems of Learning to Read and Write," *Remedial and Special Education,* 1985, vol. 6, pp. 8–17.

11. Not all researchers have been won over from perceptual to linguistic explanations of LD. For example, phonetic recognition problems—recognizing sounds and associating them with letters—are said to be caused by a general dysfunction in "temporal order processing," an impediment in perceiving sequential order (Tallal, P., "Auditory Temporal Perception, Phonics, and Reading Disabilities in Children," *Brain and Language,* 1980, vol. 9, pp. 182–98; Tallal, "Temporal or Phonetic Processing Deficit in Dyslexia? That Is the Question," *Applied Psycholinguistics,* 1984, vol. 5, pp. 167–69). This means a child might be able to process phonetic sounds individually but not sequentially, making word analysis and recognition difficult, if not impossible. Sounds in the middle or at the end of words might not be recognized, recalled, or processed within their respective places because the order of the sounds is mixed up. Other researchers, convinced that this is a retrogressive explanation in the field's progress toward a more accurate understanding of LD, have countered with studies demonstrating that phonological difficulties of disabled readers do indeed impair these readers' ability to distinguish sounds within words and so on, but that these children do not display "temporal-order-processing" deficits (Holmes, D. R., and McKeever, W. F., "Material Specific Serial Memory Deficits in Adolescent Dyslexics," *Cortex,* 1979, vol. 15, pp. 51–62; Katz, R. B., Shankweiler, D., and Liberman, I. Y., "Memory for Item Order and Phonetic Recoding in the Beginning Reader," *Journal of Experimental Child Psychology,* 1981, vol. 32, pp. 474–84; Katz, R. B., Healy, A. F., and Shankweiler, D., "On Accounting for Deficiencies in Order Memory Associated with Reading Difficulty: A Reply to Tallal," *Applied Psycholinguistics,* 1984, vol. 5, pp. 170–74).

12. Bradley, L., and Bryant, P. E., "Categorizing Sounds and Learning to Read—a Causal Connection," *Nature,* 1983, vol. 301, pp. 419–21.

13. Ibid., p. 419.

14. Goldstein, D. M., "Cognitive-Linguistic Functioning and Learning to Read in Preschoolers," *Journal of Educational Psychology,* 1976, vol. 68, pp. 680–88.

15. Ibid., p. 687.

16. For example, one study trained preschool and kindergarten prereaders in phonemic analysis of spoken syllables (such as how to put words together from segments—*huh* + *em* = *hem*—and conversely segmenting whole words), and found these children were more proficient than untrained children in learning and using spelling-sound relations in reading (Treiman, R., and Baron, J., "Phonemic-Analysis Training Helps Children Benefit from Spelling-Sound Rules," *Memory and Cognition,* 1983, vol. 4, pp. 382–89). Also see Wong, B. Y. L., and Sawatsky, D., "Sentence Elaboration and Retention of Good, Average and Poor Readers," *Learning Disability Quarterly,* 1984, vol. 7, pp. 229–36; Henderson, A. J., and Shores, R. E., "How Learning Disabled Students' Failure to Attend Suffixes Affects Their Oral Reading Performance," *Journal of Learning Disabilities,* 1982, vol. 15, pp. 178–82; Olson, J. L., Wong, B. Y. L., and Marx, R. W., "Linguistic and Metacognitive Aspects of Normally Achieving and Learning Disabled Children's Communication Process," *Learning Disability Quarterly,* 1983, vol. 6, pp. 289–304; Olofsson, A., and Lundberg, I., "Can Phonemic Awareness Be Trained in Kindergarten?" *Scandinavian Journal of Psychology,* 1983, vol. 24, pp. 35–44.

A slightly different approach to the issue of whether awareness of word sounds and structure is associated with experience or arises "spontaneously in the course of general cognitive growth" comes from a study of illiterate Portuguese peasants (Morais, J., Cary, L., Alegria, J., and Bertelson, P., "Does Awareness of Speech as a Sequence of Phones Arise Spontaneously?" *Cognition,* 1979, vol. 7, pp. 323–31). One group of peasants had attended adult illiteracy classes organized by the government, the army, or industry and had acquired a modicum of reading ability (reading levels were not specified); another had never received any instruction. When given a phonological-awareness task of adding or deleting consonants to words and nonwords to make other words or nonwords, the percentage of correct responses of the readers was high, that of the illiterates', quite low (for example, the readers scored 71 percent correct in adding consonants to nonwords; the illiterates, 19 percent). Additionally, although the scores of better readers were higher than those of poorer readers (adults who had not attained a literacy certificate), the latter group had markedly higher scores than adults who had never been instructed. Similar conclusions about the effect of educational experience on phonological awareness were reported in a study in China with adults who had experience with an alphabet and others who were taught only with Chinese characters. The former group developed phonological skills, but the latter did not (Read, C., Zhang, Y., Nie, H., and Ding, B., "The Ability to Manipulate Speech Sounds Depends on Knowing Alphabetic Spelling," paper presented at the Twenty-third International Congress of Psychology, Acapulco, Mexico, 1984).

17. Liberman and Shankweiler, "Phonology and the Problems of Learning," pp. 8–17.

18. Olofsson and Lundberg, "Can Phonemic Awareness," p. 41.

19. Bradley and Bryant, "Categorizing Sounds," p. 421 (emphasis added).

20. Morais, J., Cary, L., Alegria, J., and Bertelson, P., "Does awareness of speech," pp. 329–31.

21. Goldstein, "Cognitive-Linguistic Functioning," p. 687.

22. Vellutino, F. R., "Childhood Dyslexia: A Language Disorder," in Myklebust, H. R., ed., *Progress in Learning Disabilities,* vol. 5 (N.Y.: Grune & Stratton, 1983), p. 136.

23. For example, see Mann, V. A., and Liberman, I. Y., "Phonological Awareness and Verbal Short-Term Memory," *Journal of Learning Disabilities,* 1984, vol. 17, pp. 592–99; Olson, R. K., Davidson, B. J., Kliegl, R., and Davies, S. E., "Development of Phonetic Memory in Disabled and Normal

Readers," *Journal of Experimental Child Psychology,* 1984, vol. 37, pp. 187–206; Treiman, R., and Hirsh-Pasek, K., "Are There Qualitative Differences in Reading Behavior Between Dyslexics and Normal Readers?" *Memory & Cognition,* 1985, vol. 13, pp. 357–64.

24. Frith, "Experimental Approaches," p. 101.

25. Fox, B., and Routh, D. K., "Phonemic Analysis and Synthesis as Word-Attack Skills," *Journal of Educational Psychology,* 1976, vol. 68, pp. 70–74.

26. Also see related follow-up studies: Fox and Routh, "Phonemic Analysis and Severe Reading Disability"; Fox and Routh, "Reading Disability, Phonetic Analysis, and Dysphonetic Spelling: A Follow-up Study," *Journal of Clinical Child Psychology,* 1983, vol. 12, pp. 28–32.

27. For example, see Bradley, L. and Bryant, P., "A Tactile Approach to Reading," *British Journal of Special Education,* 1981, vol. 8, pp. 32–36.

28. Edwards, R., and Webb, J. R., *Analytical Reading Series* (N.Y.: Taintor & Co., 1866).

Another reading series published at the same time emphasized "articulation, syllabication, accent, emphasis, slur, [and] inflections . . . through simple Analysis of Words and of Phonetic Exercises." The teacher was told to "exercise the class" in "tonic," "subtonic," and "atonic" speech sounds, alone and in combination, "until each pupil can utter *consecutively* all the elementary sounds" (Parker, R. G., and Watson, J. M., *National Readers,* (N.Y.: A.S. Barnes & Co., 1868).

A recent U.S. Department of Education study on "what works" in public schools embraced phonics as the core of beginning reading (*What Works: Research About Teaching and Learning* (Washington, D.C.: U.S. Government Printing Office, 1986).

29. Chall, J., *Learning to Read: The Great Debate* (N.Y.: McGraw-Hill, 1967). An example of the debate outside the LD field can been seen in the titles of a commentary and of responses appearing in *Education Week.* The commentary, "Why Can't Johnny Read? We Taught Him Incorrectly" (June 12, 1985), was by Rudolf Flesch, a strong phonics advocate. A letter, "Systematic Phonics Alone Won't Help Johnny's Reading Problem," followed (September 4, 1985). It in turn elicited a reply, " 'Ignorant' Opposition to Phonics Instruction Hinders Literacy Efforts" (October 2, 1985).

30. For example, see Ellis, N. C., and Miles, T. R., "A Lexical Encoding Deficiency I: Experimental Evidence," in Pavlidis and Miles, eds., *Dyslexia Research;* Smith, C. R., *Learning Disabilities: The Interaction of Learner, Task, and Setting* (Boston: Little, Brown & Co., 1983); Vellutino, *Dyslexia;* Vellutino, "Childhood Dyslexia."

31. Oldfield, R. C., and Wingfield, A., "Response Latencies in Naming Objects," *The Quarterly Journal of Experimental Psychology,* 1965, vol. 17, part 4, pp. 273–81; Newcombe, F., Oldfield, R. C., Ratcliff, G., and Wingfield, A., "Recognition and Naming of Object-Drawings by Men with Focal Brain Wounds," *Journal of Neurology, Neurosurgery and Psychiatry,* 1971, vol. 34, pp. 329–40.

32. Denckla, M. B., and Rudel, R. G., "Naming of Object-Drawings by Dyslexic and Other Learning Disabled Children," *Brain and Language,* 1976, vol. 3, pp. 1–15.

33. For example, see Rudel, R. G., "Neuroplasticity: Implications for Development and Education," In Chall, J. S., and Mirsky, A.F., eds., *Education and the Brain* (Chicago: University of Chicago Press, 1978); Rudel, R. G., Denckla, M. B., and Broman, M., "The Effect of Varying Stimulus Context on Word-Finding Ability: Dyslexia Further Differentiated from Other Learning Disabilities," *Brain and Language,* 1981, vol. 13, pp. 130–144; Denckla, Rudel, and Broman, "Tests that Discriminate Between Dyslexic and Other Learning-Disabled Boys," *Brain and Language,* 1981, vol. 13, pp. 118–29.

34. The dyslexia researchers were interested in finding a diagnosis for "minimal brain dysfunction" (MBD) that would distinguish between MBD with and without dyslexia. MBD has been criticized for its unsubstantiated criteria, such as neurological "soft signs," and is rarely spoken of in LD circles these days. However, to evaluate the naming studies, I will accept the identification of one group of children as dyslexic.

35. Their similar performance can be seen in the fourth category, for which each group identified correctly 90 percent of the objects (anchor, cigarette, screw, typewriter, and windmill).

36. For ages eight through ten (the ages for which dyslexics and normal children were matched for all the analyses), the mean for normal children was 18.6; for the dyslexics it was 17.7. The normal group's median score of objects correctly identified was 19; the dyslexics' was 18. In the distribution of scores, the normals had the greater number of higher scores, but also had more scores lower than those of the dyslexics.

37. For the other two error categories, "wrong name" and "not known," the error percentages of the two groups were approximately the same.

38. In the dyslexia study the researchers discussed the dyslexics' errors for words in the less frequent categories (five, six, and seven), but for reasons not explained, comparable figures were not given for the the normal children; hence comparison to figures in the veterans' study cannot be made.

39. Denckla and Rudel, "Naming of Object-Drawings," p. 12.

40. Ibid., p. 11 (emphasis added).

41. Another example of this logic comes from research discussed later in this chapter. Analogies were drawn between brain-damaged adults and reading-disabled children, on the assumption that evidence from acquired dyslexia "can furnish suggestions for the construction of neuropsychological models of developmental dyslexia" (Doehring, D. G., Trites, R. L., Patel, P. G., and Fiedorowicz, A. M., *Reading Disabilities: The Interaction of Reading, Language, and Neuropsychological Deficits* (N.Y.: Academic Press, 1981), p. 2.

42. Denckla, M. B., and Rudel, R. G., "Rapid Automatized Naming (R.A.N.): Dyslexia Differentiated from Other Learning Disabilities," *Neuropsychologia,* 1976, vol. 14, pp. 471–79; Spring, C. and Capps, C., "Encoding Speed, Rehearsal, and Probed Recall of Dyslexic Boys," *Journal of Educational Psychology,* 1974, vol. 66, pp. 780–86; Wolf, M., "The Word Retrieval Process and Reading in Children and Aphasics," in Nelson, K., ed., *Children's Language,* vol. 3 (N.Y.: Gardner, 1981); Rubin, H., and Liberman, I. Y., "Exploring the Oral and Written Language Errors Made by Language Disabled Children," *Annals of Dyslexia,* 1983, vol. 33, pp. 111–20; Rudel, "Neuroplasticity"; Rudel, Denckla, and Broman, "The Effect of Varying Stimulus"; Denckla, Rudel, and Broman, "Tests That Discriminate."

43. The argument that slower naming translates into a naming deficit can be challenged, because concentration, attention, motivation, and problem-solving strategy also factor into naming tasks. For example, to test color naming, Denckla and Rudel used a chart of five colors (red, green, black, blue, and yellow) which were repeated (as circles or squares—the study does not say) fifty times in random sequence. The normal children required approximately fifty-five seconds to name the fifty colors, the dyslexics about sixty-five. What does this ten-second difference mean? It is not necessarily due to the dyslexics' ability to recall (retrieve). For example, if the reader is sitting in a room with a shelf of books, he or she might try naming their colors in sequence. After naming the colors of several books, the reader will find that the task requires not only the ability to name colors but also a great deal of concentration, focus, and motivation. Diligent focusing from one book to another without stop will be necessary; any lapse in concentration will interfere with the process and might make the reader lose her or his place. If each color is not attended to, there might be some confusion, especially if there are no other cues, such as a book name, in returning to the color sequence. If the reader were to look at the color of the book following the one presently named, the naming process could be speeded markedly. If to all this any personal insecurities of a poor test-taker are added, he or she will tend to go a bit slower to ensure the sequence is correct. And if the reader is not interested in the task, he or she might go through it lazily, in semipassive resistance.

Two researchers who have devoted most of their work to studying language disabilities noted: "an error in naming does not automatically reveal its source, which can only be discovered by further analysis. The experiments needed to pinpoint the source of mistakes in naming have rarely been carried out," (Liberman and Shankweiler, "Phonology and the Problems of Learning," p. 12). (They argue that phonological, not neurological problems may cause naming difficulties.)

The validity of the general naming-deficit thesis was questioned in a study that found no differences in the time it took poor and normal readers to name colors, digits, or pictures of objects (kite, hammer, giraffe). Not surprisingly, the poor readers did take more time to identify *words*—in this case, the names of the objects. Also not surprising was the finding that the more syllables a word had, the longer it took poor readers to identify it. But, most important, there were no differences in response times to pictures with objects the names of which varied in number of syllables; nor were there time differences between poor and normal readers. The researchers concluded that the contrast between response times to pictures and words seems "to rule out some general name retrieval deficit by less skilled readers" (Perfetti, C. A., Finger, E., and Hogaboam, T., "Sources of Vocalization Latency Differences Between Skilled and Less Skilled Young Readers," *Journal of Educational Psychology,* 1978, vol. 70, pp. 730–39).

The conclusions of naming research have been questioned in several other respects as well, including their use of a methodology that exaggerates group differences and the weakness of the correlation between naming speed and reading. For a summary of these criticisms see Stanovich, K. E., "Cognitive Processes and the Reading Problems of Learning Disabled Children: Evaluating the Assumption of Specificity," in Torgesen, J., and Wong, B., eds., *Learning Disabilities: Some New Perspectives* (N.Y.: Academic Press, 1986).

44. Bee, H. L., Barnard, K. E., Eyres, S. J., Gray, C. A., Hammond, M. A., Spietz, A. L., Snyder, C., and Clark, B., "Prediction of IQ and Language Skill from Perinatal Status, Child Performance, Family Characteristics, and Mother-Child Interaction," *Child Development*, 1982, vol. 53, pp. 1134–56.

45. Torgesen, J. K., "Memory Processes in Reading Disabled Children," *Journal of Learning Disabilities*, 1985, vol. 18, pp. 350–57; also see Jorm, A. F., "Specific Reading Retardation and Working Memory: A Review," *British Journal of Psychology*, 1983, vol. 74, pp. 311–42.

46. Torgesen, "Memory Processes," p. 352. For a discussion of these strategies also see: Bauer, R. H., "Memory, Acquisition, and Category Clustering in Learning-Disabled Children," *Journal of Experimental Child Psychology*, 1979(a), vol. 27, pp. 365–83; Bauer, "Information Processing As a Way of Understanding and Diagnosing Learning Disabilities," in Reid, D. K., and Swanson, H. L., eds., *Topics in Learning and Learning Disabilities: Controversy, Strategy or Capacity Deficit* (Gaithersburg, Md.: Aspen, 1982); Bauer, R. H., and Emhert, J., "Information Processing in Reading-Disabled and Nondisabled Children," *Journal of Experimental Child Psychology*, 1984, vol. 37, pp. 271–81; Dallago, M. L. L., and Moelly, B. E., "Free Recall in Boys in Normal and Poor Reading Levels as a Function of Task Manipulations," *Journal of Experimental Child Psychology*, 1980, vol. 30, pp. 62–78; Torgesen, J. K., and Goldman, T., "Verbal Rehearsal and Short-Term Memory in Reading-Disabled Children," *Child Development*, 1977, vol. 48, pp. 56–60; Torgesen, J. K., and Houck, D. G., "Processing Deficiencies of Learning-Disabled Children Who Perform Poorly on the Digit Span Test," *Journal of Educational Psychology*, 1980, vol. 72, pp. 141–60; Torgesen, J. K., Murphy, H. A., and Ivey, C., "The Influence of an Orienting Task on the Memory Performance of Children with Reading Problems," *Journal of Learning Disabilities*, 1979, vol. 12, pp. 396–401.

47. Jorm, "Specific Reading Retardation," p. 330. Also, Chi, M. T., "Short-Term Memory Limitations in Children: Capacity or Processing Deficits," *Memory & Cognition*, 1976, vol. 4, pp. 559–72: "what appears to be a [short-term memory] capacity limitation in children is actually a deficit in the processing strategies, as well as a deficit in processing speeds. Both of these deficiencies result from a limited [long-term memory] semantic and recognition knowledge base, which presumably improves with age through cumulative learning."

48. Torgesen, "Memory processes," p. 352. Also, Jorm, "Specific Reading Retardation," p. 336: "There is clearly an association between specific reading retardation and deficient performance in certain memory tasks. However, it cannot necessarily be concluded that memory deficit is a cause of reading retardation."

49. Swanson, L., "Verbal encoding effects on the visual short-term memory of learning disabled and normal readers," *Journal of Educational Psychology*, 1978, 70, 539–544; Byrne, B. & Shea, P., "Semantic and phonetic memory codes in beginning readers," *Memory & Cognition*, 1979, 7, 333–338.

50. For example, see Cermak, L. S., "Information Processing Deficits in Children with Learning Disabilities," *Journal of Learning Disabilities*, 1983, vol. 16, pp. 599–605; Liberman, I. Y., Mann, V. A., Shankweiler, D., and Werfelman, M., "Children's Memory for Recurring Linguistic and Non-linguistic Material in Relation to Reading Ability," *Cortex,* 1982, vol. 18, pp. 367–75; Katz, Shankweiler, and Liberman, "Memory for Item Order"; Mann and Liberman, "Phonological Awareness"; Jorm, "Specific Reading Retardation."

51. Stanovich, K. E., "Individual Differences in the Cognitive Processes of Reading: II. Text-Level Processes," *Journal of Learning Disabilities,* 1982, vol. 15, pp. 549–54. Also: Stanovich, "Explaining the Variance in Reading Ability in Terms of Psychological Processes: What Have We Learned?" *Annals of Dyslexia,* 1985(a), vol. 35, pp. 67–96; Torgesen, "Performance of Reading Disabled Children on Serial Memory Tasks," *Reading Research Quarterly,* 1978–79, vol. 14, pp. 57–87.

52. Bauer, R. H., "Memory Processes in Children with Learning Disabilities: Evidence for Deficient Rehearsal," *Journal of Experimental Child Psychology,* 1977, vol. 24, pp. 415–30; Bauer, R. H., "Recall After a Short Delay and Acquisition in Learning Disabled and Nondisabled Children," *Journal of Learning Disabilities,* 1979, vol. 12, pp. 30–41; Cermak, L. S., Goldberg-Warter, J., DeLuca, D., Cermak, S., and Drake, C., "The Role of Interference in the Verbal Retention Ability of Learning Disabled Children," *Journal of Learning Disabilities,* 1981, vol. 14, pp. 291–95.

53. Fisk, J. L., and Rourke, B. P., "Neuropsychological Subtyping of Learning-Disabled Children: History, Methods, Implications," *Journal of Learning Disabilities,* 1983, vol. 16, pp. 529–31.

54. Rourke, B., ed., *Neuropsychology of Learning Disabilities* (N.Y.: Guilford Press, 1985), pp. vii–viii (emphasis added).

55. Two key papers in the development of subtype analysis are: Boder, E., "Developmental Dyslexia: A Diagnostic Approach Based on Three Atypical Reading-Spelling Patterns," *Developmental Medicine and Child Neurology,* 1973, vol. 15, pp. 663–87; and Mattis, S., French, J. H., and Rapin, I., "Dyslexia in Children and Young Adults: Three Independent Neuropsychological Syndromes," *Developmental Medicine and Child Neurology,* 1975, vol. 17, pp. 150–63. These and related earlier papers will not be discussed because recent subtyping research, the focus of this section, has been recognized as advancing upon this work.

56. Fisk, J. L., and Rourke, B. P. "Identification of Subtypes of Learning-Disabled Children at Three Age Levels: A Neuropsychological, Multivariate Approach," *Journal of Clinical Neuropsychology,* 1979, vol. 1, pp. 289–310 (emphasis added).

57. Ibid., p. 291. The central assumption of another subtyping study was that "reading disabilities could result from the impairment of specific abilities that are associated with specific neurological dysfunctions," and that "different types of neurological dysfunction can lead to different types of reading disabilities" (Doehring, et al., *Reading Disabilities,* p. 2).

58. Rourke, B. P., and Fisk, J. L., "Socio-Emotional Disturbances of Learning Disabled Children: The Role of Central Processing Deficits," *Bulletin of the Orton Society,* 1981, vol. 31, pp. 77–88.

59. Satz, P., and Morris, R., "Learning Disability Subtypes: A Review." In Pirozzolo, F. J., and Wittrock, M. C., eds., *Neuropsychological and Cognitive Processes in Reading* (N.Y.: Academic Press, 1981). For support of this recommendation also see McKinney, J. D., "The Search for Subtypes of Specific

Learning Disability," *Journal of Learning Disabilities,* 1984, vol. 17, pp. 43–50.

60. Doehring, Trites, Patel, and Fiedorowicz, *Reading Disabilities,* p. 7.

61. Ibid., p. 62.

62. Ibid., p. 65.

63. Ibid., p. 143 (emphasis added).

64. For example, see Charnley, A. H., and Jones, H. A., *The Concept of Success in Adult Literacy* (Cambridge, England: Huntington, 1979); Eberle, A., and Robinson, S., *The Adult Illiterate Speaks Out: Personal Perspectives on Learning to Read and Write* (Washington, D.C.: National Institute of Education, 1980); Kozol, J., *Prisoners of Silence: Breaking the Bonds of Adult Illiteracy in the United States* (N.Y.: Continuum, 1980); Mezirow, J., Darkenwald, G. G., and Knox, A. B., *Last Gamble on Education: Dynamics of Adult Basic Education* (Washington, D.C.: Adult Education Association of the U.S.A., 1975).

65. Lyon, R., Stewart, N., and Freedman, D., "Neuropsychological Characteristics of Empirically Derived Subgroups of Learning Disabled Readers," *Journal of Clinical Neuropsychology,* 1982, vol. 4, pp. 343–65. In another study, because all the children did not immediately fall into distinct groups, the "arbitrary decision" was again made to place the child in the subtype for which his or her score was the highest to "maximize the number of subjects classified into the three types of reading disabilities," and also to avoid having a considerable number of children categorized as "mixed subtypes." Each child and each group could have been divided up in different ways depending upon where the investigators decided to draw the cutoff line for each group. The researchers chose a 40 percent cutoff for the percentage of factors making up the test score profile of a child, rather than 50 percent, which would have selected "purer" subtypes but also would have subtyped fewer children. However, at the 40 percent cutoff some children's test profiles were mixed because they could have been placed in more than one category. In these cases—26 percent, or twenty-three of eighty-eight—the child was put in the category in which he or she had the highest percentage of factors (Doehring, Trites, Patel, and Fiedorowicz, *Reading Disabilities,* p. 86).

66. Fisk and Rourke, "Identification of Subtypes."

67. Schauer, C. A., *The Developmental Relationship Between Neuropsychological and Achievement Variables: A Cluster Analysis Study,* unpublished doctoral dissertation, University of Florida, summarized in Fletcher, J. M., and Satz, P., "Cluster Analysis and the Search for Learning Disability Subtypes," in Rourke, B. P., ed., *Neuropsychology of Learning Disabilities: Essentials of Subtype Analysis* (N.Y.: Guilford, 1985) p. 56.

A related longitudinal study also found subtype "variations in ability patterns over time." For example, one subgroup had poorer verbal skills than another subgroup at age five, but by age eleven "the initial differences on verbal skills were not apparent." Conversely, at age five, both groups were "equally deficient on visual-spatial skills," but by age eleven one group had better visual-spatial skills than the other (Fletcher and Satz, "Cluster Analysis," in Rourke, *Neuropsychology of Learning Disabilities*).

68. Doehring, Trites, Patel, and Fiedorowicz, *Reading Disabilities.*

69. Ibid., p. 186.

70. Ibid., 154.

71. Ibid., 186.

72. Doehring, D. G., "Reading Disability Subtypes: Interaction of Reading and Nonreading Deficits," In Rourke, *Neuropsychology of Learning Disabilities,* p. 137.

73. For example, another group had "relatively poor performance" on the Raven Matrices, the Right-Left discrimination test, the tactual performance test, and the finger localization test. The comparative scores of the first were 56, 56, and 50; for the second they were 50, 50, and 48. On the second test, however, even these differences did not hold up in a separate analysis when the children were selected by "stringent criteria of reading disability." The group that previously had had the lowest score now had 53, the *highest* score among the groups. The third test showed the same pattern as the second.

The only test that did show a significant difference among the subgroups was the finger localization test. The meaning of this finding is ambiguous because the task involves a number of strategies for organizing information, including counting, persistence, and differentiation (keeping in mind that the thumb is counted as a finger).

What did the investigators conclude from a set of tests in which only one, of dubious interpretation, differentiated the subgroup? "Relatively poor performance by [this subgroup] on the Raven Matrices, Right-Left Discrimination, and Tactual Performance tests, along with a marked deficiency in nondominant finger localization, would be compatible with posterior cerebral dysfunction, particularly of the right hemisphere" (Doehring, Trites, Patel, and Fiedorowicz, *Reading Disabilities,* p. 186).

74. Another study, after counseling that "caution should be exercised in going beyond hypothesizing," said this about the test scores of one subgroup:

> . . . the types of visual perceptual deficits could be associated with impairment of a number of brain areas. These include (1) the frontal lobes, where the behavioral sequelae of impairment may include a decreased capacity for active visual perception and visual comprehension of complex visual stimuli such as thematic pictures and picture series . . . (2) the posterior left association region . . . [and] (3) the posterior right parietal-occipital region. (Lyon, Stewart, and Freedman, "Neuropsychological Characteristics," p. 358).

Questions about arbitrary sorting of test scores that could have landed a child in one subgroup as easily as in another, the ambiguous meaning of the "neuropsychological" tests, the weak association of neuropsychological test profiles and types of LD did not temper this or similar interpretations of other subtypes in the study. As is common in LD research, "hypothesizing" does not include alternative hypotheses of the test scores.

Another example where tests metamorphosed into measures solely of neuropsychological processing comes from a study using the information subtest of the Wechsler intelligence test. This subtest, heavily dependent on acquired general and academic information, became an "auditory-verbal" test (presumably because the child listens to a question and answers orally). The arithmetic test was transformed into a test of "sequencing" (Petrauskas, R. J., and Rourke, B. P., "Identification of Subtypes of Retarded Readers: A Neuropsychological, Multivariate Approach," *Journal of Clinical Neuropsychology,* 1979, vol. 1, pp. 17–37). Also see Lyon, Stewart, and Freedman, "Neuropsychological Characteristics," pp. 357–58). In the research by Doehring et al. in

Reading Disabilities, tests heavily dependent on knowledge of words, word sounds, and spelling became tests strictly of cognitive processing: tests of visual matching, auditory-visual matching, or visual scanning. For example, in the auditory-visual matching test, the children listened to a tape-recorded series of letters, words, and syllables, and then matched the sample to one of three printed choices. A child might hear *find* and match it to one of three words presented, *mind, film,* or *find;* or might match the syllable *cla* to *cra, cla,* or *pla.* The visual matching-to-sample tests involved matching words such as *did* or *long,* or syllables such as *sig,* to one of three choices. The visual scanning test involved finding and underlining numbers, letters, words, or word strings in a series of letters or words (for example, find *spot* in "post tops stop spot sotp psot").

75. Fletcher and Satz, "Cluster Analysis."

76. Lyon, R., and Watson, B., "Empirically Derived Subgroups of Learning Disabled Readers: Diagnostic Characteristics," *Journal of Learning Disabilities,* 1981, vol. 14, pp. 256–61; Lyon, R., Watson, B., Reitta, S., Porch, B., and Rhodes, J., "Selected Linguistic and Perceptual Abilities of Empirically Derived Subgroups of Learning Disabled Readers," *Journal of School Psychology,* 1981, vol. 19, pp. 152–66.

77. Lyon and Watson, "Empirically Derived Subgroups," p. 261. For a similar observation expressed in a recent summary of this and related work, see Lyon, G. R., "Educational Validation Subtypes of Learning Disability Subtypes," in Rourke, *Neuropsychology of Learning Disabilities.* For another example of a failure to match reading and cognitive subtype patterns see: Lovett, M. W. "A Developmental Perspective on Reading Dysfunction; Accuracy and Rate Criteria in the Subtyping of Dyslexic Children," *Brain and Language,* 1984, vol. 22, pp. 67–91. In this study, for dyslexics divided into two subtypes of reading problems, no differences were found between the groups for most of the subtyping tests, among them tests of language function and memory. Some differences were found in tests of morphology, but as I mentioned, performance on these depends heavily on sociological factors.

78. Doehring, "What Do We Know About Reading Disabilities? Closing the Gap Between Research and Practice," *Annals of Dyslexia,* 1983, vol. 33, pp. 175–83.

79. Doehring, "Subtypes of Reading Disorders: Implications for Remediation," *Annals of Dyslexia,* 1984, vol. 34, pp. 205–16. Similarly cheerless is the conclusion that the statistical procedures for subtyping do "not insure that the clusters are meaningful, or that they have any prognostic value. It is difficult to see how the discovery of LD subtypes *per se* is useful unless they can be shown to predict different developmental outcomes" (McKinney, "The Search for Subtypes," p. 48).

80. *Waverly* (N.Y.: Publishers Plate Renting Co., 1871), p. 28.

A seeming exception to all this unfruitful work is a series of papers, by leaders in subtype analysis, that did report a correlation between academic performance (such as good reading and spelling but poor arithmetic skills) and scores on neuropsychological tests. This study, however, used a method that appears to have guaranteed that this correlation would be found. Forty-five children between the ages of nine and fourteen were divided into three groups for the research. Interestingly enough, they "were selected from over 2000 children *who had received an extensive battery of neuropsychological tests*" (emphasis added). This exact wording is found in all the original studies. Thus, before the "investigations" began, the researchers knew not only the children's academic achievement patterns but also their scores on an extensive number of tests, perhaps among them the tests reported in the research papers (the "extensive battery" is never discussed). Given this procedure, one can only wonder, for example, how the researchers chose the group that demonstrated the most differentiated neuropsychological test pattern, the subgroup with achievement higher in reading and spelling than in arithmetic. Was this group of fifteen the only fifteen with this academic pattern out of two thousand children evaluated? Or were the fifteen selected because the investigators knew their neuropsychological test pattern, a pattern that would neuropsychologically explain the academic achievement? Asking this another way, if children had been selected *without* the prescreening, would the study have found the same number of them with neuropsychological test results similar to the fifteen?

The investigators published a series of papers on these forty-five children said to be reports in a *series* of investigations (for example, "This is the third study of the neuropsychological significance"). Because of that, and because publication of the papers spanned five years, it is implied that batteries of tests were administered over time. However, the age charts show that the children were the exact same ages in the first study, published in 1978, and the third study, published in 1983. In both studies, the group with "high reading and spelling and low arithmetic" averaged 140.93 months old, with a standard deviation of 18.53 months. Given these figures and their precise decimal fractions, what else can be assumed other than that the "series" of tests were actually administered at the same time?

See Rourke, B. P., and Finlayson, M. A. J., "Neuropsychological Significance of Variations in Patterns of Academic Performance: Verbal and Visual-Spatial Abilities," *Journal of Abnormal Child Psychology,* 1978, vol. 6, pp. 121–33; Strang, J. D., and Rourke, B. P., "Concept-Formation/Non-verbal Reasoning Abilities of Children Who Exhibit Specific Academic Problems with Arithmetic," *Journal of Clinical Child Psychology,* 1983, vol. 12, pp. 33–39; Strang, and Rourke, "Arithmetic Disability Subtypes: The Neuropsychological Significance of Specific Arithmetical Impairment in Childhood," in Rourke, *Neuropsychology of Learning Disabilities;* Rourke, B. P. and Strang, J. D., "Neuropsychological Significance of Variations in Patterns of Academic Performance: Motor, Psychomotor, and Tactile-Perceptual Abilities," *Journal of Pediatric Psychology,* 1978, vol. 3, pp. 62–66.

4 Technology and the Identification of Neurological Deficits

1. Schulman, S., "Facing the Invisible Handicap," *Psychology Today,* February 1986, pp. 58–64.

2. Hynd, G. W., and Hynd, C. R., "Dyslexia: Neuroanatomical/Neurolinguistic Perspectives," *Reading Research Quarterly,* 1984 (a), vol. 19, pp. 482–49; Hynd and Hynd, "Dyslexia: Two Priorities for the 1980's," *International Journal of Neuroscience,* 1984 (b), vol. 23, pp. 223–30.

3. Blakeslee, S., "Brain Studies Shed Light on Disorders," *New York Times* (Fall Education Survey), November 11, 1984, p. 45.

4. Witty, P. A., and Kopel, D., "Sinistral and Mixed Manual-Ocular Behavior in Reading Disability," *Journal of Educational Psychology,* 1936, vol. 27, pp. 119–34; Gates, A. I., and Bond, G. L., "Relation of Handedness, Eyesighting, and Acuity Dominance to Reading," *Journal of Educational Psychology,* 1936, vol. 27, pp. 450–56; Balow, I. H., "Lateral Dominance Characteristics and Reading Achievement in First Grade," *Journal of Psychology,* 1963, vol. 55, pp. 323–28; Belmont, I. H., and Birch, H. G., "Lateral Dominance, Lateral Awareness and Reading Disability," *Child Development,* 1965, vol. 36, pp. 57–71; Coleman, R. I., and Deutsch, C. P., "Lateral Dominance and Right-Left Discrimination: A Comparison of Normal and Retarded Readers," *Perceptual and Motor Skills,* 1964, vol. 19, pp. 43–50; de Hirsch, K., Jansky, J. J., and Langford, W. S., *Predicting Reading Failure* (NY: Harper & Row, 1966); Crinella, F. M., Beck, F. W., and Robinson, J. W., "Unilateral Dominance Is Not Related to Neuropsychological Integrity," *Child Development,* 1971, vol. 42, pp. 2033–54.

5. Zurif, E. B., and Carson, G., "Dyslexia in Relation to Cerebral Dominance and Temporal Analysis," *Neuropsychologia,* 1970, vol. 8, pp. 351–61; Witelson, S. F., and Rabinovitch, S., "Hemispheric Speech Lateralization in Children with Auditory-Linguistic Deficits," *Cortex,* 1972, vol. 8, pp. 412–26; Yeni-Komshian, G. H., Isenberg, D., and Goldberg, H., "Cerebral Dominance and Reading Disability: Left Visual Field Deficit in Poor Readers," *Neuropsychologia,* 1975, vol. 13, pp. 83–94; Obrzut, J. E., Hynd, G. W., Obrzut, A., and Pirozzolo, F. J., "Effect of Directed Attention on Cerebral Asymmetries in Normal and Learning-Disabled Children," *Developmental Psychology,* 1981, vol. 17, pp. 118–25.

6. A study that divided disabled readers into subgroups found that "ear asymmetry, as measured by dichotic right-ear advantage, did not discriminate normal from dyslexic groups" and that "laterality differences as inferred from REA on a dichotic task may not be a consistent factor in differentiating diagnostic reading groups" (Obrzut, J. E., "Dichotic Listening and Bisensory Memory Skills in Qualitatively Diverse Dyslexic Readers," *Journal of Learning Disabilities,* 1979, vol. 12, pp. 304, 312). Another study reports a few dichotic-listening differences in subgroups of disabled readers but presented only summary scores of group differences and not a single piece of information about their respective ear scores. Therefore, there is no way of knowing, as was possible from the data in the other subgroup study, exactly how the groups differed in laterality (Malatesha, R. N., and Dougan, D. R., "Clinical Subtypes of Developmental Dyslexia: Resolution of an Irresolute Problem," in Malatesha, R. N., and Aaron, P. G., eds., *Reading Disorders: Varieties and Treatments* (N.Y.: Academic Press, 1982).

7. Leong, C.K., "Lateralization in Severely Disabled Readers in Relation to Functional Cerebral Development and Synthesis of Information," in Knights and Bakker, *Neuropsychology of Learning Disorders.*

8. Hiscock, M., and Kinsbourne, M., "Asymmetries of Selective Listening and Attention Switching in Children," *Developmental Psychology,* 1980, vol. 16, pp. 70–82. Also see Hynd, G. W., Obrzut, J. E., Weed, W., and Hynd, C. R., "Development of Cerebral Dominance: Dichotic Listening Asymmetry in Normal and Learning Disabled Children," *Journal of Experimental Child*

Psychology, 1979, vol. 28, pp. 445–54; Nagafuchi, M., "Development of Dichotic and Monaural Hearing Abilities in Young Children," *Acta Otolaryngologica,* 1970, vol. 69, pp. 409–14; Geffner, D., and Hochberg, I., "Ear Laterality Preference of Children from Low and Middle Socio-Economic Levels on a Verbal Dichotic Listening Task," *Cortex,* 1971, vol. 7, pp. 193–203; Kinsbourne, M., "The Ontogeny of Cerebral Dominance," *Annals of the New York Academy of Sciences,* 1975, vol. 263, pp. 244–50.

9. One criticism is that the findings of dichotic-listening experiments do not square with what is known about brain hemispheres and language function (Satz, P., "Laterality Tests: An Inferential Problem," *Cortex,* 1977, vol. 13, pp. 208–12.). It has been confirmed that in a random group of 100 right-handed adults, *"at least* 95 would be expected to be left-brained for speech" (p. 209). Dichotic-listening research has found superior right-ear hearing in only about 70 percent of right-handers tested, suggesting that this percentage had speech functioning lateralized in the left hemisphere. Therefore, one could not predict whether a right-handed individual had left- or right-brained speech on the basis of a dichotic-listening test. For example, there is a 97 percent probability that people with a right-ear advantage have left-brain speech. (This statistic can be determined without dichotic-listening tests.) However, if a right-handed individual had a left-ear advantage, dichotic-listening tests would suggest a 10 percent probability that the person had right-brain speech (and of course a 90 percent likelihood of having left-brain speech). The figures come from several studies. In one, sodium amytal, a barbiturate, was injected into the arteries supplying blood to one side of the brain. The drug incapacitates one hemisphere for a few minutes, allowing administration of a test to determine lateralization functioning. See Wada, J., and Rasmussen, T., "Intracarotid Injection of Sodium Amytal for the Lateralization of Cerebral Speech Dominance: Experimental and Clinical Observations," *Journal of Neurosurgery,* 1960, vol. 17, pp. 266–82; Branch, C., Milner, B., and Rasmussen, J., "Intracarotid Sodium Amytal for the Lateralization of Cerebral Speech Dominance," *Journal of Neurosurgery,* 1964, vol. 21, pp. 399–405). Other research was done with aphasics (Kinsbourne, M., and Hiscock, M., "Cerebral Lateralization and Cognitive Development," in Chall, J. S., and Mirsky, A. F., eds., *Education and the Brain* [Chicago: National Society for the Study of Education, 1978]).

A slight twist to this conceptual contradiction is in a study that reported 69 percent of the right-handed good readers were right-ear superior, while "only 58% of the [right-handed] poor readers" showed this superiority (Bryden, M. P., "Laterality Effects in Dichotic Listening: Relations with Handedness and Reading Ability in Children," *Neuropsychologia,* 1970, vol. 8, pp. 443–50). If it is true that left-hemisphere-lateralized language functioning is essential for learning to read, the study leaves unexplained how 31 percent of the right-handers managed to become good readers without this structural organization. In addition, of course, the 11 percent difference between the groups explains little about the possible cause of the reading differences.

10. Hiscock, M., and Kinsbourne, M., "Laterality and Dyslexia: A Critical View," *Annals of Dyslexia,* 1982, vol. 32, pp. 177–228.

Normal children were asked to listen to digit names from a headphone. The children who were asked to listen first to sounds from the right headphone obtained a much higher (statistically significant) right-ear score than those asked to listen first with their left ear. These results were said to show that the children either had an "exaggerated right-ear advantage or no right-ear advantage at all, depending on the order in which they monitored left and right ears" (Hiscock, M., and Bergstrom, K. J., "The Lengthy Persistence of Primary Effects in Dichotic Listening," *Neuropsychologia,* 1982, vol. 20, pp. 43–53).

11. An example suggesting that experience influences dichotic listening comes from a study of adult musicians and nonmusicians who listened to violin melodies. After each presentation of two melodies heard simultaneously, each two seconds in length, the groups heard a single violin melody and were asked to match it to one of those heard dichotically. Musicians had more correct answers with the right ear than nonmusicians and also demonstrated right-ear superiority over the left. Nonmusicians performed better with the left ear. It is not important for the issue discussed here whether the researchers' hypothesis is exactly correct that musically adept individuals make greater use of a "left hemisphere sequential analytic mechanism." The main general conclusion for our purposes is that the experiment demonstrates an association between experience and brain-area function. (Johnson, P. R., "Dichotically-Stimulated Ear Differences in Musicians and Nonmusicians," *Cortex,* 1977, vol. 13, pp. 385–89).

12. Kinsbourne, M., "Cerebral Dominance, Learning, and Cognition," in Myklebust, H. R., ed., *Progress in Learning Disabilities* (N.Y.: Grune & Stratton, 1975), vol. 3; Caplan, B., and Kinsbourne, M., "Cerebral Lateralization, Preferred Cognitive Mode, and Reading Ability in Normal Children," *Brain and Language,* 1981, vol. 14, pp. 349–70; Morais, J., and Bertelson, P., "Laterality Effects in Dichotic Listening," *Perception,* 1973, vol. 2, pp. 107–11; Bryden, M. P., "Laterality Effects in Dichotic Listening: Relations with Handedness and Reading Ability in Children," *Neuropsychologia,* 1970, vol. 8, pp. 443–50; Inglis, J., and Sykes, D. H., "Some Sources of Variation in Dichotic Listening Performance in Children," *Journal of Experimental Child Psychology,* 1967, vol. 5, pp. 480–88; Hiscock, M., and Kinsbourne, M., "Selective Listening Asymmetry in Preschool Children," *Developmental Psychology,* 1977, vol. 13, pp. 217–24.

13. Hiscock and Kinsbourne, "Asymmetries of Selective Listening," p. 80.

14. Prior, M. R., Frolley, M., and Sanson, A., "Language Lateralization in Specific Reading Retarded Children and Backward Readers," *Cortex,* 1983, vol. 19, pp. 149–63.

15. Obrzut, J. E., and Hynd, G. W. "The Neurobiological and Neuropsychological Foundations of Learning Disabilities," *Journal of Learning Disabilities,* 1983, vol. 16, pp. 515–20.

16. Naylor, H., Lambert, N., Sassone, D. M., and Hardyck, C., "Lateral Asymmetry in Perceptual Judgments of Reading Disabled, Hyperactive and Control Children," *International Journal of Neuroscience,* 1980, vol. 10, pp. 135–43; Marcel, T., and Rajan, P., "Lateral Specialization for Recognition of Words and Faces in Good and Poor Readers," *Neuropsychologia,* 1975, vol. 13, pp. 489–97, Kershner, J. R., "Cerebral Dominance in Disabled Readers, Good Readers, and Gifted Children: Search for a Valid Model," *Child Development,* 1977, vol. 48, pp. 61–67; Bouma, H., and Legein, Ch. P., "Foveal and Parafoveal Recognition of Letters and Words by Dyslexics and by Average Readers," *Neuropsychologia,* 1977, vol. 15, pp. 69–80; Olson, M. E., "Laterality Differences in Tachistoscopic Word Recognition in Normal and Delayed Readers in Elementary School," *Neuropsychologia,* 1973, vol. 11, pp. 343–50.

17. In one study the right-visual-half-field scores were approximately the same for good and disabled readers for both words and numbers. Since the assumption in this research is that right-visual-half-field accuracy indicates active left-hemisphere processing, these results would seem to be a good sign for the disabled readers. But there was more to it: the disabled readers' left-visual-half-field scores were lower; conversely, this meant the good readers' were higher—that is, closer to their left-visual-half-field scores. By examining the data charts one could conclude that the normal readers had "mixed laterality" because their right and left-visual-half-field scores were approximately the same. However, the researchers interpreted the "significantly larger" degree of lateralization in the disabled readers to mean that they "suffer from some kind of processing deficit in the right hemisphere" because their relatively lower left-visual-half-field score suggested that "stimuli projected to the right visual cortex are the ones with which the poor readers have the most difficulty" (Yeni-Komshian, Isenberg, and Goldberg, "Cerebral Dominance and Reading Disability," p. 92).

The other study found asymmetrical lateralization for both good and disabled readers with verbal stimuli. Contrary to the previous study, while the disabled readers had lower right-visual-half-field scores, the left-half-field scores were about the same for both groups. This meant that disabled readers had less right-over-left (11.3 vs. 7.4) and good readers had greater right-over-left (14.35 vs. 7.85) activations. If we were to interpret the similar left-visual-half-field scores with the logic of the previous study they would mean that the poor readers do not have a processing deficit in the right hemisphere. However, here too there was more to it: the disabled readers did have lower right-half-field scores, which indicated that the good readers had "more asymmetrically" stored linguistic information (Marcel, T., Katz, L., and Smith, M., "Laterality and Reading Proficiency," *Neuropsychologia,* 1974, vol. 12, pp. 131–39).

18. McKeever, W. F. and VanDeventer, A. D., "Dyslexic Adolescents: Evidence of Impaired Visual and Auditory Language Processing Associated with Normal Lateralization of Responsivity," *Cortex,* 1975, vol. 11, pp. 361–78. Also see McKeever, W. F., and Huling, M. D., "Lateral Dominance in Tachistoscopic Word Recognition of Children at Two Levels of Ability," *Quarterly Journal of Experimental Psychology,* 1970, vol. 22, pp. 600–04.

An analysis of individual scores (an easy analysis to make because each group had no more than nine children) revealed the following. In the bilateral word-recognition test, the right-visual-half-field scores of three normal readers surpassed the dyslexics' scores. Without these three, the range of scores for dyslexics and normals is the same. In addition, three dyslexics and three normal readers had right-left scores *exactly the same.* Two of the normal readers had greater left- than right-half-field scores, the reverse of the other normal readers and of all dyslexics but one. Thus, only by group-score averages that include the three high scores in the normal group do the group scores appear drastically different.

19. Hiscock and Kinsbourne, "Laterality and Dyslexia."

20. Marcel, Katz, and Smith, "Laterality and Reading Proficiency"; White, M. J., "Laterality Differences in Perception," *Psychological Bulletin,* 1969, vol. 72, pp. 387–405; Salmaso, D., and Umilta, C., "Vowel Processing in the Left and Right Visual Fields," *Brain and Language,* 1982, vol. 16, pp. 147–57;

Kershner, J., Thomae, R., and Callaway, R., "Nonverbal Fixation Control in Young Children Induces a Left-Field Advantage in Digit Recall," *Neuropsychologia,* 1977, vol. 15, pp. 569–76; Hardyck, C., Tzeng, O. J. L., and Wang, W. S-Y., "Cerebral Lateralization of Function and Bilingual Decision Processes: Is Thinking Lateralized?" *Brain and Language,* 1978, vol. 5, pp. 56–71; Klein, D., Moscovitch, M., and Vigna, C., "Attentional Mechanisms and Perceptual Asymmetries in Tachistoscopic Recognition of Words and Faces," *Neuropsychologia,* 1976, vol. 14, pp. 55–66; Hellige, J. B., Cox, P. J., and Litvac, L., "Information Processing in the Cerebral Hemispheres: Selective Hemispheric Activation and Capacity Limitations," *Journal of Experimental Psychology: General,* 1979, vol. 108, pp. 251–79; Naylor, Lambert, Sassone, and Hardyck, "Lateral Asymmetry in Perceptual Judgments."

21. Ibid., p. 186.

22. Consider, for example, the semantic content of the language used in the experiments. Abstract nouns produce higher right-visual-half-field test scores than concrete, imaginable nouns. This suggests that the right hemisphere "is able to recognize a number of simple words"; that "the right cerebral hemisphere can contribute to the recognition of some types of words when they are presented" in the left visual field; and, that right-hemisphere functioning varies in its contribution to word identification. Therefore, a finding of smaller right-visual-field functioning "in poor readers may . . . be attributable to their having recognized . . . predominantly concrete, imageable words." In contrast, normal readers may have greater right-visual-field functioning because they are able to "recognize relatively more abstract, nonimageable words as well as concrete words" (Young, A. W., and Ellis, A. W., "Asymmetry of Cerebral Hemispheric Function in Normal and Poor Readers," *Psychological Bulletin,* 1981, vol. 89, pp. 183–90).

23. Ibid., p. 188.

24. Ibid., p. 188.

25. Ayers, F. W., and Torres, F. "The Incidence of EEG Abnormalities in a Dyslexic and a Control Group," *Journal of Clinical Psychology,* 1967, vol. 23, pp. 334–36; Hughes, J. R., "Electroencephalographic and Neurophysiological Studies in Dyslexia," in Benton, A. L., and Pearl, D., eds., *Dyslexia: An Appraisal of Current Knowledge* (N.Y.: Oxford, 1978).

26. Freeman, R. D., "Special Education and the Electroencephalogram: Marriage of Convenience," *Journal of Special Education,* 1967, vol. 2, pp. 61–73.

27. Hughes, "Electroencephalographic and Neurophysiological."

28. Coles, G. S., "The Learning-Disabilities Test Battery: Empirical and Social Issues," *Harvard Educational Review,* 1978, vol. 48, pp. 313–40.

29. Conner, C. K., "Critical Review of Electroencephalographic and Neurophysiological Studies in Dyslexia," in Benton and Pearl, *Dyslexia: An Appraisal.*

30. Pirozzolo, F. J., and Hansch, E. C., "The Neurobiology of Developmental Reading Disorders," in Malatesha, R. N., and Aaron, P. G., eds., *Reading Disorders: Varieties and Treatments* (N.Y.: Academic Press, 1982) pp. 215–232. (Emphasis added.)

31. Duane, D., "Neurobiological Correlates of Reading Disorders," *Journal of Educational Research,* 1983, vol. 77, pp. 5–15.

32. Coles, "The Learning-Disabilities Test Battery."

33. Restak, R. M., *The Brain: The Last Frontier* (N.Y.: Doubleday, 1979), p. 301; Restak, "Brain Potentials: Signaling Our Inner Thoughts," *Psychology Today,* March 1979, pp. 42–90.

34. John, E. R., et al., "Neurometrics: Numetrical Taxonomy Identifies Different Profiles or Brain Functions Within Groups of Behaviorally Similar People," *Science,* 1977, vol. 196, pp. 1393–410; John, E. R., *Neurometrics: Clinical Applications of Quantitative Electrophysiology* (Hillsdale, N.J.: Lawrence Erlbaum, 1977).

35. Regan, D., "Electrical Responses Evoked from the Human Brain," *Scientific American,* 1979, vol. 241, pp. 134–46.

36. John, *Neurometrics,* p. 202.

37. Ibid., p. 207.

38. Ibid., p. 209.

39. Ibid., p. 196.

40. For other comments on subject selection in neurometric research see Duane, "Neurobiological Correlates"; Johnstone, J., Galin, D., Fein, G., Yingling, C., Herron, J., and Marcus, M., "Regional Brain Activity in Dyslexic and Control Children During Reading Tasks: Visual Probe Event-Related Potentials," *Brain and Language,* 1984, vol. 21, pp. 233–54.

41. Neurometrics is cited either as evidence of the EEG heterogeneity in dyslexics, and therefore of the need for subtyping, or in an occasional remark about the vision of "some neuropsychologists" who feel that neurometrics will emerge as "a new way of evaluating children. . . . They foresee a potential in neurometrics for instructional treatments based on the precise brain cause of a learning problem" (Smith, C. R., *Learning Disabilities: The Interaction of Learner, Task, and Setting* (Boston: Little, Brown & Co., 1983).

42. Restak, R. M., *The Brain* (N.Y.: Bantam, 1984).

43. Regan, "Electrical Responses," p. 134.

44. Ibid, p. 146.

45. The higher left than right brain-hemisphere activation in normal readers than in disabled readers occurred when the children looked at simple three- or four-letter words (Cohen, J., and Breslin, P. W., "Visual Evoked Responses in Dyslexic Children," *Annals of the New York Academy of Sciences,* 1984, vol. 425, pp. 338–43).

46. For example, Weber, B. A., and Omenn, G. S., "Auditory and Visual Evoked Responses in Children with Familial Reading Disabilities," *Journal of Learning Disabilities,* 1977, vol. 10, pp. 153–58: "The findings of both studies in this investigation do not confirm the rather dramatic and consistent findings of Conners . . . of left parietal flattening" in evoked responses.

47. Sobotka, K. R., and May, J. G., "Visual Evoked Potentials and Reaction Time in Normal and Dyslexic Children," *Psychophysiology,* 1977, vol. 14, pp. 18–24.

48. See Sobotka and May, "Visual Evoked Potentials" for a summary of this research.

Even in a very early evoked-potential study, one that prompted replication research, the suggestion was made that the disabled learners' attitude and behavior related to "attentiveness, low arousal, or other motivational factors" may explain evoked-response results (Conners, C. K., "Cortical Visual Evoked Response in Children with Learning Disorders," *Psychophysiology,* 1971, vol. 7, pp. 418–28).

Follow-up research acknowledged that it was possible "that the disabled readers in some sense were less attentive" during the experimental tasks than the normal readers and that "attention factors can affect" evoked responses (Preston, M. S., Guthrie, J. T., and Childs, B., "Visual Evoked Responses (VERs) in Normal and Disabled Readers," *Psychophysiology,* 1974, vol. 11, pp. 452–457). A few years after this study, its principal investigators, in a comparison of adult normal and disabled readers, found both groups had larger brain-wave amplitudes in the left hemisphere in response to words than to flashing lights. They observed that the "heightened amplitude on the left side for the word condition . . . may be a reflection of the attentional decision-making processes required in the word task in contrast to the relatively passive task of viewing light flashes." Also, the closer left-right amplitudes in the disabled readers for both words and flashes might have occurred, they suggested, because "word stimuli may have a negative *affective* association for disabled readers"; thus the less active response by the disabled readers to words produced a lower amplitude. Although the researchers noted the influence of affect, they concluded that it was "unlikely that attentional differences between normal and disabled readers can account for the results, since both groups were able to identify . . . with almost 100% accuracy" the words used in the experiment. This explanation makes little sense in light of the inability of the researchers to know how the dyslexics responded to the words when they were embedded in a series of words. For example, in a string of similar words, all of which were presented at two-second intervals (for example, the target word *bin* was embedded with *bid, bit,* and *ban*), disabled readers were not likely to identify quickly words with similar consonant and vowel configurations (Preston, M. S., Guthrie, J. T., Kirsch, I., Gertman, D., and Childs, B., "VERs in Normal and Disabled Adult Readers," *Psychophysiology,* 1977, vol. 14, pp. 8–14).

In a study done at the U.S. Navy Electronics Laboratory Center in San Diego, four male experimental psychologists and two graduate students were used as subjects in a task that required them to respond to light flashes from one visual field but not the other. In order to test the impact "general arousal" and attention might have on evoked responses, the investigators administered "a strong but harmless electric shock" to the left ankle if the subject's reaction time exceeded a certain length. In spite of the shocking methods, scientific knowledge was advanced when the data showed that "greater evoked responses were obtained under threat of shock than under no threat." In contrast, "irrelevant stimuli" (those in the visual field that were to be ignored) quite frequently produced no discernible evoked response. The general conclusions drawn from the study were

> Cortical evoked potentials are dramatically related to specific attention and to a lesser extent to general arousal level. The combined effects of these two variables determine whether the net change in evoked potential amplitude will be zero, an increase, or a decrease.

See Eason, R. G., Harter, M. R., and White, C. T., "Effects of Attention and Arousal on Visually Evoked Cortical Potentials and Reaction Time in Man," *Physiology and Behavior,* 1969, vol. 4, pp. 283–89.

49. Shucard, D. W., Cummins, K. R., and McGee, M. G. "Event-Related Brain Potentials Differentiate Normal and Disabled Readers," *Brain and Language,* 1984, vol. 21, pp. 318–34.

50. Johnstone, J., Galin, D., Fein, G., Yingling, C., Herron, J., and Marcus, M. "Regional Brain Activity in Dyslexic and Control Children During Reading Tasks: Visual Probe Event-Related Potentials," *Brain and Language,* 1984, vol. 21, pp. 233–54. The investigators explained: "It is likely that dyslexics either carry out subprocesses of reading at different rates or carry out qualitatively different subprocesses. Such differences in cognitive processing may account for" group differences in evoked responses during a reading task.

51. The increased reading difficulty meant "more reliance on phonological decoding for both groups. . . . Since left temporal lobe mechanisms are known to be important in phonetic analysis and the ability to read aloud," the researchers speculated that the evoked potential effect for both groups at the temporal lobe "may be related to this dimension of difficulty" (ibid. p. 249).

52. Hiscock and Kinsbourne, "Laterality and Dyslexia," p. 181.

53. Restak, *The Brain,* p. 352.

54. Ibid., p. 243.

55. Johnstone, et al., "Regional Brain Activity," p. 235.

56. Duffy, F. H., Denckla, M. B., Bartels, P. H., Sandini, G., and Kiessling, L. S., "Dyslexia: Automated Diagnosis by Computerized Classification of Brain Electrical Activity," *Annals of Neurology,* 1980 (a), vol. 7, pp. 421–28; Duffy, Denckla, Bartels, and Sandini, "Dyslexia: Regional Differences in Brain Electrical Activity by Topographic Mapping," *Annals of Neurology,* 1980 (b), vol. 7, pp. 412–20.

57. Duffy, Denckla, Bartels, and Sandini, "Dyslexia: Regional Differences," p. 417.

58. Ibid.

59. Luria, A. R. *The Working Brain* (N.Y.: Basic Books, 1973).

60. Duffy, Denckla, Bartels, and Sandini, "Dyslexia: Regional Differences," p. 417.

61. Some studies have found that alpha waves are associated with attention deficits—which, we have seen, have not been demonstrated to be of neurological origin (Fuller, P. W., "Attention and the EEG Alpha Rhythm in Learning Disabled Children," *Journal of Learning Disabilities,* 1978, vol. 11, pp. 303–12).

62. Sklar, B., Hanley, J., and Simmons, W. W., "An EEG Experiment Aimed Toward Identifying Dyslexic Children," *Nature* (London), 1972, vol. 240, pp. 414–16; Sklar, Hanley, and Simmons, "A Computer Analysis of EEG Spectral Signatures from Normal and Dyslexic Children," *IEEE Transactions on Biomedical Engineering,* 1973, BME-20, pp. 20–26; Leisman, G., and Ashkenazi, M., "Aetiological Factors in Dyslexia: IV. Cerebral Hemispheres Are Functionally Equivalent," *Neuroscience,* 1980, vol. 11, pp. 157–64.

63. Restak, *The Brain,* p. 354.

64. This asymmetry has been confirmed to be present not only at birth but also in fetuses and neonates examined at ten to forty-eight weeks after conception (Hier, D. B., LeMay, M., Rosenberger, P. B., and Perlo, V. P. "Developmental Dyslexia: Evidence for a Subgroup with a Reversal of Cerebral Asymmetry," *Archives of Neurology,* 1978, vol. 35, pp. 90–92).

65. Four of the ten "reported delays in the acquisition of speech, while only one of the other 14 dyslexic patients had delayed speech acquisition" (Ibid., p. 92).

66. Ibid.

67. Rosenberger, P. B., and Hier, D. B., "Cerebral Asymmetry and Verbal Intellectual Deficits," *Annals of Neurology,* 1980, vol. 8, pp. 300–04.

68. Hynd and Cohen, *Dyslexia,* p. 86. Also Masland, R. L., "Neurological Aspects of Dyslexia," in Pavlidis and Miles, *Dyslexia Research,* pp. 35–66; Galaburda, A., "Developmental Dyslexia: Current Anatomical Research," *Annals of Dyslexia,* 1983, vol. 33, pp. 41–53; Sobotowicz, W. S., and Evans, J. R., *Cortical Dysfunctioning in Children with Specific Reading Disability* (Springfield, Ill.: Charles C Thomas, 1982).

69. Rosenberger and Hier, "Cerebral Asymmetry," p. 303.

70. Ibid.

71. "Of the 26 [dyslexic] boys in the present study, six gave a history of language delay but only one of the these subjects had reversed asymmetry. The other two children in the sample with reversed asymmetry had normal language milestones, implying a lack of association between posterior hemisphere width and delayed language." The study divided the dyslexics into subgroups according to reading problems with phonics, spelling, and sight vocabulary, but no association with asymmetry was found. The researchers did find a higher proportion of symmetric occipital-lobe width in the dyslexics, and they suggested there might be some validity in the theory of the relationship between structure size and functional differences. But beyond offering this suggestion, there was no amplification of it. In sum, the study concluded that computerized tomography was "not warranted in the clinical investigation of children with reading disabilities unless an underlying disorder associated with significant neurological signs [was] uncovered" (Haslam, R. H. A., Dalby, J. T., Johns, R. D., and Rademaker, A. W., "Cerebral Asymmetry in Developmental Dyslexia," *Archives of Neurology,* 1981, vol. 38, pp. 679–82).

72. Thompson, J. S., Ross, R. J., and Horowitz, S. J., "The Role of Computed Axial Tomography in the Study of the Child with Minimal Brain Dysfunction," *Journal of Learning Disabilities,* 1980, vol. 13, pp. 334–37.

73. Denckla, M. B., LeMay, M., and Chapman, C. A., "Few CT Scan Abnormalities Found Even in Neurologically Impaired Learning Disabled Children," *Journal of Learning Disabilities,* 1985, vol. 18, pp. 132–35.

74. Thompson, Ross, and Horowitz, "The Role of Computed Axial Tomography," p. 336.

75. Denckla, LeMay, and Chapman, "Few CT Scan Abnormalities," p. 133.

76. One radiologist categorized "15 scans as normal, 9 scans as slightly abnormal and one scan as borderline atrophic" (possible tissue atrophy). The other radiologist categorized "13 scans as normal, 12 as slightly abnormal and none as atrophic" (ibid).

77. Ibid., p. 134 (emphasis added). The twelve were of a total thirty-two children scanned, but the scans of only twenty-five were read by both radiologists.

78. Drake, W. E., "Clinical and Pathological Findings in a Child with a Developmental Learning Disability," *Journal of Learning Disabilities,* 1968, vol. 1, pp. 486–502.

79. The Orton Dyslexia Society, "The Neurological Basis of the Talents of Dyslexics," *Perspectives on Dyslexia,* August 1984. The following discussion of the history of the research division and the brain-autopsy project, and all quotations in my discussion, come from this issue of *Perspectives.*

In 1970 "the seeds of the Research Division . . . were sown" when the then-president of the society "recommended that the procedures for organ donating be explored to determine the feasibility of a brain bank to be used in neuroanatomical research." Seven years later, while exploring ways to finance the project, and because "enthusiasm for this concept was rapidly mounting," the society called together "specialists renowned in the fields of dyslexia and brain function" for a "brain-storming session."

This 1977 meeting culminated with the agreement that the society "should undertake a program of basic research in anatomical analysis of dyslexic and nondyslexic brains." Fortuitously, before a final decision was made, members of the Harvard Medical School Department of Neurology at Beth-Israel Hospital obtained the brain of a dyslexic who had died in an accident, and even more fortuitously, they indeed found a number of abnormalities, thereby confirming, at least in this single case, the "farsighted" view of Dr. Orton that dyslexia was "neurologically rather than psychologically based." This "first study of the brain of a diagnosed dyslexic" was published in 1979 and "was considered so significant that the Society decided to name Harvard as the institution to conduct the brain research." With a contribution of $100,000 from the Underwood Canning Company, and another $50,000 gift from the Powder River Corporation, a "food oriented company . . . founded by a dyslexic," the laboratory opened in 1982. Additional funds have come from the National Institute of Health. Within two years it "received its first brain of a diagnosed dyslexic female and its first brain from outside the United States, that of a German male dyslexic." For the Orton Dyslexia Society, the autopsy project is among the "current research . . . proving Dr. Orton correct."

The brain-donor program has "several thousand dyslexic individuals and their relatives, all of whom have agreed to donate their brains in the event of their death" (Galaburda, A. M., Sherman, G. F., Rosen, G. D., Aboitiz, F., and Geschwind, N., "Developmental Dyslexia: Four Consecutive Patients with Cortical Anomalies," *Annals of Neurology,* 1985, vol. 18, pp. 222–33).

In addition, because the laboratory is interested in controlled studies, it has sought nondyslexics who would donate their brains. Donor cards have been issued, and in those states with an organ-donor designation area on automobile drivers licenses, participants may state their bequests.

80. Galaburda, A. M., and Kemper, T. L. "Cytoarchitectonic Abnormalities in Developmental Dyslexia: A Case Study," *Annals of Neurology,* 1979, vol. 6, pp. 94–100.

81. Ibid., p. 94.

82. Ibid., p. 94–95.

83. Orton Society, "The neurological basis," p. 3.

84. Galaburda and Kemper, "Cytoarchitectonic Abnormalities," p. 100. For a similar discussion of this case see Galaburda, A., and Eidelberg, D., "Symmetry and Asymmetry in the Human Posterior Thalamus," *Archives of Neurology,* 1982, vol. 39, pp. 333–36.

85. Galaburda and Kemper, "Cytoarchitectonic Abnormalities," p. 98.

86. Ibid., p. 99.

87. Penfield, W., and Jasper, H., *Epilepsy and the Functional Anatomy of the Human Brain* (Boston: Little, Brown & Co., 1954).

88. Galaburda and Kemper, "Cytoarchitectonic Abnormalities," p. 99.

89. Ibid.

90. Drake, "Clinical and Pathological Findings."

91. Galaburda and Kemper, "Cytoarchitectonic Abnormalities," p. 99.

92. Ibid.

93. These points are omitted from all of Galaburda's papers subsequent to the original one.

The discussion of the case in the November 11, 1984, *New York Times* supplement on the learning disabled reads:

> [They] obtained the brain of a dyslexic man who died in an accident. By cutting the tissue into nearly 3,000 slices, they were able to identify structural abnormalities. Cells were out of place or misaligned in several regions, particularly in structures of the brain's left side known to have language function. [p. 45]

A *Journal of Learning Disabilities* article said the Galaburda and Kemper findings

> made a truly significant contribution in the microscopic study of the brain of a well-documented dyslexic. They reported that their patient had symmetrical temporal lobes (usually the left temporal region is slightly enlarged). Inspection of the brain revealed many neurodevelopmental abnormalities localized only in the left language dominant hemisphere. The patterns of convolutions was unusual and many small gyria (micropolygyri) existed. Microscopic abnormalities existed as well, primarily in the left temporal region and parietal area. [Obrzut, J. E., and Hynd, G. W., "The Neurobiological Foundations of Learning Disabilities," p. 516.]

94. Galaburda, Sherman, Rosen, Aboitiz, and Geschwind, "Four consecutive patients," p. 228.

95. Galaburda, A. M., "Developmental Dyslexia: A Review of Biological Interactions," *Annals of Dyslexia,* 1985, vol. 35, pp. 21–33; Galaburda, Sherman, Rosen, Aboitiz, and Geschwind, "Four consecutive cases."

96. Galaburda, Sherman, Rosen, Aboitiz, and Geschwind, "Four consecutive patients," p. 223.

97. Ibid.

98. Ibid.

99. Ibid.

100. Orton Society, "The neurological basis," p. 4.

101. Galaburda, Sherman, Rosen, Aboitiz, and Geschwind, "Four consecutive patients," p. 223.

102. Ibid.

103. Ibid.

104. Ibid., p. 229.

105. Dublin, W. B., *Fundamentals of Neuropathology* (Springfield, Ill.: Charles C Thomas, 1967); Larroche, J. C., "Cytoarchitectonic Abnormalities (Abnormalities of Cell Migration)," In Vinken, P. J., and Bruyn, G. W., eds., *Handbook of Clinical Neurology* (Amsterdam, North-Holland, 1977).

106. McGuinness, D., *When Children Don't Learn: Understanding the Biology and Psychology of Learning Disabilities* (N.Y.: Basic Books, 1985), p. 111.

107. Replication is a sine qua non of scientific research. Unless a study can be replicated, and its conclusions verified by independent investigators, the study cannot be said to meet scientific criteria. Unfortunately, the brain-autopsy research is different from all other LD research. As the Orton Dyslexia Society learned when it sent a questionnaire to over 300 major medical schools, only one (Harvard) was studying the relationship of brain anatomy and dyslexia. To my knowledge the situation has not changed very much.

At best, independent replication and verification of the autopsied dyslexic brains is likely to be a drawn out process because the procedure for studying dyslexic brains is, to quote an Orton publication, "so demanding of time that only 3–5 brains can be completed per year," assuming of course that that many are available ("The neurological basis," p. 3). It would appear, therefore, that the best way to establish the validity of the autopsy findings would be to make the case materials available for peer review.

For these reasons, and to discuss the research in this book, in May 1985 I wrote to Dr. Galaburda, explained I was writing a book on LD, and asked if I might have access to the case records. Aware of the importance of confidentiality, I said I would agree to whatever arrangements he suggested.

After a few months went by and it became clear I would not receive a reply, I wrote to Sylvia O. Richardson, the president of the Orton Dyslexia Society, because the research project was under its auspices. I asked if the society had a policy on scholarly review of the case materials. If independent reviews were not allowed, I asked to know the reasons for this decision.

Dr. Richardson responded (with copies to Dr. Galaburda and other parties associated with the society's research division), informing me that the society had "no policy as yet with regard to the case materials and autopsy slides." Because "this situation has not arisen before," the matter had been referred to the society's research advisory council for a policy statement. "When they have come up with a policy statement which has been approved by our national Board of Directors," I was told, it would be sent to me. Since this was not a refusal of my request, I asked if, for now, in lieu of a formal policy, the society had a de facto policy either of making the materials available or of withholding them. Simply, I wished to know if I might have access to the case studies.

I received a letter from the legal counsel for the society, to whom my last letter had been referred. The attorney wrote that my inquiry raised "serious ethical questions," one of which concerned subject and next-of-kin rights: Possibly the dyslexics would be "readily identifiable from their case histories" even if their names were not revealed. Shouldn't permission be received from the next of kin to release the case histories, even for "those non-readily identifiable subjects of the study?" Another ethical question raised was, in what form should permission be received ("is notarization necessary")? A third question: What is the "legal exposure of the Society and its Research Division" if any or all case histories were "released without permission"? A fourth ethical issue: "What are Dr. Galaburda's rights? . . . Can the materials be released without his permission and/or desire?" Then there were the "rights of the next of kin of Dr. Geschwind" (who had participated in the project and had died in 1985). Finally, Was it appropriate to release the materials "at a time when the study is not complete, especially in view of the fact that the study is intended to be of a long-term nature, i.e., many years?" These and other questions had to be resolved before the board of directors could arrive at a policy.

I replied by reviewing the unusual replication problems, which for most LD research would not arise. I suggested that because I was only asking permission to review four cases, and since I too would find a review without proper permission to be unethical, it seemed sensible to believe that the matter could easily be expedited. Concerning subject and next-of-kin rights, a letter to the latter could be drawn, asking permission to make the materials available for scientific review. Permission could contain the proviso that after a professional review of the materials, only information the research division decided would not reveal the identity of the deceased or that of their families could be used for publication.

The issue of the "long-term nature" of the study did not seem applicable to my request because only those materials that pertained to *published* papers would be reviewed. Since the published papers of the research division presented hypotheses, data, and conclusions for the scientific community to consider at the time of publication and not until the "study" had been completed, it was reasonable for the materials to be available before "many years" had gone by. Otherwise, it would be difficult for this work to meet scientific criteria. (I added that I was not aware of any research division publication that had ever mentioned a projected termination point for the "study" and asked the counsel to inform me if one existed.)

Finally, it seemed to me that given the difficulty of replicating and confirming the findings of this unusual research, peer review and validation of the findings would be in the best professional interest of Dr. Galaburda and of Dr. Geschwind's's next of kin. Why, I asked, would these parties possibly object to a process that would enhance their professional standing?

In March 1986, I received a reply from Richard L. Masland, M.D., chairman of the research advisory committee of the Orton Dyslexia Society. He informed me that having selected Dr. Galaburda to be responsible for the study of neuroanatomical changes in dyslexia, the committee's policy is "to allocate to the principal investigator not only the responsibility but also the authority to make the best possible use of the material sent to him. Within this mandate, I am sure that Dr. Galaburda will be anxious to help you in any way that he can properly do so."

Shortly afterward, having gone full circle, I sent a certified letter to Dr. Galaburda, to whom the committee had sent a copy of their letter, asking him what policy he had formulated for reviewing the case materials. He never responded.

108. The autopsy was conducted by Sandra Witelson and Marc Colonnier (personal communication with Witelson of McMaster University, Hamilton, Ontario). The autopsy was mentioned in McGuinness's book, *When Children Don't Learn.* However, McGuinness's report that Witelson found that "the splenium of the corpus collosum was abnormally small" is not correct.

109. The term "deficit-driven" is, I believe, Mary Poplin's (Poplin, M., "Reductionism from the Medical Model to the Classroom: The Past, Present and Future of Learning Disabilities," *Research Communications in Psychology, Psychiatry and Behavior,* 1985, vol. 10, pp. 37–70.

5 Drugs and LD Explanations

1. Wender, P. H., "The Minimal Brain Dysfunction Syndrome," *Annual Review of Medicine,* 1975, vol. 26, pp. 45–62.

2. Ibid., p. 57.

3. Millman, H. L., "Minimal Brain Dysfunction in Children—Evaluation and Treatment," *Journal of Learning Disabilities,* 1970, vol. 3, pp. 91–99.

4. Gadow, K. D., "Effects of Stimulant Drugs on Academic Performance in Hyperactive and Learning Disabled Children," *Journal of Learning Disabilities,* 1983, vol. 16, p. 290.

5. Wender, "Minimal Brain Dysfunction," p. 58; Wender, "The Minimal Brain Dysfunction Syndrome in Children," *Journal of Nervous and Mental Disease,* 1972, vol. 155, pp. 55–71.

6. See Millman, "Minimal Brain Dysfunction"; Silver, L. B., "The Neurologic Learning Disability Syndrome," *American Family Physician,* 1971, vol. 4, pp. 95–101; Cochran, A., "Recognizing MBD in the Problem Child," *RN,* 1972, pp. 2–5; Frazier, S., "Minimal Brain Dysfunction," *Medical Times,* 1975, vol. 103, pp. 70–81; Haller, J. S., and Axelrod, P., "Minimal Brain Dysfunction Syndrome," *American Journal of Disabled Children,* 1975, vol. 129, pp. 1319–24; Lewis, J. A., and Young, R., "Deanol and Methylphenidate in Minimal Brain Dysfunction," *Clinical Pharmacology and Therapeutics,* 1975, vol. 17, pp. 534–40.

7. Schrag, P., and Divoky, D., *The Myth of the Hyperactive Child* (N.Y.: Pantheon, 1975).

8. IMS America Ltd. Copyright market statistics used with permission of publisher (Ambler, Pa., 1977).

9. Gadow, K. D., "Prevalence of Drug Treatment for Hyperactivity and Other Childhood Behavior Disorders," in Gadow, K. D., and Loney, J., eds., *Psychosocial Aspects of Drug Treatment for Hyperactivity* (Boulder, Co.: Westview Press, 1981).

10. O'Leary, K. D., "Pills or Skills for Hyperactive Children," *Journal of Applied Behavior,* 1980, vol. 13, pp. 191–204.

11. Elevation of MBD to an explanation of several social maladies probably peaked in the early 1970s with the publication of Camilla Anderson's book, *Society Pays: The High Costs of Minimal Brain Damage in America* (N.Y.: Walker, 1972). Anderson argued that MBD was a common and widespread disability and appeared "to play a major role in producing our socially handicapped people"—that is, the "disadvantaged," the poor, and welfare recipients. It is time, she implored, "that we begin to look at poverty not only as a cause of trouble, but also, in many instances, as a natural and almost inevitable result of certain personal inadequacies, chief of which is MBD."

It should be noted that even now, the volumes of evidence against the notion that MBD is strictly a medical problem have not touched the faithful.

A recent assessment, reproving past misconceptions but nonetheless urging retention of the term and concept, observed that neither criticism nor "its outright abandonment in DSM-III . . . have failed to result in dismissal of the term by many pediatric specialists. The term remains popular in both research and clinical circles and is applied to varying degrees, and with perhaps somewhat different meanings, across a broad range of pediatric disciplines" (Taylor, H. G., "MBD: Meanings and Misconceptions," *Journal of Clinical Neuropsychology,* 1983, vol. 5, pp. 271–87).

For additional discussions of MBD see Coles, G. S., "The Learning-Disabilities Test Battery: Empirical and Social Issues," *Harvard Educational Review,* 1978, vol. 48, pp. 313–40; McGuinness, D., *When Children Don't Learn;* Lewontin, Rose, and Kamin, *Not in Our Genes;* Schrag and Divoky, *The Myth of the Hyperactive Child.*

12. Aman, M. G., "Psychotropic Drugs in the Treatment of Reading Disorders," in Malatesha, R. N., and Aaron, P.G., eds., *Reading Disorders: Varieties and Treatments* (N.Y.: Academic Press, 1982), p. 457. (Emphasis in original.)

13. Barkley, R. A., and Cunningham, C. E., "Do Stimulant Drugs Improve the Academic Performance of Hyperkinetic Children?" *Clinical Pediatrics,* 1978, vol. 17, pp. 85–92.

14. Ibid., pp. 85, 89.

15. Freeman, R. D., "Drug Effects on Learning in Children: A Selective Review of the Past Thirty Years," *Journal of Special Education,* 1966, vol. 1, pp. 17–44; Grinspoon, L., and Singer, S. B., "Amphetamines in the Treatment of Hyperkinetic Children," *Harvard Educational Review,* 1973, vol. 43, pp. 515–55.

16. Aman, M. G., "Psychotropic Drugs and Learning Problems—A Selective Review," *Journal of Learning Disabilities,* 1980, vol. 13, pp. 87–97; Gadow, "Effects of Stimulant Drugs."

17. Ayllon, T., Layman, D., and Kandel, H. J., "A Behavioral-Educational Alternative to Drug Control of Hyperactive Children," *Journal of Applied Behavior Analysis,* 1975, vol. 8, pp. 137–46; Wolraich, M., Drummond, T., Salomon, M. K., O'Brien, M. L., Sivage, C., "Effects of Methylphenidate Alone and in Combination with Behavior Modification Procedures on the Behavior and Academic Performance of Hyperactive Children," *Journal of Abnormal Child Psychology,* 1978, vol. 6, pp. 149–61; Brown, R. T., Wynne, M. E., and Medenis, R., "Methylphenidate and Cognitive Therapy: A Comparison of Treatment Approaches with Hyperactive Boys," *Journal of Abnormal Child Psychology,* 1985, vol. 13, pp. 69–87; Gadow, "Effects of Stimulant Drugs."

18. Aman, "Hyperactivity: Nature of the Syndrome and Its Natural History," *Journal of Autism and Developmental Disorders,* 1984, vol. 14, pp. 39–56; Weiss, G., Kruger, E., Danielson, U., and Elman, M., "Effect of Long Term Treatment of Hyperactive Children with Methylphenidate," *Canadian Medical Association Journal,* 1975, vol. 112, pp. 159–65; Rie, H. E., Rie, E. D., Stewart, S., "Effects of Methylphenidate on Underachieving Children," *Journal of Consulting and Clinical Psychology,* 1976, vol. 44, pp. 250–60; Rie, H. E., Rie, E. D., Stewart, S., and Ambuel, J. P., "Effects of Ritalin on Underachieving Children: A Replication," *American Journal of Orthopsychiatry,* 1976, vol. 46, pp. 313–22; Charles, L., and Schain, R., "A Four-Year Follow-up Study of the Effects of Methylphenidate on the Behavior and Academic

Achievement of Hyperactive Children," *Journal of Abnormal Child Psychology,* 1981, vol. 9, pp. 495–505; Quinn, P. O., and Rapoport, J. L., "One-Year Follow-up of Hyperactive Boys Treated with Imipramine or Methylphenidate," *American Journal of Psychiatry,* 1975, vol. 132, pp. 241–45; Abikoff, H., and Gittelman, R., "The Normalizing Effects of Methylphenidate on the Classroom Behavior of ADD Children," *Journal of Abnormal Child Psychology,* 1985, vol. 13, pp. 33–44; Brown, Wynne, and Medenis, "Methylphenidate and Cognitive Therapy."

19. *Physicians' Desk Reference* (Oradell, NJ: Medical Economics Co., 1985), thirty-ninth edition, p. 865.

20. Insight into the inclination to prescribe drugs comes from a cross-cultural study of U.S. and Italian physicians and psychologists. These professionals were asked to describe the diagnosis and treatment they would be likely to provide for a hypothetical case of a nine-year-old boy who had a normal IQ, was performing one or two years below expected grade level, and displayed behavioral and cognitive symptoms such as excessive motion, impulsivity, restlessness, short tolerance and quick frustration, short attention span, and specific learning disabilities. The U.S. professionals were more inclined than the Italians to offer a primary diagnosis of LD and a secondary diagnosis for hyperactivity, to choose an organic interpretation of the etiology, and to advocate the use of medication (O'Leary, K. D., Vivian, D., and Cornoldi, C., "Assessment and Treatment of 'Hyperactivity' in Italy and the United States," *Journal of Clinical Child Psychology,* 1984, vol. 13, pp. 56–60.)

21. O'Leary, "Pills or Skills."

22. IMS America Ltd., *National Prescription Audit: General Information Report* (Ambler, Pa., 1981).

23. *A Twelve Week, Double-Blind, Parallel Group, Multicenter Study to Compare the Efficacy and Safety of Piracetam with Placebo in Children with Specific Written Language Difficulties (Dyslexia)* (Belgium: UCB-Pharmaceutical, 1980).

24. *Nootropil: Basic Scientific and Clinical Data* (Brussels: UCB-Pharmaceutical, 1980), p. 21.

25. Dimond, S. J., and Brouwers, E. Y. M., "Increase in the Power of Human Memory in Normal Man Through the Use of Drugs," *Psychopharmacology,* 1976, vol. 49, pp. 307–09.

Another study with college students found some statistically significant effects for Piracetam over placebos in a similar memory task and in a perceptual-motor task requiring them to copy symbols within a short time. Yet, in contrast to initial Piracetam-group gains found immediately after the words were memorized, no significant recall advantage was found for the group when the time following memorization was lengthened (Hyde, J. R. G., "The Effect of an Acute Dose of Piracetam on Human Performance" (unpublished doctoral dissertation, University of London School of Pharmacy, 1980).

For similar results with adult groups, see Wilsher, C., Atkins, G., and Manfield, P., "Piracetam as an Aid to Learning in Dyslexia: Preliminary Report," *Psychopharmacology,* 1979, vol. 65, pp. 107–09.

26. The U.S. consultant to UCB is G.H. Besselaar Associates, "consultants to the international pharmaceutical and medical device industries," in Princeton, N.J.

27. Simeon, J., Waters, B., and Resnick, M. "Effects of Piracetam in Children with Learning Disorders," *Psychopharmacology Bulletin,* 1980, vol. 16, pp. 65–66.

28. Wilsher, Atkins, and Manfield, "Dyslexia: Piracetam Promotion of Reading Skills," manuscript, 1980; Wilsher, Atkins, and Manfield, "Effect of Piracetam on Dyslexic's Reading Ability," *Journal of Learning Disabilities,* 1985, vol. 18, pp. 19–25.

29. The reading results are for the Neale Analysis of Reading Ability, which is composed of subtests in comprehension, reading rate (speed of reading a story), and accuracy (Neale, M. D., *Neale Analysis of Reading*) (London: Macmillan Education Ltd., 1966).

30. The British Abilities Scale Word-Reading Test (Elliot, C. D., Murray, D. S., and Pearson, L. S., *British Abilities Scales Manual 3: Directions for Administration and Scoring* (Winsor, England: NFER Publishing Co., 1978).

31. Several cognitive ability tests were used, each categorized as a measure of either left- or right-hemisphere functioning. These were the block-design test from the Wechsler intelligence test (described by the researchers as "a test of spatial ability"); coding from the Wechsler ("a test of short term memory, freedom from distraction and speed of processing"), and auditory sequential memory (an adaptation of a Wechsler subtest). The investigators categorized the block-design test as a right-hemisphere task, and coding and auditory sequential memory as left-hemisphere tasks.

The spelling test was the Schonell spelling test.

32. DiIanni, M., Wilsher, C. R., Blank, M. S., Conners, C. K., Chase, C. H., Funkenstein, H. H., Helfgott, E., Holmes, J. M., Lougee, L., Maletta, G. J., Milewski, J., Pirozzolo, F. J., Rudel, R. G., and Tallal, P. "The Effects of Piracetam in Children with Dyslexia," *Journal of Clinical Psychopharmacology,* 1985, vol. 5, pp. 272–78.

The guidelines of a UCB research protocol for a double-blind twelve-week trial of the drug versus a placebo was followed at each site, but along with the overall study each site undertook a special project of its own.

33. Mixed results were found among the sites for similar tests of verbal memory and word-identification tests; Piracetam benefits reported at one site were not confirmed elsewhere (Rudel, R. G., and Helfgott, E., "Effect of Piracetam on Verbal Memory of Dyslexic Boys," *Journal of the American Academy of Child Psychiatry,* 1984, vol. 23, pp. 695–99; Helfgott, E., Rudel, R. G., and Krieger, J., "Effect of Piracetam on the Single Word and Prose Reading of Dyslexic Children," *Psychopharmacology Bulletin,* 1984, vol. 20, pp. 688–90; Di Ianni, et al., "The Effects of Piracetam"; Chase, C. H., Schmitt, R. L., Russell, G., and Tallal, P., "A New Chemotherapeutic Investigation: Piracetam Effects on Dyslexia," *Annals of Dyslexia,* 1984, vol. 34, pp. 29–48.

Perhaps the most notable Piracetam improvement in a special project was found on the similarities subtest of the WISC, in which children are asked how two objects are similar. However, while a Piracetam effect was reported for this single subtest, whether the drug improved verbal abilities, which are part of the subtest, is questionable because no drug advantage was found on the vocabulary subtest, in which children are asked for verbal definitions of words (Wilsher, C. R., and Milewski, J., "Effects of Piracetam on Dyslexics' Verbal Conceptualizing Ability," *Psychopharmacology Bulletin,* 1983, vol. 19, pp. 3–4).

34. Chase, Schmitt, Russell, and Tallal, "A New Chemotherapeutic Investigation."

35. Conners, C. K., Blouin, A. G., Winglee, M., Lougee, L., O'Donnell, D., and Smith, A., "Piracetam and Event-Related Potentials in Dyslexic Children," *Psychopharmacology Bulletin,* 1984, vol. 20, pp. 667–73.

36. Di Ianni, et al., "The Effects of Piracetam," p. 277.

37. Wilsher, C. R., *Piracetam Treatment of Specific Written Language Difficulties (Dyslexia)—A Discussion,* pamphlet, no date.

If Piracetam is not useful in improving reading, it may yet make its mark in improving the lifting of heavy weights. In a leaflet circulating through the gym underground, powerlifters were instructed on how to beat drug-testing and which drugs to use. Piracetam was discussed as a drug that had become very popular among European athletes. The side effects undesired by others are exactly what many powerlifters want. The leaflet advises, Piracetam "assists in maintaining strength and *aggression* during the period off anabolic steroids." Considering the expertise in pharmacology powerlifters and other athletes have acquired, and their dedication to finding elixirs for improving performance, it would be unwise to disregard the "findings" of these gym experiments. Strength athletes might be casual about drug risks but they nonetheless are quite knowledgeable about their benefits.

38. Ibid.

39. "Doctor Fights for Dyslexia Theory," *New York Times,* November 24, 1985.

40. Levinson, H. N., *A Solution to the Riddle of Dyslexia* (N.Y.: Springer-Verlag, 1980); Levinson, *Smart But Feeling Dumb* (N.Y.: Warner Books, 1984).

41. "Two Doctors Offer Dyslexia Theory," *New York Times,* April 29, 1974, p. 20; "A Reading Problem Is Traced to a Disorder of the Inner Ear," *Philadelphia Inquirer,* November 7, 1983, p. 8-C; "Drug Eases Dyslexia, Doctor Says," *Detroit News,* April 25, 1983, p. 1-A; "New Treatment for Dyslexia," *McCall's,* reprinted in a booklet from Levinson's Medical Dyslexic Treatment Center; "More on Dyslexia," *Family Weekly,* January 24, 1982, p. 27.

42. Levinson, *A Solution,* p. 22.

43. Ibid., p. 23.

44. Ibid., p. 22.

Like the U.S. shuttle program, Levinson's "dyslexic 'space flight' " encountered difficulties "almost from the blast-off phase" of his "research probe." One difficulty in the blast-off was his own internal criticism of his "flight"; the other was external criticism from the dyslexia "big guns." However, these "critical forces" did not deter him; "unfortunately, the author's space capsule was only shaken, not shattered or driven from orbit" (ibid., pp. 287–89).

45. Ibid., p. 23.

46. Ibid., p. 73.

47. Ibid., p. 292.

48. Ibid., p. 107.

49. Levinson has devised an instrument, called a 3-D scanner, in hope of proving "that there truly existed [eye] tracking difficulties in dyslexics." However, by his own account he failed to do so. "The 3-D Optical Scanner projects a moving series of elephants (or any target) which the eyes of the tested individual are reflexively forced to follow. As the speed of the moving elephants is increased, the speed at which the eye is forced to track these accelerated elephants must correspondingly increase. Ultimately the speed of the moving elephants exceeds the ability of the eye to follow them. Blurring is then experienced; the point at which this happens is called the blurring speed" (*Smart But Feeling Dumb,* p. 94). Levinson reported finding that "the average dyslexic had one-half the blurring speed or tracking capacity of non-dyslexic individuals, proving that there existed an eye-tracking defect in dyslexics" (ibid.).

Perhaps the fundamental error in this method of assessment is that "blurring speed" is not evidence of c-v dysfunction. As one critic observed, since the target passes across the person's visual field, it "constitutes visual stimulation, not vestibular" (Polatajko, H. J., "A Critical Look at Vestibular Dysfunction in Learning-Disabled Children," *Developmental Medicine & Child Neurology,* 1985, vol. 27, pp. 283–92).

Be that as it may, he found that for young dyslexics (mean age 7.8) the target object blurred at a slower speed than it did for either normal children or older dyslexics (mean age 13). However, and most important, the blurring-speed scores of the dyslexics improved with age, increasingly approximating those of the normal children at the older age levels (*A Solution,* pp. 134–35). Did this mean that as dyslexics grew older their eye-tracking became normal? Not at all! Levinson saw the decreasing differential between scores—the "age-blurring speed relationship"—as a display of his "concepualization of blurring-speed compensation" (ibid., p. 135). If normal readers exhibited a visual-tracking dysfunction, they actually were dyslexic but had undergone "academic compensation" (ibid., p. 140). Levinson explained that disabled readers who showed no eye-tracking dysfunction actually had one, only they compensated for it by compensatory focusing. In other words, they learned to focus on a single target or on part of an object in the moving series of targets rather than on all the objects in the sequence. Certainly inconsistencies in eye-tracking results did not mean Levinson's visual-tracking measures and children's reading problems had nothing to do with each other.

He looked for "electronystagmographic and blurring-speed pharmacologic correlations." Alas: "the expected ability to objectively record and quantitatively measure these responses [to medication] via ENG and blurring speeds did not materialize. All too often ENG parameters did not reflect the pharmacologically triggered dramatic changes in C-V dyslexic functioning. Blurring speeds were often found to vary independently of clinical therapeutic responses" (ibid., p. 252).

50. Ibid., p. 253.

51. Ibid., p. 206; Levinson, *Smart But Feeling Dumb,* pp. 108–109.

52. Levinson, *Smart But Feeling Dumb,* p. 34.

53. Ibid., p. 32.

54. Ibid., p. 239.

55. One testimonial, consistent with his eye-tracking theory, reads: "Before taking the medication, I'd continually lose my place when reading and I'd have to go back over the same page a million times." Another states, "[My son] is able to read without confusion or losing his place."

Other testimonials came from "two adult dyslexic clinical-therapeutic examples." These cases were supposed to have something to do with reading disability but in neither is the connection apparent, except to Levinson. A thirty-five-year-old woman wrote that since taking anti-motion medicine she found her "periods of vertigo or dizziness and light headedness have seemed to have disappeared" and she had a greater desire to read and an ability to do so for longer times (ibid., p. 242). However, most of the letter was an account not of reading problems but of numerous somatic and emotional disorders totally unrelated to reading; at least she herself made no causal connection in either direction. The second case was that of a forty-three-year-old woman with a variety of coordination and orientation problems but, said the case description, with "normal reading-score functioning" (ibid., p. 243). Why did both women with clear c-v dyslexic signs read normally? Why were they used as examples of reading disability? Of course—they had "compensated" for their "reading-score deficiency" (ibid., p. 245).

56. See Ottenbacher, K., Abbott, C., Haley, D., Watson, P. J., "Human Figure Drawing Ability and Vestibular Processing Dysfunction in Learning-Disabled Children," *Journal of Clinical Psychology,* 1984, vol. 40, pp. 1084–89; Ottenbacher, "Identifying Vestibular Processing Dysfunction in Learning-Disabled Children," *American Journal of Occupational Therapy,* 1978, vol. 32, pp. 217–21; Wilson, E. B., "Some Impressions of the Effects of Sensory Integrative Therapy for Children with Learning Disabilities," *Australian Occupational Therapy Journal,* 1979, vol. 26, pp. 239–43; Ayres, A. J., "Learning Disabilities and the Vestibular System," *Journal of Learning Disabilities,* 1978, vol. 11, pp. 18–29.

57. Among its "numerous flaws" is its method of rotating a person "in a lighted room with eyes open, thus providing both visual and vestibular stimulation (Polatajko, "A Critical Look," p. 284). Also see Royeen, C. B., Lesinski, G., Ciani, S., and Schneider, D., "Relationship of the Southern California Sensory Integration Tests, the Southern California Postrotary Nystagmus Test, and Clinical Observations Accompanying Them to Evaluations in Otolaryngology, Ophthalmology, and Audiology: Two Descriptive Case Studies," *American Journal of Occupational Therapy,* 1981, vol. 35, pp. 443–50.

58. Brown, B., Haegerstrom-Portnoy, G, Yingling, C. D., Herron, J., Galin, D., and Marcus, M., "Dyslexic Children Have Normal Vestibular Responses to Rotation," *Archives of Neurology,* 1983, vol. 40, pp. 370–73.

59. Levinson, *Smart But Feeling Dumb,* p. 129.

60. Polatajko, "A Critical Look," p. 290. Also see Brown, et al., "Dyslexic Children Have Normal"; Stockwell, C. W., Sherard, E. S., and Schuler, J. V., "Electronystagmographic Findings in Dyslexic Children," *Transactions of the American Academy of Ophthalmology and Otolaryngology,* 1976, vol. 82, pp. 239–43.

61. Polatajko, "A Critical Look," p. 283.

62. Masland, R., and Usprich, C., book review of *A Solution to the Riddle Dyslexia, Bulletin of the Orton Society,* 1981, vol. 31, pp. 256–61.

63. Ibid., p. 259.

6 Genes, Gender, and the "Affliction of Geniuses"

1. Critchley, M. "Isolation of the Specific Dyslexic," in Keeney, A. H., and Keeney, V. T., eds., *Dyslexia: Diagnosis and Treatment of Reading Disorders* (St. Louis: Mosby, 1968), p. 17.

2. Bannatyne, A., "The Spatially Competent LD Child," *Academic Therapy,* 1978, vol. 14, pp. 133–55. In the mid-1960s Bannatyne described a type of learning disability he termed "genetic dyslexia." He subsequently changed the term to "spatially competent learning disabled" (SCLD), but the major characteristics of the disorder basically remained the same. In brief, Bannatyne maintained that the SCLD child had a "spatially dominant right hemisphere" of the brain, which "tends to suppress verbal ability in the left hemisphere, which in turn processes auditory-vocal content inadequately" (p. 134). Research by others has failed to support Bannatyne's explanation. For example, see Decker, S. D. and Corley, R. P., "Bannatyne's 'Genetic Dyslexic' Subtype: A Validation Study," *Psychology in the Schools,* 1984, vol. 21, pp. 300–04.

3. Goldberg, H. K., Shiffman, G. B., and Bender, M., *Dyslexia: Interdisciplinary Approaches to Reading Disabilities* (N.Y.: Grune & Stratton, 1983), p. 122. For similar statements about the likelihood that genetic factors cause reading disabilities see Kushnick, T., "Genetic Counseling: The Case for Primary Prevention," in New Jersey Association for Children with Learning Disabilities, *Handbook on Learning Disabilities: A Prognosis for the Child, the Adolescent, the Adult* (Englewood Cliffs, NJ: Prentice-Hall, 1974); Duane, D., "Written Language Underachievement: An Overview of the Theoretical and Practical Issues," in Duffy, F. H., and Geschwind, N., eds., *Dyslexia: A Neuroscientific Approach to Clinical Evaluation* (Boston: Little, Brown, 1985).

4. Simpson, E., *Reversals: A Personal Account of Victory Over Dyslexia* (Boston: Houghton Mifflin, 1979), pp. vii, 37.

5. McCready, E. B., "Efforts in the Zone of Language (Word-Deafness and Word-Blindness) and Their Influence in Education and Behavior," *American Journal of Psychiatry,* 1926, vol. 6, pp. 267–77; Orton, S. T., "Familial Occurrence of Disorders in the Acquisition of Language," *Eugenics,* 1930, vol. 3, pp. 140–47; Newman, H. H., Freeman, F. N., and Holzinger, K. J., *Twins: A Study of Heredity and Environment* (Chicago: University of Chicago, 1937); Eustis, R. S., "Specific Reading Disability," *New England Journal of Medicine,* 1947, vol. 237, pp. 243–49; Norrie, E., "Ordblindhedens (Dyslexiens) Arvegang," *Laesepaedagogen,* 1954, vol. 2, p. 61; Husen, T., "Abilities of Twins," *Journal of Psychology,* 1960, vol. 1, pp. 125–35; Vandenberg, S. G., "The Hereditary Abilities Study: Hereditary Components in a Psychological Test Battery," *American Journal of Human Genetics,* 1962, vol. 14, pp. 220–37; Op't Hof, J. O. and Guldenpfenning, W. M., "Dominant Inheritance of Specific Reading Disability," *South African Medical Journal,* 1972, vol. 46, pp. 737–38.

6. Finucci, J. M., Guthrie, J. T., Childs, A. L., Abbey, H., and Childs, B., "The Genetics of Specific Reading Disability," *Annals of Human Genetics,* 1976, vol. 40, pp. 1–23.

7. Ibid., p. 18.

8. Symmes, J. S., and Rapoport, J. L., "Unexpected Reading Failure," *American Journal of Orthopsychiatry,* 1972, vol. 42, pp. 82–91.

9. Ibid., p. 88.

10. Ibid., p. 89.

11. DeFries, J. C., McClearn, G. E., and Wilson, J. E., "Genetic Analysis of Reading Disabilities" (Boulder: University of Colorado, 1976), final report to the Spencer Foundation; DeFries, J. C., Singer, S. M., Foch, T. T., and Lewitter, F. I., "Familial Nature of Reading Disability," *British Journal of Psychiatry,* 1978, vol. 132, pp. 361–67; Foch, T. T., DeFries, J. C., McClearn, G. E., and Singer, S. M., "Familial Patterns of Impairment in Reading Disability," *Journal of Educational Psychology,* 1977, vol. 69, pp. 316–29; DeFries, J. C., and Decker, S. N., "Genetic Aspects of Reading Disability," in Malatesha, R. N., and Aaron, P. G., eds., *Reading Disorders* (N.Y.: Academic Press, 1982).

12. Symmes and Rapoport, "Unexpected Reading Failure," p. 88.

13. Finucci, et al., "The Genetics of Specific Reading Disability."

14. Symmes and Rapoport, "Unexpected Reading Failure," p. 88.

15. DeFries and Decker, "Genetic Aspects," p. 267.

16. Ibid., p. 277.

17. DeFries, et al., "Genetic Analysis," p. 38.

18. A critique by geneticists of these family studies may be found in Smith, S. D., and Goldgar, D. E., "Single Gene Analyses and Their Application to Learning Disabilities," in Smith, ed., *Genetics and Learning Disabilities* (San Diego: College-Hill Press, 1986).

19. For earlier twins studies see Newman, H. H., Freeman, F. N., and Holzinger, K. J., *Twins: A Study of Heredity and Environment* (Chicago: University of Chicago, 1937); Norrie, E., "Ordblindhedens," in Thompson, L. J., ed., *Reading Disability* (Springfield, Ill.: Charles C Thomas, 1959); Husen, T., "Abilities of Twins," *Scandinavian Journal of Psychology,* 1960, vol. 1, pp. 125–35; Vandenberg, S. G., "The Hereditary Abilities Study: Hereditary Components in a Psychological Test Battery," *American Journal of Human Genetics,* 1962, vol. 14, pp. 220–37.

20. Matheny, A. P., and Dolan, A. B., "A Twin Study of Genetic Influences in Reading Achievement," *Journal of Learning Disabilities,* 1974, vol. 7, pp. 99–102.

21. Matheny, A. P., Dolan, A. B., and Wilson, R. S., "Twins with Academic Learning Problems: Antecedent Characteristics," *American Journal of Orthopsychiatry,* 1976, vol. 46, pp. 464–69.

22. Bakwin, H., "Reading Disability in Twins," *Developmental Medicine and Child Neurology,* 1973, vol. 15, pp. 184–87.

23. Loehlin, J. C., and Nichols, R. C., *Heredity, Environment, and Personality: A Study of 850 Sets of Twins* (Austin: University of Texas, 1976).

24. Kamin, L. J., "Psychology as Social Science: The Jensen Affair, 10 Years After," presidential address presented at the Eastern Psychological Association, Philadelphia, April 1979.

25. Loehlin and Nichols, *Heredity, Environment, and Personality,* p. 52.

26. Kamin, "Psychology as Social Science," p. 12.

27. Nichols, R. C., *The Inheritance of General and Specific Ability,* National Merit Scholarship Report, 1965, vol. 1, pp. 1–9.

28. "The F-ratio was only 1.25. For a one-tailed probability of .05 F should be approximately 1.30."

29. For further discussion see Kamin, L., "MZ and DZ Twins," in Eysenck, H. J., and Kamin, L., *The Intelligence Controversy* (N.Y.: John Wiley, 1981).

30. Smith, S. D., and Pennington, B. F., "Genetic Influences on Learning Disabilities II: Behavior Genetics and Clinical Implications," *Learning Disabilities,* 1983, vol. 2, pp. 43–55; Smith, S. D., Kimberling, W. J., Pennington, B. F., and Lubs, H. A., "Specific Reading Disability: Identification of an Inherited Form Through Linkage Analysis," *Science,* 1983, vol. 219, pp. 1345–47; Smith, Pennington, Kimberling, and Lubs, "A Genetic Analysis of Specific Reading Disability," in Ludlow, C. L., and Cooper, J. A., eds., *Genetic Aspects of Speech and Language Disorders* (N.Y.: Academic Press, 1983).

31. Smith and Pennington, "Genetic Influences," p. 48.

32. Smith, Pennington, et al., "A Genetic Analysis," p. 170.

33. Ibid.

34. Smith, Kimberling, et al, "Specific Reading Disability," p. 1345.

35. Burian, R. M., "A Methodological Critique of Sociobiology," in Caplan, A. L., ed., *The Sociobiology Debate* (N.Y.: Harper & Row, 1978), pp. 380–81.

Geneticists may reply that genetic effects have been identified in schizophrenia, crime, alcoholism, and affective disorders, all of which are "behaviors," and the same may hold for "reading disability." However, this begs the question because the validity of neither the empirical evidence nor the theoretical basis of the "genetic effects" of these and other variant behaviors has been established. It is beyond the scope of this book to discuss this literature. See, for example, Rose, S. ed., *Towards a Liberatory Biology* (NY: Allison & Busby, 1982); Rose, ed., *Against Biological Determinism* (NY: Allison & Busby, 1982); Lewontin, Rose, and Kamin, *Not in Our Genes*; Kamin, L. J., "Is Crime in the Genes? The Answer May Depend on Who Chooses What Evidence," *Scientific American,* 1986, vol. 254, pp. 22–27; Nassi, A. J., and Abramowitz, S. I., "From Phrenology to Psychosurgery and Back Again," *American Journal of Orthopsychiatry,* 1976, vol. 46, pp. 591–607.

36. (Emphasis added.)

37. Smith, Kimberling, et al., "Specific Reading Disability," p. 1347; Smith, Pennington, et al., "A Genetic Analysis," p. 174.

38. Finucci, J. M., and Childs, B., "Are There Really More Dyslexic Boys Than Girls," in Ansara, A., Geschwind, A., Albert, M., Gartell, N., eds., *Sex Differences in Dyslexia* (Towson, Maryland: Orton Dyslexia Society, 1981).

39. McGuinness, D., *When Children Don't Learn: Understanding the Biology and Psychology of Learning Disabilities* (N.Y.: Basic Books, 1985).

40. Ibid., p. 21.

41. Ibid., p. 5.

42. Ibid., p. 8.

43. Ibid., p. 25.

44. Ibid., pp. 45, 106.

45. Ibid., pp. 106, 436.

46. Kertesz, A., "Are There Sex Differences in Acquired Alexia?" in Ansara, et al., *Sex Differences in Dyslexia.*

47. Ibid., p. 15 (emphasis added).

48. Ibid., p. 17.

49. Personal communication with Kertesz, May 5, 1986.

50. Mateer, C. A., Polen, S. B., and Ojemann, G. A., "Sexual Variation in Cortical Localization of Naming as Determined by Stimulation Mapping," *Behavioral and Brain Sciences,* 1982, vol. 2, pp. 311–12.

51. For example, two reviews on the subject disagree with her interpretation. One study, titled "Sex-Related Differences in Cerebral Hemispheric Asymmetry and Their Possible Relation to Dyslexia," concluded: sex differences are few; these few can be explained by gender differences in strategy and attention used in performing the research tasks, "rather than to true differences in lateralization" (Bryden, M. P., in Ansara, et al., *Sex Differences in Dyslexia.*

Citing his own research as an example, Bryden noted that his "male subjects showed a larger right ear effect in the divided attention condition" (that is, where attention was divided between two ears). However, this sex-related difference disappeared under focused-attention instruction. Thus, the sex-related differences that have been observed in previous dichotic studies "may have been due to sex-related differences in the way in which attention was deployed in the task." A study by another investigator found "only very small difference favoring a greater right-ear effect in males" when a similar procedure was used. Bryden concluded: "It would seem that males show a greater right-ear effect in verbal dichotic listening when strategy effects and attentional biases are permitted to influence the results, but this sex-related difference is less likely to be observed under more controlled conditions" (p. 84).

Another review, on sex differences in verbal laterality, found that in general the literature did "not support 'the traditional sex difference' of greater lateralization of verbal processes in males" and was "most compatible with a conclusion of no sex differences" (McKeever, W. F., "Sex and Cerebral Organization: Is It Really so Simple," in Ansara, et al., *Sex Differences in Dyslexia.* Of sex studies on auditory verbal laterality in adults, only one of seven studies found a sex difference, "with males being reported as being more lateralized than females." On the other hand, in six studies of children, only one found a sex difference, "and in this instance *females* were more lateralized than males" (p. 99, emphasis in original).

52. These were tests on the comprehension of meaning, auditory-vocal memory, and the application of correct linguistic categories to objects (McGuinness, *When Children Don't Learn,* p. 83).

53. Mittler, P., and Ward, J., "The Use of the Illinois Test of Psycholinguistic Abilities on British Four-Year-Old Children: A Normative and Factorial Study," *British Journal of Educational Psychology,* 1970, vol. 40, pp. 43–54.

54. McGuinness, *When Children Don't Learn,* p. 89.

55. Moore, T., "Language and Intelligence: A Longitudinal Study of the First 8 Years," *Human Development,* 1967, vol. 10, pp. 88–106.

56. Using her own research to bolster her theory, McGuinness fails to explain or realize that its evidence could as easily be interpreted to refute her theory. In a study of auditory perception, male and female college students at an English university were asked to listen for a target sound (*a* as in *day*, or *i* as in *night*) in a sequence of words and to decide which words contained them. Upon determining that male college students made more errors (for reasons that are left unexplored), McGuinness observed: "When university students with high linguistic ability fail at a simple task of matching a word heard to the visual image of that word, this may provide some indication of the difficulty that might be experienced by a certain class of dyslexics who can read but are incapable of written communication" (McGuinness, D., and Courtney, A., "Sex Differences in Visual and Phonetic Search," *Journal of Mental Imagery,* 1983, vol. 7, p. 103). That *may* be—however, McGuinness ignores the fact that *no* association apparently existed between performance on the task and "high linguistic ability" found in both sexes of the English university students. Without this connection, exactly what the test measured and what it has to do with "high linguistic ability" remains dubious at best.

57. Maccoby, E. E., and Jacklin, C. N., *The Psychology of Sex Differences* (Stanford, Ca.: Stanford University Press, 1974), pp. 84–85.

58. Benbow, C. P., and Stanley, J. C., "Sex Differences in Mathematical Ability: More Fact," *Science,* 1983, vol. 222, pp. 1029–31.

59. One review found no evidence "to support the contention that boys are more oriented toward vision, girls towards hearing" or that "differences in sensitivity to these two kinds of stimulation" were the "foundation of any sex differences in language acquisition. . . . Beginning in early infancy, the two sexes show a remarkable degree of similarity in the basic intellectual processes of perception, learning, and memory" (Maccoby and Jacklin, *The Psychology of Sex Differences,* pp. 35, 61).

Studies of language development as determined, for example, by children's use of phonemes and consonants, the age at which the first word was spoken, or the expression of intelligible speech suggested either there were no differences in many of the measures or that the rate of language acquisition was not substantially different between boys and girls (Fairweather, H., "Sex Differences in Cognition," *Cognition*, 1976, vol. 4, pp. 231–80).

Another review concerning the social-interaction theory found that "despite the alleged 'hunger' of girls for auditory stimuli" there was no "impressive evidence of a sex difference in attentiveness or responsiveness to auditory stimulation . . . [nor in infancy] did either sex consistently [show] more interest in social stimuli (i.e. faces and voices) or nonsocial stimuli than the other" (Maccoby and Jacklin, *The Psychology of Sex Differences,* pp. 26, 38).

A recent study of functional use of language in preschool boys and girls even showed a reverse pattern to that McGuinness believes exists. Reflecting adult modes of behavior, boys were found to be more talkative, sociable, and assertive (Cook, A. S., Fritz, J. J., McCormack, B. L., and Visperas, C., "Early Gender Differences in the Functional Usage of Language," *Sex Roles,* 1985, vol. 12, pp. 909–19).

60. Hyde, J. S., "How Large Are Cognitive Gender Differences?" *American Psychologist,* 1981, vol. 36, pp. 892–901. Also see Sherman, J., *Sex-Related Cognitive Differences: An Essay on Theory and Evidence* (Springfield, Ill.: Charles C Thomas, 1978); Plomin, R., and Foch, T. T., "Sex Differences and Individual Differences," *Child Development,* 1981, vol. 52, pp. 383–85.

61. Plomin and Foch, "Sex Differences," p. 383.

62. Rosenthal, R., and Rubin, D. B., "Further Meta-analytic Procedures for Assessing Cognitive Gender Differences," *Journal of Educational Psychology,* 1982, vol. 74, pp. 708–12.

63. Ibid., p. 711 (emphasis added).

For a discussion of methodological issues confounding conclusions about sex differences see Jacklin, C. N., "Methodological Issues in the Study of Sex-Related Differences," *Developmental Review,* 1981, vol. 1, pp. 266–73.

64. Canning, P. M., Orr, R. R., and Rourke, B. P., "Sex Differences in the Perceptual, Visual-Motor, Linguistic and Concept-Formation Abilities of Retarded Readers?" *Journal of Learning Disabilities,* 1980, vol. 13, pp. 563–67.

65. Ryckman, D.B., "Sex Differences in a Sample of Learning Disabled Children," *Learning Disability Quarterly,* 1981, vol. 4, pp. 48–52.

66. For discussions of math and spatial abilities in females see Beckwith, J., "Gender and Math Performance: Does Biology Have Implications for Educational Policy?" *Journal of Education,* 1983, vol. 165, pp. 158–74; Alper, J. S., "Sex Differences in Brain Asymmetry: A Critical Analysis," *Feminist Studies,* 1985, vol. 11, pp. 7–37; Fausto-Sterling, A., *Myths of Gender* (N.Y.: Basic Books, 1985); Bleier, R., *Science and Gender* (N.Y.: Pergamon Press, 1984). In addition, other work I have cited in this section, such as the reanalyses of verbal abilities in males and females, contains discussions of math and spatial abilities.

67. The primary sources of the men-of-eminence theory are two articles by Lloyd J. Thompson with the same title, "Language Disabilities in Men of Eminence." One was published in the *Journal of Learning Disabilities* (1971, vol. 4, pp. 39–50) and the other in *Bulletin of the Orton Society* (1969, vol. 19, pp. 113–20). Thompson's interpretations have been endlessly repeated, seemingly without anyone bothering to read any other biographical material to assess the validity of his accounts.

68. Clark, R. W., *Einstein: The Life and Times* (N.Y.: Crowell, 1971).

69. Ibid., p. 10.

70. Ibid., p. 12.

71. Ibid., p. 13.

72. Ibid., p. 14.

73. Ibid., p. 24.

74. Thompson, "Language Disabilities," p. 42.

75. Vanderbilt, B. M., *Thomas Edison, Chemist* (Washington, D.C.: American Chemical Society, 1971), p. 4.

76. Conot, R., *A Streak of Luck* (N.Y.: Seaview Books, 1979), p. 6.

77. Vanderbilt, *Thomas Edison,* p. 4.

78. Ibid.

79. Conot, *A Streak of Luck,* p. 7 (emphasis added).

80. Once he and a girl threw the entire school into an uproar when they lowered a baited fishhook from the second story, and hauled up a squawking, flapping chicken.

81. Ibid., p. 8.

82. Ibid., p. 9.

83. Ibid., p. 20.

84. Simpson, E. *Reversals: A Personal Account of Victory Over Dyslexia* (Boston: Houghton Mifflin, 1979).

85. Ibid., p. vii.

86. Simpson explains: "I should be prepared for death, not life. I was taught the catechism well above my grade level (which I learned without difficulty) and by special dispensation I was confirmed at age six, it being thought I probably wouldn't survive to the statutory age of eight" (ibid., p. 26).

87. Ibid., p. 24.

88. "When the bell rang for supper, in desperation she gave me ink and stationery. On the first piece of paper I pressed down so awkwardly I made a hole. On the second, I made a shameful blot. In the end, with me in tears and Mother Serafina beside herself with vexation, she cupped her hand around mine and guided it over the letters" (ibid., p. 25).

89. According to Thompson, in his biographical novel of Rodin, David Weiss, probably without realizing what he was revealing, conjured "up a typical picture of dyslexia" (*Naked Came I: A Novel of Rodin* [William Morrow, 1963]). Rodin's father, a police messenger, was himself illiterate. Hoping his son would grow up to be a police official, he was intent on giving his son the necessary education. When Auguste entered a nearby Jesuit school when he was about six, he had great difficulty memorizing the catechism and understanding arithmetic. When Rodin became the worst pupil in the school his father was reported to have said, "I have an idiot for a son." Rodin's uncle thought the Jesuits were to blame and undertook his nephew's education in a school he directed. After four years the uncle was forced to admit the Jesuits were right; Rodin knew no Latin and his spelling and composition were "horrible." The uncle told Rodin's father, "He is ineducable." Rodin did "learn to read and write to some extent."

Thompson suggests that confused brain dominance might have played a role in Rodin's dyslexia. As evidence he points to Rodin's famous sculpture "The Thinker," in which the right elbow rests on the left knee—"a most awkward and uncomfortable position for a right-sided person. Did Rodin have some confusion in sidedness?"

From early youth onward, Rodin's attention seemed to be focused entirely on nature and art. His father, on the other hand, desiring that his son not involve himself in frivolous diversion, opposed his absorption with drawing. Once when he was annoyed and disgusted with his five-year-old son's drawing, he threw the boy's sketches and crayons into the fire and sent him to bed without supper. The father, "mystified by Auguste's need to draw" told his son, "If I find any drawing around the house, I will spank you to an inch of your life. I must put you in school as soon as possible, before you become an idiot" (Weiss, *Naked Came I,* p. 9).

Taught by "solemn-faced monks," as one biographer described them (Leslie, A., *Rodin: Immortal Peasant,* Prentice-Hall, 1937), the "lessons did not appeal to his imagination. At nine years of age he scarcely knew anything. His attention seemed to be focused entirely on more interesting subjects." Weiss described the school as "a poor man's school, despising leisure and any other such nonsense, determined to turn out boys who would work hard, be content with their place, and be deeply devout. Art was taboo. When Auguste drew in his geography class, sketching a map of the Holy Roman Empire, it was torn up. When he did it again, a ruler descended harshly on his fingers. They hurt so much he could not hold a pencil for a week. Yet he had to draw; it had become the only thing that mattered. The next time Auguste was caught, he was whipped" (Weiss, *Naked Came I,* pp. 9–10).

Later in life, Rodin himself recalled: "I played truant a great deal at school. When it came to mathematics, which I never could understand, I made a point of being absent. I only wanted to study leaves, trees, architecture" (Tirel, J., *The Last Years of Rodin,* New York: Robert M. McBride, 1925, p. 20). His mother often found him "lying on the floor, copying pictures from old newspapers which had been used as wrapping for her market purchases."

For the young Rodin, life was more interesting than school:

> The maddening convention of education was imposed upon Auguste with small success. He was absorbed by his own discoveries, and the desolating rules of *a* and *b* and cubic fractions had to be drummed into his square unwilling head. At one thing he was adept, and that solitary accomplishment won him naught but punishment. [Leslie, *Rodin,* p. 8]

Rodin's father reportedly called him an idiot, but Weiss described the circumstances in which it occurred. Rodin began staying away from school and one day had gone to look at Notre Dame—"he liked the pinnacles, the light, far-reaching buttresses, and the great west front with its towers, as if everything had been measured with a view to grandeur." While he was viewing Notre Dame, the school informed his father of his truancy. When he returned home his father said, "I have an idiot for a son. He does not even know this is a day for school. He cannot even add and subtract." Without another word he thrashed his son with his heavy belt.

The change, at the age of nine, to his uncle's school was no improvement for young Rodin. He was especially distraught over leaving his sister, who had been his inseparable companion, and he spent the four years at the school in "gloomy loneliness" (Leslie, *Rodin,* p. 11). This was a mistake because "a conventional education was really wasted on him." The dull school existence made him unbearably unhappy, but this did not seem to bother his cousins and classmates. Added to this was a derision he encountered from his schoolmates who were of a higher social class and who mocked him openly.

At thirteen he returned to his parents' home in Paris. His formal education may have ended, but he was still unable to spell or add. When he announced his determination to study art, his father at first opposed the decision, then finally gave way.

90. In LD lore Hans Christian Andersen was very behind in his school work and was regarded at one time as a dullard. Even as an adult he spelled poorly and, according to McDonald Critchley:

> his manuscripts revealed many errors of a type which are characteristic of dyslexia. Naturally enough, these mistakes were usually detected and rectified by the editor. Occasionally, however, they escaped notice. Thus when Hans Christian Andersen wrote an account of his visit to Charles Dickens in London, names of English persons and places were often rendered incorrectly. These shortcomings were not always recognized by his publishers, so that they appeared in their original form in print. Among the numerous errors one may quote "Shack-

speare"; "Machbeth"; "Tamps" or "Temps" (Thames); "Manschester"; "Brackfest" (breakfast). [Critchley, *The Dyslexic Child,* p. 100]

Discussing Critchley's description of Andersen, Thompson commented: "Critchley presents clear evidence of characteristic dyslexia of extreme degree in the spelling of Hans Christian Andersen." The paragraph quoted above is the entirety of Critchley's "clear evidence."

In *Fairy Tale of My Life: An Autobiography,* Andersen describes himself as becoming enamored of the theater at an early age (N.Y.: Paddington Press, 1975). When his father died and his mother "went out washing," he was left entirely to himself, playing with his "little theater" at home, acting out comedies with dolls and doll clothes he had made for it, reading plays, and even writing one of his own, a tragedy. Thanks to a neighbor of the "educated class," who opened her library to him, he read Shakespeare and acted out the Bard's plays in his little puppet theater. His exact age at this time is not given but he appears to have been about ten or eleven.

Andersen became a street actor of sorts, reciting his written pieces, acting out whole scenes of Shakespeare, and singing songs in the street and in a factory where he was sent to work so that his mother might know where he was and what he was doing. For reasons that are not explained, he attended school erratically at this time. His talents had attracted the attention of several upper-class families in town and he was called to their houses to entertain them. One family took a particular interest in him and introduced him to a Danish prince with the advice, "If the prince should ask you what you have a liking for, answer him that your highest desire is to enter the grammar school." Denmark was sharply divided by class and the grammar school was reserved for children of "superior families." When asked the question, Andersen replied as he was advised. In his autobiography, Andersen describes the prince's reply: He said "my singing and declamation of poetry was really good and beautiful, but for all that was no mark of genius, and that I must keep in mind that studying was a long and expensive course! In the mean time he would take care of me if I would learn a handy trade, for instance that of a turner" (p. 20).

Instead of the grammar school, Andersen was sent to a "charity school," where he learned only religion, writing, and arithmetic. Instruction was poor and he continued to "scarcely spell a word correctly." He recalls looking at the "scholars of the grammar school" while they played in the church yard, and wishing he were among these "fortunate ones—not for the sake of play, but for the sake of the many books they had, and for what they might be able to become in the world."

When he was fourteen he decided he wanted to go to Copenhagen, a city far from his town, to enter the theater, although exactly what he might do—become a singer, actor, or playwright—was not clear in his young mind. But he had convinced himself: "It was the theater for which I was born; it was there that I should become a famous man." His mother wept but nonetheless gave him permission to go.

Andersen's is an extraordinary story of which I can give but a glimpse here (I strongly recommend the autobiography). At fourteen, with the optimism and naiveté of a child, he began seeking out men and women connected with the theater who would help him, seeking them out by simply going straight to their homes, knocking on the door, and telling them his wish to be a singer, a dancer, an actor. Usually he was endearing enough to be invited in to perform. He received special encouragement from artists who, as Andersen put it, had themselves "risen from poverty."

While experimenting and abandoning various art forms, he continued to read, having gotten permission to use various libraries, and began to write in earnest. Writers and intellectuals recognized Andersen's creativity and promise, but told him that he had to attend school in order to acquire the skills and intellectual discipline his writing required. Andersen recalls that at sixteen years old he wrote a tragedy in which "there was scarcely a word in it correctly written." Each day he heard what a good thing it would be for him if he could study, but no one came forth to provide the funds for him to do so. Finally, the director of the Theater Royal took an interest in him, arranged for him to receive free instruction in the grammar school, and recommended him to King Frederick VI, who granted him an annual sum to support himself. Thus, at seventeen he began grammar school, finding himself placed in the lowest class, among small children. Such a circumstance was not unusual for a fortunate child of the lower class. The headmaster himself, of peasant background, had not begun grammar school until he was twenty-three! In six years Andersen completed school, passed his examinations, and at last was considered—as he considered himself—a "student." A year later, at twenty-four, his first book was published, was read and praised throughout Copenhagen, was reprinted twice, and was published in Sweden. Andersen ends this chapter of his life with the following description:

> All houses began to be open to me; I flew from circle to circle in happy self-contentment. Under all these external and internal affections, I still however devoted myself industriously to study, so that without any teacher I passed my second academic examination, "Examen philologicum et philosophicum," with highest marks. [p. 65]

91. Nelson Rockefeller was a poor speller and reader all his life.

His father, concerned that his son was left-handed, attempted to change a condition that at the time was regarded as unfortunate. After failing to get Nelson to respond to instruction that he eat with his right hand, Mr. Rockefeller arrived at a new solution. At mealtime a rubber band with a string attached to it was put around Nelson's wrist. Mr. Rockefeller held the string and each time his son started to use his left hand for eating, he would pull the string. One biographer said he tugged gently, pulling the left hand away from the utensil for which it was reaching (Morris, J. A., *Nelson Rockefeller* (N.Y.: Harper, 1960), p. 13. Rockefeller himself recalled: "If I ate with my left hand he pulled the elastic with the string and let it snap" (Kramer, M., and Roberts, S., *I Never Wanted to Be Vice-President of Anything* (N.Y.: Basic Books, 1976), p. 39.

His father's continued efforts succeeded in reducing Nelson's left-handedness. "He did most things with his right hand but he played tennis left-handed and he learned to write—not very well—with either hand." He was "more or less ambidextrous" (Morris, *Rockefeller,* p. 13).

92. George S. Patton had a "definite language disability." His parents constantly read to him and delayed his schooling until he was twelve. Although the parents said they did this out of principle, "one wonders if the father might have had a reading problem or recognized one in his son and rationalized it and tried to circumvent it." At any rate, at twelve, George could not read and he never learned to read well. The hostility and frustration of "Old Blood and

Guts" derived from his language disability probably led to his acting out these feelings in warfare.

Patton's father and grandfather had graduated from Virginia Military Institute. George and his sister played soldier when they were young children, his sister being a major and George a private. Each morning their father saluted them and asked how the private and major were. His father made him a wooden sword and taught him how to build a fort. He also taught him how to shoot a rifle. Patton's grandfather had fought as an officer in the Confederate Army and died in battle [Blumenson, M., *Patton: The Man Behind the Legend, 1885–1945* (William Morrow, 1985), p. 16]. A great-grandfather, great-uncles, and uncles had all been in the military. In "addition to these warriors, many cousins held senior rank in the [Civil] War—at least three Slaughters, one Mercer, and three Pattons. The bloodlines were running pure, rich, and true" (p. 21). Enriched no doubt by the spice of dyslexia.

In a recent biography, Patton is described as dyslexic. It is claimed that his parents kept him out of school to spare him from the taunts and ridicule their son surely would have received from his classmates. The truthfulness of this is open to some question. According to the biographical account in *Cradles of Eminence,* from which Thompson obtained many of the men-of-eminence biographical sketches Patton's father

> believed that ontogeny recapitulates phylogeny, that each boy lives out the history of the human race and must start life as a savage enjoying fire, water, earth, the simple speech rhythms of the native chant and the nursery jingle. He did not believe in teaching children to read until they were adolescent and could read history books for themselves. [Goertzel, V., and Goertzel, M. G., *Cradles of Eminence* (Boston: Little, Brown, 1962), pp. 5–6]

It is difficult to know which account is true. The recent biography does not deal with this explanation. However, it is a fact that Patton did not attend school until he was 12. Beginning his education so late caused him several years of academic difficulty. Nonetheless, he completed high school, was accepted to West Point, and at the end of his first year passed his academic requirement. In his second year he ranked in the middle of his class.

In his last year at West Point he was able to write prose such as the following from his personal notebook: "In order for a man to become a great soldier . . . it is necessary . . . to read military history in its earliest and hence crudest form and to follow it down in natural sequence permitting his mind to grow with his subject until he can grasp with out effort the most abstruce question of the science of war because he is already permiated with all its elements" (Blumenson, *Patton,* p. 59). There are spelling errors here *(with out, abstruce,* and *permiated)* but whether within the entirety of the paragraph—in relation to its expression and overall correct spelling—these errors represent a neurologically based language disability, is at least questionable.

It appears certain that his "language disability" did not extend to reading because, following the precept in the above paragraph, "he read widely in military history all his life" (Ibid., p. 59).

93. Considering Woodrow Wilson's "general brilliance," his marked delay in learning his letters until he was nine and in learning to read until he was eleven cannot be attributed to the family's excessive reading to Wilson or to "poverty of stimulation." Thompson notes that "many moderately bright children learn to read on their own initiative before entering the first grade at the age of six." In his higher education Wilson excelled only in subjects that had to do with speech and made his name as a great debater. "Dyslexics frequently become fluent speakers, perhaps, in part, as a compensation for poor facility in reading and writing."

Wilson's parents believed that "children should not be confined in schoolrooms" (Bragdon, H. W., *Woodrow Wilson: The Academic Years* [Cambridge: Harvard University Press, 1967]). Consequently, he was kept home and read to so that he would acquire a strong educational foundation. Wilson did not go to school until he was nine and was reading in two years. The young Wilson was an average student but was intellectually curious and satisfied that curiosity at the age of fourteen in part by reading in the seminary library where his father taught. In his early teens he read Cooper, Marryat, and Scott. Whatever educational difficulties he had in childhood and adolescence appear to be attributable to a "secluded childhood, lack of systematic early education [due to the family relocating several times], and delicate health." But by sixteen he began to do better academically and at seventeen his report card at Davidson College showed that he had grades of 96 in Composition and English, 90 in Latin, 87 in Greek, 74 in mathematics, and 92 in declamation. Unfortunately, he became ill at the time and had to abandon school for a year and a half. Thus, not until he was nineteen was he healthy and sufficiently well prepared to enter Princeton (Cranston, R., *The Story of Woodrow Wilson* [Simon & Schuster, 1945]).

94. When William Butler Yeats was a child, sometime before the age of eight or nine, his father and several of his uncles and aunts tried, without success, to teach him to read. In his autobiography, Yeats attributes the failure to his difficulty to attend to anything less interesting than his own thoughts. Whether or not this is correct, this failure occurred before Yeats was eight! About that time, after he "had got beyond books of one syllable," he began reading a multivolumed encyclopedia.

By Yeats's account, he was reading successfully when he began school but his father had stern ideas about what constituted a proper education:

> When I first went to school, he tried to keep me from reading boys' papers, because a paper, by its very nature, as he explained to me, had to be made for the average boy or man and so could not but thwart one's growth. He took away my paper and I had not courage to say that I was but reading and delighting in a prose retelling of the *Iliad.* [*Autobiography* (N.Y.: Collier Books, 1965) p. 31]

By fifteen he had read "Darwin and Wallace, Huxley and Haeckel" (p. 39).

95. When Lee Harvey Oswald's mother divorced her husband she was left without support. Trying to adjust her life to being single and to support her children meant frequent relocation. Oswald "transferred from one public school to another" and by fifth grade "had attended six different public schools" in the Dallas–Fort Worth area (Epstein, E. J., *Legend: The Secret World of Lee Harvey Oswald* [N.Y.: McGraw-Hill, 1978], p. 58). His mother then moved to New York City and in the fall of 1952 he was transferred to a school in the Bronx, where he failed to attend for more than half the time. The following January the family moved again and Oswald was again transferred to another school, "which he refused to attend, perhaps because his classmates made fun of his Southern ways." In the spring of 1953 Oswald was picked up for truancy. The psychiatrist who examined the thirteen-year-old boy wrote in his report:

> Lee is a youngster with superior mental endowments, functioning presently in the bright-normal range of mental efficiency. His abstract thinking capacity and his vocabulary are well-developed. No retardation in school subjects could be found despite truancy. [p. 59]

Oswald returned to school the following September and "made considerable progress." Oswald remained at the school for slightly more than a semester, when his mother moved to New Orleans where, despite continued school problems, he "became a voracious reader of books." When he turned sixteen, he signed his mother's name to a note stating that the family was moving out of town and dropped out of school. Unemployed, Oswald spent "all of his time at home reading 'deep books' " (p. 61).

96. Arguments for and against maturational-lag theories may be found in the following: Satz, P., Taylor, H. G., Friel, J., and Fletcher, J. M., "Some Developmental and Predictive Precursors of Reading Disabilities: A Six-Year Follow-up," in Benton, A. L., and Pearl, D., eds., *Dyslexia: An Appraisal of Current Knowledge* (NY: Oxford University Press, 1978); DiPasquale, G. W., Moule, A. D., and Flewelling, R. W., "The Birthdate Effect," *Journal of Learning Disabilities,* 1980, vol. 13, pp. 4–12; Waber, D. P., "Maturation: Thoughts on Renewing an Old Acquaintanceship." in Caplan, D., ed., *Biological Studies of Mental Processes* (Cambridge: MIT Press, 1982); Waber, D. P., "Sex Differences in Cognition: A Function of Maturation Rate?" *Science,* 1976, vol. 192, pp. 572–73.; Diamond, G. H., "The Birthdate Effect—A Maturational Effect?" *Journal of Learning Disabilities,* 1983, vol. 16, pp. 161–164; Gredler, G. R., "The Birthdate Effect: Fact or Artifact?" *Journal of Learning Disabilities,* 1980, vol. 13, pp. 239–42; Green, D. R., and Simmons, S. V., "Chronological Age and School Entrance," *Elementary School Journal,* 1962, vol. 63, pp. 41–47; Jinks, P. C., "An Investigation into the Effect of Date of Birth on Subsequent School Performance," *Educational Research,* 1964, vol. 6, pp. 220–25; Webb, G., *Learning Disabilities—Uniquely American or Cross-Cultural?* (unpublished doctoral dissertation, Boston College, 1976); Gordon, M., Post, E. M., Crouthamel, C., and Richman, R. A., "Do Children with Constitutional Delay Really Have More Learning Problems?" *Journal of Learning Disabilities,* 1984, vol. 17, pp. 291–93; Rourke, B. P., "Reading Retardation in Children: Developmental Lag or Deficit?" in Knights and Bakker, eds., *The Neuropsychology of Learning Disorders.*

97. Ferreri, C. A., and Wainwright, R. B., *Breakthrough for Dyslexia and Learning Disabilities* (Pompano Beach, Florida: Exposition Press of Florida, 1984).

7 Families, Children, and Learning: An Overview of the Theory of Interactivity

1. Peele, S., "Reductionism in the Psychology of the Eighties: Can Biochemistry Eliminate Addiction, Mental Illness, and Pain?" *American Psychologist,* 1981, vol. 36, pp. 807–18.

2. Bronfenbrenner, U., *The Ecology of Human Development* (Cambridge: Harvard University Press, 1979), p. 16.

3. Ibid.

4. Leontiev. A. N., *Activity, Consciousness, and Personality* (Englewood Cliffs, N. J.: Prentice-Hall, 1978), p. 14. In the following discussion, I am heavily indebted to the theoretical work of Leontiev and Vygotsky. Where I have not quoted their work directly, these two psychologists remain influences for many ideas in my outline of the interactivity theory of LD.

5. Nisbet, R., *Sociology as an Art Form* (N.Y.: Oxford University Press, 1976).

6. Romand Coles, personal communication, September 12, 1986.

7. Nisbet, *Sociology,* p. 17.

8. Conner, F. P., "Improving School Instruction for Learning Disabled Children: The Teachers College Institute," *Exceptional Education Quarterly,* 1983, vol. 4, pp. 23–44.

At another institute, the "learning strategies approach" is based on a model "that views behavior as a function of the interaction between the characteristics of learner variables and environmental variables" (Schumaker, J. B., and Deshler, D. D., *Setting Demand Variables: A Major Factor in Program Planning for the LD Adolescent,* unpublished manuscript, University of Kansas, Institute for Research in Learning Disabilities, 1983).

9. Rumelhart, D., "Toward an Interactive Model of Reading," in Dornic, S., ed., *Attention and Performance VI* (Hillsdale, N.J.: Erlbaum, 1977).

10. Bruner, J., *In Search of Mind* (N.Y.: Harper & Row, 1983).

11. Gottfried, A. W., and Gottfried, A. E., "Home Environment and Cognitive Development in Young Children of Middle-Socioeconomic-Status Families," in Gottfried, A. W., ed., *Home Environment and Early Cognitive Development* (N.Y.: Academic Press, 1984).

12. Also see Barnard, K., Bee, H., and Hammond, M., "Home Environment and Cognitive Development in a Healthy, Low-Risk Sample: The Seattle Study," in Gottfried, *Home Environment.* The investigators studied healthy working- and middle-class families who appeared to provide a healthy environment for their children. The study showed moderate to strong correlations between the quality of the home environment and later measures of cognition.

13. Wachs, T. D., "Proximal Experience and Early Cognitive-Intellectual Development: The Social Environment," in Gottfried, *Home Environment.*

14. Carew, J. V., "Experience and the Development of Intelligence in Young Children at Home and in Day Care," *Monographs of the Society for Research in Child Development,* 1980, vol. 45, no. 187, pp. 6–7; MacPhee, D., Ramey, C. T., and Yeates, K. O., "Home Environment and Early Cognitive Development: Implications for Intervention," in Gottfried, *Home Environment.*

15. Kronick, D., *Three Families* (San Rafael, Calif.: Academic Therapy Publications, 1976).

16. Ibid., p. 12.

17. Ibid.

18. Each family had "two parents and two biological children, with the learning-disabled child being between nine and eleven years of age." In each instance Doreen Kronick, the researcher, had access to the "learning disabled child's psychological assessment to ensure that the child was learning disabled." Kronick spent forty hours in each home and observed the families over a period of six weeks.

19. Ibid., p. 13.

20. Ibid., pp. 23, 25.

21. Ibid., pp. 40, 46.

22. Ibid., p. 61.

23. Ibid., pp. 36, 88.

24. Miller, D. R., and Westman, J. C., "Reading Disability as a Condition of Family Stability," *Family Process,* 1964, vol. 3, pp. 66–76; Miller and Westman, "Family Teamwork and Psychotherapy," *Family Process,* 1966, vol. 5, pp. 49–59.

25. Miller and Westman, "Family Teamwork," p. 58.

26. Miller and Westman, "Reading Disability," p. 72.

27. Miller and Westman, "Family Teamwork," p. 50.

28. Ibid., pp. 50, 58.

29. Feuerstein, R., *The Dynamic Assessment of Retarded Performers* (Baltimore: University Park Press, 1979), p. 231.

30. Ibid., p. 238.

31. Ibid., p. 239.

32. Ibid., pp. 339–40.

33. Eisenstein, Z., "Some Notes on the Relations of Capitalist Patriarchy," in Eisenstein, Z. R., ed., *Capitalist Patriarchy and the Case for Socialist Feminism* (N.Y.: Monthly Review Press, 1979).

34. Chodorow, N., "Mothering, Male Dominance, and Capitalism," in Eisenstein, *Capitalist Patriarchy.*

35. "These participants in the work force need such support because their work is alienating and affectless, and would be otherwise unbearable. Women's role in the family, then, serves as an important siphon for work discontent . . . to ensure worker stability. It also removes the need for employers themselves to attend to such stability or to create contentedness" (ibid., pp. 96–97).

36. Eisenstein, "Some Notes on the Relations," p. 48.

37. Cowan, R. S., *More Work for Mother* (N.Y.: Basic Books, 1983).

For example, food preparation and cleanup is less time consuming than it had been, but the time saved has been lost to "an increase in time devoted to shopping and record keeping." Washing machines and wash-and-wear clothing have not reduced laundry time "perhaps because people now have more clothes" or "wash them more often" (Heiss, J., "Family Roles and Behavior," in Boudreau, F. A., Sennott, R. S., and Wilson, M, eds., *Sex Roles and Social Patterns* (N.Y.: Praeger, 1986).

38. Cowan, *More Work,* p. 212.

39. Margolis, M. L., *Mothers and Such* (Berkeley: University of California, 1985), p. 168.

With the development of technology and increased identification as "housewife," American women in this century have been further burdened by the increasing exhortation in advertising and women's magazines that they become model homemakers, not simply cooking for their families but making wholesome nutritious or gourmet meals, not simply scrubbing floors but creating "an attractive environment in which their families could thrive" (ibid., p. 155).

40. Dally, A., *Inventing Motherhood: The Consequences of an Ideal* (N.Y.: Schocken, 1982), p. 201.

41. De Beauvoir, S., *The Second Sex* (N.Y.: Knopf, 1961), p. 489.

42. Women who work outside the home carry a double burden. Society regards them as part-time mothers, as mothers who put their most important responsibility on the back burner, and a majority of them internalize these social biases and carry not only the blame for their children's failures, which other mothers carry, but also that of being absent mothers. The traditional nuclear family's division of labor, arising as it has from social, economic, and cultural relationships, demands multiple and inordinate homemaking responsibilities and personal limitations for one adult regardless of whether that one adult works outside the home.

43. In spite of some recent individual and isolated cases where both parents work outside and inside the home equally, most of the home responsibilities have remained women's, even when it has meant working a forty-hour week outside and a forty-hour week inside the home. Needless to say, since more and more women continue to enter the labor market, the social and personal implications of how children are cared for have become more intricate. Women have shown themselves much more ready to assume traditionally male roles than males have been willing to assume those traditionally female roles that are ultimately connected with the child's cognitive development.

44. Kuhn, A., "Structures of Patriarchy and Capital in the Family," in Kuhn, A., and Wolpe, A., eds., *Feminism and Materialism* (Boston: Routledge & Kegan Paul, 1978).

45. Ibid., p. 63.

8 Schools and Schooling in Interactivity

1. Kohl, H., "And Not So Gladly Teach," *Nation,* May 24, 1986, p. 736.

2. Bowles, S., and Gintis, H., *Schooling in Capitalist America* (N.Y.: Basic Books, 1976); Carnoy, M., *Education as Cultural Imperialism* (N.Y.: McKay, 1974); Karabel, J. K., and Halsey, A. H., eds., *Power and Ideology in Education* (N.Y.: Oxford University Press, 1977); Sarup, M., *Marxism and Education* (London: Routledge & Kegan Paul, 1978).

3. Anyon, J., "Social Class and the Hidden Curriculum of Work," *Journal of Education,* 1980, vol. 162, pp. 67–92.

4. Ibid., p. 88.

5. Carlson, D. " 'Updating' Individualism and the Work Ethic: Corporate Logic in the Classroom," *Curriculum Inquiry,* 1982, vol. 12, pp. 125–160; Mickelson, R. A., "Social Stratification Processes in Secondary Schools: A Comparison of Beverly Hills High School and Morningside High School," *Journal of Education,* 1980, vol. 162, pp. 83–101.

6. Greer, C., *The Great School Legend* (N.Y.: Viking Press, 1972), p. 36.

7. Ibid., p. 59.

8. Snow, C. E., "Literacy and Language: Relationships During the Preschool Years," *Harvard Educational Review,* 1983, vol. 53, pp. 165–89.

9. Pedersen, E., Faucher, T. A., and Eaton, W. W., "A New Perspective on the Effects of First-Grade Teachers on Children's Subsequent Adult Status," *Harvard Educational Review,* 1978, vol. 48, pp. 1–31.

10. Ibid., p. 19.

11. Brookover, W. B., "Can We Make Schools Effective for Minority Students?" *Journal of Negro Education,* 1985, vol. 54, pp. 257–68.

12. Rist, R. C., *The Urban School: A Factory for Failure* (Cambridge: MIT Press, 1973).

13. Bloomberg Jr., W., "The School as a Factory," paper prepared for the Interdistrict Institute, Homewood-Flossmoor, Illinois, 1967.

14. Freire, P., *Pedagogy of the Oppressed* (N.Y.: Herder and Herder, 1971), pp. 57–58.

15. Sirotnik, K. A., "What You See Is What You Get—Consistency, Persistency, and Mediocrity in Classrooms," *Harvard Educational Review,* 1985, vol. 53, pp. 16–31.

16. Ibid., p. 20.

17. Mehan, H., *Learning Lessons* (Cambridge: Harvard University Press, 1979).

18. Moore, D. T., "Discovering the Pedagogy of Experience," *Harvard Educational Review,* 1981, vol. 51, pp. 286–300.

19. Durkin, D., "What Classroom Observations Reveal About Reading Comprehension Instruction," *Reading Research Quarterly,* 1978–1979, vol. 14, pp. 481–533.

20. Ibid., p. 506.

21. Brophy, J., "Interactions of Male and Female Students with Male and Female Teachers," in Wilkinson, L. C., and Marrett, C. B., eds., *Gender Influences in Classroom Interaction* (N.Y.: Academic Press, 1985).

22. Bank, B. J., Biddle, B. J., and Good, T. L., "Sex Roles, Classroom Instruction, and Reading Achievement," *Journal of Educational Psychology,* 1980, vol. 72, pp. 119–32.

23. Leinhardt, G., Mar Seewald, A., and Engel, M., "Learning What's Taught: Sex Differences in Instruction," *Journal of Educational Psychology,* 1979, vol. 71, pp. 432–39.

24. Ibid., p. 432.

25. Bank, Biddle, and Good, "Sex Roles," p. 122.

26. Ibid., p. 123.

27. Ibid, pp. 125.

28. Ibid.

29. Solomon, D., and Kendall, A. J., *Individual Characteristics and Children's Performance in Varied Educational Settings* (Rockville, Md.: Montgomery County Public Schools, 1976). Summarized by Bank, Biddle, and Good, p. 126.

30. Bank, Biddle, & Good, "Sex Roles," p. 127.

31. Coles, G. S., "The Polyphony of Learning in the Learning Disabled," *Learning Disability Quarterly,* 1984, vol. 7, pp. 321–28.

32. Vygotsky, L. S., *Thought and Language* (Cambridge: MIT Press, 1962), pp. 150–151.

33. Leontiev, A. N., *Activity, Consciousness, and Personality* (Englewood Cliffs, N.J.: Prentice-Hall, 1978).

34. Ibid., p. 89.

35. Ibid., p. 88.

36. For other case studies that discuss reading behavior that can be misinterpreted as symtomatic of dyslexia see Johnston, P., "Understanding Reading Disability: A Case Study Approach," *Harvard Educational Review,* 1985, vol. 55, pp. 153–177; Coles, G. S., "Adult Illiteracy and Learning Theory: A Study of Cognition and Activity," *Science and Society,* 1983–84, vol. 47, pp. 451–82; Hood, L., McDermott, R., and Cole, M., "Let's Try to Make It a Good Day—Some Not So Simple Ways," *Discourse Processes,* 1980, vol. 3, pp. 155–168.

For discussions of the application of case studies to LD and other problems see Guralnick, M. J., "The Application of Single-Subject Research Designs to the Field of Learning Disabilities," *Journal of Learning Disabilities,* 1978, vol. 11, pp. 414–21; Runyon, W. M., "In Defense of the Case Study Method," *American Journal of Orthopsychiatry,* 1982, vol. 52, pp. 440–46.

37. Ibid., p. 85.

38. Ibid., p. 89.

39. Ibid., p. 87.

40. By itself, the theory of the zone of proximal development as laid out by Vygotsky represents a substantial but not particularly radical departure from current LD theory and practice. The theory could be incorporated into the field by narrowly focusing on mediating instruction and its impact on the cognitive development of the LD child while at the same time *disregarding* all other influences, such as schools and teachers, and those forces affecting them. However, the theory and approach of the zone of cognitive development is presently almost totally disregarded in the LD field, a fact which is characteristic of the generally conservative nature of LD research and practice.

41. The concepts self-efficacy, as developed by Albert Bandura, and learned helplessness are similar to my notion of powerlessness. I prefer the latter term because it is more connotative of the entire complex of power relationships within the classroom and not solely attributes of the individual.

42. Licht, B. G., and Dweck, C. S., "Determinants of Academic Achievement: The Interaction of Children's Achievement Orientations with Skill Area," *Developmental Psychology,* 1984, vol. 20, pp. 628–36.

43. Torgesen, J., and Goldman, T., "Verbal Rehearsal and Short-Term Memory," *Child Development,* 1977, vol. 48, pp. 56–60; Torgesen, J. K., Murphy, H. A., and Ivey, C., "The Influence of an Orienting Task on the Memory Performance of Children with Reading Problems," *Journal of Learning Disabilities,* 1979, vol. 12, pp. 396–401; Torgesen, "Conceptual and Educational Implications of the Use of Efficient Task Strategies by Learning Disabled Children," *Journal of Learning Disabilities,* 1980, vol. 13, pp. 364–71; Torgesen, J. K., and Houck, D. G., "Processing Deficiencies of Learning-Disabled Children Who Perform Poorly on the Digit Span Test," *Journal of Educational Psychology,* 1980, vol. 72, pp. 141–60; Graham, S., and Freeman, S., "Strategy Training and Teacher vs. Student Controlled Study Conditions: Effects on LD Students' Spelling Performance," *Learning Disability Quarterly,* 1986, vol. 9, pp. 15–22.

44. Griswold, P. C., Gelzheiser, L. M., and Shepherd, M. J., "How Good Is the Evidence for a Production Deficiency Among Learning Disabled Students?" *Journal of Educational Psychology,* 1985, vol. 77, pp. 553–61.

45. Rueda, R., and Mehan, H., "Metacognition and Passing: A Context Specific Interpretation of Learning Disabilities," unpublished manuscript, 1985.

46. For discussion of learning disabled children and self-esteem see Korhonen, T., "A Follow-up Study of Finnish Children with Specific Learning Disabilities," *Acta Paedopsychiatria,* 1984, vol. 50, pp. 255–63.

For discussions of motivation see Adelman, H. S., "The Concept of Intrinsic Motivation: Implications for Practice and Research Related to Learning Disability," *Learning Disability Quarterly,* 1978, vol. 1, pp. 43–54; Adelman, H. S., and Taylor, L., "Classifying Students by Inferred Motivation to Learn," *Learning Disability Quarterly,* 1983, vol. 6, pp. 201–06; Adelman and Taylor, "Enhancing Motivation of Overcoming Learning and Behavior Problems," *Journal of Learning Disabilities,* 1983, vol. 16, pp. 384–92; Licht, B. G., and Kistner, J. A., "Motivational Problems of Learning-Disabled Children: Individual Differences and Their Implications for Treatment," in Torgesen, J. K., and Wong, B. Y. L., eds., *Psychological and Educational Perspectives on Learning Disabilities* (N.Y.: Academic Press, 1986).

9 Reconsidering Neurology

1. Rosenzweig, M. R., "Experience, Memory, and the Brain," *American Psychologist,* 1984, vol. 39, pp. 365–76; Rosenzweig, M. R., Bennett, E. L., and Diamond, M. C. "Brain Changes in Response to Experience," *Scientific American,* 1972, vol. 226, pp. 22–30.

2. Money, J., and Annecillo, C., "IQ Change of Domicile in the Syndrome of Reversible Hyposomatotropinism (Psychosocial Dwarfism): Pilot Investigation," *Psychoneuroendocrinology,* 1976, vol. 1, pp. 427–29; Money, J., "Child Abuse: Growth Failure, IQ Deficit, and Learning Disability," *Journal of Learning Disabilities,* 1982, vol. 15, pp. 579–82.

3. Money, "Child Abuse," p. 581.

4. Money and Annecillo, "IQ Change of Domicile."

5. Coles, C. S., and Goldstein, L., "Hemispheric EEG Activation and Literacy Development," *The International Journal of Clinical Neuropsychology,* 1985, vol. 7, pp. 3–7.

6. Lassen, N. A., Ingvar, D. H., and Skinhoj, E., "Brain Function and Blood Flow," *Scientific American,* 1978, vol. 239, pp. 62–71.

7. Goldstein, L., "Some Relationships Between Quantified Hemispheric EEG and Behavioral States in Man," in Gruzelier, J., Florheury, P., eds.,

Hemispheric Asymmetries of Function and Psychopathology (N.Y.: Elsevier, 1979).

8. Campbell, R., "The Lateralization of Emotion: A Critical Review," *International Journal of Psychology,* 1982, vol. 17, pp. 211–29.

9. The EEG data showed reduced features of abnormal right-hemisphere amplitude.

10. See Hiscock, M., and Kinsbourne, M., "Laterality and Dyslexia: A Critical View," *Annals of Dyslexia,* 1982, vol. 32, pp. 177–228; Naylor, H., "Reading Disability and Lateral Asymmetry: An Information Processing Analysis," *Psychological Bulletin,* 1980, vol. 87, pp. 531–45; Satz, P., "Cerebral Dominance and Reading Disability: An Old Problem Revisited," in Knights and Bakker, *Neuropsychology of Learning Disorders.*

11. Marlowe, M., and Errera, J., "Low Lead Levels and Behavior Problems in Children," *Behavior Disorders,* 1982, vol. 7, pp. 163–72; Marlowe, M., Folio, R., Hall, D., and Errera, J., "Increased Lead Burdens and Trace-Mineral Status in Mentally Retarded Children," *Journal of Special Education,* 1982, vol. 16, pp. 87–99.

12. Marlowe, M., Cossairt, A., Welch, K., and Errera, J., "Hair Mineral Content as a Predictor of Learning Disabilities," *Journal of Learning Disabilities,* 1984, vol. 17, pp. 418–21.

13. Ibid.

14. Ely, D. L., Mostardi, R. A., Woebkenberg, N., and Worstell, D., "Aerometric and Hair Trace Metal Content in Learning-Disabled Children," *Environmental Research,* 1981, vol. 25, pp. 325–29; Ernhart, C. B., Landa, B., and Schell, N. B., "Subclinical Levels of Lead and Developmental Deficit: A Multivariate Follow-up Reassessment," *Pediatrics,* 1981, vol. 67, pp. 911–19.

15. Capel, I. D., Pinnock, M. H., Dorrell, H. M., Williams, D. C., and Grant, E. C. G., "Comparison of Concentrations of Some Trace, Bulk, and Toxic Metals in the Hair of Normal and Dyslexic Children," *Clinical Chemistry,* 1981, vol. 27, pp. 879–81.

16. Thatcher, R. W., Lester, M. L., McAlaster, R., Horst, R., and Ignasias, S. W., "Intelligence and Lead Toxins in Rural Children," *Journal of Learning Disabilities,* 1983, vol. 16, pp. 355–59.

A reexamination of a study that five years earlier had reported a relationship between moderate levels of lead exposure and cognitive impairment in preschool urban black children found "no significant association of preschool lead level and outcome measures—including cognitive measures, reading tests, and teacher behavior ratings" (Ernhart, C. B., Landa, B., and Wolf, A. W., "Subclinical Lead Level and Developmental Deficit: Re-analyses of Data," *Journal of Learning Disabilities,* 1985, vol. 18, pp. 475–79; Ernhart, Landa, and Schell, "Subclinical Levels of Lead"; Ernhart, C. B., and Morrow-Tlucak, M., "The Caretaking Environment and Exposure of Children to Lead," *Science Reviews Limited* (forthcoming).

Unfortunately, the work of the first chief author of this research was and remains partially supported by the lead industry, which casts a shadow on the objectivity of the research (Marshall, E., "EPA Faults Classic Lead Poisoning Study," *Science,* 1983, vol. 222, pp. 906–07).

17. Ibid.

18. Pihl, R. O., "Hair Element Content in Learning Disabled Children," *Science,* 1977, vol. 198, pp. 204–06; ; Ely, et al., "Aerometric and Hair Trace Metal Content"; Thatcher, R. W., and Lester, M. L., "Nutrition, Environmental Toxins and Computerized EEG: A Mini-Max Approach to Learning Disabilities," *Journal of Learning Disabilities,* 1985, vol. 18, pp. 287–97; Capel, et al., "Comparison of Concentration."

19. Marlowe, et al., "Hair Mineral Content."

20. Capel, et al., "Comparison of Concentrations."

21. Ely, et al., "Aerometric and Hair Trace Metal Content." Furthermore, overlap of cadmium levels between normal and learning-disabled groups left problematic why normal children with the same cadmium levels as those of learning-disabled children are not learning disabled.

22. Lester, M. L., Thatcher, R. W., and Monroe-Lord, L., "Refined Carbohydrate Intake, Hair Cadmium Levels, and Cognitive Functioning in Children," *Nutrition and Behavior,* 1982, vol. 1, pp. 3–13; Lester, M. I., Horst, R. L., and Thatcher, R. W., "Protective Effects of Zinc and Calcium Against Heavy Metal Impairment of Children's Cognitive Function," *Nutrition and Behavior,* 1986, vol. 3, pp. 145–61.

23. Some answers to the seeming contradictions in toxic-metal research lie in the complex association of these metals with each other and with nutrients. For example, toxic metals possibly interact synergistically. Thus lead by itself might not be associated with cognitive performance but the combination of lead and aluminum might be (Moon, C., Marlowe, M., Stellern, J., and Errera, J., "Main and Interaction Effects of Metallic Pollutants on Cognitive Functioning," *Journal of Learning Disabilities,* 1985, vol. 18, pp. 217–21). An example of the relationship between metals and nutrients is the inverse correlation between phosphorus and lead found in mentally retarded children: children with high levels of phosphorus had lower lead levels, making it appear that increased phosphorus could result in lower lead levels. Significantly, no children had both high lead and high phosphorus levels. The researchers noted that "this finding is in agreement with experimental animal studies which have demonstrated that diets deficient in phosphorus result in higher tissue concentrations of lead at equivalent levels of intake:" (Marlowe, et al., "Increased Lead Burdens," p. 95).

The antagonistic biochemical relationship of zinc and cadmium also illustrates the role nutrients may play in determining the concentration of toxic metals. Though cadmium can displace zinc in biochemical reactions and interfere with the metabolic processes zinc normally catalyzes, generous amounts of zinc in the diet can prevent cadmium from doing so. Therefore, "the zinc to cadmium ratio in foods is critical for determining" the amount of cadmium in the body (Thatcher and Lester, "Nutritional Environmental Toxins," p. 292).

These kinds of nutrient-metal relationships are not uncommon: "certain dietary factors have been found to ameliorate heavy metal toxicity by afffecting rates of absorption or excretion of these pollutants. A dietary deficiency of zinc, copper, iron, calcium and vitamin C has been found to enhance toxicity of lead or cadmium; whereas, an excess dietary intake of these micronutrients has been shown in laboratory animals to be protective" (ibid., p. 291).

24. Hambidge, K. M., "Hair Analyses: Worthless for Vitamins, Limited for Minerals," *American Journal of Clinical Nutrition,* 1982, vol. 36, pp. 943–49.

25. Ibid., p. 946.

26. "[I]t is essential to know which tissue concentrations, stores, or body pools of each trace element, if any, do correlate with hair concentrations. Unfortunately, no such information is available currently for the majority of elements. Until data are available, it is premature to reach final conclusions on the value of hair analysis" (ibid., p. 946).

27. Feingold, B. F., *Why Your Child Is Hyperactive* (N.Y.: Random House, 1974).

28. Cott, A., *Dr. Cott's Help for Your Learning Disabled Child: The Orthomolecular Treatment* (N.Y.: Times Books, 1985).

29. Kershner, J., and Hawke, W., "Megavitamins and Learning Disorders: A Controlled Double-Blind Experiment," *Journal of Nutrition,* 1979, vol. 109, pp. 819–26. The research was especially interested in testing claims made in papers by Alan Cott. His recent book, *Dr. Cott's Help,* advances similar claims found in his earlier papers.

30. Prinz, R. J., Roberts, W. A., and Hantmann, E., "Dietary Correlates of Hyperactive Behavior in Children," *Journal of Consulting and Clinical Psychology,* 1980, vol. 48, pp. 760–69; Barling, J., and Bullen, G., "Dietary Factors and Hyperactivity: A Failure to Replicate," *The Journal of Genetic Psychology,* 1985, vol. 146, pp. 117–23; Rapoport, J. L., "Effects of Dietary Substances in Children," *Journal of Psychiatric Research,* 1982–83, vol. 17, pp. 187–91.

31. Mattes, J. A., "The Feingold Diet: A Current Reappraisal," *Journal of Learning Disabilities,* 1983, vol. 16, pp. 319–23.

The National Advisory Committee on Hyperkinesis and Food Additives concluded there was little need for further research on the subject because the results were overwhelmingly negative. Its conclusions however should not be surprising since the committee was established and supported by the Nutrition Foundation, an organization of major (mostly junk-) food manufacturers (National Advisory Committee, *Final Report to the Nutrition Foundation* [N.Y.: The Nutrition Foundation, 1980]).

Also negative, but slightly less so, were the conclusions of reviewers whose statistical analysis of the studies did not, in their estimation, "offer support for the Feingold hypothesis" because the diet "produces a small treatment effect." Where any appreciable improvement was found it was related to "overt aspects of behavior (i.e., symptoms of hyperactivity)" rather than to "cognition (e.g., attention or learning ability)" for which there were "essentially no treatment effects" (Kavale, K. A., and Forness, S. R., "Hyperactivity and Diet Treatment: A Meta-analysis of the Feingold Hypothesis," *Journal of Learning Disabilities,* 1983, vol. 16, pp. 324–30).

32. Conners, C. K., *Food Additives and Hyperactive Children* (N.Y.: Plenum Press, 1980).

33. Weiss, B., "Food Additives and Environmental Chemicals as Sources of Childhood Behavior Disorders," *Journal of the American Academy of Child Psychiatry,* 1982, vol. 21, pp. 144–52.

34. Rimland, B., "The Feingold Diet: An Assessment of the Reviews by Mattes, by Kavale and Forness, and Others," *Journal of Learning Disabilities,* 1983, vol. 16, pp. 331–33.

35. Quoted in Rimland, "The Feingold Diet," p. 331.

Another of Rimland's criticisms was that the dosage levels even of the few artificial colors studied were "ridiculously small." Most of the studies used doses of 1.6 to 26 milligrams of food colors per day, the latter amount being the Nutritional Foundation's estimate of per-capita daily consumption of these colorings. However, this estimate was considerably below that of the Food and Drug Administration, which found the daily consumption of food colors to be "59 mg/day for children ages one to five and 76 mg/day for children six to 12 years old." These average amounts were far exceeded by some children who, at ages six to twelve, used as much as 312 milligrams a day. Rimland emphasized Feingold's sentiments: the issue was not food coloring alone but the "denatured, refined, additive-laden artificial foods" (ibid., p. 333).

36. Weiss, B., "Feingold Diet Research Seen as Inadequate," *Journal of Learning Disabilities,* 1983, vol. 16, pp. 574–75.

37. Ely, et al., "Aerometric and Hair Trace Metal Content," p. 333.

38. Food industries use growth-stimulating hormones and antibiotics in cattle and chicken; use more than 2,700 chemicals in meat processing; use artificial dyes, flavors, and preservatives in a multitude of foods; use chemicals, sugar, and caffeine in soft drinks; make white breads from processed flour from which the bran and germ have been removed, resulting in the loss of important amounts of protein, vitamins, and minerals, leaving little more than starchy calories, even in those processed foods in which vitamins and minerals are added back into them (Silverstein, B., *Fed Up: The Food Forces That Make You Fat, Sick and Poor* (Boston: South End Press, 1984); Null, G., *The Complete Guide to Health and Nutrition* (N.Y.: Delacorte Press, 1984).

39. Though an increasing number of people are avoiding blatant junk foods and a vegetarian minority avoids contaminated meats, they usually still have no choice but to eat contaminated vegetables and fruits.

40. More specific interventions are possible, such as chelation therapy, an intravenous method for removing toxic metals from the body.

41. Gladiators did fight lions.

10 The Function of the LD Field

1. Baran, P. A., and Sweezy, P. M., *Monopoly Capital: An Essay on the American Economic and Social Order* (N.Y.: Monthly Review, 1967).

2. Aronowitz, S., *Food, Shelter, and the American Dream* (N.Y.: Seabury Press, 1974), p. 19.

3. Mowry, G. E., *The Urban Nation: 1920–1960* (N.Y.: Hill and Wang, 1965), p. 203.

4. From 1951 to 1964, while the U.S. labor force grew by about 10 million workers, blue-collar employment declined to a point below that of 1951 (Galbraith, J. K., *The New Industrial State* [Boston: Houghton Mifflin, 1967]).

5. Baran and Sweezy, *Monopoly Capital,* p. 300.

6. Gottman, J., *Megalopolis: The Urbanized Northeastern Seaboard of the United States* (N.Y.: Twentieth Century Fund, 1961), p. 679, quoted in Baran and Sweezy, *Monopoly Capital,* p. 304.

7. Parker, R., *The Myth of the Middle Class* (N.Y.: Harper & Row, 1972). For a discussion of the distribution of wealth see G. Kolko, *Wealth and Power in America* (N.Y.: Praeger, 1964), p. 7.

8. Jezer, M., *The Dark Ages: Life in the United States 1945–1960* (Boston: South End Press, 1982), p. 193.

9. Whyte, W. H., *The Organization Man* (N.Y.: Simon & Schuster, 1956).

10. Hughes, R., and Brewin, R., *The Tranquilizing of America* (N.Y.: Warner, 1979); Powell, E. H., *The Design of Discord* (N.Y.: Oxford University Press, 1970); Jezer, *The Dark Ages.*

11. For a discussion of education and income see Innes, J. T., Jacobson, P. B., and Pellegrin, R. J., *The Economic Returns to Education* (Eugene: University of Oregon Press, 1965).

12. Kenneth B. Clark's foreword to Sexton, P.O., *Education and Income: Inequalities in Our Public Schools* (N.Y.: Viking, 1961).

13. *National Assessment of Educational Progress: Reading Rate and Comprehension* (Washington, D.C.: U.S. Government Printing Office, 1972), report 02-R-09.

14. Silberman, C. E., *Crisis in the Classroom* (N.Y.: Random House, 1970).

15. Kozol, J., *Death at an Early Age* (N.Y.: Houghton Mifflin, 1967); Kohl, H., *36 Children* (N.Y.: New American Library, 1967); Herndon, J., *The Way It Spozed to Be* (N.Y.: Simon and Schuster, 1968).

16. The literature on the educational issues and demands of blacks during this period is voluminous. Two anthologies that contain many of the issues and demands are Rubinstein, A. T., ed., *Schools Against Children: The Case for Community Control* (N.Y.: Monthly Review Press, 1970); and Woock, R. R., ed., *Education and the Urban Crisis* (Scranton, PA: International Textbook Company, 1970).

17. Lerner, J. W., *Children with Learning Disabilities* (Boston: Houghton Mifflin, 1976), ch. 2.

18. Ibid., pp. 24–25.

19. Smith, C. R., *Learning Disabilities* (Boston: Little, Brown & Co., 1983), p. 13.

20. Carrier, J. G., "Explaining Educability: An Investigation of Political Support for the Children with Learning Disabilities Act of 1969," *British Journal of Sociology of Education,* 1983, vol. 4, pp. 125–140.

21. For a review of many of these developments, see *Mind and Behavior: Readings from Scientific American* (San Francisco: W.H. Freeman, 1980).

22. Among the historical examples is the late-nineteenth-century theory of craniology, with its guiding technique, the "cephalic index." Craniology claimed that humans could be classified as roundheads (brachycephalics), longheads (dolichocephalics), and in-between heads (mesocephalics), and that these physical classifications correlated with fundamental social and intellectual characteristics (Chase, A., *The Legacy of Malthus: The Social Costs of the New Scientific Racism* (N.Y.: Alfred A. Knopf, 1977), pp. 94–97, 181–88). From this theory came illuminating conclusions, such as that longheads tended to be urban residents because they "showed a stronger inclination to city life and a greater aptitude for success" than roundheads. Craniology remained part of

the prevailing wisdom of anthropology for decades, even after Franz Boas conclusively repudiated it.

Analogous examples of blaming people's biology for their failures are criminal atavism (Nassi, A. J., and Abramowitz, S. I., "From Phrenology to Psychosurgery and Back Again: Biological Studies of Criminality," *American Journal of Orthopsychiatry,* 1976, vol. 46, pp. 591–606); inherited pellagra (Chase, *The Legacy of Malthus*); and immigrant and racial intelligence (Kamin, L. J., *The Science and Politics of I.Q.* (N.Y.: Wiley, 1974). In each instance we look back at these simplistic reductionist explanations of a problem and are appalled, angered, and perhaps amused by the investigations, conclusions, and statements made under the guise of "scientific thought." Yet, in their time the theories were presented and received as credible and became part of an acceptable social outlook.

23. For expressions and discussions of these explanations see Green, P., *The Pursuit of Inequality* (N.Y.: Pantheon, 1978); Ardrey, R., *The Territorial Imperative* (N.Y.: Atheneum, 1966); Lorenz, K., *On Aggression* (N.Y.: Harcourt, Brace & World, 1966); Morris, D., *The Naked Ape* (N.Y.: McGraw-Hill, 1968); Piven, F. F., and Cloward, R. A., *Regulating the Poor* (N.Y.: Vintage, 1971); Valenstein, E. S., *Brain Control* (N.Y.: John Wiley, 1973); Ryan, W., *Blaming the Victim* (N.Y.: Vintage, 1971); London, P., *Behavior Control* (N.Y.: New American Library, 1969); Hernnstein, R. J., *IQ in the Meritocracy* (Boston: Little, Brown & Co., 1974); Jensen, A. R., "How Much Can We Boost IQ and Scholastic Achievement?" *Harvard Educational Review,* 1969, vol. 39, pp. 1–23; Chorover, S. L., *From Genesis to Genocide* (Cambridge: Massachusetts Institute of Technology, 1979); Schrag, P., *Mind Control* (N.Y.: Pantheon, 1978); Scheff, T., ed., *Labeling Madness* (Englewood Cliffs, N.J.: Prentice-Hall, 1975); Tobach, E., Topoff, H. R., Gianutsos, J., and Gross, C. G., *The Four Horsemen* (N.Y.: Behavioral Publications, 1974).

24. Carrier, J. G., "Comparative Special Education: Ideology, Differentiation and Allocation in England and the United States," in Barton, L., and Tomlinson, S., eds., *Special Education and Social Interests* (N.Y.: Nichols, 1984).

25. For discussion of the class character of Progressive-period educational reforms see Katz, M. B., *Class, Bureaucracy, and Schools: The Illusion of Educational Change in America* (N.Y.: Praeger, 1971); Karrier, C. J., Violas, P. C., and Spring, J., *Roots of Crisis: American Education in the Twentieth Century* (Chicago: Rand McNally, 1973); Spring, J., *Education and the Rise of the Corporate State* (Boston: Beacon, 1972).

26. For a summary of this viewpoint see Nearing, S., *New Education: A Review of the Progressive Education Movements of the Day* (N.Y.: Row, Peterson & Co., 1915).

27. Sigmon, S. B., *A Radical Perspective on the Development of American Special Education with a Focus on the Concept of "Learning Disabilities,"* unpublished dissertation, Rutgers University 1985; Carrier, J., *Learning Disability* (Westport, Conn.: Greeenwood Press, 1986), p. 103.

28. Arab-Ogly, E. "Ideological Manipulation of the Masses," *Political Affairs,* 1976, vol. 55, pp. 45–58.

29. Carrier, "Explaining Educability."

30. Shor, I., *Culture Wars: School and Society in the Conservative Restoration, 1969–1984* (Boston: Routledge & Kegan Paul, 1986).

31. Armstrong, T., "How Real Are Learning Disabilities?" *Learning 85*, 1985, vol. 14, pp. 45–47.

32. Coles, G. S., "The Learning-Disabilities Test Battery: Empirical and Social Issues," *Harvard Educational Review*, 1978, vol. 48, pp. 313–40. The ten most frequently recommended and used tests and evaluations reviewed in the paper were the Illinois Test of Psycholinguistic Abilities, the Bender Visual-Motor Gestalt Test, the Frostig Developmental Test of Visual Perception, the Wepman Auditory Discrimination Test, the Lincoln-Oseretsky Motor Development Scale, the Graham-Kendall Memory for Designs Test, the Purdue Perceptual-Motor Survey, the Wechsler Intelligence Scale for Children, an evaluation by a neurologist, and an electroencephalogram.

33. Davis, W. A., and Shepard, L. A., "Specialists' Use of Tests and Clinical Judgment in the Diagnosis of Learning Disabilities," *Learning Disability Quarterly*, 1983, vol. 6, pp. 128–38; German, D., Johnson, B., and Schneider, M., "Learning Disability vs. Reading Disability: A Survey of Practitioners' Diagnostic Populations and Test Instruments," *Learning Disability Quarterly*, 1985, vol. 8, pp. 141–57.

34. For examples, see McGue, M., Shinn, M., and Ysseldyke, J., "Use of Cluster Scores on the Woodcock-Johnson Psycho-Educational Battery with Learning Disabled Students," *Learning Disability Quarterly*, 1982, vol. 5, pp. 274–87; Marson, D., and Ysseldyke, J., "Concerns in Interpreting Subtest Scatter on the Tests of Cognitive Ability from the Woodcock-Johnson Psycho-Educational Battery," *Journal of Learning Disabilities*, 1984, vol. 17, pp. 588–91; Ysseldyke, J. E., Algozzine, B., and Shinn, M., "Validity of the Woodcock-Johnson Psycho-Educational Battery for Learning Disabled Youngsters," *Learning Disability Quarterly*, 1981, vol. 4, pp. 244–49; Olson, J., Mercer, C., Paulson, D., "Process Testing: Is the Detroit the Answer?" *Learning Disability Quarterly*, 1981, vol. 4, pp. 44–47.

35. The Luria-Nebraska Neuropsychological Battery is an illustration of the inadequacies of the newer instruments in diagnosing LD. The test is a fairly comprehensive evaluation of neuropsychological functioning and has been shown to be correlated closely with other neuropsychological assessments, particularly the extensively-used Halstead-Reitan Neuropsychological Test Battery (Golden, C. J., Purisch, A. D., and Hammeke, T. A., *The Luria-Nebraska Neuropsychological Battery: A Manual for Clinical and Experimental uses* [Lincoln: University of Nebraska Press, 1979]; Reitan, R. M. and Davison, L. A., *Clinical Neuropsychology: Current Status and Applications* [N.Y.: Wiley, 1974]; Golden, C. J., *Diagnosis and Rehabilitation in Clinical Neuropsychology* [Springfield, Ill.: Charles C. Thomas, 1981]; Stambrook, M., "The Luria-Nebraska Neuropsychological Battery: A Promise That *May* Be Partly Fulfilled," *Journal of Clinical Neuropsychology*, 1983, vol. 5, pp. 247–269).

The Luria-Nebraska test has successfully identified distinct kinds of brain damage and has been used to establish the neuropsychological profiles of LD children. It has subtests to assess motor, rhythm, tactile, visual, receptive speech, expressive language, memory, writing, reading, arithmetic, intellectual processes, and right-hemisphere and left-hemisphere functioning. Among all these, significant differences between LD and normal children have been found mainly in three subtests: reading, writing, and expressive language (Nolan, D. R., Hammeke, T. A., and Barkley, R. A., "A Comparison of the Patterns of the Neuropsychological Performance in Two Groups of Learning Disabled Children," *Journal of Clinical Child Psychology,* 1983, vol. 12, pp. 22–27; Geary, D. C., Jennings, S. M., Schultz, D. D., and Alper, T. G., "The Diagnostic Accuracy of the Luria-Nebraska Neuropsychological Battery—Children's Revision for Nine- to Twelve-Year-Old Learning-Disabled Children," *School Psychology Review,* 1984, vol. 13, pp. 375–380).

The first two results are not surprising (writing assesses children's ability to spell and write from dictation). Since the third subtest, expressive language, is closely associated with a variety of reading skills—repeating a series of phonemes, filling in the blanks in a sentence—it is impossible to conclude whether it is expressive language problems that cause reading problems or vice versa. Some tasks in the expressive language subtest clearly demonstrate expressive language problems disconnected from reading skills—generating a sentence from several words, rearranging two mixed-up sentences. However, as was true for the other language tests reviewed earlier, the reasons for poor performance on language tasks are numerous, as researchers on the Luria-Nebraska have proposed, not merely due to a single "neuropsychological impairment of functions mediated by the posterior left cerebral hemisphere" (Nolan, et al., "A comparison of the patterns," p. 26).

The differences found for these subtests do not overshadow the results on the ten other subscales, which failed to differentiate learning disabled from normal children. A single study found that learning disabled children did more poorly than normal children on the rhythm subtest, but the meaning of the finding for LD is questionable because this subtest requires discrimination of pitch, melody, and rhythm, as well as the reproduction and recall of melodies, tasks heavily influenced by attention and experience (Geary, D. C., and Gilger, J. W., "The Luria-Nebraska Neuropsychological Battery—Children's Revision: Comparison of Learning Disabled and Normal Children Matched on Full Scale IQ," *Perceptual and Motor Skills,* 1984, vol. 58, pp. 115–118; for a discussion of the experiential basis of tone discrimination see: Leontiev, A. N., "On the Biological and Social Aspects of Human Development: The Training of Auditory Ability," in Cole, M., and Maltzman, I., [eds.], *Handbook of Contemporary Soviet Psychology* [N.Y.: Basic Books, 1969]). I use the Luria-Nebraska in my clinical program. As someone without musical abilities—I was placed in the "listeners" section in school music classes—I have never been able to hear differences in portions of the subtest. Fortunately for me, the subtest contains a cassette tape (with answers) for administering.

The last finding worth noting concerns the tactile perception subtest, which includes finger agnosia and fingertip number writing, measures which, we will recall from an earlier discussion, had been reported to distinguish the learning disabled. In one study of the Luria-Nebraska, (Nolan, "A Comparison of the Patterns"), these measures did not reveal any group differences.

36. Torgesen, J. K., introduction to Ysseldyke, J. E., "Current Practices in Making Psychoeducational Decisions About Learning Disabled Students," *Journal of Learning Disabilities,* 1983, vol. 16, p. 226.

37. Ysseldyke, J. E., Thurlow, M. L., Graden, J. L., Wesson, C., Deno, S. L., and Algozzine, B., "Generalizations from Five Years of Research on Assessment and Decision Making," 1982, Institute for Research on Learning Disabilities, University of Minnesota, research report no. 100.

38. Ysseldyke, et al., "Generalizations from Five Years," p. 6. Also see Algozzine, B., and Ysseldyke, J. E., "Learning Disabilities as a Subset of School Failure: The Oversophistication of a Concept," 1982, Institute for Research on Learning Disabilities, research report no. 69.

39. Ysseldyke, J. E., Algozzine, B., Shinn, M., and McGue, M., "Similarities and Differences Between Underachievers and Students Labeled Learning Disabled: Identical Twins with Different Mothers," 1979, Institute for Research on Learning Disabilities, research report no. 13.

40. Shinn, M. R., Ysseldyke, J. E., Deno, S., and Tindal, G., "A Comparison of Psychometric and Functional Differences Between Students Labeled Learning Disabled and Low Achieving," 1982, Institute for Research on Learning Disabilities, research report no. 71.

41. Algozzine, B., Ysseldyke, J. E., and Shinn, M., "Identifying Children with Learning Disabilities: When Is a Discrepancy Severe?" *Journal of School Psychology,* 1982, vol. 20, pp. 299–305. Also see Epps, S., Ysseldyke, J. E., and Algozzine, B., "An Analysis of the Conceptual Framework Underlying Definitions of Learning Disabilities," 1982, Institute for Research on Learning Disabilities, research report no. 98; Furlong, M. J., and Yanagida, E. H., "Psychometric Factors Affecting Multidisciplinary Team Identification of Learning Disabled Children," *Learning Disability Quarterly,* 1985, vol. 8, pp. 37–44.

42. Another graphic demonstration of LD tests' inability to differentiate LD students from others was an investigation of cognitive ability and scholastic achievement test scores for 248 students enrolled in regular third-, fifth-, and twelfth-grade classes (Ysseldyke, J. E., Algozzine, B., and Epps, S., "A Logical and Empirical Analysis of Current Practices in Classifying Students as Handicapped," Institute for Research on Learning Disabilities, research report no. 2, 1982). These students were considered normal because their scores on achievement tests were within the normal range for their grades and they had not been identified as learning disabled by the schools. Nonetheless, when the students were classified according to various operational definitions of LD (translations of LD concepts into test scores), many of these children met criteria for LD classification: 16 percent of the third-graders, 18 percent of the fifth-graders, and 28 percent of the twelfth-graders could have been identified as learning disabled. In laboratory studies in which school personnel were presented with test information about students whom the researchers said had been referred for a possible learning disability, although "all data indicated normal test performance, more than half of the decisionmakers declared the normal student eligible for special education services." (Ysseldyke et al., "Generalizations from Five Years," p. 5).

The researchers concluded:

> From its inception, the LD classification has been an ill-defined, poorly conceptualized, incredibly popular *idea.* There are millions of children who perform poorly [academically]. . . . There is no defensible system for classifying or categorizing these students; there are no defensible inclusionary/exclusionary principles to guide our efforts to classify them [Ysseldyke, Algozzine, and Epps, "A Logical and Empirical Analysis," p. 16].

43. Mann, L., Davis, C. H., Boyer, C. W., Metz, C. M., and Wolford, B., "LD or not LD, That Was the Question: A Retrospective Analysis of Child Service

Demonstration Centers' Compliance with the Federal Definition of Learning Disabilities," *Journal of Learning Disabilities,* 1983, vol. 16, pp. 14–17.

44. Epps, S., Ysseldyke, J. E., and Algozzine, B., "Public-Policy Implications of Different Definitions of Learning Disabilities," Institute for Research on Learning Disabilities, 1982, research report no. 99.

45. Perlmutter, B. F., and Parus, M. V., "Identifying Children with Learning Disabilities: A Comparison of Diagnostic Procedures Across School Districts," *Learning Disability Quarterly,* 1983, vol. 6, pp. 321–28.

46. Furlong and Yanagida, "Psychometric Factors."

47. Thurlow, M. L., Ysseldyke, J. E., and Casey, A., "Teachers' Perceptions of Criteria for Identifying Learning Disabled Students," *Psychology in the Schools,* 1984, vol. 21, pp. 349–55.

48. Ysseldyke, J. E., Algozzine, B., Richey, L., and Graden, J., "Declaring Students Eligible for Learning Disability Services: Why Bother with the Data?" *Learning Disability Quarterly,* 1982, vol. 5, pp. 37–44.

49. Shinn, et al., "A Comparison of Psychometric and Functional Differences," p. 20.

50. Pugach, M. C., "The Limitations of Federal Special Education Policy: The Role of Classroom Teachers in Determining Who Is Handicapped," *Journal of Special Education,* 1985, vol. 19, pp. 123–37.

51. Ysseldyke, et al., "Declaring Students Eligible," p. 42.

52. Shepard, L., "An Evaluation of the Regression of Discrepancy Method for Identifying Children with Learning Disabilities," *Journal of Special Education,* 1980, vol. 14, pp. 79–91.

53. Brosnan, F. L., "Overrepresentation of Low-Socioeconomic Minority Students in Special Education Programs in California," *Learning Disability Quarterly,* 1983, vol. 6, pp. 517–25.

54. Tucker, J. A., "Ethnic Proportions in Classes for the Learning Disabled: Issues in Nonbiased Assessment," *Journal of Special Education,* 1980, vol. 14, pp. 93–105.

55. Tucker, "Ethnic Proportions in Classes," p. 104.

56. Patrick, J., and Reschly, D., "Relationship of State Demographic Variables to School-System Prevalence of Mental Retardation," *American Journal of Mental Deficiency,* 1982, vol. 86, pp. 351–60; Wright, P., and Santa Cruz, R., "Ethnic Composition of Special Education Programs in California," *Learning Disability Quarterly,* 1983, vol. 6, pp. 387–94.

57. Argulewicz, E. N., "Effects of Ethnic Membership, Socioeconomic Status, and Home Language on LD, EMR, and EH Placements," *Learning Disability Quarterly,* 1983, vol. 6, pp. 195–200.

58. Ibid., p. 199.

59. Wright and Santa Cruz, "Ethnic Composition"; Brosnan, "Overrepresentation of Low-Socioeconomic Minority Students."

60. Ysseldyke, J. E., "Current Practices in Making Psychoeducational Decisions About Learning Disabled Students," *Journal of Learning Disabilities,* 1983, vol. 16, pp. 226–33.

61. Feagans, L., and McKinney, J. D., "The Pattern of Exceptionality Across Domains in Learning Disabled Children," *Journal of Applied Developmental*

Psychology, 1981, vol. 1, pp. 313–28; McKinney, J. D., and Feagans, L., "Academic and Behavioral Characteristics of Learning Disabled Children and Average Achievers: Longitudinal Studies," *Learning Disability Quarterly,* 1984, vol. 7, pp. 251–65; Hartzell, H. E., and Compton, C., "Learning Disability: 10-Year Follow Up," *Pediatrics,* 1984, vol. 74, pp. 1058–64.

62. Ysseldyke, "Current Practices in Making Psychoeducational Decisions," p. 229.

63. McLeod, J. "Learning Disability Is for Educators," *Journal of Learning Disabilities,* 1983, vol. 16, pp. 23–24.

64. Ysseldyke, J. E., and Algozzine, B. "LD or not LD: That's not the Question!" *Journal of Learning Disabilities,* 1983, vol. 16, pp. 29–31. Also see Keogh, B. K., "Future of the LD Field: Research and Practice," *Journal of Learning Disabilities,* 1986, vol. 19, pp. 455–60.

65. Ysseldyke and Algozzine, "LD or not LD," p. 31.

66. Algozzine and Ysseldyke, "The Future of the LD Field: Screening and Diagnosis," *Journal of Learning Disabilities,* 1986, vol. 19, pp. 394–98.

67. Randel, D. M., *Harvard Concise Dictionary of Music* (Cambridge: Harvard University Press, 1978).

68. Hopkins, T. K., "Theories of Historical Change," paper delivered at the 101 Years After Marx in the Social Sciences conference, SUNY at Buffalo, March 1984.

69. The Heritage Foundation is a conservative think tank, linked with and speaking for many conservative groups, that has influenced the Reagan administration's national and foreign policy. As the foundation itself recounted in 1984: "Four years ago, newly elected President Reagan received from the Heritage Foundation a blueprint for the running of the federal government. . . . Of the more than 2,000 recommendations offered, the Reagan Administration enacted or acted positively on more than 60 percent ("Reagan and Education: The Second Chance," *Education Update,* 1984, vol. 7, p. 1). The blueprint was contained in a 1,100-page volume titled *Mandate for Leadership: Policy Management in a Conservative Administration.*

70. This strategy is akin to conservative agreement with liberal criticism of state mental institutions several years ago. However, de-institutionalization for conservatives meant not only considerable reduction of funds for state hospitals but also minimal funds for after-care programs to assist released patients.

71. "The Education Crisis: Washington Shares the Blame," *The Backgrounder* (Heritage Foundation), May 11, 1984, no. 351; Gardner, E. M., *A New Agenda for Education* (Washington, D.C.: The Heritage Foundation, 1984).

72. Montagu, A., and Matson, F., *The Dehumanization of Man* (N.Y.: McGraw-Hill, 1983), p. 108.

Bibliography

Aaron, P. G., "The Neuropsychology of Developmental Dyslexia." In R. N. Malatesha and P. G. Aaron, eds., *Reading Disorders: Varieties and Treatments.* N.Y.: Academic Press, 1982.

Abikoff, H., and Gittelman, R., "The Normalizing Effects of Methylphenidate on the Classroom Behavior of ADDH Children," *Journal of Abnormal Child Psychology,* 1985, vol. 13, pp. 33–44.

"ACLD Adopts New Definition of Learning Disabilities," *LD Forum,* 1985, vol. 10, pp. 12–13.

Adler-Grinberg, D., and Stark, L., "Eye Movements, Scanpaths, and Dyslexia," *American Journal of Optometry & Physiological Optics,* 1978, vol. 55, pp. 557–570.

Algozzine, B., and Ysseldyke, J. E., "The Future of the LD Field: Screening and Diagnosis," *Journal of Learning Disabilities,* 1986, vol. 19, pp. 394–398.

Algozzine, B., and Ysseldyke, J., "Learning Disabilities as a Subset of School Failure: The Oversophistication of a Concept," Institute for Research on Learning Disabilities, University of Minnesota, 1982, research report no. 69.

Algozzine, B., Ysseldyke, J. E., and Shinn, M., "Identifying Children with Learning Disabilities: When Is a Discrepancy Severe?" *Journal of School Psychology,* 1982, vol. 20, pp. 299–305.

American Psychiatric Assocation, *Diagnostic and Statistical Manual of Mental Disorders* (third edition). Washington, D.C.: APA, 1980.

Aman, M. G., "Hyperactivity: Nature of the Syndrome and Its Natural History," *Journal of Autism and Developmental Disorders,* 1984, vol. 14, pp. 39–56.

Aman, M. G., "Psychotropic Drugs and Learning Problems—A Selective Review," *Journal of Learning Disabilities,* 1980, vol. 13, pp. 87–97.

Aman, M. G., "Psychotropic Drugs in the Treatment of Reading Disorders." In R. N. Malatesha and P. G. Aaron, eds., *Reading Disorders: Varieties and Treatments.* N.Y.: Academic Press, 1982.

Ames, L. B. "Learning Disability—Very Big Around Here," *Research Communications in Psychology, Psychiatry & Behavior,* 1985, vol. 10, pp. 17–37.

Anderson, C., *Society Pays: The High Costs of Minimal Brain Damage in America.* N.Y.: Walker, 1972.

Andolina, C., "Syntactic Maturity and Vocabulary Richness of Learning Disabled Children," *Journal of Learning Disabilities,* 1980, vol. 13, pp. 372–77.

Arab-Ogly, E. "Ideological Manipulation of the Masses," *Political Affairs,* 1976, vol. 55, pp. 45–58.

Argulewicz, E. N., "Effects of Ethnic Membership, Socioeconomic Status, and Home Language on LD, EMR, and EH placements," *Learning Disability Quarterly,* 1983, vol. 6, pp. 195–200.

Armstrong, T., "How Real Are Learning Disabilities?" *Learning 85,* 1985, vol. 14, pp. 45–47.

Aronowitz, S., *Food, Shelter, and the American Dream.* N.Y.: Seabury Press, 1974.

"Attention disorders need better measures and theory," *APA Monitor,* January 1985, p. 16.

Ayllon, T., Layman, D., and Kandel, H. J., "A Behavioral-Educational Alternative to Drug Control of Hyperactive Children," *Journal of Applied Behavior Analysis,* 1975, vol. 8, pp. 137–46.

Ayres, A. J., "Learning Disabilities and the Vestibular System," *Journal of Learning Disabilities,* 1978, vol. 11, pp. 18–29.

Ayers, F. W., and Torres, F. "The Incidence of EEG Abnormalities in a Dyslexic and a Control Group, *Journal of Clinical Psychology,* 1967, vol. 23, pp. 334–36.

Bakwin, H., "Reading Disability in Twins," *Developmental Medicine and Child Neurology,* 1973, vol. 15, pp. 184–87.

Balow, I. H., "Lateral Dominance Characteristics and Reading Achievement in First Grade," *Journal of Psychology,* 1963, vol. 55, pp. 323–28.

Bank, B. J., Biddle, B. J., and Good, T. L., "Sex Roles, Classroom Instruction, and Reading Achievement," *Journal of Educational Psychology,* 1980, vol. 72, pp. 119–32.

Bannatyne, A., *Language, Reading and Learning Disabilities.* Springfield, Ill.: Charles C Thomas, 1971.

Bannatyne, A., "The Spatially Competent LD Child," *Academic Therapy,* 1978, vol. 14, pp. 133–55.

Baran, P. A., and Sweezy, P. M., *Monopoly Capital: An Essay on the American Economic and Social Order.* N.Y.: Monthly Review, 1967.

Barker, M., "Biology and Ideology: The Uses of Reductionsim." In S. Rose, ed., *Against Biological Determinism.* NY: Allison & Busby, 1982.

Barkley, R. A., and Cunningham, C. E., "Do Stimulant Drugs Improve the Academic Performance of Hyperkinetic Children?" *Clinical Pediatrics,* 1978, vol. 17, pp. 85–92.

Barling, J., and Bullen, G., "Dietary Factors and Hyperactivity: A Failure to Replicate," *The Journal of Genetic Psychology,* 1985, vol. 146, pp. 117–23.

Baron, J., "Orthographic and Word-specific Mechanisms in Children's Reading of Words," *Child Development,* 1979, vol. 50, pp. 60–72.

Bauer, R. H., "Information Processing as a Way of Understanding and Diagnosing Learning Disabilities." In D. K. Reid and H. L. Swanson, eds., *Topics in Learning and Learning Disabilities: Controversy, Strategy or Capacity Deficit.* Gaithersburg, Md.: Aspen, 1982.

Bauer, R. H., "Memory, Acquisition, and Category Clustering in Learning-Disabled Children." *Journal of Experimental Child Psychology,* 1979(a), vol. 27, pp. 365–83.

Bauer, R. H., "Memory Processes in Children with Learning Disabilities: Evidence for Deficient Rehearsal," *Journal of Experimental Child Psychology,* 1977, vol. 24, pp. 415–30.

Bauer, R. H., "Recall After a Short Delay and Acquisition in Learning Disabled and Nondisabled Children," *Journal of Learning Disabilities,* 1979(b), vol. 12, pp. 30–41.

Bauer, R. H., and Emhert, J., "Information Processing in Reading-Disabled and Nondisabled Children," *Journal of Experimental Child Psychology,* 1984, vol. 37, pp. 271–81.

Bee, H. L., Barnard, K. E., Eyres, S. J., Gray, C. A., Hammond, M. A., Spietz, A. L., Snyder, C., and Clark, B. "Prediction of IQ and Language Skill from Perinatal Status, Child Performance, Family Characteristics, and Mother-Child Interaction," *Child Development,* 1982, vol. 53, pp. 1134–56.

Belmont, I. H., and Birch, H. G., "Lateral Dominance, Lateral Awareness and Reading Disability," *Child Development,* 1965, vol. 36, pp. 57–71.

Black, F. W., "Reversal and Rotation Errors by Normal and Retarded Readers," *Perceptual and Motor Skills,* 1973, vol. 36, pp. 895–98.

Black, J. L., Collins, W. K., DeRoach, J. N., and Zubrick, S. R., "Dyslexia: Saccadic Eye Movements," *Perceptual and Motor Skills,* 1984, vol. 58, pp. 903–10.

Blakeslee, S., "Brain Studies Shed Light on Disorders," *New York Times,* "The Learning Disabled (Education Fall Survey)," November 11, 1984, p. 45.

Bloomberg, Jr., W., "The School as a Factory," paper prepared for the Inter-district Institute, Homewood-Flossmoor, Illinois, 1967.

Boder, E., "Developmental Dyslexia: A Diagnostic Approach Based on Three Atypical Reading-Spelling Patterns," *Developmental Medicine and Child Neurology,* 1973, vol. 15, pp. 663–87.

Bond, G. L., and Tinker, M. A., *Reading Difficulties: Their Diagnosis and Correction.* N.Y.: Appleton-Century-Crofts, 1957.

Bouma, H., and Legein, Ch. P., "Foveal and Parafoveal Recognition of Letters and Words by Dyslexics and by Average Readers," *Neuropsychologia,* 1977, vol. 15, pp. 69–80.

Bowles, S., and Gintis, H., *Schooling in Capitalist America.* N.Y.: Basic Books, 1976.

Bradley, L., and Bryant, P. E., "Categorizing Sounds and Learning to Read—A Causal Connection," *Nature,* 1983, vol. 301, pp. 419–21.

Bradley, L., and Bryant, P. E., "Difficulties in Auditory Organization as a Possible Cause of Reading Backwardness," *Nature,* 1978, vol. 271, pp. 746–47.

Bradley, L., and Bryant, P., "A Tactile Approach to Reading," *British Journal of Special Education,* 1981, vol. 8, pp. 32–36.

Branch, C., Milner, B., and Rasmussen, J., "Intracarotid Sodium Amytal for the Lateralization of Cerebral Speech Dominance," *Journal of Neurosurgery,* 1964, vol. 21, pp. 399–405.

Bronfenbrenner, U., *The Ecology of Human Development.* Cambridge: Harvard University Press, 1979.

Brophy, J., "Interactions of Male and Female Students with Male and Female Teachers." In L. C. Wilkinson and C. B. Marrett, eds., *Gender Influences in Classroom Interaction.* N.Y.: Academic Press, 1985.

Brosnan, F. L., "Overrepresentation of Low-Socioeconomic Minority Students in Special Education Programs in California," *Learning Disability Quarterly,* 1983, vol. 6, pp. 517–25.

Brown, B., Haegerstrom-Portnoy, G., Adams, A. J., Yingling, C. D., Galin, D., Herron, J., and Marcus, M. "Predictive Eye Movements Do Not Discriminate Between Dyslexic and Control Children," *Neuropsychologia,* 1983, vol. 21, pp. 121–28.

Brown, B., Haegerstrom-Portnoy, G., Yingling, C. D., Herron, J., Galin, D., and Marcus. M. "Tracking Eye Movements Are Normal in Dyslexia Children," *American Journal of Optometry & Physiological Optics,* 1983, vol. 60, pp. 376–83.

Brown, B., Haegerstrom-Portnoy, G., Yingling, C.D., Herron, J., Galin, D., and Marcus, M., "Dyslexic Children Have Normal Vestibular Responses to Rotation," *Archives of Neurology,* 1983(c), vol. 40, pp. 370–73.

Brown, R. T., Wynne, M. E., and Medenis, R., "Methylphenidate and Cognitive Therapy: A Comparison of Treatment Approaches with Hyperactive Boys," *Journal of Abnormal Child Psychology,* 1985, vol. 13, pp. 69–87.

Bryden, M. P., "Laterality Effects in Dichotic Listening: Relations with Handedness and Reading Ability in Children," *Neuropsychologia,* 1970, vol. 8, pp. 443–50.

Bryden, M. P., "Sex-related Differences in Cerebral Hemisphere Asymmetry and Their Possible Relation to Dyslexia." In A. Ansara, A. Geschwind, M. Albert, N., and Gartell, N., eds., *Sex Differences in Dyslexia.* Towson, Maryland: Orton Dyslexia Society, 1981.

Burian, R. M., "A Methodological Critique of Sociobiology." In A. L. Caplan, ed., *The Sociobiology Debate.* N.Y.: Harper & Row, 1978.

Byrne, B., and Shea, P., "Semantic and Phonetic Memory Codes in Beginning Readers," *Memory & Cognition,* 1979, vol. 7, pp. 333–38.

Campbell, R., "The Lateralisation of Emotion: A Critical Review," *International Journal of Psychology,* 1982, vol. 17, pp. 211–29.

Canning, P. M., Orr, R. R., and Rourke, B. P. "Sex Differences in the Perceptual, Visual-Motor, Linguistic and Concept-Formation Abilities of Retarded Readers?" *Journal of Learning Disabilities,* 1980, vol. 13, pp. 563–67.

Capel, I. D., Pinnock, M. H., Dorrell, H. M., Williams, D. C., and Grant, E. C. G., "Comparison of Concentrations of Some Trace, Bulk, and Toxic Metals in the Hair of Normal and Dyslexic Children," *Clinical Chemistry,* 1981, vol. 27, pp. 879–81.

Caplan, B., and Kinsbourne, M., "Cerebral Lateralization, Preferred Cognitive Mode, and Reading Ability in Normal Children," *Brain and Language,* 1981, vol. 14, pp. 349–70.

Carew, J. V., "Experience and the Development of Intelligence in Young Children at Home and in Day Care," *Monographs of the Society for Research in Child Development,* 1980, vol. 45, no. 187, pp. 6–7.

Carrier, J. G. "Comparative Special Education: Ideology, Differentiation and Allocation in England and the United States." In L. Barton and S. Tomlinson, eds., *Special Education and Social Interests.* N.Y.: Nichols, 1984.

Carrier, J. G. "Explaining Educability: An Investigation of Political Support for the Children with Learning Disabilities Act of 1969," *British Journal of Sociology of Education,* 1983, vol. 4, pp. 125–40.

Cazden, C., "Peekaboo as an Instructional Model: Discourse Development at Home and at School. In *Papers and Reports on Child Language Development,* no. 17, Stanford University, Department of Linguistics. Summarized in B. Rogoff and W. Garder, "Adult Guidance of Cognitive Development." In B. Rogoff and J. Lave, eds., *Everyday cognition.* Cambridge: Harvard University Press, 1984.

Cermak, L. S., "Information Processing Deficits in Children with Learning Disabilities," *Journal of Learning Disabilities,* 1983, vol. 16, pp. 599–605.

Cermak, L. S., Goldberg-Warter, J., DeLuca, D., Cermak, S., and Drake, C., "The Role of Interference in the Verbal Retention Ability of Learning Disabled Children," *Journal of Learning Disabilities,* 1981, vol. 14, pp. 291–95.

Chall, J. S., *Learning to Read: The Great Debate.* N.Y.: McGraw-Hill, 1967.

Chall, J. S., and Mirsky, A. F., eds., *Education and the Brain.* Chicago: University of Chicago Press, 1978.

Charles, L., and Schain, R., "A Four-year Follow-up Study of the Effects of Methylphenidate on the Behavior and Academic Achievement of Hyperactive Children," *Journal of Abnormal Child Psychology,* 1981, vol. 9, pp. 495–505.

Charnley, A. H., and Jones, H. A., *The Concept of Success in Adult Literacy.* Cambridge, England: Huntington, 1979.

Chase, A., *The Legacy of Malthus: The Social Costs of the New Scientific Racism.* N.Y.: Knopf, 1977.

Chase, C. H., Schmitt, R. L., Russell, G., and Tallal, P., "A New Chemotherapeutic Investigation: Piracetam Effects on Dyslexia," *Annals of Dyslexia,* 1984, vol. 34, pp. 29–48.

Chi, M. T., "Short-term Memory Limitations in Children: Capacity or Processing Deficits," *Memory & Cognition,* 1976, vol. 4, pp. 559–72.

Chorover, S. L., *From Genesis to Genocide.* Cambridge: MIT Press, 1980.

Clark, K. B., foreword to P.O. Sexton, *Education and Income: Inequalities in Our Public Schools.* N.Y.: Viking, 1961.

Clark, R. W., *Einstein: The Life and Times.* N.Y.: Crowell, 1971.

Clarke, L., *Can't Read, Can't Write, Can't Talk Too Good Either.* Baltimore: Penguin, 1974.

Clements, S. D., "Minimal Brain Dysfunction in Children." In S. G. Sapir and A. C. Nitzburg, *Children with Learning Problems.* N.Y.: Brunner/Mazel, 1973.

Clements, S. D., *Minimal Brain Dysfunction in Children: Terminology and Identification.* Washington, D.C.: U.S. Government Printing Office, 1966.

Cochran, A., "Recognizing MBD in the Problem Child," *RN,* 1972, pp. 2–5.

Cohen, J., and Breslin, P. W. "Visual Evoked Responses in Dyslexic Children," *Annals of the New York Academy of Sciences,* 1984, vol. 425, pp. 338–43.

Coleman, R. I., and Deutsch, C. P., "Lateral Dominance and Right-Left Discrimination: A Comparison of Normal and Retarded Readers," *Perceptual and Motor Skills,* 1964, vol. 19, pp. 43–50.

Coles, G. S., "Adult Illiteracy and Learning Theory: A Study of Cognition and Activity," *Science and Society,* 1983–84, vol. 47, pp. 451–82.

Coles, G. S., "Evaluation of Genetic Explanations of Reading and Learning Problems," *Journal of Special Education,* 1980, vol. 14, pp. 365–83.

Coles, G. S. "The Learning-Disabilities Test Battery: Empirical and Social Issues," *Harvard Educational Review,* 1978, vol. 48, pp. 313–40.

Coles, G. S., "The Polyphony of Learning in the Learning Disabled," *Learning Disability Quarterly,* 1984, vol. 7, pp. 321–28.

Coles, G. S., and Goldstein, L., "Hemispheric EEG Activation and Literacy Development," *The International Journal of Clinical Neuropsychology,* 1985, vol. 7, pp. 3–7.

Conners, C. K., "Cortical Visual Evoked Response in Children with Learning Disorders," *Psychophysiology,* 1971, vol. 7, pp. 418–28.

Conners, C. K. "Critical Review of 'Electroencephalographic and Neurophysiological Studies in Dyslexia.' " In A. L. Benton and D. Pearl, eds.. *Dyslexia: An Appraisal of Current Knowledge.* N.Y.: Oxford, 1978.

Conners, C. K., *Food Additives and Hyperactive Children.* N.Y.: Plenum Press, 1980.

Conners, C. K., Blouin, A. G., Winglee, M., Lougee, L., O'Donnell, D., and Smith, A., "Piracetam and Event-related Potentials in Dyslexic Children," *Psychopharmacology Bulletin,* 1984, vol. 20, pp. 667–73.

Conot, R., *A Streak of Luck.* N.Y.: Seaview Books, 1979.

Copeland, A. P., and Reiner, E. M., "The Selective Attention of Learning-Disabled Children: Three Studies," *Journal of Abnormal Child Psychology,* 1984, vol. 12, pp. 455–70.

Cott, A., *Dr. Cott's Help for Your Learning Disabled Child.* N.Y.: Times Books, 1985.

Crinella, F. M., Beck, F. W., and Robinson, J. W., "Unilateral Dominance Is Not Related to Neuropsychological Integrity," *Child Development,* 1972, vol. 42, pp. 2033–54.

Critchley, M., *The Dyslexic Child,* Springfield, Ill.: Charles C Thomas, 1970.

Critchley, M. "Isolation of the Specific Dyslexic." In A. H. Keeney and V. T. Keeney, eds., *Dyslexia: Diagnosis and Treatment of Reading Disorders.* St. Louis: Mosby, 1968.

Cruickshank, W. M., Foreword in W. H. Gaddes, *Learning Disabilities and Brain Function: A Neuropsychological Approach.* N.Y.: Springer-Verlag, 1980.

Dallago, M. L. L., and Moelly, B. E., "Free Recall in Boys in Normal and Poor Reading Levels as a Function of Task Manipulations," *Journal of Experimental Child Psychology,* 1980, vol. 30, pp. 62–78.

Davis, W. A., and Shepard, L. A., "Specialists' Use of Tests and Clinical Judgment in the Diagnosis of Learning Disabilities," *Learning Disability Quarterly,* 1983, vol. 6, pp. 128–38.

Decker, S. D., and Corley, R. P., "Bannatyne's 'Genetic Dyslexic' Subtype: A Validation Study," *Psychology in the Schools,* 1984, vol. 21, pp. 300–04.

DeFries, J. C., and Decker, S. N., "Genetic Aspects of Reading Disability." In R. N. Malatesha and P. G. Aaron, eds., *Reading Disorders.* N.Y.: Academic Press, 1982.

DeFries, J. C., McClearn, G. E., and Wilson, J. E., "Genetic Analysis of Reading Disabilities." Final report to the Spencer Foundation. Boulder: University of Colorado, 1976.

DeFries, J. C., Singer, S. M., Foch, T. T., and Lewitter, F. I., "Familial Nature

of Reading Disability," *British Journal of Psychiatry,* 1978, vol. 132, pp. 361–67.
deHirsch, K., Jansky, J. J., and Langford, W. S., *Predicting Reading Failure.* NY: Harper & Row, 1966.
Deikel, S. M., and Freidman, M. P. "Selective Attention in Children with Learning Disabilities," *Perceptual Motor Skills,* 1976, vol. 42, pp. 675–78.
Denckla, M. B., LeMay, M., and Chapman, C. A., "Few CT Scan Abnormalities Found Even in Neurologically Impaired Learning Disabled Children," *Journal of Learning Disabilities,* 1985, vol. 18, pp. 132–35.
Denckla, M. B. and Rudel, R. G., "Naming of Object-Drawings by Dyslexic and Other Learning Disabled Children," *Brain and Language,* 1976, vol. 3, pp. 1–15.
Denckla, M. B., and Rudel, R. G., "Rapid 'Automatized' Naming (R.A.N.): Dyslexia Differentiated from Other Learning Disabilities," *Neuropsychologia,* 1976, vol. 14, pp. 471–79.
Denckla, M. B., Rudel, R. G., and Broman, M., "Tests That Discriminate Between Dyslexic and Other Learning-Disabled Boys," *Brain and Language,* 1981, vol. 13, pp. 118–29.
Diamond, G. H., "The Birthdate Effect—A Maturational Effect?" *Journal of Learning Disabilities,* 1983, vol. 16, pp. 161–64.
DiIanni, M., Wilsher, C. R., Blank, M. S., Conners, C. K., Chase, C. H., Funkenstein, H. H., Helfgott, E., Holmes, J. M., Lougee, L., Maletta, G. J., Milewski, J., Pirozzolo, F. J., Rudel, R. G., and Tallal, P. "The Effects of Piracetam in Children with Dyslexia," *Journal of Clinical Psychopharmacology,* 1985, vol. 5, pp. 272–78.
Dimond, S. J., and Brouwers, E. Y. M. "Increase in the Power of Human Memory in Normal Man Through the Use of Drugs," *Psychopharmacology,* 1976, vol. 49, pp. 307–09.
DiPasquale, G. W., Moule, A. D., and Flewelling, R. W., "The Birthdate Effect," *Journal of Learning Disabilities,* 1980, vol. 13, pp. 4–12.
"Doctor Fights for Dyslexia Theory," *New York Times,* November 24, 1985.
Doehring, D. G., "Reading Disability Subtypes: Interaction of Reading and Nonreading Deficits." In B. Rourke, ed., *Neuropsychology of Learning Disabilities: Essentials of Subtype Analysis.* N.Y.: Guilford, 1985.
Doehring, D. G., "Subtypes of Reading Disorders: Implications for Remediation," *Annals of Dyslexia,* 1984, vol. 34, pp. 205–16.
Doehring, D. G., "What Do We Know About Reading Disabilities? Closing the Gap Between Research and Practice," *Annals of Dyslexia,* 1983, vol. 33, pp. 175–83.
Doehring, D. G., Trites, R. L., Patel, P. G., and Fiedorowicz, A. M., *Reading Disabilities: The Interaction of Reading, Language, and Neuropsychological Deficits.* New York: Academic Press, 1981.
Drake, W. E., "Clinical and Pathological Findings in a Child with a Developmental Learning Disability," *Journal of Learning Disabilities,* 1968, vol. 1, pp. 486–502.
Drew, A. L., "A Neurological Appraisal of Familial Congenital Word-Blindness," *Brain,* 1956, vol. 79, pp. 440–60.
"Drug Eases Dyslexia, Doctor Says," *Detroit News,* April 25, 1983, p. 1-A.
Duane, D., "Neurobiological Correlates of Reading Disorders," *Journal of Educational Research,* 1983, vol. 77, pp. 5–15.

Duane, D., "Written Language Underachievement: An Overview of the Theoretical and Practical Issues." In F. H. Duffy and N. Geschwind, eds., *Dyslexia: A Neuroscientific Approach to Clinical Evaluation.* Boston: Little, Brown, 1985.

Dublin, W. B., *Fundamentals of Neuropathology.* Springfield, Ill.: Charles C Thomas, 1967.

Duffy, F. H., Denckla, M. B., Bartels, P. H., and Sandini, G., "Dyslexia: Regional Differences in Brain Electrical Activity by Topographic Mapping," *Annals of Neurology,* 1980, vol. 7, pp. 412–20.

Duffy, F. H., Denckla, M. B., Bartels, P. H., Sandini, G., and Kiessling, L. S. "Dyslexia: Automated Diagnosis by Computerized Classification of Brain Electrical Activity," *Annals of Neurology,* 1980, vol. 7, pp. 421–28.

"Dyslexia: Is the Inner Ear the Culprit," *Instructor and Teacher,* January 1982. Reprinted in a booklet from Levinson's Medical Dyslexic Treatment Center.

Eason, R. G., Harter, M. R., and White, C. T., "Effects of Attention and Arousal on Visually Evoked Cortical Potentials and Reaction Time in Man," *Physiology and Behavior,* 1969, vol. 4, pp. 283–89.

Eberle, A., and Robinson, S., *The Adult Illiterate Speaks Out: Personal Perspectives on Learning to Read and Write.* Washington, D.C.: National Institute of Education, 1980.

"The Education Crisis: Washington Shares the Blame," *The Backgrounder* (Heritage Foundation), no. 351, May 11, 1984.

Edwards, R., and Webb, J. R., *Analytical Reading Series.* N.Y.: Taintor & Co., 1866.

Elliot, C. D., Murray, D. S., and Pearson, L. S. *British Abilities Scales Manual 3: Directions for Administration and Scoring.* Winsor, England: NFER Publishing Co., 1978.

Ellis, N. C., and Miles, T. R., "A Lexical Encoding Deficiency I: Experimental Evidence." In G. Th. Pavlidis and T. R. Miles, eds., *Dyslexia Research and Its Application to Education.* N.Y.: John Wiley, 1981.

Ely, D. L., Mostardi, R. A., Woebkenberg, N., and Worstell, D., "Aerometric and Hair Trace Metal Content in Learning-Disabled Children," *Environmental Research,* 1981, vol. 25, pp. 325–29.

Epps, S., Ysseldyke, J. E., and Algozzine, B., "An Analysis of the Conceptual Framework Underlying Definitions of Learning Disabilities," Institute for Research on Learning Disabilities, University of Minnesota 1982, research report no. 98.

Epps, S., Ysseldyke, J. E., & Algozzine, B., "Public-Policy Implications of Different Definitions of Learning Disabilities," Institute for Research on Learning Disabilities, University of Minnesota, 1982, research report no. 99.

Ernhart, C. B., Landa, B., and Schell, N. B., "Subclinical Levels of Lead and Developmental Deficit: A Multivariate Follow-up Reassessment," *Pediatrics,* 1981, vol. 67, pp. 911–19.

Ernhart, C. B., Landa, B., Wolf, A. W., "Subclinical Lead Level and Developmental Deficit: Re-analyses of Data," *Journal of Learning Disabilities,* 1985, vol. 18, pp. 475–79.

Ernhart, C. B., and Morrow-Tlucak, M., "The Caretaking Environment and Exposure of Children to Lead," *Science Reviews Limited,* in press.

Eustis, R. S., "Specific Reading Disability," *New England Journal of Medicine,* 1947, vol. 237, pp. 243–49.

Fairweather, H., "Sex Differences in Cognition," *Cognition,* 1976, vol. 4, pp. 231–80.
Farnham-Diggory, S., *Learning Disabilities: A Psychological Perspective.* Cambridge: Harvard University Press, 1978.
Feagans, L., and McKinney, J. D., "The Pattern of Exceptionality Across Domains in Learning Disabled Children," *Journal of Applied Developmental Psychology,* 1981, vol. 1, pp. 313–28.
Feagans, L., and Short, E. J., "Developmental Differences in the Comprehension and Production of Narratives by Reading-Disabled and Normally Achieving Children," *Child Development,* 1984, vol. 55, pp. 1727–36.
Feingold, B. F., *Why Your Child Is Hyperactive.* N.Y.: Random House, 1974.
Feuerstein, R., *The Dynamic Assessment of Retarded Performers.* Baltimore: University Park Press, 1979.
Finucci, J. M., and Childs, B., "Are There Really More Dyslexic Boys Than Girls?" In A. Ansara, A. Geschwind, M. Albert, and N. Gartell, eds., *Sex Differences in Dyslexia.* Towson, Md.: Orton Dyslexia Society, 1981.
Finucci, J. M., Guthrie, J. T., Childs, A. L., Abbey, H., and Childs, B., "The Genetics of Specific Reading Disability," *Annals of Human Genetics,* 1976, vol. 40, pp. 1–23.
Fisk, J. L., and Rourke, B. P. "Identification of Subtypes of Learning-Disabled Children at Three Age Levels: A Neuropsychological, Multivariate Approach," *Journal of Clinical Neuropsychology,* 1979, vol. 1, pp. 289–310.
Fisk, J. L., and Rourke, B. P. "Neuropsychological Subtyping of Learning-Disabled Children: History, Methods, Implications," *Journal of Learning Disabilities,* 1983, vol. 16, pp. 529–31.
Fleisher, L. S., Soodak, L. C., and Jelin, M. A., "Selective Attention Deficits in Learning Disabled Children: Analysis of the Data Base," *Exceptional Children,* 1984, vol. 52, pp. 136–41.
Fletcher, J. M., and Satz, P., "Cluster Analysis and the Search for Learning Disability Subtypes." In B. Rourke, ed., *Neuropsychology of Learning Disabilities: Essentials of Subtype Analysis.* N.Y.: Guilford, 1985.
Foch, T. T., DeFries, J. C., McClearn, G. E., and Singer, S. M., "Familial Patterns of Impairment in Reading Disability," *Journal of Educational Psychology,* 1977, vol. 69, pp. 316–29.
Forness, S. R., and Cantwell, D. P., "DSM III Psychiatric Diagnoses and Special Education Categories," *Journal of Special Education,* 1982, vol. 16, pp. 49–63.
Fox, B., and Routh, D. K., "Phonemic Analysis and Severe Reading Disability," *Journal of Psycholinguistic Research,* 1980, vol. 9, pp. 115–19.
Fox, B., and Routh, D. K., "Phonemic Analysis and Synthesis as Word-Attack Skills," *Journal of Educational Psychology,* 1976, vol. 68, pp. 70–74.
Fox, B., and Routh, D. K., "Reading Disability, Phonetic Analysis, and Dysphonetic Spelling: A Follow-up Study," *Journal of Clinical Child Psychology,* 1983, vol. 12, pp. 28–32.
Frazier, S., "Minimal Brain Dysfunction," *Medical Times,* 1975, vol. 103, pp. 70–81.
Freeman, R. D., "Drug Effects on Learning in Children: A Selective Review of the Past Thirty Years," *Journal of Special Education,* 1966, vol. 1, pp. 17–44.
Freeman, R. D., "Special Education and the Electroencephalogram: Marriage of Convenience," *Journal of Special Education,* 1967, vol. 2, pp. 61–73.

Freire, P., *Pedagogy of the Oppressed.* N.Y.: Herder and Herder, 1971.
Frith, U., "Experimental Approaches to Developmental Dyslexia: An Introduction," *Psychological Research,* 1981, vol. 43, pp. 97–109.
Fuller, P. W., "Attention and the EEG Alpha Rhythm in Learning Disabled Children," *Journal of Learning Disabilities,* 1978, vol. 11, pp. 303–12.
Furlong, M. J., and Yanagida, E. H., "Psychometric Factors Affecting Multidisciplinary Team Identification of Learning Disabled Children," *Learning Disability Quarterly,* 1985, vol. 8, pp. 37–44.
Gadow, K. D., "Effects of Stimulant Drugs on Academic Performance in Hyperactive and Learning Disabled Children," *Journal of Learning Disabilities,* 1983, vol. 16, pp. 290–99.
Gadow, K. D., "Prevalence of Drug Treatment for Hyperactivity and Other Childhood Behavior Disorders." In K. D. Gadow and J. Loney, eds., *Psychosocial Aspects of Drug Treatment for Hyperactivity.* Boulder, Col.: Westview Press, 1981.
Galaburda, A. M., "Developmental Dyslexia: Current Anatomical Research," *Annals of Dyslexia,* 1983, vol. 33, pp. 41–53.
Galaburda, A. M., "Developmental Dyslexia: A Review of Biological Interactions," *Annals of Dyslexia,* 1985, vol. 35, pp. 21–33.
Galaburda, A. M., and Eidelberg, D., "Symmetry and Asymmetry in the Human Posterior Thalamus," *Archives of Neurology,* 1982, vol. 39, pp. 333–36.
Galaburda, A. M., and Kemper, T. L. "Cytoarchitectonic Abnormalities in Developmental Dyslexia: A Case Study," *Annals of Neurology,* 1979, vol. 6, pp. 94–100.
Galaburda, A. M., Sherman, G. F., Rosen, G. D., Aboitiz, F., and Geschwind, N., "Developmental Dyslexia: Four Consecutive Cases with Cortical Anomalies," *Annals of Neurology,* 1985, vol. 18, pp. 222–33.
Galbraith, J. K., *The New Industrial State.* Boston: Houghton Mifflin, 1967.
Gaddes, W. H., *Learning Disabilities and Brain Function: A Neuropsychological Approach.* N.Y.: Springer-Verlag, 1980.
Gaddes, W. H., "Prevalence Estimates and the Need for Definition of Learning Disabilities." In R. M. Knights and D. J. Bakker, eds., *The Neuropsychology of Learning Disorders.* Baltimore: University Park Press, 1976.
Gardner, E. M., *A New Agenda for Education.* Washington, D.C.: The Heritage Foundation, 1984.
Gates, A. I., and Bond, G. L., "Relation of Handedness, Eyesighting, and Acuity Dominance to Reading," *Journal of Educational Psychology,* 1936, vol. 27, pp. 450–56.
Geary, D. C., and Gilger, J. W., "The Luria-Nebraska Neuropsychological Battery-Children's Revision: Comparison of Learning Disabled and Normal Children Matched on Full Scale IQ," *Perceptual and Motor Skills,* 1984, vol. 58, pp. 115–18.
Geary, D. C., Jennings, S. M., Schultz, D. D., and Alper, T. G., "The Diagnostic Accuracy of the Luria-Nebraska Neuropsychological Battery-Children's Revision for 9 to 12 Year Old Learning Disabled Children," *School Psychology Review,* 1984, vol. 13, pp. 375–80.
Geffner, D., and Hochberg, I., "Ear Laterality Preference of Children from Low and Middle Socio-economic Levels on a Verbal Dichotic Listening Task," *Cortex,* 1971, vol. 7, pp. 193–203.
German, D., Johnson, B., and Schneider, M., "Learning Disability vs. Reading

Disability: A Survey of Practitioners' Diagnostic Populations and Test Instruments," *Learning Disability Quarterly,* 1985, vol. 8, pp. 141–57.

Geschwind, N., "Why Orton Was Right," *Annals of Dyslexia,* 1982, vol. 32, pp. 13–30.

Gibson, E. J., and Levin, H. *The Psychology of Reading.* Cambridge: MIT Press, 1975.

Godfrey, J. J., Syrdal-Lasky, A. K., Millay, K. K., and Knox, C. M., "Performance of Dyslexic Children on Speech Perception Tests," *Journal of Experimental Child Psychology,* 1981, vol. 32, pp. 401–24.

Goldberg, H. K., Shiffman, G. B., and Bender, M., *Dyslexia: Interdisciplinary Approaches to Reading Disabilities.* N.Y.: Grunc & Stratton, 1983.

Golden, C. J., *Diagnosis and Rehabilitation in Clinical Neuropsychology.* Springfield, Ill.: Charles C Thomas, 1981.

Golden, C. J., Purisch, A. D., and Hammeke, T. A., *The Luria-Nebraska Neuropsychological Battery: A Manual for Clinical and Experimental Uses.* Lincoln: University of Nebraska Press, 1979.

Goldstein, D. M., "Cognitive-Linguistic Functioning and Learning to Read in Preschoolers," *Journal of Educational Psychology,* 1976, vol. 68, pp. 680–88.

Goldstein, D. M., "Cognitive-Linguistic Functioning and Learning to Read in Preschoolers," *Journal of Educatinal Psychology,* 1976, vol. 68, pp. 680–88.

Goldstein, L., "Some Relationships Between Quantified Hemispheric EEG and Behavioral States in Man." In J. Gruzelier and P. Florheury, eds., *Hemispheric Asymmetries of Function and Psychopathology.* N.Y.: Elsevier, 1979.

Gordon, M., Post, E. M., Crouthamel, C., and Richman, R. A., "Do Children with Constitutional Delay Really Have More Learning Problems?" *Journal of Learning Disabilities,* 1984, vol. 17, pp. 291–93.

Gottfried, A. W., and Gottfried, A. E., "Home Environment and Cognitive Development in Young Children of Middle-Socioeconomic-Status Families." In A. W. Gottfried, ed., *Home Environment and Early Cognitive Development.* N.Y.: Academic Press, 1984.

Gottman, J., *Megalopolis: The Urbanized Northeastern Seaboard of the United States.* N.Y.: 1961, p. 679 quoted in Baran and Sweezy, *Monopoly Capital.*

Gould, S. J., *The Mismeasure of Man.* N.Y.: W. W. Norton, 1981.

Gray, W. S., *Remedial Cases in Reading: Their Diagnosis and Treatment.* Supplementary educational monograph, no. 22. Chicago: University of Chicago, 1922.

Gray, W. S., *Summary of Investigations Relating to Reading.* Supplementary educational monograph, no. 28. Chicago: University of Chicago, 1925.

Gredler, G. R., "The Birthdate Effect: Fact or Artifact?" *Journal of Learning Disabilities,* 1980, vol. 13, pp. 239–42.

Green, D. R., and Simmons, S. V., "Chronological Age and School Entrance," *Elementary School Journal,* 1962, vol. 63, pp. 41–47.

Grinspoon, L., and Singer, S. B., "Amphetamines in the Treatment of Hyperkinetic Children," *Harvard Educational Review,* 1973, vol. 43, pp. 515–55.

Hagger, T. D., "Congenital Word Blindness or Specific Developmental Dyslexia: A Review," *The Medical Journal of Australia,* 1968, vol. 1, pp. 783–89.

Hallahan, D. P., Gajar, A. H., Cohen, S. B., and Tarver, S. G., "Selective Attention and Locus of Control in Learning Disabled and Normal Children," *Journal of Learning Disabilities,* 1978, vol. 11, pp. 231–36.

Hallahan, D. P., Kauffman, J. M., and Ball, D. W. "Selective Attention and Cognitive Tempo of Low Achieving and High Achieving Sixth Grade Males," *Perceptual and Motor Skills,* 1973, vol. 36, pp. 579–83.

Hallahan, D. P., and Sapona, R., "Self-monitoring of Attention with Learning Disabled Children: Past Research and Current Issues," *Journal of Learning Disabilities,* 1983, vol. 16, pp. 616–20.

Hallahan, D., Tarver, S. G., Kauffman, J. M., and Graybeal, N. L., "A Comparison of the Effects of Reinforcement and Response Cost of the Selective Attention of Learning Disabled Children," *Journal of Learning Disabilities,* 1978, vol. 11, pp. 430–38.

Haller, J. S., and Axelrod, P., "Minimal Brain Dysfunction Syndrome," *American Journal of Disabled Children,* 1975, vol. 129, pp. 1319–24.

Hambidge, K. M., "Hair Analyses: Worthless for Vitamins, Limited for Minerals," *American Journal of Clinical Nutrition,* 1982, vol. 36, pp. 943–49.

Hammill, D. D., Leigh, J. E., McNutt, G., and Larsen, S. C., "A New Definition of Learning Disabilities," *Learning Disabilities Quarterly,* 1981, vol. 4, pp. 336–42.

Hardyck, C., Tzeng, O. J. L., and Wang, W. S-Y., "Cerebral Lateralization of Function and Bilingual Decision Processes: Is Thinking Lateralized?" *Brain and Language,* 1978, vol. 5, pp. 56–71.

Haslam, R. H. A., Dalby, J. T., Johns, R. D., and Rademaker, A. W. "Cerebral Asymmetry in Developmental Dyslexia," *Archives of Neurology,* 1981, vol. 38, pp. 679–82.

Hatchette, R. K., and Evans, J. R., "Auditory-Visual and Temporal-Spatial Pattern Matching Performance of Two Types of Learning-Disabled Children," *Journal of Learning Disabilities,* 1983, vol. 16, pp. 537–41.

Hebben, N. A., Whitman, R. D., Milberg, W. P., Andresko, M., and Galpin, R., "Attentional Dysfunction in Poor Readers," *Journal of Learning Disabilities,* 1981, vol. 14, pp. 287–90.

Helfgott, J. A., "Phonemic Segmentation and Blending Skills of Kindergarten Children: Implications for Beginning Reading Acquisition," *Contemporary Educational Psychology,* 1976, vol. 1, pp. 157–69.

Helfgott, E., Rudel, R. G., and Krieger, J., "Effect of Piracetam on the Single Word and Prose Reading of Dyslexic Children," *Psychopharmacology Bulletin,* 1984, vol. 20, pp. 688–90.

Hellige, J. B., Cox, P. J., and Litvac, L., "Information Processing in the Cerebral Hemispheres: Selective Hemispheric Activation and Capacity Limitations," *Journal of Experimental Psychology: General,* 1979, vol. 108, pp. 251–79.

Henderson, A. J., and Shores, R. E., "How Learning Disabled Students' Failure to Attend Suffixes Affects Their Oral Reading Performance," *Journal of Learning Disabilities,* 1982, vol. 15, pp. 178–82.

Herndon, J., *The Way It Spozed to Be.* N.Y.: Simon and Schuster, 1968.

Hier, D. B., LeMay, M., Rosenberger, P. B., and Perlo, V. P. "Developmental Dyslexia: Evidence for a Subgroup with a Reversal of Cerebral Asymmetry," *Archives of Neurology,* 1978, vol. 35, pp. 90–92.

Hinshelwood, J., "A Case of Congenital Word-Blindness," *The British Medical Journal,* 1904, vol. 2, pp. 1303–07.

Hinshelwood, J., "A Case of 'Word' Without 'Letter' Blindness," *Lancet,* 1898, vol. 1, pp. 422–25.

Hinshelwood, J., "A Case of Word-Blindness, with Right Homonymous Hemianopsia," *British Medical Journal,* 1904, vol. 2, pp. 1304–07.
Hinshelwood, J., *Congenital Word-Blindness.* London: H. K. Lewis & Co., 1917.
Hinshelwood, J., "Congenital Word-Blindness," *Lancet,* 1900, vol. 1, pp. 1506–08.
Hinshelwood, J., "Congenital Word-Blindness, with Reports of Two Cases," *Ophthalmic Review,* 1902, vol. 21, pp. 91–99.
Hinshelwood, J., "Four Cases of Congenital Word-Blindness Occurring in the Same Family," *British Medical Journal,* 1907, vol. 2, pp. 1229–32.
Hinshelwood, J., "The Treatment of Word-Blindness, Acquired and Congenital," *British Medical Journal,* 1912, vol. 2, pp. 1033–35.
Hinshelwood, J., "Two Cases of Hereditary Congenital Word-Blindness," *British Medical Journal,* 1911, vol. 1, pp. 608–9.
Hinshelwood, J., "The Visual Memory for Words and Figures," *British Medical Journal,* 1896, vol. 2, pp. 1543–44.
Hinshelwood, J., "Word-Blindness and Visual Memory," *Lancet,* 1895, vol. 2, pp. 1564–70.
Hiscock, M., and Bergstrom, K. J., "The Lengthy Persistence of Primary Effects in Dichotic Listening," *Neuropsychologia,* 1982, vol. 20, pp. 43–53.
Hiscock, M., and Kinsbourne, M., "Asymmetries of Selective Listening and Attention Switching in Children," *Developmental Psychology,* 1980, vol. 16, pp. 70–82.
Hiscock, M., and Kinsbourne, M., "Laterality and Dyslexia: A Critical View," *Annals of Dyslexia,* 1982, vol. 32, pp. 177–228.
Hiscock, M., and Kinsbourne, M., "Selective Listening Asymmetry in Preschool Children," *Dovelopmental Psychology,* 1977, vol. 13, pp. 217–24.
Holmes, D. R., and McKeever, W. F., "Material Specific Serial Memory Deficits in Adolescent Dyslexics," *Cortex,* 1979, vol. 15, pp. 51–62.
Hughes, J. R. "Electroencephalographic and Neurophysiological Studies in Dyslexia." In A. L. Benton, and D. Pearl, eds., *Dyslexia: An Appraisal of Current Knowledge.* N.Y.: Oxford, 1978.
Hughes, R., and Brewin, R., *The Tranquilizing of America.* N.Y.: Warner, 1979.
Husen, T., "Abilities of Twins," *Journal of Psychology,* 1960, vol. 1, pp. 125–35.
Hyde, J. R. G., *The Effect of an Acute Dose of Piracetam on Human Performance.* Unpublished doctoral dissertation, University of London School of Pharmacy, 1980.
Hynd, G. W., and Cohen, M., *Dyslexia: Neuropsychological Theory, Research, and Clinical Differentiation.* N.Y.: Grune & Stratton, 1983.
Hynd, G. W., and Hynd, C. R., "Dyslexia: Neuroanatomical/Neurolinguistic Perspectives," *Reading Research Quarterly,* 1984(a), vol. 19, pp. 482–98.
Hynd, G. W., and Hynd, C. R., "Dyslexia: Two Priorities for the 1980's," *International Journal of Neuroscience,* 1984(b), vol. 23, pp. 223–30.
Hynd, G. W., Obrzut, J. E., Weed, W., and Hynd, C. R., "Development of Cerebral Dominance: Dichotic Listening Asymmetry in Normal and Learning Disabled Children," *Journal of Experimental Child Psychology,* 1979, vol. 28, pp. 445–54.

IMS America Ltd. Copyright market statistics used with permission of publisher. Ambler, Pa., 1977.
Inglis, J., and Sykes, D. H., "Some Sources of Variation Indichotic Listening Performance in Children," *Journal of Experimental Child Psychology,* 1967, vol. 5, pp. 480–88.
Innes, J. T., Jacobson, P. B., and Pellegrin, R. J., *The Economic Returns to Education.* Eugene: University of Oregon Press, 1965.
Jacoby, R., *Social Amnesia.* Boston: Beacon Press, 1975.
Javal, E., "Essai sur la Physiologie de la Lecture," *Annales D'Oculistique,* 1879, vol. 87, pp. 242–53.
Jezer, M., *The Dark Ages: Life in the United States 1945–1960.* Boston: South End Press, 1982.
Jinks, P. C., "An Investigation into the Effect of Date of Birth on Subsequent School Performance," *Educational Research,* 1964, vol. 6, pp. 220–25.
John, E. R., *Neurometrics: Clinical Applications of Quantitative Electrophysiology.* Hillsdale, N.J.: Lawrence Erlbaum, 1977.
John, E. R., et al., "Neurometrics: Numerical Taxonomy Identifies Different Profiles or Brain Functions Within Groups of Behaviorally Similar People," *Science,* 1977, vol. 196, pp. 1393–1410.
Johnson, B., Schneider, M., and German, D., "The Debate Over Learning Disability vs. Reading Disability: A Survey of Practitioners' Populations and Remedial Methods," *Learning Disability Quarterly,* 1983, vol. 6, pp. 258–64.
Johnson, P. R., "Dichotically-Stimulated Ear Differences in Musicians and Nonmusicians," *Cortex,* 1977, vol. 13, pp. 385–89.
Johnston, P. R., "Understanding Reading Disability: A Case Study Approach," *Harvard Educational Review,* 1985, vol. 55, pp. 153–77.
Johnstone, J., Galin, D., Fein, G., Yingling, C., Herron, J., and Marcus, M., "Regional Brain Activity in Dyslexic and Control Children During Reading Tasks: Visual Probe Event-Related Potentials," *Brain and Language,* 1984, vol. 21, pp. 233–54.
Jorm, A. F., "Specific Reading Retardation and Working Memory: A Review," *British Journal of Psychology,* 1983, vol. 74, pp. 311–42.
Kamin, L. J., "Is Crime in the Genes? The Answer May Depend on Who Chooses What Evidence," *Scientific American,* 1986, vol. 254, pp. 22–27.
Kamin, L. J., "MZ and DZ Twins." In H. J. Eysenck and L. J. Kamin, *The Intelligence Controversy.* N.Y.: John Wiley, 1981.
Kamin, L. J., "Psychology as Social Science: The Jensen Affair, 10 Years After." Presidential address presented at the Eastern Psychological Association, Philadelphia, April 1979.
Kamin, L. J., *The Science and Politics of I.Q.,* N.Y.: Wiley, 1974.
Karabel, J. K., and Halsey, A. H., eds., *Power and Ideology in Education.* N.Y.: Oxford University Press, 1977.
Karrier, C. J., Violas, P. C., and Spring, J., *Roots of Crisis: American Education in the Twentieth Century.* Chicago: Rand McNally, 1973.
Katz, M. B., *Class, Bureaucracy, and Schools: The Illusion of Educational Change in America.* N.Y.: Praeger, 1971.
Katz, R. B., Healy, A. F., and Shankweiler, D., "On Accounting for Deficiencies in Order Memory Associated with Reading Difficulty: A Reply to Tallal," *Applied Psycholinguistics,* 1984, vol. 5, pp. 170–74.
Katz, R. B., Shankweiler, D., and Liberman, I. Y., "Memory for Item Order

and Phonetic Recoding in the Beginning Reader," *Journal of Experimental Child Psychology,* 1981, vol. 32, pp. 474–84.

Kaufman, H. S., and Biren, P. L., "Persistent Reversers: Poor Readers, Writers, Spellers?" *Academic Therapy,* 1976–77, vol. 12, pp. 209–17.

Kavale, K. A., and Forness, S. R., "Hyperactivity and Diet Treatment: A Meta-analysis of the Feingold Hypothesis," *Journal of Learning Disabilities,* 1983, vol. 16, pp. 324–30.

Kavale, K. A., and Forness, S. R., "Learning Disability and the History of Science: Paradigm or Paradox?" *Remedial and Special Education,* 1985, vol. 6, pp. 12–23.

Keogh, B. K., "Future of the LD Field: Research and Practice," *Journal of Learning Disabilities,* 1986, vol. 19, pp. 455–60.

Kershner, J., and Hawke, W., "Megavitamins and Learning Disorders: A Controlled Double-Blind Experiment," *Journal of Nutrition,* 1979, vol. 109, pp. 819–26.

Kershner, J., Thomae, R., and Callaway, R., "Nonverbal Fixation Control in Young Children Induces a Left-Field Advantage in Digit Recall," *Neuropsychologia,* 1977, vol. 15, pp. 569–76.

Kershner, J. R., "Cerebral Dominance in Disabled Readers, Good Readers, and Gifted Children: Search for a Valid Model," *Child Development,* 1977, vol. 48, pp. 61–67.

Kertesz, A., "Are There Sex Differences in Acquired Alexia?" In A. Ansara, A. Geschwind, M. Albert, N. Gartell, eds., *Sex Differences in Dyslexia.* Towson, Maryland: Orton Dyslexia Society, 1981.

Kinsbourne, M., "Cerebral Dominance, Learning, and Cognition." In H. R. Myklebust, ed., *Progress in Learning Disabilities,* vol. 3. N.Y.: Grune & Stratton, 1975.

Kinsbourne, M., "The Ontogeny of Cerebral Dominance," *Annals of the New York Academy of Sciences,* 1975, vol. 263, pp. 244–50.

Kinsbourne, M., and Hiscock, M., "Cerebral Lateralization and Cognitive Development." In Chall, J. S., and Mirsky, A. F., eds., *Education and the Brain.* Chicago: National Society for the Study of Education, 1978.

Kirk, S. A., McCarthy, J. J., and Kirk, W. D., *Illinois Test of Psycholinguistic Abilities.* Urbana: University of Illinois Press, 1968.

Kistner, J. A., "Attentional Deficits of Learning-Disabled Children: Effects of Rewards and Practice," *Journal of Abnormal Child Psychology,* 1985, vol. 13, pp. 19–31.

Klein, D., Moscovitch, M., and Vigna, C., "Attentional Mechanisms and Perceptual Asymmetries in Tachistoscopic Recognition of Words and Faces," *Neuropsychologia,* 1976, vol. 14, pp. 55–66.

Knight-Arest, I., "Communicative Effectiveness of Learning Disabled and Normally Achieving 10- to 13-Year-Old Boys," *Learning Disability Quarterly,* 1984, vol. 7, pp. 237–45.

Knights, R. M., and Bakker, D. J., eds., *The Neuropsychology of Learning Disorders: Theoretical Approaches.* Baltimore: University Park Press, 1976.

Kochnower, J., Richardson, E., and DiBenedetto, B., "A Comparison of the Phonic Decoding Ability of Normal and Learning Disabled Children," *Journal of Learning Disabilities,* 1983, vol. 16, pp. 348–51.

Kohl, H., "And Not So Gladly Teach," *The Nation,* May 24, 1986, pp. 736–39.

Kohl, H., *36 Children.* N.Y.: New American Library, 1967.

Kolko, G., *Wealth and Power in America.* N.Y.: Praeger, 1964.

Koppell, S., "Testing the Attentional Deficit Notion," *Journal of Learning Disabilities,* 1979, vol. 12, pp. 43–48.
Kozol, J., *Death at an Early Age.* N.Y.: Houghton Mifflin, 1967.
Kozol, J., *Prisoners of Silence: Breaking the Bonds of Adult Illiteracy in the United States.* N.Y.: Continuum, 1980.
Kronick, D., *Three Families.* San Rafael, Calif.: Academic Therapy Publications, 1976.
Kushnick, T., "Genetic Counseling: The Case for Primary Prevention." In New Jersey Association for Children with Learning Disabilities, *Handbook on Learning Disabilities: A Prognosis for the Child, the Adolescent, the Adult.* Englewood Cliffs, NJ: Prentice-Hall, 1974.
Lahey, B. B., Kupfer, D. L., Beggs, V. E., and Landon, D., "Do Learning Disabled Children Exhibit Peripheral Deficits in Selective Attention? An Analysis of Eye Movements During Reading," *Journal of Abnormal Child Psychology,* 1982, vol. 10, pp. 1–10.
Larroche, J. C., "Cytoarchitectonic Abnormalities (Abnormalities of Cell Migration)." In P. J. Vinken and G. W. Bruyn, eds., *Handbook of Clinical Neurology.* Amsterdam, North-Holland, 1977.
Lassen, N. A., Ingvar, D. H., and Skinhoj, E., "Brain Function and Blood Flow," *Scientific American,* 1978, vol. 239, pp. 62–71.
"The Learning Disabled (Education Fall Survey)," *New York Times,* November 11, 1984, pp. 1, 44–58.
Lefton, L. A., Lahey, B. B., and Stagg, D. I., "Eye Movements in Reading Disabled and Normal Children: A Study of Systems and Strategies," *Journal of Learning Disabilities,* 1978, vol. 11, pp. 549–58.
Leisman, G., and Ashkenazi, M., "Aetiological Factors in Dyslexia: 4. Cerebral Hemispheres Are Functionally Equivalent," *Neuroscience,* 1980, vol. 11, pp. 157–64.
Leisman, G., and Schwartz, J., "Aetiological Factors in Dyslexia: 1. Saccadic Eye Movement Control," *Perceptual and Motor Skills,* 1978, vol. 47, pp. 403–07.
Leong, C. K., "Cognitive Processing, Language Awareness, and Reading in Grade 2 and Grade 4 Children," *Contemporary Educational Psychology,* 1984, vol. 9, pp. 369–83.
Leong, C. K., "Lateralization in Severely Disabled Readers in Relation to Functional Cerebral Development and Synthesis of Information." In R. M. Knights, and D. J. Bakker, eds., *The Neuropsychology of Learning Disorders.* Baltimore: University Park Press, 1976.
Leontiev, A. N., *Activity, Consciousness, and Personality.* Englewood Cliffs, N. J.: Prentice-Hall, 1978.
Leontiev, A. N., "On the Biological and Social Aspects of Human Development: The Training of Auditory Ability." In M. Cole and I. Maltzman, eds., *Handbook of Contemporary Soviet Psychology.* N.Y.: Basic Books, 1969.
Lerner, J. W., *Children with Learning Disabilities.* Boston: Houghton Mifflin, 1976.
Lester, M. I., Horst, R. L., and Thatcher, R. W., "Protective Effects of Zinc and Calcium Against Heavy Metal Impairment of Children's Cognitive Function," *Nutrition and Behavior,* 1986, vol. 3, pp. 145–61.
Lester, M. L., Thatcher, R. W., and Monroe-Lord, L., "Refined Carbohydrate Intake, Hair Cadmium Levels, and Cognitive Functioning in Children," *Nutrition and Behavior,* 1982, vol. 1, pp. 3–13.

Levinson, H. N., *Smart But Feeling Dumb.* N.Y.: Warner Books, 1984.

Levinson, H. N., *A Solution to the Riddle Dyslexia.* N.Y.: Springer-Verlag, 1980.

Lewis, J. A., and Young, R., "Deanol and Methylphenidate in Minimal Brain Dysfunction," *Clinical Pharmacology and Therapeutics,* 1975, vol. 17, pp. 534–40.

Lewontin, R. C., Rose, S., and Kamin, S., *Not in Our Genes.* N.Y.: Pantheon, 1984.

Liberman, I. Y., Mann, V. A., Shankweiler, D., and Werfelman, M., "Children's Memory for Recurring Linguistic and Non-linguistic Material in Relation to Reading Ability," *Cortex,* 1982, vol. 18, pp. 367–75.

Liberman, I. Y., and Shankweiler, D., "Phonology and the Problems of Learning to Read and Write," *Remedial and Special Education,* 1985, vol. 6, pp. 8–17.

Liberman, I. Y., Shankweiler, D., Orlando, C., Harris, K. S., and Berti, F. B., "Letter Confusions and Reversals of Sequence in the Beginning Reader: Implications for Orton's Theory of Developmental Dyslexia," *Cortex,* 1971, vol. 7, pp. 127–42.

"The Link . . . Undetected Learning Disabilities and Juvenile Delinquency," *Their World,* 1985, pp. 52–56.

Loehlin, J. C., and Nichols, R. C., *Heredity, Environment, and Personality: A Study of 850 Sets of Twins.* Austin: University of Texas, 1976.

Lovett, M. W., "A Developmental Perspective on Reading Dysfunction: Accuracy and Rate Criteria in the Subtyping of Dyslexic Children," *Brain and Language,* 1984, vol. 22, pp. 67–91.

Lovrich, D., and Stamm, J. S., "Event-Related Potential and Behavioral Correlates of Attention in Reading Retardation," *Journal of Clinical Neuropsychology,* 1983, vol. 5, pp. 13–37.

Lundberg, I., Olofsson, A., and Wall, S., "Reading and Spelling Skills in the First School Years, Predicted from Phonemic Awareness Skills in Kindergarten," *Scandinavian Journal of Psychology,* 1980, vol. 21, pp. 159–73.

Luria, A. R., *The Working Brain.* N.Y.: Basic Books, 1973.

Lyon, C. R., "Educational Validation Subtypes of Learning Disability Subtypes." In B. R. Rourke, ed., *Neuropsychology of Learning Disabilities: Essentials of Subtype Analysis.* N.Y.: Guilford Press, 1985.

Lyon, R., Stewart, N., and Freedman, D. "Neuropsychological Characteristics of Empirically Derived Subgroups of Learning Disabled Readers," *Journal of Clinical Neuropsychology,* 1982, vol. 4, pp. 343–65.

Lyon, R., and Watson, B., "Empirically Derived Subgroups of Learning Disabled Readers: Diagnostic Characteristics," *Journal of Learning Disabilities,* 1981, vol. 14, pp. 256–61.

Lyon, R., Watson, B., Reitta, S., Porch, B., and Rhodes, J., "Selected Linguistic and Perceptual Abilities of Empirically Derived Subgroups of Learning Disabled Readers," *Journal of School Psychology,* 1981, vol. 19, pp. 152–66.

Malatesha, R. N., and Dougan, D. R., "Clinical Subtypes of Developmental Dyslexia: Resolution of an Irresolute Problem." In R. N. Malatesha and P. G. Aaron, eds., *Reading Disorders: Varieties and Treatments.* N.Y.: Academic Press, 1982.

Manis, F. R., and Morrison, F. J., "Reading Disability: A Deficit in Rule Learning?" In L. S. Siegel and F. J. Morrison, eds., *Cognitive Development in Atypical Children.* N.Y.: Springer-Verlag, 1985.

Mann, L., Davis, C. H., Boyer, C. W., Metz, C. M., and Wolford, B., "LD or Not LD, That Was the Question: A Retrospective Analysis of Child Service Demonstration Centers' Compliance with the Federal Definition of Learning Disabilities," *Journal of Learning Disabilities,* 1983, vol. 16, pp. 14–17.

Mann, V. A., and Liberman, I. Y., "Phonological Awareness and Verbal Short-Term Memory," *Journal of Learning Disabilities,* 1984, vol. 17, pp. 592–99.

Mann, V. A., Shankweiler, D., and Smith, S. T., "The Association Between Comprehension of Spoken Sentences and Early Reading Ability: The Role of Phonetic Representation," *Journal of Child Language,* 1984, vol. 11, pp. 627–43.

Marcel, T., Katz, L., and Smith, M., "Laterality and Reading Proficiency," *Neuropsychologia,* 1974, vol. 12, pp. 131–39.

Marcel, T., and Rajan, P., "Lateral Specialization for Recognition of Words and Faces in Good and Poor Readers," *Neuropsychologia,* 1975, vol. 13, pp. 489–97.

Marlowe, M., Cossairt, A., Welch, K., and Errera, J., "Hair Mineral Content as a Predictor of Learning Disabilities," *Journal of Learning Disabilities,* 1984, vol. 17, pp. 418–21.

Marlowe, M., and Errera, J., "Low Lead Levels and Behavior Problems in Children," *Behavior Disorders,* 1982, vol. 7, pp. 163–72.

Marlowe, M., Folio, R., Hall, D., and Errera, J., "Increased Lead Burdens and Trace-Mineral Status in Mentally Retarded Children," *Journal of Special Education,* 1982, vol. 16, pp. 87–99.

Marshall, E., "EPA Faults Classic Lead Poisoning Study," *Science,* 1983, vol. 222, pp. 906–07.

Marshall, W., and Ferguson, J. H., "Hereditary Word-Blindness as a Defect of Selective Association," *Journal of Nervous and Mental Disorders,* 1939, vol. 89, pp. 164–73.

Marson, D., and Ysseldyke, J., "Concerns in Interpreting Subtest Scatter on the Tests of Cognitive Ability from the Woodcock-Johnson Psychoeducational Battery," *Journal of Learning Disabilities,* 1984, vol. 17, pp. 588–91.

Masland, R. L., "Neurological Aspects of Dyslexia." In G. Th. Pavlidis and T. R. Miles, eds., *Dyslexia Research and Its Applications to Education.* N.Y.: John Wiley, 1981.

Masland, R., and Usprich, C., book review of *A Solution to the Riddle Dyslexia, Bulletin of the Orton Society,* 1981, vol. 31, pp. 256–61.

Matheny, A. P., and Dolan, A. B., "A Twin Study of Genetic Influences in Reading Achievement," *Journal of Learning Disabilities,* 1974, vol. 7, pp. 99–102.

Matheny, A. P., Dolan, A. B., and Wilson, R. S., "Twins with Academic Learning Problems: Antecedent Characteristics," *American Journal of Orthopsychiatry,* 1976, vol. 46, pp. 464–69.

Mattes, J. A., "The Feingold Diet: A Current Reappraisal," *Journal of Learning Disabilities,* 1983, vol. 16, pp. 319–23.

Mattis, S., French, J. H., and Rapin, I., "Dyslexia in Children and Young Adults: Three Independent Neuropsychological Syndromes," *Developmental Medicine and Child Neurology,* 1975, vol. 17, pp. 150–63.

McCready, E. B., "Efforts in the Zone of Language (Word-Deafness and Word-Blindness) and Their Influence in Education and Behavior," *American Journal of Psychiatry,* 1926, vol. 6, pp. 267–77.

McGuinness, D., *When Children Don't Learn: Understanding the Biology and Psychology of Learning Disabilities.* N.Y.: Basic Books, 1985.

McKeever, W. F., and Huling, M. D., "Lateral Dominance in Tachistoscopic Word Recognition of Children at Two Levels of Ability," *Quarterly Journal of Experimental Psychology,* 1970, vol. 22, pp. 600–04.

McKeever, W. F., and VanDeventer, A. D., "Dyslexic Adolescents: Evidence of Impaired Visual and Auditory Language Processing Associated with Normal Lateralization of Responsivity," *Cortex,* 1975, vol. 11, pp. 361–78.

McKinney, J. D., "The Search for Subtypes of Specific Learning Disability," *Journal of Learning Disabilities,* 1984, vol. 17, pp. 43–50.

McKinney, J. D., and Feagans, L., "Academic and Behavioral Characteristics of Learning Disabled Children and Average Achievers: Longitudinal Studies," *Learning Disability Quarterly,* 1984, vol. 7, pp. 251–65.

McLeod, J. "Learning Disability Is for Educators," *Journal of Learning Disabilities,* 1983, vol. 16, pp. 23–24.

Meier, J. H., "Prevalence and Characteristics of Learning Disabilities Found in Second Grade Children," *Journal of Learning Disabilities,* 1971, vol. 4, pp. 1–16.

Mercer, C. D., Hughes, C., and Mercer, A. R., "Learning Disabilities Definitions Used by State Education Departments," *Learning Disability Quarterly,* 1985, vol. 8, pp. 45–55.

Mercer, M., and Liebowitz, M. R., "Solving the Mysteries of the Mind," *Family Circle,* July 21, 1981, pp. 92–136.

Mezirow, J., Darkenwald, G. G., and Knox, A. B., *Last Gamble on Education: Dynamics of Adult Basic Education.* Washington, D.C.: Adult Education Association of the U.S.A., 1975.

Miller, D. R., and Westman, J. C., "Reading Disability as a Condition of Family Stability," *Family Process,* 1964, vol. 3, pp. 66–76.

Miller, D. R., and Westman, J. C., "Family Teamwork and Psychotherapy," *Family Process,* 1966, vol. 5, pp. 49–59.

Miller, J., *States of Mind.* N.Y.: Pantheon, 1983.

Millman, H. L., "Minimal Brain Dysfunction in Children—Evaluation and Treatment," *Journal of Learning Disabilities,* 1970, vol. 3, pp. 91–99.

Mills, C. W., *The Sociological Imagination.* N.Y.: Oxford University Press, 1959.

Mind and Behavior: Readings from Scientific American. San Francisco: W.H. Freeman, 1980.

Money, J., "Child Abuse: Growth Failure, IQ Deficit, and Learning Disability," *Journal of Learning Disabilities,* 1982, vol. 15, pp. 579–82.

Money, J., and Annecillo, C. "IQ Change of Domicile in the Syndrome of Reversible Hyposomatotropinism (Psychosocial Dwarfism): Pilot Investigation," *Psychoneuroendocrinology,* 1976, vol. 1, pp. 427–29.

Montagu, A., and Matson, F., *The Dehumanization of Man.* New York: McGraw-Hill, 1983.

Moon, C., Marlowe, M., Stellern, J. and Errera, J., "Main and Interaction Effects of Metallic Pollutants on Cognitive Functioning," *Journal of Learning Disabilities,* 1985, vol. 18, pp. 217–21.

Morais, J., and Bertelson, P., "Laterality Effects in Diotic Listening," *Perception,* 1973, vol. 2, pp. 107–11.

Morais, J., Cary, L., Alegria, J., and Bertelson, P., "Does Awareness of Speech as a Sequence of Phones Arise Spontaneously?" *Cognition,* 1979, vol. 7, pp. 323–31.

"More on Dyslexia," *Family Weekly,* January 24, 1982, p. 27.

Morgan, W. P., "A Case of Congenital Word-Blindness," *British Medical Journal,* 1896, vol. 2, p. 1378.

Mowry, G. E., *The Urban Nation: 1920–1960.* N.Y.: Hill & Wang, 1965.

Moyer, S. B., and Newcomer, P. L., "Reversals in Reading: Diagnosis and Remediation," *Exceptional Children,* 1977, vol. 43, pp. 424–29.

Nagafuchi, M., "Development of Dichotic and Monaural Hearing Abilities in Young Children," *Acta Otolaryngologica,* 1970, vol. 69, pp. 409–14.

Nassi, A. J., and Abramowitz, S. I., "From Phrenology to Psychosurgery and Back Again," *American Journal of Orthopsychiatry,* 1976, vol. 46, pp. 591–607.

National Advisory Committee on Handicapped Children, *Special Education for Handicapped Children* (first annual report). Washington, D.C.: U.S. Department of Health, Education, and Welfare, 1968.

National Assessment of Educational Progress: Reading Rate and Comprehension (report 02-R-09). Washington, D.C.: U.S. Government Printing Office, 1972.

National Prescription Audit: General Information Report, Ambler, Pa: IMS America, Ltd., 1981.

Naylor, H., "Reading Disability and Lateral Asymmetry: An Information Processing Analysis," *Psychological Bulletin,* 1980, vol. 87, pp. 531–45.

Naylor, H., Lambert, N., Sassone, D. M., and Hardyck, C., "Lateral Asymmetry in Perceptual Judgments of Reading Disabled, Hyperactive and Control Children," *International Journal of Neuroscience,* 1980, vol. 10, pp. 135–43.

Neale, M. D., *Neale Analysis of Reading.* London: Macmillan Education Ltd., 1966.

Nearing, S., *New Education: A Review of the Progressive Education Movements of the Day.* N.Y.: Row, Peterson & Co., 1915.

"The Neurological Basis of the Talents of Dyslexics," *Perspectives on Dyslexia* (Orton Dyslexia Society), August 1984.

"New treatment for dyslexia," *McCall's.* Reprinted in a booklet from Levinson's Medical Dyslexic Treatment Center.

Newcombe, F., Oldfield, R. C., Ratcliff, G., and Wingfield, A., "Recognition and Naming of Object-Drawings by Men with Focal Brain Wounds," *Journal of Neurology, Neurosurgery and Psychiatry,* 1971, vol. 34, pp. 329–40.

Newman, H. H., Freeman, F. N., and Holzinger, K. J., *Twins: A Study of Heredity and Environment.* Chicago: University of Chicago, 1937.

Newman, S. A., "Idealism in Modern Biology," unpublished manuscript, 1986.

Nichols, R. C., *The Inheritance of General and Specific Ability.* National Merit Scholarship Report, 1965, vol. 1, pp. 1–9.

Nolan, D. R., Hammeke, T. A., and Barkley, R. A., "A Comparison of the Patterns of the Neuropsychological Performance in Two Groups of Learning Disabled Children," *Journal of Clinical Child Psychology,* 1983, vol. 12, pp. 22–27.

Nootropil: Basic Scientific and Clinical Data. Brussels: UCB Pharmaceutical, 1980.

Norrie, E., "Ordblindhedens." In L. J. Thompson, *Reading Disability.* Springfield, Ill.: Charles C Thomas, 1959.

Null, G., *The Complete Guide to Health and Nutrition.* N.Y.: Delacorte Press, 1984.

Obrzut, J. E., "Dichotic Listening and Bisensory Memory Skills in Qualitatively Diverse Dyslexic Readers," *Journal of Learning Disabilities,* 1979, vol. 12, pp. 304–14.

Obrzut, J. E., and Hynd, G. W., "The Neurobiological and Neuropsychological Foundations of Learning Disabilities," *Journal of Learning Disabilities,* 1983, vol. 16, pp. 515–20.

Obrzut, J. E., Hynd, G. W., Obrzut, A., and Pirozzolo, F. J., "Effect of Directed Attention on Cerebral Asymmetries in Normal and Learning-Disabled Children," *Developmental Psychology,* 1981, vol. 17, pp. 118–25.

Oldfield, R. C., and Wingfield, A., "Response Latencies in Naming Objects," *Quarterly Journal of Experimental Psychology,* 1965, vol. 17, part 4, pp. 273–81.

O'Leary, K. D., "Pills or Skills for Hyperactive Children," *Journal of Applied Behavior,* 1980, vol. 13, pp. 191–204.

O'Leary, K. D., Vivian, D., and Cornoldi, C. "Assessment and Treatment of 'Hyperactivity' in Italy and the United States," *Journal of Clinical Child Psychology,* 1984, vol. 13, pp. 56–60.

Olofsson, A., and Lundberg, I., "Can Phonemic Awareness Be Trained in Kindergarten?" *Scandinavian Journal of Psychology,* 1983, vol. 24, pp. 35–44.

Olsen, J. L., Wong, B. Y. L., and Marx, R. W., "Linguistic and Metacognitive Aspects of Normally Achieving and Learning Disabled Children's Communication Process," *Learning Disability Quarterly,* 1983, vol. 6, pp. 289–304.

Olson, J., Mercer, C., and Paulson, D., "Process Testing: Is the Detroit the Answer?" *Learning Disability Quarterly,* 1981, vol. 4, pp. 44–47.

Olson, M. E., "Laterality Differences in Tachistoscopic Word Recognition in Normal and Delayed Readers in Elementary School," *Neuropsychologia,* 1973, vol. 11, pp. 343–50.

Olson, R. K., "Disabled Reading Processes and Cognitive Profiles." In D. Gray and J. Kavanaugh, eds., *Biobehavioral Measures of Dyslexia.* Parkton, Md.: York, 1986.

Olson, R. K., Davidson, B. J., Kliegl, R., and Davies, S. E., "Development of Phonetic Memory in Disabled and Normal Readers," *Journal of Experimental Child Psychology,* 1984, vol. 37, pp. 187–206.

Olson, R. K., Kliegl, R., and Davidson, B. J., "Dyslexics' and Normal Readers' Eye Movements," *Journal of Experimental Psychology: Human Perception and Performance,* 1983, vol. 9, pp. 816–25.

Op't Hof, J. O., and Guldenpfenning, W. M., "Dominant Inheritance of Specific Reading Disability," *South African Medical Journal,* 1972, vol. 46, pp. 737–38.

The Orton Dyslexia Society and the Problem of Dyslexia (pamphlet). Baltimore: Orton Dyslexia Society, n.d.

Orton, S. T., "Familial Occurrence of Disorders in the Acquisition of Language," *Eugenics,* 1930, vol. 3, pp. 140–47.

Orton, S. T., "An Impediment to Learning to Read—A Neurological Explanation of the Reading Disability," *School and Society,* 1928, vol. 28, pp. 286–90.

Ottenbacher, K., "Identifying Vestibular Processing Dysfunction in Learning-

Disabled Children," *American Journal of Occupational Therapy,* 1978, vol. 32, pp. 217–21.

Ottenbacher, K., Abbott, C., Haley, D., and Watson, P. J., "Human Figure Drawing Ability and Vestibular Processing Dysfunction in Learning-Disabled Children," *Journal of Clinical Psychology,* 1984, vol. 40, pp. 1084–89.

Parker, R., *The Myth of the Middle Class.* N.Y.: Harper & Row, 1972.

Parker, R. G. & Watson, J. M., *National Readers,* N.Y.: A.S. Barnes & Co., 1868.

Patrick, J. & Reschly, D., "Relationship of state demographic variables to school-system prevalence of mental retardation," *American Journal of Mental Deficiency,* 1982, 86, 351–360.

Pavlidis, G. Th., "Do Eye Movements Hold the Key to Dyslexia?" *Neuropsychologia,* 1981 (a), vol. 19, pp. 57–64.

Pavlidis, G. Th., "Erratic Sequential Eye-Movements in Dyslexics: Comments and Reply to Stanley et al.," *British Journal of Psychology,* 1983, vol. 74, pp. 189–93.

Pavlidis, G. Th., "Eye Movements in Dyslexia: Their Diagnostic Significance," *Journal of Learning Disabilities,* 1985, vol. 18, pp. 42–50.

Pavlidis, G. Th., "How Can Dyslexia Be Objectively Diagnosed?" *Reading,* 1979, vol. 13, pp. 3–15.

Pavlidis, G. Th., "Sequencing Eye Movements and the Early Objective Diagnosis of Dyslexia." In G. Th. Pavlidis and T. R. Miles, eds., *Dyslexia Research and Its Applications to Education.* London: John Wiley & Sons, 1981.

Pavlidis, G. Th., and Miles, T. R., eds., *Dyslexia Research and Its Applications to Education.* N.Y.: John Wiley & Sons, 1981.

Pedersen, E., Faucher, T. A., Eaton, W. W., "A New Perspective on the Effects of First-grade Teachers on Children's Subsequent Adult Status," *Harvard Educational Review,* 1978, vol. 48, pp. 1–31.

Pelham, W. E., "Selective Attention Deficits in Poor Readers? Dichotic Listening, Speeded Classification, and Auditory and Visual Central and Incidental Learning Tasks," *Child Development,* 1979, vol. 50, pp. 1050–61.

Penfield, W., and Jasper, H., *Epilepsy and the Functional Anatomy of the Human Brain.* Boston: Little, Brown & Co., 1954.

Perfetti, C. A., Finger, E., and Hogaboam, T., "Sources of Vocalization Latency Differences Between Skilled and Less Skilled Young Readers," *Journal of Educational Psychology,* 1978, vol. 70, pp. 730–39.

Perlmutter, B. F., and Parus, M. V., "Identifying Children with Learning Disabilities: A Comparison of Diagnostic Procedures Across School Districts," *Learning Disabilities Quarterly,* 1983, vol. 6, pp. 321–28.

Petrauskas, R. J., and Rourke, B. P., "Identification of Subtypes of Retarded Readers: A Neuropsychological, Multivariate Approach," *Journal of Clinical Neuropsychology,* 1979, vol. 1, pp. 17–37.

Physicians' Desk Reference, thirty-ninth edition. Oradell, NJ: Medical Economics Co., 1985.

Pihl, R. O., "Hair Element Content in Learning Disabled Children," *Science,* 1977, vol. 198, pp. 204–06.

Pirozzolo, F. J., and Hansch, E. C. "The Neurobiology of Developmental Reading Disorders." In R. N. Malatesha and P. G. Aaron, eds.. *Reading Disorders: Varieties and Treatments.* N.Y.: Academic Press, 1982.

"Plain Talk About Children with Learning Disabilities." Washington, D.C.: U.S. Government Printing Office, 1979.

Polatajko, H. J., "A Critical Look at Vestibular Dysfunction in Learning-

Disabled Children," *Developmental Medicine & Child Neurology,* 1985, vol. 27, pp. 283–92.

Pollatsek, A., "What Can Eye Movements Tell Us About Dyslexia?" In K. Rayner, ed., *Eye Movements in Reading: Perceptual and Language Processes.* N.Y.: Academic Press, 1983.

Poplin, M., "Reductionism from the Medical Model to the Classroom: The Past, Present and Future of Learning Disabilities," *Research Communications in Psychology, Psychiatry and Behavior,* 1985, vol. 10, pp. 37–70.

Powell, E. H., *The Design of Discord.* N.Y.: Oxford University Press, 1970.

Preston, M. S., Guthrie, J. T., and Childs, B., "Visual Evoked Responses (VERs) in Normal and Disabled Readers," *Psychophysiology,* 1974, vol. 11, pp. 452–57.

Preston, M. S., Guthrie, J. T., Kirsch, I., Gertman, D., and Childs, B., "VERs in Normal and Disabled Adult Readers," *Psychophysiology,* 1977, vol. 14, pp. 8–14.

Prinz, R. J., Roberts, W. A., and Hantmann, E., "Dietary Correlates of Hyperactive Behavior in Children," *Journal of Consulting and Clinical Psychology,* 1980, vol. 48, pp. 760–769.

Prior, M. R., Frolley, M., and Sanson, A., "Language Lateralization in Specific Reading Retarded Children and Backward Readers," *Cortex,* 1983, vol. 19, pp. 149–63.

Pugach, M. C., "The Limitations of Federal Special Education Policy: The Role of Classroom Teachers in Determining Who Is Handicapped," *Journal of Special Education,* 1985, vol. 19, pp. 123–37.

Quinn, P. O., and Rapoport, J. L., "One-year Follow-up of Hyperactive Boys Treated with Imipramine or Methylphenidate," *American Journal of Psychiatry,* 1975, vol. 132, pp. 241–45.

Randel, D. M., *Harvard Concise Dictionary of Music.* Cambridge: Harvard University Press, 1978.

Rapoport, J. L., "Effects of Dietary Substances in Children," *Journal of Psychiatric Research,* 1982–83, vol. 17, pp. 187–91.

Raven, J. C., *Coloured Progressive Matrices.* N.Y.: Psychological Corp., 1960.

Read, C., Zhang, Y., Nie, H., and Ding, B., "The Ability to Manipulate Speech Sounds Depends on Knowing Alphabetic Spelling," paper presented at the 23rd International Congress of Psychology, Acapulco, Mexico, 1984.

"A Reading Problem Is Traced to a Disorder of the Inner Ear," *Philadelphia Inquirer,* November 7, 1983, p. 8-C.

"Reagan and Education: The Second Chance," *Education Update,* 1984, vol. 7, p. 1.

Regan, D., "Electrical Responses Evoked from the Human Brain," *Scientific American,* 1979, vol. 241, pp. 134–46.

Reitan, R. M., and Davison, L. A., *Clinical Neuropsychology: Current Status and Applications.* N.Y.: John Wiley & Sons, 1974.

Restak, R. M., *The Brain: The Last Frontier.* N.Y.: Doubleday, 1979.

Restak, R., *The Brain.* N.Y.: Bantam, 1984.

Restak, R. M., "Brain Potentials: Signaling Our Inner Thoughts," *Psychology Today,* March 1979, pp. 42–90.

Richardson, E., DiBenedetto, B., and Bradley, C. M., "The Relationship of Sound Blending to Reading Achievement," *Review of Educational Research,* 1977, vol. 47, pp. 319–34.

Rie, H. E., Rie, E. D., and Stewart, S., "Effects of Methylphenidate on Underachieving Children," *Journal of Consulting and Clinical Psychology,* 1976, vol. 44, pp. 250–60.

Rie, H. E., Rie, E. D., Stewart, S., and Ambuel, J. P., "Effects of Ritalin on Underachieving Children: A Replication," *American Journal of Orthopsychiatry,* 1976, vol. 46, pp. 313–22.

Riege, W. H., "Environmental Influences on Brain and Behavior of Year-old Rats," *Developmental Psychobiology,* 1971, vol. 2, pp. 113–28.

Rimland, B., "The Feingold Diet: An Assessment of the Reviews by Mattes, by Kavale and Forness and Others," *Journal of Learning Disabilities,* 1983, vol. 16, pp. 331–33.

Rist, R. C., *The Urban School: A Factory for Failure.* Cambridge, Mass.: MIT Press, 1973.

Rose, S., ed., *Against Biological Determinism.* N.Y.: Allison & Busby, 1982.

Rose, S., ed., *Towards a Liberatory Biology.* N.Y.: Allison & Busby, 1982.

Rosenberger, P. B., and Hier, D. B., "Cerebral Asymmetry and Verbal Intellectual Deficits," *Annals of Neurology,* 1980, vol. 8, pp. 300–04.

Rosenzweig, M. R., "Experience, Memory, and the Brain," *American Psychologist,* 1984, vol. 39, pp. 365–76.

Rosenzweig, M. R., Bennett, E. L., and Diamond, M. C., "Brain Changes in Response to Experience," *Scientific American,* 1972, vol. 226, pp. 22–30.

Rourke, B., ed., *Neuropsychology of Learning Disabilities.* N.Y.: Guilford Press, 1985.

Rourke, B. P., "Reading Retardation in Children: Developmental Lag or Deficit?" In R. M. Knights and D. J. Bakker, eds., *The Neuropsychology of Learning Disorders.* Baltimore: University Park Press, 1976.

Rourke, B. P., and Finlayson, M. A. J., "Neuropsychological Significance of Variations in Patterns of Academic Performance: Verbal and Visual-Spatial Abilities," *Journal of Abnormal Child Psychology,* 1978, vol. 6, pp. 121–33.

Rourke, B. P., and Fisk, J. L., "Socio-emotional Disturbances of Learning Disabled Children: The Role of Central Processing Deficits," *Bulletin of the Orton Society,* 1981, vol. 31, pp. 77–88.

Rourke, B. P. and Strang, J. D., "Neuropsychological Significance of Variations in Patterns of Academic Performance: Motor, Psychomotor, and Tactile-perceptual Abilities," *Journal of Pediatric Psychology,* 1978, vol. 3, pp. 62–66.

Royeen, C. B., Lesinski, G., Ciani, S., and Schneider, D., "Relationship of the Southern California Sensory Integration Tests, the Southern California Postrotary Nystagmus Test, and Clinical Observations Accompanying Them to Evaluations in Otolaryngology, Ophthalmology, and Audiology: Two Descriptive Case Studies," *American Journal of Occupational Therapy,* 1981, vol. 35, pp. 443–50.

Rubin, H., and Liberman, I. Y., "Exploring the Oral and Written Language Errors Made by Language Disabled Children," *Annals of Dyslexia,* 1983, vol. 33, pp. 111–20.

Rubinstein, A. T., ed., *Schools Against Children: The Case for Community Control.* N.Y.: Monthly Review Press, 1970.

Rudel, R. G., "Neuroplasticity: Implications for Development and Education." In J. S. Chall and A. F. Mirsky, eds., *Education and the Brain.* Chicago: University of Chicago Press, 1978.

Rudel, R. G., and Helfgott, E., "Effect of Piracetam on Verbal Memory of

Dyslexic Boys," *Journal of the American Academy of Child Psychiatry,* 1984, vol. 23, pp. 695–99.

Rudel, R. G., Denckla, M. B., and Broman, M., "The Effect of Varying Stimulus Context on Word-finding Ability: Dyslexia Further Differentiated from Other Learning Disabilities," *Brain and Language,* 1981, vol. 13, pp. 130–44.

Rumelhart, D., "Toward an Interactive Model of Reading." In S. Dornic, ed., *Attention and Performance VI.* Hillsdale, N.J.: Erlbaum, 1977.

Rutter, M., and Yule, W., "The Concept of Specific Reading Retardation," *Journal of Child Psychology and Psychiatry,* 1975, vol. 16, pp. 181–97.

Ryan, W., *Blaming the Victim.* N.Y.: Random House, 1971.

Salmaso, D., and Umilta, C., "Vowel Processing in the Left and Right Visual Fields," *Brain and Language,* 1982, vol. 16, pp. 147–57.

Sampson, E. E., "Cognitive Psychology as Ideology," *American Psychologist,* 1981, vol. 36, pp. 730–43.

Samuels, S. J., and Edwall, G., "The Role of Attention in Reading with Implications for the Learning Disabled Student," *Journal of Learning Disabilities,* 1981, vol. 14, pp. 353–68.

Samuels, S. J., and Miller, N. L., "Failure to Find Attention Differences Between Learning Disabled and Normal Children on Classroom and Laboratory Tasks," *Exceptional Children,* 1985, vol. 51, pp. 358–75.

Sarup, M., *Marxism and Education.* London: Routledge & Kegan Paul, 1978.

Satz, P., "Cerebral Dominance and Reading Disability: An Old Problem Revisited." In R. M. Knights and D. J. Bakker, eds., *The Neuropsychology of Learning Disorders.* Baltimore: University Park Press, 1976.

Satz, P., "Laterality Tests: An Inferential Problem," *Cortex,* 1977, vol. 13, pp. 208–12.

Satz, P., and Morris, R., "Learning Disability Subtypes: A Review." In F. J. Pirozzolo and M. C. Wittrock, eds., *Neuropsychological and Cognitive Processes in Reading.* N.Y.: Academic Press, 1981.

Satz, P., Taylor, H. G., Friel, J., and Fletcher, J. M., "Some Developmental and Predictive Precursors of Reading Disabilities: A Six Year Follow-up." In A. L. Benton and D. Pearl, eds., *Dyslexia: An Appraisal of Current Knowledge.* NY: Oxford University Press, 1978.

Schauer, C. A., *The Developmental Relationship Between Neuropsychological and Achievement Variables: A Cluster Analysis Study.* Unpublished doctoral dissertation, University of Florida. Summarized in J. M. Fletcher and P. Satz, "Cluster Analysis and the Search for Learning Disability Subtypes." In B. Rourke, ed., *Neuropsychology of Learning Disabilities: Essentials of Subtype Analysis.* N.Y.: Guilford, 1985.

Schrag, P., and Divoky, D., *The Myth of the Hyperactive Child.* N.Y.: Pantheon, 1975.

Schulman, S., "Facing the Invisible Handicap," *Psychology Today,* February 1986, pp. 58–64.

Schworm, R. W., "The Effects of the Selective Attention on the Decoding Skills of Children with Learning Disabilities," *Journal of Learning Disabilities,* 1979, vol. 12, pp. 639–44.

Shankweiler, D., Liberman, I. Y., Mark, L. S., Fowler, C. A., and Fischer, F. W., "The Speech Code and Learning to Read," *Journal of Experimental Psychology: Human Learning and Memory,* 1979, vol. 5, pp. 531–45.

Sheer, D. E., "Focused Arousal and 40-Hz EEG." In R. M. Knights and D. J. Bakker, eds., *The Neuropsychology of Learning Disorders: Theoretical Approaches,* Baltimore: University Park Press, 1976.

Shepard, L., "An Evaluation of the Regression of Discrepancy Method for Identifying Children with Learning Disabilities," *Journal of Special Education,* 1980, vol. 14, pp. 79–91.

Shepard, L. A., and Smith, M. L., "An Evaluation of the Identification of Learning Disabled Students in Colorado," *Learning Disabilities Quarterly,* 1983, vol. 6, pp. 115–38.

Shinn, M. R., Ysseldyke, J., Deno, S., and Tindal, G., "A Comparison of Psychometric and Functional Differences Between Students Labeled Learning Disabled and Low Achieving," Institute for Research on Learning Disabilities, University of Minnesota, 1982, research report no. 71.

Shor, I., *Critical Teaching and Everyday Life.* Boston: South End Press, 1980.

Shor, I., *Culture Wars: School and Society in the Conservative Restoration 1969–1984.* Boston: Routledge & Kegan Paul, 1986.

Shucard, D. W., Cummins, K. R., McGee, M. G., "Event-related Brain Potentials Differentiate Normal and Disabled Readers," *Brain and Language,* 1984, vol. 21, pp. 318–34.

Sigmon, S. B., *A Radical Perspective on the Development of American Special Education with a Focus on the Concept of "Learning Disabilities."* Unpublished doctoral dissertation, Rutgers University, 1985.

Silberman, C. E., *Crisis in the Classroom.* N.Y.: Random House, 1970.

Silver, L. B., "The Neurologic Learning Disability Syndrome," *American Family Physician,* 1971, vol. 4, pp. 95–101.

Silverstein, B., *Fed Up: The Food Forces That Make You Fat, Sick and Poor.* Boston: South End Press, 1984.

Simeon, J., Waters, B., and Resnick, M., "Effects of Piracetam in Children with Learning Disorders," *Psychopharmacology Bulletin,* 1980, vol. 16, pp. 65–66.

Simms, R. B., and Crump, W. D., "Syntactic Development in the Oral Language of Learning Disabled and Normal Students at the Intermediate and Secondary Level," *Learning Disability Quarterly,* 1983, vol. 6, pp. 155–65.

Simpson, E., *Reversals: A Personal Account of Victory Over Dyslexia.* Boston: Houghton Mifflin, 1979.

Sinclair, E., Guthrie, D., and Forness, S. R., "Establishing a Connection Between Severity of Learning Disabilities and Classroom Attention Problems," *Journal of Educational Research,* 1984, vol. 78, pp. 18–21.

Sklar, B., Hanley, J., and Simmons, W. W., "A Computer Analysis of EEG Spectral Signatures from Normal and Dyslexic Children," *IEEE Transactions on Biomedical Engineering,* 1973, vol. 1, pp. 20–26.

Sklar, B., Hanley, J., and Simmons, W. W., "An EEG Experiment Aimed Toward Identifying Dyslexic Children," *Nature* (London), 1972, vol. 240, pp. 414–16.

Smith, C. R., *Learning Disabilities: The Interaction of Learner, Task, and Setting.* Boston: Little, Brown & Co., 1983.

Smith, S. D., and Goldgar, D. E., "Single Gene Analyses and Their Application to Learning Disabilities." In S. D. Smith, ed., *Genetics and Learning Disabilities.* San Diego: College-Hill Press, 1986.

Smith, S. D., Kimberling, W. J., Pennington, B. F., and Lubs, H. A., "Specific Reading Disability: Identification of an Inherited Form Through Linkage Analysis," *Science,* 1983(a), vol. 219, pp. 1345–47.

Smith, S. D., and Pennington, B. F., "Genetic Influences on Learning Disabilities II: Behavior Genetics and Clinical Implications," *Learning Disabilities,* 1983, vol. 2, pp. 43–55.

Smith, S. D., Pennington, B. F., Kimberling, W. J., and Lubs, H. A., "A Genetic Analysis of Specific Reading Disability." In C. L. Ludlow and J. A. Cooper, eds., *Genetic Aspects of Speech and Language Disorders.* N.Y.: Academic Press, 1983.

Sobotka, K. R., and May, J. G., "Visual Evoked Potentials and Reaction Time in Normal and Dyslexic Children," *Psychophysiology,* 1977, vol. 14, pp. 18–24.

Sobotowicz, W. S., and Evans, J. R., *Cortical Dysfunctioning in Children with Specific Reading Disability.* Springfield, Ill.: Charles C. Thomas, 1982.

Spears, C. E., and Weber, R. E., "The Nature of Learning Disabilities." In R. E. Weber, *Handbook on Learning Disabilities.* Englewood Cliffs, N.J.: Prentice-Hall, 1974.

Spreen, O., "The Dyslexias: A Discussion of Neurobehavioral Research." In A. L. Benton and D. Pearl, eds., *Dyslexia: An Appraisal of Current Knowledge.* N.Y.: Oxford University Press, 1978.

Spring, C., and Capps, C., "Encoding Speed, Rehearsal, and Probed Recall of Dyslexic Boys," *Journal of Educational Psychology,* 1974, vol. 66, pp. 780–86.

Spring, J., *Education and the Rise of the Corporate State.* Boston: Beacon, 1972.

Stambrook, M., "The Luria-Nebraska Neuropsychological Battery: A Promise That *May* Be Partly Fulfilled," *Journal of Clinical Neuropsychology,* 1983, vol. 5, pp. 247–69.

Stanovich, K. E., "Cognitive Processes and the Reading Problems of Learning Disabled Children: Evaluating the Assumption of Specificity." In J. Torgesen and B. Wong, eds., *Learning Disabilities: Some New Perspectives.* N.Y.: Academic Press, 1986.

Stanovich, K. E., "Explaining the Variance in Reading Ability in Terms of Psychological Processes: What Have We Learned?" *Annals of Dyslexia,* 1985, vol. 35, pp. 67–96.

Stanovich, K. E., "Individual Differences in the Cognitive Processes of Reading: 1. Word Decoding," *Journal of Learning Disabilities,* 1982, vol. 15, pp. 485–93.

Stanovich, K. E., "Individual Differences in the Cognitive Processes of Reading: 2. Text-level Processes," *Journal of Learning Disabilities,* 1982, vol. 15, pp. 549–54.

Stanley, G., Smith, G. A., and Howell, E. A., "Eye-movements and Sequential Tracking in Dyslexic and Control Children," *British Journal of Psychology,* 1983, vol. 74, pp. 181–87.

Stockwell, C. W., Sherard, E. S., and Schuler, J. V., "Electronystagmographic Findings in Dyslexic Children," *Transactions of the American Academy of Ophthalmology and Otolaryngology,* 1976, vol. 82, pp. 239–43.

Strang, J. D., and Rourke, B. P., "Arithmetic Disability Subtypes: The Neuropsychological Significance of Specific Arithmetical Impairment in Childhood." In B. P. Rourke, ed., *Neuropsychology of Learning Disabilities: Essentials of Subtype Analysis.* N.Y.: Guilford Press, 1985.

Strang, J. D., and Rourke, B. P. "Concept Formation/Non-verbal Reasoning Abilities of Children Who Exhibit Specific Academic Problems with Arithmetic," *Journal of Clinical Child Psychology,* 1983, vol. 12, pp. 33–39.

Sutherland, J., and Algozzine, B., "The Learning Disabled Label as a Biasing Factor in the Visual Motor Performance of Normal Children," *Journal of Learning Disabilities,* 1979, vol. 12, pp. 17–23.

Swanson, L., "Verbal Encoding Effects on the Visual Short-term Memory of Learning Disabled and Normal Readers," *Journal of Educational Psychology,* 1978, vol. 70, pp. 539–44.

Symmes, J. S., and Rapoport, J. L., "Unexpected Reading Failure," *American Journal of Orthopsychiatry,* 1972, vol. 42, pp. 182–91.

Tallal, P., "Auditory Temporal Perception, Phonics, and Reading Disabilities in Children," *Brain and Language,* 1980, vol. 9, pp. 182–98.

Tallal, P., "Temporal or Phonetic Processing Deficit in Dyslexia? That Is the Question," *Applied Psycholinguistics,* 1984, vol. 5, pp. 167–69.

Tarnopol, L., and Tarnopol, M., *Reading Disabilities: An International Perspective.* Baltimore: University Park Press, 1976.

Tarver, S. G., Hallahan, D. P., Cohen, S. B., and Kaufman, J. M., "The Development of Visual Selective Attention and Verbal Rehearsal in Learning Disabled Boys," *Journal of Learning Disabilities,* 1977, vol. 10, pp. 491–500.

Tarver, S. G., Hallahan, D. P., Kauffman, J. M., and Ball, D. W., "Verbal Rehearsal and Selective Attention in Children with Learning Disabilities: A Developmental Lag," *Journal of Experimental Child Psychology,* 1976, vol. 22, pp. 375–85.

Taylor, H. G., "MBD: Meanings and Misconceptions," *Journal of Clinical Neuropsychology,* 1983, vol. 5, pp. 271–87.

Thatcher, R. W., and Lester, M. L., "Nutrition, Environmental Toxins and Computerized EEG: A Mini-max Approach to Learning Disabilities," *Journal of Learning Disabilities,* 1985, vol. 18, pp. 287–97.

Thatcher, R. W., Lester, M. L., McAlaster, R., Horst, R., and Ignasias, S. W., "Intelligence and Lead Toxins in Rural Children," *Journal of Learning Disabilities,* 1983, vol. 16, pp. 355–59.

Thompson, J. S., Ross, R. J., and Horowitz, S. J., "The Role of Computed Axial Tomography in the Study of the Child with Minimal Brain Dysfunction," *Journal of Learning Disabilities,* 1980, vol. 13, pp. 334–37.

Thompson, L. J., "Did Lee Harvey Oswald Have a Specific Language Disability?," *Bulletin of the Orton Society,* 1964, vol. 14, pp. 89–90.

Thompson, L. J., "Language Disabilities in Men of Eminence," *Journal of Learning Disabilities,* 1971, vol. 4, pp. 39–50.

Thurlow, M. L., Ysseldyke, J. E., and Casey, A., "Teachers' Perceptions of Criteria for Identifying Learning Disabled Students," *Psychology in the Schools,* 1984, vol. 21, pp. 349–55.

Tinker, M. A., "Recent Studies of Eye Movements in Reading," *Psychological Bulletin,* 1958, vol. 55, pp. 215–31.

Tobach, E., Gianutsos, J., Topoff, H., and Gross, C. G., *The Four Horsemen: Racism, Sexism, Militarism and Social Darwinism.* N.Y.: Behavioral Publications, 1974.

Torgesen, J. K., introduction to J. E. Ysseldyke, "Current Practices in Making

Psychoeducational Decisions About Learning Disabled Students," *Journal of Learning Disabilities,* 1983, vol. 16, pp. 226.

Torgesen, J. K., "Memory Processes in Reading Disabled Children," *Journal of Learning Disabilities,* 1985, vol. 18, pp. 350–57.

Torgesen, J. K., "Performance of Reading Disabled Children on Serial Memory Tasks," *Reading Research Quarterly,* 1978–1979, vol. 14, pp. 57–87.

Torgesen, J., and Goldman, T., "Verbal Rehearsal and Short-term Memory in Reading-Disabled Children," *Child Development,* 1977, vol. 48, pp. 56–60.

Torgesen, J. K., and Houck, D. G., "Processing Deficiencies of Learning-Disabled Children Who Perform Poorly on the Digit Span Test," *Journal of Educational Psychology,* 1980, vol. 72, pp. 141–60.

Torgesen, J. K., Murphy, H. A., and Ivey, C., "The Influence of an Orienting Task on the Memory Performance of Children with Reading Problems," *Journal of Learning Disabilities,* 1979, vol. 12, pp. 396–401.

Treiman, R., "Onsets and Rimes as Units of Spoken Syllables: Evidence from Children," *Journal of Experimental Child Psychology,* 1985, vol. 39, pp. 161–81.

Treiman, R., and Baron, J., "Phonemic-Analysis Training Helps Children Benefit from Spelling-Sound Rules," *Memory & Cognition,* 1983, vol. 4, pp. 382–89.

Treiman, R., and Hirsh-Pasek, K., "Are There Qualitative Differences in Reading Behavior Between Dyslexics and Normal Readers," *Memory & Cognition,* 1985, vol. 13, pp. 357–64.

Tucker, J. A., "Ethnic Proportions in Classes for the Learning Disabled: Issues in Nonbiased Assessment," *Journal of Special Education,* 1980, vol. 14, pp. 93–105.

A Twelve Week, Double-blind, Parallel Group, Multicenter Study to Compare the Efficacy and Safety of Piracetam with Placebo in Children with Specific Written Language Difficulties (Dyslexia). Brussels: UCB Pharamaceutical, 1980.

"Two Doctors Offer Dyslexia Theory," *New York Times,* April 29, 1974, p. 20.

Understanding Learning Disabilities (pamphlet). N.Y.: Foundation for Children with Learning Disabilities, n.d.

U.S. Office of Special Education and Rehabilitative Services, *Seventh Annual Report to Congress on the Implementation of the Education of the Handicapped Act.* Washington, D.C.: U.S. Department of Education, 1985.

Vandenberg, S. G., "The Hereditary Abilities Study: Hereditary Components in a Psychological Test Battery," *American Journal of Human Genetics,* 1962, vol. 14, pp. 220–37.

Vanderbilt, B. M., *Thomas Edison, Chemist.* Washington, D.C.: American Chemical Society, 1971.

Vellutino, F. R., "Childhood Dyslexia: A Language Disorder." In H. R. Myklebust, ed., *Progress in Learning Disabilities,* vol. 5. N.Y.: Grune & Stratton, 1983.

Vellutino, F. R., *Dyslexia.* Cambridge: MIT Press, 1979.

Vernon, M. D., *Backwardness in Reading.* London: Cambridge University Press, 1957.

Vrana, F., and Pihl, R. O. "Selective Attention Deficit in Learning Disabled Children: A Cognitive Interpretation," *Journal of Learning Disabilities,* 1980, vol. 13, pp. 387–91.

Vygotsky, L. S., *Mind in Society.* Cambridge: Harvard University Press, 1978.

Vygotsky, L. S., *Thought and Language.* Cambridge: MIT Press, 1962.

Waber, D. P., "Maturation: Thoughts on Renewing an Old Acquaintanceship." In D. Caplan, ed., *Biological Studies of Mental Processes.* Cambridge: MIT Press, 1982.

Waber, D. P., "Sex Differences in Cognition: A Function of Maturation Rate?" *Science,* 1976, vol. 192, pp. 572–73.

Wachs, T. D., "Proximal Experience and Early Cognitive-Intellectual Development: The Social Environment." In A. W. Gottfried, ed., *Home Environment and Early Cognitive Development.* N.Y.: Academic Press, 1984.

Wada, J., and Rasmussen, T., "Intracarotid Injection of Sodium Amytal for the Lateralization of Cerebral Speech Dominance: Experimental and Clinical Observations," *Journal of Neurosurgery,* 1960, vol. 17, pp. 266–82.

Weaver, P. A., and Rosner, J., "Relationships Between Visual and Auditory Perceptual Skills and Comprehension in Students with Learning Disabilities," *Journal of Learning Disabilities,* 1979, vol. 12, pp. 617–19.

Webb, G., *Learning Disabilities—Uniquely American or Crosscultural?,* unpublished doctoral dissertation, Boston College, 1976.

Weber, B. A., and Omenn, G. S. "Auditory and Visual Evoked Responses in Children with Familial Reading Disabilities," *Journal of Learning Disabilities,* 1977, vol. 10, pp. 153–58.

Weiss, B., "Feingold Diet Research Seen as Inadequate," *Journal of Learning Disabilities,* 1983, vol. 16, pp. 574–75.

Weiss, B., "Food Additives and Environmental Chemicals as Sources of Childhood Behavior Disorders," *Journal of the American Academy of Child Psychiatry,* 1982, vol. 21, pp. 144–52.

Weiss, G., Kruger, E., Danielson, U., and Elman, M., "Effect of Long Term Treatment of Hyperactive Children with Methylphenidate," *Canadian Medical Association Journal,* 1975, vol. 112, pp. 159–65.

Wender, P. H., "The Minimal Brain Dysfunction Syndrome," *Annual Review of Medicine,* 1975, vol. 26, pp. 45–62.

Wender, P. H., "The Minimal Brain Dysfunction Syndrome in Children," *Journal of Nervous and Mental Disease,* 1972, vol. 155, pp. 55–71.

What Works: Research About Teaching and Learning. Washington, D.C.: U.S. Government Printing Office, 1986.

White, M., "Identification of Dyslexia: A Ninety-Minute Procedure," *Journal of Learning Disabilities,* 1983, vol. 16, pp. 32–34.

White, M. J., "Laterality Differences in Perception," *Psychological Bulletin,* 1969, vol. 72, pp. 387–405.

Whyte, W. H., *The Organization Man.* N.Y.: Simon & Schuster, 1956.

Wiig, E. H., Becker-Redding, U., and Semel, E. M., "A Cross-cultural, Crosslinguistic Comparison of Language Abilities of 7- to 8- and 12- to 13-year-old Children with Learning Disabilities," *Journal of Learning Disabilities,* 1983, vol. 16, pp. 576–85.

Wiig, E. H., Semel, E. M., and Abele, E., "Perception and Interpretation of Ambiguous Sentences by Learning Disabled Twelve-year-olds," *Learning Disability Quarterly,* 1981, vol. 4, pp. 3–12.

Williams, J. P., "Phonemic Analysis and How It Relates to Reading," *Journal of Learning Disabilities,* 1984, vol. 17, pp. 240–45.

Wilsher, C. R., *Piracetam Treatment of Specific Written Language Difficulties (Dyslexia)—A Discussion,* pamphlet, n.d.

Wilsher, C., Atkins, G., and Manfield, P., "Dyslexia: Piracetam Promotion of Reading Skills," unpublished manuscript, 1980.

Wilsher, C., Atkins, G., and Manfield, P., "Effect of Piracetam on Dyslexics' Reading Ability," *Journal of Learning Disabilities,* 1985, vol. 18, pp. 19–25.

Wilsher, C., Atkins, G., and Manfield, P., "Piracetam as an Aid to Learning in Dyslexia: Preliminary Report," *Psychopharmacology,* 1979, vol. 65, pp. 107–09.

Wilsher, C. R., and Milewski, J., "Effects of Piracetam on Dyslexics' Verbal Conceptualizing Ability," *Psychopharmacology Bulletin,* 1983, vol. 19, pp. 3–4.

Wilson, E. B., "Some Impressions of the Effects of Sensory Integrative Therapy for Children with Learning Disabilities," *Australian Occupational Therapy Journal,* 1979, vol. 26, pp. 239–43.

Wilson, E. O., *Sociobiology: The New Synthesis.* Cambridge: Harvard University Press, 1975.

Witelson, S. F., "Developmental Dyslexia: Two Right Hemispheres and None Left," *Science,* 1977, vol. 195, pp. 309–11.

Witelson, S. F., "Sex and the Single Hemisphere: Right Hemisphere Specialization for Spatial Processing," *Science,* 1976, vol. 193, pp. 425–27.

Witelson, S. F., "Abnormal Right Hemisphere Specialization in Developmental Dyslexia." In R. M. Knights and D. J. Bakker, eds., *The Neuropsychology of Learning Disorders.* Baltimore: University Park Press, 1976.

Witelson, S. F., and Rabinovitch, S., "Hemispheric Speech Lateralization in Children with Auditory-Linguistic Deficits," *Cortex,* 1972, vol. 8, pp. 412–26.

Witty, P.A., and Kopel, D., "Sinistral and Mixed Manual-Ocular Behavior in Reading Disability," *Journal of Educational Psychology,* 1936, vol. 27, pp. 119–34.

Wolf, M., "The Word Retrieval Process and Reading in Children and Aphasics." In K. Nelson, ed., *Children's Language,* vol. 3. N.Y.: Gardner, 1981.

Wolraich, M., Drummond, T., Salomon, M. K., O'Brien, M. L., and Sivage, C., "Effects of Methylphenidate Alone and in Combination with Behavior Modification Procedures on the Behavior and Academic Performance of Hyperactive Children," *Journal of Abnormal Child Psychology,* 1978, vol. 6, pp. 149–61.

Wong, B. Y. L., and Sawatsky, D., "Sentence Elaboration and Retention of Good, Average and Poor Readers," *Learning Disability Quarterly,* 1984, vol. 7, pp. 229–36.

Woock, R. R., ed., *Education and the Urban Crisis.* Scranton, Pa.: International Textbook Company, 1970.

Wright, P., and Santa Cruz, R., "Ethnic Composition of Special Education Programs in California," *Learning Disabilities Quarterly,* 1983, vol. 6, pp. 387–94.

Yeni-Komshian, G. H., Isenberg, D., and Goldberg, H., "Cerebral Dominance and Reading Disability: Left Visual Field Deficit in Poor Readers," *Neuropsychologia,* 1975, vol. 13, pp. 83–94.

Young, A. W. and Ellis, A. W., "Asymmetry of Cerebral Hemispheric Function in Normal and Poor Readers," *Psychological Bulletin,* 1981, vol. 89, pp. 183–90.

Ysseldyke, J. E., "Current Practices in Making Psychoeducational Decisions

About Learning Disabled Students," *Journal of Learning Disabilities,* 1983, vol. 16, pp. 226–33.

Ysseldyke, J. E., and Algozzine, B., "LD or Not LD: That's Not the Question!" *Journal of Learning Disabilities,* 1983, vol. 16, pp. 29–31.

Ysseldyke, J. E., Algozzine, B., and Epps, S., "A Logical and Empirical Analysis of Current Practices in Classifying Students as Handicapped," Institute for Research on Learning Disabilities, University of Minnesota, 1982, research report no. 92.

Ysseldyke, J. E., Algozzine, B., Richey, L., and Graden, J., "Declaring Students Eligible for Learning Disability Services: Why Bother with the Data?" *Learning Disability Quarterly,* 1982, vol. 5, pp. 37–44.

Ysseldyke, J. E., Algozzine, B., and Shinn, M., "Validity of the Woodcock-Johnson Psycho-educational Battery for Learning Disabled Youngsters," *Learning Disability Quarterly,* 1981, vol. 4, pp. 244–49.

Ysseldyke, J. E., Algozzine, B., Shinn, M., and McGue, M., "Similarities and Differences Between Underachievers and Students Labeled Learning Disabled: Identical Twins with Different Mothers," Institute for Research on Learning Disabilities, University of Minnesota, 1979, research report no. 13.

Ysseldyke, J. E., Thurlow, M. L., Graden, J. L., Wesson, C., Deno, S. L., and Algozzine, B., "Generalizations from Five Years of Research on Assessment and Decision Making," Institute for Research on Learning Disabilities, University of Minnesota, 1982, research report no. 100.

Zendel, I. H., and Pihl, R. O., "Visual and Auditory Matching in Learning Disabled and Normal Children," *Journal of Learning Disabilities,* 1983, vol. 16, pp. 158–60.

Zurif, E. B., and Carson, G., "Dyslexia in Relation to Cerebral Dominance and Temporal Analysis," *Neuropsychologia,* 1970, vol. 8, pp. 351–61.

Index

ABOUT THE AUTHOR

Gerald S. Coles is Associate Professor of Clinical Psychiatry at the Robert Wood Johnson (formerly Rutgers) Medical School, and Youth and Education Coordinator at UMDNJ Community Mental Health Center. His articles have appeared in *The Harvard Educational Review, Science and Society, The Journal of Special Education, Learning Disability Quarterly,* and many other professional journals. He lives in Highland Park, N.J., and this is his first book.